JOHN
VOLUME TWO

D1342220

Expository Thoughts on the Gospels

JOHN

VOLUME TWO

J. C. Ryle

THE BANNER OF TRUTH TRUST

THE BANNER OF TRUTH TRUST
3 Murrayfield Road, Edinburgh EH12 6EL
P.O. Box 621, Carlisle, Pennsylvania 17013, U.S.A

*

First published 1869
First Banner of Truth Trust edition 1987
Reprinted 1999
ISBN 0 85151 505 3

*

Printed in Finland by WSOY

TABLE OF CONTENTS OF EXPOSITIONS

1 After these things Jesus walked in Galilee: for he would not walk in Jewry, because the Jews sought to kill him.

2 Now the Jews' feast of tabernacles was at hand.

3 His brethren therefore said unto him, Depart hence, and go into Judæa, that thy disciples also may see the works that thou doest.

4 For *there is* no man *that* doeth any thing in secret, and he himself seeketh to be known openly. If thou do these things, shew thyself to the world.

5 For neither did his brethren believe in him.

6 Then Jesus said unto them, My time is not yet come: but your time is alway ready.

7 The world cannot hate you; but me it hateth, because I testify of it, that the works thereof are evil.

8 Go ye up unto this feast: I go not up yet unto this feast; for my time is not yet full come.

9 When he had said these words unto them, he abode *still* in Galilee.

10 But when his brethren were gone up, then went he also up unto the feast, not openly, but as it were in secret.

11 Then the Jews sought him at the feast, and said, Where is he?

12 And there was much murmuring among the people concerning him: for some said, He is a good man: others said, Nay; but he deceiveth the people.

13 Howbeit no man spake openly of him for fear of the Jews.

THE chapter we now begin is divided from the preceding one by a wide interval of time. The many miracles which our Lord wrought, while He "walked in Galilee," are passed over by St. John in comparative silence. The events which he was specially inspired to record, are those which took place in or near Jerusalem.

We should observe in this passage *the desperate hardness and unbelief of human nature.* We are told that even our Lord's "brethren did not believe in Him."

Holy and harmless and blameless as He was in life, some of his nearest relatives, according to the flesh, did not receive Him as the Messiah. It was bad enough that His own people, "the Jews, sought to kill Him." But it was even worse that "His brethren did not believe."

That great Scriptural doctrine, man's need of preventing and converting grace, stands out here, as if written with a sunbeam. It becomes all who question that doctrine to look at this passage and consider. Let them observe that seeing Christ's miracles, hearing Christ's teaching, living in Christ's own company, were not enough to make men believers. The mere possession of spiritual privileges never yet made any one a Christian. All is useless without the effectual and applying work of God the Holy Ghost. No wonder that our Lord said in another place, "No man can come to Me, except the Father which hath sent Me draw him." (John vi. 44.)

The true servants of Christ in every age will do well to remember this. They are often surprised and troubled to find that in religion they stand alone. They are apt to fancy that it must be their own fault that all around them are not converted like themselves. They are ready to blame themselves because their families remain worldly and unbelieving. But let them look at the verse before us. In our Lord Jesus Christ there was no fault either in temper, word, or deed. Yet even Christ's own "brethren did not believe in Him."

Our blessed Master has truly learned by experience how to sympathize with all His people who stand alone.

This is a thought "full of sweet, pleasant, and unspeak-able comfort." He knows the heart of every isolated believer, and can be touched with the feeling of his trials. He has drunk this bitter cup. He has passed through this fire. Let all who are fainting and cast down, because brothers and sisters despise their re-ligion, turn to Christ for comfort, and pour out their hearts before Him. He "Himself hath suffered being tempted" in this way, and He can help as well as feel. (Heb. ii. 18.)

We should observe, for another thing, in this passage, *one principal reason why many hate Christ.* We are told that our Lord said to His unbelieving brethren, "The world cannot hate you ; but Me it hateth, because I testify of it, that the works thereof are evil."

These words reveal one of those secret principles which influence men in their treatment of religion. They help to explain that deadly enmity with which many during our Lord's earthly ministry regarded Him and His Gospel. It was not so much the high doctrines which He preached, as the high standard of practice which He proclaimed, which gave offence. It was not even His claim to be received the Messiah which men dis-liked so much, as His witness against the wickedness of their lives. In short, they could have tolerated His opinions if He would only have spared their sins.

The principle, we may be sure, is one of universal application. It is at work now just as much as it was eighteen hundred years ago.. The real cause of many people's dislike to the Gospel, is the holiness of living

which it demands. Teach abstract doctrines only, and
few will find any fault. Denounce the fashionable sins
of the day, and call on men to repent and walk consis-
tently with God, and thousands at once will be offended.
The true reason why many profess to be infidels and
abuse Christianity, is the witness that Christianity bears
against their own bad lives.—Like Ahab, they hate it,
" because it does not prophesy good concerning them,
but evil." (1 Kings xxii. 8.)

We should observe, lastly, in this passage, *the strange
variety of opinions about Christ, which were current from
the beginning.* We are told that " there was much
murmuring among the people concerning Him · for
some said, He is a good man ; others said, Nay, but He
deceiveth the people." The words which old Simeon
had spoken thirty years before, were here accomplished
in a striking manner. He had said to our Lord's mother,
" This child is set for the fall and rising again of many
in Israel ; and for a sign which shall be spoken against ;
—that the thoughts of many hearts may be revealed."
(Luke ii. 34, 35.) In the diversities of opinion about
our Lord which arose among the Jews, we see the good
old man's saying fulfilled

In the face of such a passage as this, the endless
differences and divisions about religion, which we see
on all sides, in the present day, ought never to surprise us. The open hatred of some toward Christ,—
the carping, fault-finding, prejudiced spirit of others,—
the bold confession of the few faithful ones,—the timid,
man-fearing temper of the many faithless ones,—the

unceasing war of words and strife of tongues with which the Churches of Christ are so sadly familiar,—are only modern symptoms of an old disease. Such is the corruption of human nature, that Christ is the cause of divisions among men, wherever He is preached.. So long as the world stands, some, when they hear of Him, will love, and some will hate,—some will believe, and some will believe not. That deep prophetical saying of His will be continually verified : "Think not that I am come to send peace on earth : I came not to send peace, but a sword." (Matt. x. 34.)

What think we of Christ ourselves ? This is the one question with which we have to do. Let us never be ashamed to be of that little number who believe on Him, hear His voice, follow Him, and confess Him before men. While others waste their time in vain jangling and unprofitable controversy, let us take up the cross and give all diligence " to make our calling and election sure." The children of this world may hate us, as it hated our Master, because our religion is a standing witness against them. But the last day will show that we chose wisely, lost nothing, and gained a crown of glory that fadeth not away.

NOTES. JOHN VII. 1—13.

1.—[*After these things Jesus walked in Galilee.*] These words cover a space of about six months. The events of the last chapter took place about the time of the Passover, in spring. The events of the chapter we now begin took place in autumn, at the feast of taber-nacles. What our Lord did in Galilee during these six months St. John passes over in silence. His Gospel, with the exception of the 1st, 2nd, 4th, and 6th chapters, is almost entirely taken up with our Lord's doings in or near Jerusalem. He was at this period of His ministry, entirely absent from Jerusalem, it would seem, for about eighteen months.

The expression "walked" must be taken figuratively. It simply means, that our Lord "lived, dwelt, sojourned, was going to and fro, and passing His time." The Greek word is in the imperfect tense, and denotes a continuous action or habit.

[*He would not walk in Jewry.*] This would be more literally rendered, "He did not will, or desire, or choose to walk." The use of the word "Jewry" by our translators is to be regretted, and seems uncalled for. The Greek word so rendered is the same that is rendered "Judæa" in the third verse.

[*Because the Jews sought to kill Him.*] By "the Jews" we must understand the leaders and rulers of the Jewish nation. There is no proof that the lower orders felt the same enmity that the upper classes did against our Lord. "The common people heard Him gladly." (Mark xii. 37.) The depth and bitterness of this hatred against Christ may be seen in their wish to kill Him. It seems to have been a settled plan with the Jews from the time when the miracle was wrought at the pool of Bethesda. (John v. 16, 18.) They could neither answer Him, nor silence Him, nor prevent the common people listening to Him. They resolved therefore to kill Him.

Our Lord's example recorded in this verse shows clearly that Christians are not meant to court martyrdom, or wilfully expose themselves to certain death, under the idea that it is their duty. Many primitive martyrs seem not to have understood this.

2.—[*Jews' feast of tabernacles.*] This expression, like many others in St. John's Gospel, shows that he wrote for the Gentiles, who knew little of Jewish customs and feasts. Hence "the Jews' feast."

The feast of tabernacles was one of the three great feasts in the Jewish year, when, by God's command, all pious Jews went up to Jerusalem. (Deut. xvi. 16.) It was held in autumn, after the completion of the harvest, in the seventh month. The time of the Jewish "Passover" answered to our Easter, "Pentecost" to our Whitsuntide, and "Tabernacles" to our Michaelmas. The seventh month was remarkable for the number of ordinances which the law of Moses required the Jews to observe. On the first day was the feast of trumpets, on the tenth day was the day of atonement, and on the fifteenth began the feast of tabernacles.

There are several things peculiar to the feast of tabernacles. which ought to be remembered in reading this chapter, because

some of them throw light on it.   (1) It was an occasion of special
mirth and rejoicing with the Jews.   They were ordered to dwell
in booths, or tabernacles made of branches, for seven days, in
remembrance of their dwelling in temporary booths when they
came out of Egypt, and to "rejoice before the Lord."   (Lev. xxiii.
39—43.   (2) It was a feast at which more sacrifices were offered up
than at any of the Jewish feasts.   (Num. xxix. 12—34.)   (3) It
was a feast at which, once every seven years, the law was publicly
read to the whole people.   (4) It was a feast at which water was
drawn from the pool of Siloam every day with great solemnity, and
poured upon the altar, while the people sung the 12th chapter of
Isaiah.   (5) It was a feast which followed close on the great day
of atonement, when the peculiarly typical ordinances of the scape-
goat, and the High Priest going once in the year into the holy of
holies, were fresh in the minds of the people.   These things should
be carefully noted, and remembered, as we read through the
chapter.

Josephus calls the feast of tabernacles "the holiest and greatest
feast of the Jews."   It was a Rabbinical saying, "The man who
has not seen these festivities does not know what a jubilee is."

Whether this very year, when our Lord went to the feast
of tabernacles, was the precise seventh year in which the public
reading of the law took place, we cannot now know for certainty.
Whether the custom of dwelling in booths was literally kept up when
our Lord was on earth may also be matter of question.   It certainly
had not been observed for many years in the days of Nehemiah.
(Neh. viii. 17.)   But that this feast was kept up with extraordinary
festivity and rejoicing in the latter days of the Jewish dispensation
is testified by all Jewish writers.

It was in the middle of this public rejoicing, and the concourse
of Jews from every part of the world, that the things recorded
in this chapter took place.   It stands to reason that all that our
Lord said and did this week must have been more than usually
public, and would necessarily attract great attention.

Wordsworth, Burgon, and others, consider the feast of tabernacles to have been a very significant type of our Lord's incarnation.
I confess that I am unable to see it.   If the feast was typical at
all, which is not certain, I venture the conjecture that it was
meant to be a type of our Lord's second advent.   My reasons are
these :—

(a) It was the last in order of the Jewish feasts every year, and
formed the completion of the annual routine of Mosaic ordinances.
It wound up all.

(*b*) It was kept at the end of harvest, when the year's work was done, and the fruits were all gathered in.

(*c*) It was an occasion of special rejoicing and festivity, more than any of the feasts. The dwelling in booths seems to have been a circumstance of the feast less essential than the rejoicing.

(*d*) It followed immediately after the feast of trumpets, and the day of atonement. On that day the High Priest went into the holy of holies and then came out to bless the people. (See Isa. xxvii. 13 ; 1 Thes. iv. 16.)

(*e*) It followed immediately after the jubilee every fiftieth year. That jubilee, and proclamation of liberty to all, was in the seventh month.

(*f*) It is that special feast which, after the Jews are restored and Jerusalem rebuilt, the nation are yet to keep in the future kingdom of Christ. (Zech. xiv. 16.)

I venture this conjecture with much diffidence ; but I think it deserves consideration. In the six points I have mentioned, I see much more of the second advent than of the first. To my eyes the feast of passover was a type of Christ crucified ; the feast of pentecost,—of Christ sending forth the Holy Ghost in this dispensation ; the feast of tabernacles,—of Christ coming again to gather His people in one joyous company, to reap the harvest of the earth, to wind up this dispensation, to come forth and bless His people, and to proclaim a jubilee to all the earth.

3.--[*His brethren.*] Who these " brethren " were is a matter of dispute. Some think, as Alford, Stier, and others, that they were literally our Lord's own brethren, and the children of Mary by Joseph, born after our Lord's birth. (See Psalm lxix. 8.)—Some think, as Theophylact and others, that they were the children of Joseph by a former marriage, and brought up by Mary under the same roof with our Lord.--Others think, as Augustine, Zwingle, Musculus, and Bengel, that the word " brethren " does not necessarily mean more than cousins or kinsmen. (See 1 Chron. xxiii. 22.) This is the most probable opinion. I take these " brethren " to have been relatives and kinsmen of Joseph and Mary, living at Nazareth, or Capernaum, or elsewhere in Galilee,—who naturally observed all our Lord's doings with interest and curiosity, but at present did not believe on Him. To suppose, as some do, that these brethren were some of our Lord's Apostles, is to my mind a most improbable theory, and flatly contrary to the 5th verse of this chapter.

If Mary really had sons after the birth of our Lord, it certainly seems strange that our Lord should commend her to the care of John, on the cross, and not to her own sons, His half-brethren. That at the later part of His ministry He had some "brethren" who were not Apostles, but believed, is clear from Acts i. 14. But whether they were the "brethren" of the text before us, we have no means of ascertaining.

[*Depart...go into Judea, that Thy disciples, etc.*] This recommendation, as well as the next verse, looks like the advice of men who as yet were not convinced of our Lord's Messiahship. The expression "that Thy disciples may see," seems also to indicate that the speakers were not yet of the number of our Lord's disciples. The language is that of bystanders looking on, waiting to see how the question is to be settled, before they make up their own minds. It is as though they said, " Make haste, rally a party round Thee, show some public proof that Thou art the Christ, and gather adherents." The "works" here mentioned must evidently mean miracles. This speech seems to imply that our Lord had a party of disciples in Judea and at Jerusalem. Many, it should be remembered, " believed on Him " at the first passover He attended (John ii. 23.)

4.—[*For there is no man, etc.*] This sentence is a kind of proverbial saying. Every one knows that if a man seeks to be known openly, it is no use to do his work secretly.

[*If Thou do these things, show Thyself to the world.*] There seems to be a latent sneer about this sentence. " If thou really art doing miracles to prove Thyself the Messiah, do not continue to hide Thyself here in Galilee. Go up to Jerusalem, and do miracles there." That the speakers said this from an honest zeal for God's glory, and a sincere desire to have our Lord known by others as well as themselves, is a view that I cannot think probable.

Some think that the words " if Thou doest," mean " since Thou doest," and see a parallel in Coloss. iii. 1,—where " if " does not imply any doubt whether the Colossians were " risen with Christ." Lampe thinks it means, " if Thou really and truly, not illusively, doest miracles."

The false standard of an unconverted man is very manifest in this and the preceding verse. Such an one has no idea of waiting for man's praise and favour, and being content without it if it does not come. He thinks that a religion should have the praise of the world, and labour to get it. The man of God remembers that true religion does not " cry, nor strive," nor court publicity.

5.—[*For neither...brethren believe.*] These words appear to me to admit of only one meaning. They mean, that these brethren of our Lord had at present no faith at all. They did not yet believe that Jesus was the Christ. They had no grace. They were not converted. The idea of some that the words mean, "His brethren did not fully and entirely believe in Him," seems to me utterly without foundation. It cannot, moreover, be reconciled with the language that soon follows.—"The world cannot hate you," etc. Such language cannot be applied to disciples. The whole teaching of the Bible shows clearly that it was quite possible to be a relative of Christ according to the flesh and yet not be converted. He that does God's will is as dear to Christ as "brother, or sister, or mother." (Mark iii. 35.)

How frequently even the natural brethren of God's most eminent saints have been graceless and ungodly, every Bible-reader must often have observed. The cases of the brothers of Abel, Isaac, Jacob, Joseph, and David, will occur to our minds.

We should learn from a verse like this the desperate hardness of man's heart, the absolute necessity of grace to make any one a disciple, and the extreme danger of familiarity with high spiritual privileges. We should remember too, that a man may be a truly good and holy man, and yet not have converted relatives. No one can give grace to his own family. "A prophet is not without honour but in his own country." (Mark vi. 4.) Even our Lord was not believed by all around Him. He can truly sympathise with all His people who are in a similar position.

6.—[*My time is not yet come.*] These words must mean that our Lord did everything during His earthly ministry according to a pre-ordained plan, and that He could take no step except in harmony with that plan. He doubtless spoke with a Divine depth of meaning that none but Himself could comprehend, and that must have been unintelligible at the time to His "brethren." To them His words would probably convey nothing more than the idea that for some reason or other He did not think the present a favourable opportunity for going to Jerusalem.

[*Your time is alway ready.*] This sentence must mean that to unconverted people, like our Lord's brethren, it could make no matter what time they went up. All times were alike. They would excite no enmity, and run no risk.

A Christian not possessing foreknowledge, can only pray for guidance and direction as to the steps of his life, and the ways and times of his actions; and having prayed, then make the best use of his judgment, trusting that a faithful God will not let him make mistakes.

7.—[*The world cannot hate you.*] These words surely settle the question as to the present state of our Lord's brethren. They were yet unconverted. Our Lord says, in another place, "If ye were of the world, the world would love his own." (John xv. 19.)

[*Me it hateth, because I testify...works...evil.*] The true reason of this enmity of many of the Jews against Christ is here distinctly indicated. It was not merely His claims to be received as the Messiah. It was not merely the high and spiritual doctrine He preached. It was rather His constant testimony against the sinful lives and wicked practices of the many in His day. That adultery, covetousness, and hypocrisy, were rife and common among the leading Pharisees, is evident from many expressions in the Gospels. It was our Lord's witness against these darling sins that enraged His enemies.

The wickedness of human nature is painfully shown in this sentence. Christ was "hated." It is an utter delusion to suppose that there is any innate response to perfect moral purity, or any innate admiration of "the true, the pure, the just, the kind, the good, and the beautiful," in the heart of man. God gave man, 1800 years ago, a perfect pattern of purity, truth, and love, in the person of our Lord while He was upon earth. And yet we are told He was "hated."

True Christians must never be surprised if they are "hated" like their Lord. "The disciple is not above his Master."— "Marvel not, my brethren, if the world hate you." (Matt. x. 24; 1 John iii. 13.) In fact the more like Christ they are, the more likely to be "hated." Moreover, they must not be cast down and make themselves miserable, under the idea that it is their inconsistencies the world hates, and that if they were more consistent and lovely in life the world would like them better. This is a complete mistake, and a common delusion of the devil. What the world hates about Christians is neither their doctrines nor their faults, but their holy lives. Their lives are a constant testimony against the world, which makes the men of the word feel uncomfortable, and therefore the world hates them.

Let us note that unpopularity among men is no proof that a Christian is wrong, either in faith or practice. The common notion of many, that it is a good sign of a person's character to be well-spoken of by everybody, is a great error. When we see how our Lord was regarded by the wicked and worldly of His day, we may well conclude that it is a very poor compliment to be told that we are liked by everybody. There can surely be very little " witness" about our lives if even the wicked like us. "Woe unto you when all men shall speak well of you." (Luke vi. 26.) That sentence is too much forgotten.

Erasmus used to say, that Luther might have had an easy life, if he had not touched the Pope's crown, and the monks' bellies.

Bengel observes, "Those who please all men, at all times, ought deservedly to look on themselves with suspicion."

8.—[*Go ye up...this feast.*] These words can hardly be called a command. They rather mean, "If you wish to go at once, go, and do not tarry for Me."

[*I go not up yet...my time is not yet full come.*] Here the reason already given and commented on is repeated. Our Lord did not say He would not go to the feast, but, Not yet. There was "a time" for all His actions and every step of His ministry, and that time had not yet fully arrived; or, as the Greek literally means, was not "fulfilled." True Christians should remember that, like their Master on this occasion, they and worldly men cannot well work and act and move together. They will often find it so. Their principles are different. Their reasons and motives of action are different. They will often find that "two cannot walk together except they are agreed."

It seems strange that any reasonable person should see difficulty in this passage, as if it threw a colour of doubt on our Lord's veracity. Yet Augustine has a Homily on the subject in defence of our Lord. Surely the simplest and most natural view is, that our Lord meant, " I am not going up yet ;" and "am not going, at any rate, in the public caravan with yourselves." This is Chrysostom's view and Theophylact's. At an early period Porphyry tried to fasten on our Lord the charge of inconstancy of purpose, out of this passage. An enemy of Christianity must be sadly at a loss for objections, if he can find no better than one founded on this place.

9.—[*When...said these words...abode...Galilee.*] This means, that He staid at the place where this conversation took place, while His brethren started on their journey to Jerusalem. What the place in Galilee was we are not told.

10.—[*But when...brethren...gone up, then went He.*] We are not told what interval there was between our Lord's setting off for Jerusalem, and His brethren's departure. The words before us would seem to indicate that He set off very soon after them. One reason perhaps for our Lord not going with them, was His desire to avoid being made a public show by His relatives. They had very likely a carnal desire to call attention to Him, and to rally a party of adherents round Him, for their own worldly ends. To avoid affording any opportunity for this, our Lord would not go in their company. He had not forgotten, no doubt, that in Galilee there was a party who once would fain have " taken Him by force to make Him a king." (John vi. 15.) He wished to keep clear of that party.

[*Not openly, but...in secret.*] This probably only means that our Lord did not go in the caravan, or large company of His kinsmen, who according to custom went up together from Galilee, but in a more private manner.—How large the caravans or gatherings of fellow-travellers going up to the three great feasts must have been, we may easily see from the account of our Lord being not missed by Mary and Joseph at first, when He went up to Jerusalem with them at the age of twelve. "Supposing Him to have been *in their company*, they went a day's journey, and sought Him among their kinsfolk and acquaintance." (Luke ii. 44.)—Our Lord never sought publicity but once, and that was when He entered Jerusalem, at the last passover, just before His crucifixion. Then he wanted to draw attention to the great sacrifice He was about to offer up on the cross. The contrast between His conduct on that occasion and the present one is very remarkable.

When it says that "He went in secret," it does not necessarily mean that He went alone. There is no reason to suppose that His own chosen Apostles had gone without Him. It only means that He did not go up publicly in the company of all "His kinsfolk and acquaintance" from Galilee.

11.—[*Then the Jews sought Him.*] If, as usually is the case in St. John, the " Jews " here mean the rulers and Pharisees, there can be little doubt that they sought Jesus in order to kill Him, as the first verse tells us they wished to do. They naturally concluded that, like all devout Jews, He would come up to Jerusalem to the feast.

[*Where is He?*] Here, as in many other places, the Greek word rendered "he" implies dislike and contempt. It is as if they said, "that fellow" (See Matt. xxvii. 63), "that deceiver."

12.—[*There was much murmuring.*] As a general rule the Greek word rendered "murmuring" means an under-current of discontent or dislike, not openly expressed. (Thus, Acts vi. 1.) But here, and at ver. 32, it does not seem to mean more than muttering, and private conversation, implying only that people were not satisfied about our Lord, and privately talked much to one another about Him.

[*The people.*] This word in the Greek is in the plural, and evi
dently means the multitude, or crowd of persons who were gathered
at Jerusalem on account of the feast, in contradistinction to the
rulers who were called "the Jews."

[*Some...good man: others...deceiveth...people.*] These expressions
show the feeling of the common people towards our Lord, and are
doubtless indicative of the classes from which the two opinions
came. The class of simple-minded, true-hearted Israelites, who
had sufficient independence to think for themselves, would say of
our Lord, "He is a good man." So also would the Galileans,
probably, who had seen and heard most of our Lord's ministry.
On the other hand, the class of carnal Jews who thought nothing
of true religion, and were led like a mob at the beck of the
priests and Pharisees, would probably take their cue from the
Rulers, and say, "He deceiveth the people," simply because they
were told so. Such, probably, was the feeling of the lower orders
at Jerusalem.

Let it be noted that Christ is, and always has been, the cause
of division of opinion, wherever He has come or has been preached.
To some He is a savour of "life," and to others of "death." (2 Cor.
ii. 16.) He draws out the true character of mankind. They either
like Him or dislike Him. Strife and conflict of opinion are the
certain consequences of the Gospel really coming among men with
power. The fault is not in the Gospel, but in human nature. Still-
ness and quiet are signs not of life but of death. The sun calls
forth miasma and malaria from the swamps it shines upon ; but
the fault is not in the sun, but in the land. The very same rays
call forth fertility and abundance from the corn field.

13.—[*Howbeit no man...openly...fear...Jews.*] This expression of
course applies specially to those who favoured our Lord. Those
who hated Him would not fear to say so openly. This verse shows
the length to which the enmity of the Jewish rulers against our
Lord had already gone. It was a notorious fact among the lower
orders that the heads of the nation hated Jesus, and that it was a
dangerous thing to talk favourably of Him, or to manifest any
interest in Him. The fear of man is a powerful principle among
most people. Rulers have little idea how many things are secretly
talked of sometimes among subjects, and kept back from them.
Two hundred years ago, the Stuarts could persecute all open and
out-spoken favourers of the English Puritans ; but they could not
prevent the lower orders secretly talking of them, and imbibing
prejudices in their favour.

JOHN VII. 14—24.

14 ¶ Now about the midst of the feast Jesus went up into the temple, and taught.

15 And the Jews marvelled, saying, How knoweth this man letters, having never learned?

16 Jesus answered them, and said, My doctrine is not mine, but his that sent me.

17 If any man will do his will, he shall know of the doctrine, whether it be of God, or *whether* I speak of myself.

18 He that speaketh of himself seeketh his own glory: but he that seeketh his glory that sent him, the same is true, and no unrighteousness is in him.

19 Did not Moses give you the law, and *yet* none of you keepeth the law?

Why go ye about to kill me?

20 The people answered and said, Thou hast a devil: who goeth about to kill thee?

21 Jesus answered and said unto them, I have done one work, and ye all marvel.

22 Moses therefore gave unto you circumcision (not because it is of Moses, but of the fathers); and ye on the sabbath day circumcise a man.

23 If a man on the sabbath day receive circumcision, that the law of Moses should not be broken; are ye angry at me, because I have made a man every whit whole on the sabbath day?

24 Judge not according to the appearance, but judge righteous judgment.

WE learn, first, in this passage, that *honest obedience to God's will is one way to obtain clear spiritual knowledge.* Our Lord says, "If any man will do His will, he shall know of the doctrine, whether it be of God, or whether I speak of myself."

The difficulty of finding out "what is truth" in religion, is a common subject of complaint among men. They point to the many differences which prevail among Christians on matters of doctrine, and profess to be unable to decide who is right. In thousands of cases this professed inability to find out truth becomes an excuse for living without any religion at all.

The saying of our Lord before us is one that demands the serious attention of persons in this state of mind. It supplies an argument whose edge and point they will find it hard to evade. It teaches that one secret of getting the key of knowledge, is to practise honestly what we know, and that if we conscientiously use the light that we now have, we shall soon find more light coming down into our minds.—In short, there is a sense in which it is true, that by *doing* we shall come to *knowing.*

There is a mine of truth in this principle. Well would it be for men if they would act upon it. Instead of saying, as some do, "I must first know everything clearly, and then I will act,"—we should say, "I will diligently use such knowledge as I possess, and believe that in the using fresh knowledge will be given to me." How many mysteries this simple plan would solve! How many hard things would soon become plain if men would honestly live up to their light, and "follow on to know the Lord!" (Hosea vi. 3.)

It should never be forgotten that God deals with us as moral beings, and not as beasts or stones. He loves to encourage us to self-exertion and diligent use of such means as we have in our hands. The plain things in religion are undeniably very many. Let a man honestly attend to them, and he shall be taught the deep things of God. Whatever some may say about their inability to find out truth, you will rarely find one of them who does not know better than he practises. Then if he is sincere, let him begin here at once. Let him humbly use what little knowledge he has got, and God will soon give him more.—"If thine eye be single, thy whole body shall be full of light." (Matt. vi. 22.)

We learn, secondly, in this passage, that *a self-exalting spirit in ministers of religion is entirely opposed to the mind of Christ.* Our Lord says, "He that speaketh of himself seeketh his own glory; but he that seeketh His glory that sent him, the same is true, and no unright-eousness is in him."

The wisdom and truth of this sentence will be evident at once to any reflecting mind. The minister truly called of God will be deeply sensible of His Master's majesty and his own infirmity, and will see in himself nothing but unworthiness. He, on the other hand, who knows that he is not "inwardly moved by the Holy Ghost," will try to cover over his defects by magnifying himself and his office. The very desire to exalt ourselves is a bad symptom. It is a sure sign of something wrong within.

Does any one ask illustrations of the truth before us? He will find them, on the one side, in the scribes and Pharisees of our Lord's times. If one thing more than another distinguished these unhappy men, it was their desire to get praise for themselves.—He will find them, on the other side, in the character of the Apostle St. Paul. The keynote that runs through all his Epistles is personal humility and zeal for Christ's glory: "I am less than the least of all saints—I am not meet to be called an Apostle—I am chief of sinners—we preach not ourselves but Christ Jesus the Lord, and ourselves your servants for Jesus' sake." (Ephes. iii. 8; 1 Cor. xv. 9; 1 Tim. i. 15; 2 Cor. iv. 5.)

Does any one ask for a test by which he may discern the real man of God from the false shepherd in the present day? Let him remember our Lord's weighty words, and notice carefully what is the main object that a minister loves to exalt. Not he who is ever crying,

"Behold the Church! behold the Sacraments! behold the ministry!" but he who says, "Behold the Lamb!" —is the pastor after God's own heart. Happy indeed is that minister who forgets self in his pulpit, and desires to be hid behind the cross. This man shall be blessed in his work, and be a blessing.

We learn, lastly, in this passage, *the danger of forming a hasty judgment.* The Jews at Jerusalem were ready to condemn our Lord as a sinner against the law of Moses, because He had done a miracle of healing on the Sabbath-day. They forgot in their blind enmity that the fourth commandment was not meant to prevent works of necessity or works of mercy. A work on the Sabbath our Lord had done, no doubt, but not a work forbidden by the law. And hence they drew down on themselves the rebuke, "Judge not according to the appearance, but judge righteous judgment."

The practical value of the lesson before us is very great. We shall do well to remember it as we travel through life, and to correct our estimate of people and things by the light which it supplies.

We are often too ready to be deceived by an appearance of good. We are in danger of rating some men as very good Christians, because of a little outward profession of religion, and a decent Sunday formality,— because, in short, they talk the language of Canaan, and wear the garb of pilgrims. We forget that all is not good that appears good, even as all is not gold that glitters, and that daily practice, choice, tastes, habits, conduct, private character, are the true evidence of what a man is.—In a word, we forget our Lord's saying, "Judge not according to the appearance."

We are too ready, on the other hand, to be deceived by the appearance of evil. We are in danger of setting down some men as no true Christians, because of a few faults or inconsistencies, and "making them offenders because of a word." (Isa. xxix. 21.) We must remember that the best of men are but men at their very best, and that the most eminent saints may be overtaken by temptation, and yet be saints at heart after all. We must not hastily suppose that all is evil, where there is an occasional appearance of evil. The holiest man may fall sadly for a time, and yet the grace within him may finally get a victory. Is a man's general character godly?—Then let us suspend our judgment when he falls, and hope on. Let us "judge righteous judgment."

In any case let us take care that we pass fair judgment on ourselves. Whatever we think of others, let us beware of making mistakes about our own character. There, at any rate, let us be just, honest, and fair. Let us not flatter ourselves that all is right, because all is apparently right before men. "The Lord," we must remember, "looketh on the heart." (1 Sam. xvi. 7.) Then let us judge ourselves with righteous judgment, and condemn ourselves while we live, lest we be judged of the Lord and condemned for ever at the last day. (1 Cor. xi. 31.)

Notes John vii. 14—24.

14.—[*About.. midst of...feast.*] This would be about the fourth day of the week, as the feast lasted seven days. Some who consider the feast of tabernacles a type of Christ's incarnation, tnink this circumstance is typical of our Lord's earthly ministry lasting three years and a half, answering to the three days and a half during which our Lord taught publicly here in Jerusalem.   I doubt myself whether the circumstance is typical at all.   If the feast of tabernacles is typical, I believe it points to the second advent of Christ much more than to the first.

[*Jesus went up...temple.*]   This means the outer court of the temple, where pious Jews were in the habit of assembling in order to hear the doctors of the law and others, and to discuss religious subjects.   This is the place where our Lord was, when Joseph and Mary found Him, at twelve years of age, "in the temple." (Luke ii. 46.)   It was probably a large open court yard, with piazzas or verandas around it, for shelter against heat and cold.

[*Taught.*]   What our Lord taught we are not told.   Expositions of Scriptnre, as Luke iv. 17—21, and such lessons as those contained in the Sermon on the Mount, and the parables, were most likely the kind of things that He "taught" first, on such occasions as this.   It admits of doubt whether He taught such deep things as those contained in the 5th and 6th chapters of St. John, unless publicly attacked, or put on His defence.

Alford thinks this was "the first time" that our Lord "taught publicly at Jerusalem."   Yet this seems at least questionable when we consider the 2nd and 5th chapters of John.

15.—[*The Jews marvelled.*]   The wisdom and knowledge of Scripture which our Lord showed must have been the principal cause of wonder.   Yet, we may well believe, there was something wonderful in His manner and style of speaking.

[*How knoweth this man letters?*]   The word rendered "letters ' here, must probably be taken in the sense of "learning."   It is so used in Acts xxvi. 24.   In John v. 47 it is rendered "writings." In 2 Tim. iii. 15 it is "Scriptures."   The original idea is a "written character," a letter of an alphabet.   It is thus used in Luke xxiii. 38 of the inscription on the cross, written "in letters of Greek," etc.

[*Having never learned.*]   The Jews must have meant by this, that our Lord had never attended any of the great theological schools which the scribes and Pharisees kept up in Jerusalem,— to which St. Paul refers, when he says, He was "brought up in this city at the feet of Gamaliel." (Acts xxii. 3.)   They did not of course mean that any one brought up at Nazareth must necessarily have been totally ignorant.   That our Lord could read and write is clear from Luke iv. 16, and John viii. 6.   But the Jerusalem

Jews, in their pride and self-conceit, set down any one as comparatively ignorant who had not been trained in their great metro-
politan schools.   People are very apt to condemn any one as
"ignorant" who disagrees with them in religion.

According to Tholuck, it was a rule of the Talmud, "that no
man could appear as a teacher who had not for some years been a
colleague of a Rabbi."

16.—[*My doctrine is not mine, but His that sent Me.*] Our Lord meant
by these words, "My doctrine is not mine only.   The teaching
that I am proclaiming is not a thing of my own private invention,
and the product of my own isolated mind.   It is the doctrine of
my Father who sent Me.   It deserves attention because it is His
message.   He that despiseth it, despiseth not only Me, but Him
whose messenger I am."--The great truth of His own inseparable
and mysterious union with God the Father, is here once more
pointed at.   It is like, "I can of my own self do nothing" (John
v. 30,) and "as my Father hath taught me I speak these things"
(John viii. 28,) and "I have not spoken of myself ; but the Father
which sent Me, He gave Me a commandment, what I should say,
and what I should speak." (John xii. 49.)

Some think that our Lord only meant, "The sense of Scripture
which I give is not my own, but the sense in which God at first
gave it."   But this is a very meagre view of the sentence, though
an Arian or Socinian may like it.

Cyril remarks : "In saying that He was sent by the Father, He
does not show Himself inferior to the Father.   For this mission is
not that of a servant, though it might be called so, as He 'took
on Him the form of a servant.'   But He is 'sent,' as a word is out
of the mind, or a sunbeam out of the sun."

Augustine remarks: "This sentence undoeth the Sabellian
heresy.   The Sabellians have dared to say that the Son is the same
as the Father : the names two, the reality one.   If the names
were two, and the reality one, it would not be said, 'My doctrine
is not mine.'   If Thy doctrine be not Thine, Lord, whose is it,
unless there be another whose it may be ?"

Hengstenberg thinks that our Lord had in view the famous
prophecy of Moses in which God says of Messiah, "I will put
my words in His mouth." (Deut. xviii. 18.)

Let us carefully note with what peculiar reverence we should
receive and study every word that fell from our Lord's lips.   When
He spoke, He did not speak His own mind only, as one of His
Apostles or prophets did.   It was God the Father speaking with

and through Him.   No wonder when we read such expressions as this that St. John calls our Lord " the Word."

17.—[*If any man will do His will.*]   The English language here fails to give the full force of the Greek.   It is literally, " If any man is willing to do,—has a mind and desire and inclination to do God's will."   It is not the simple future of the verb, " do."   There are two distinct verbs.   The stress, therefore, in reading the sentence, must not be laid entirely on "*doing*" God's will.   It is " if any man is *willing* to do."

[*He shall know of the doctrine.*]   This means he shall know "concerning and about" the doctrine I am proclaiming.

[*Whether it be of God, or whether I speak of myself.*]   This means "whether the doctrine is from God, as I say it is,—the doctrine of God the Father, which He has commissioned and sent Me to proclaim to man,—or whether I speak from myself, on my own isolated responsibility, without any license or commission."   The translation "speak of myself," is unfortunately equivocal.   The expression does not mean "about and concerning" myself, but "from" myself.

By "doing the will of God," our Lord must mean, "obeying and performing as far as in us lies, that will of God," which we have expressly declared to us in the Word of God." (17th Article.)   Such "doing" He declares is the way to knowledge.   It is the same idea as the "doing truth" of John iii. 21.

The principle here laid down is one of immense importance.   We are taught that clear knowledge depends greatly on honest obedience, and that distinct views of Divine truth cannot be expected, unless we try to practise such things as we know.   Living up to our light we shall have more light.   Striving to do the few things we know, we shall find the eyes of our understanding enlightened, and shall know more.   Did the Jews profess to feel perplexed, and not to know whether our Lord was sent from God?   Let them honestly do God's will, and seek knowledge in the path of sincere obedience in such matters as were clear and plain.—So doing they would be guided into all truth, and find their doubts removed.

We learn from these words how greatly they err who profess to be waiting till their mental difficulties are removed before they become decided Christians.   They must change their plan.   They must understand that knowledge comes through humble obedience as well as through the intellect.   Let them begin by honestly doing God's will, as far as they know that will, and in so doing they will find their minds enlightened.

We learn, furthermore, that God tests men's sincerity by making obedience part of the process by which religious knowledge is obtained. Are we really willing to do God's will so far as we know it ? If we are, God will take care that our knowledge is increased. If we are not willing to do His will, we show clearly that we do not want to be God's servants. Our hearts and not our heads are in fault.

We learn, finally, the great principle on which many will be condemned at the last day. They did not live up to their light. They did not use such knowledge as they possessed, and so were left dark and dead in sins. There is probably not one in a thousand among unconverted people, who does not know far better than he practises. Such men surely, if lost, will have none to blame but themselves !

In interpreting this verse, I believe we must be careful not to lay more meaning on the expression "do His will," than our Lord meant it to bear. I say this because I observe many respectable commentators place such a very wide and comprehensive sense upon "doing God's will," that they miss entirely our Lord's purpose in speaking the words. They start with saying, that to "do God's will" we must have faith in Christ, new hearts, grace reigning within us, and the like, and thus represent our Lord as saying in effect, "If any man will become a true believer, and a converted man, he shall 'know of the doctrine,'" etc. I venture to think that such interpretation completely misses the mark, and is going round in a circle. Of course any true believer knows true doctrine. I believe that our Lord's object was simply to encourage the honest-minded, sincere, single-eyed *inquirer* after truth. To such a man, though at present very ignorant, He says, "If you really have a desire to do God's will, to please Him, and to follow any light He gives you, you will be taught of Him, you will find out the truth. My doctrine may be hid from the wise and prudent, but it is revealed to babes." (Matt. xi. 25.) I hold, in short, that we should take as simple a view as possible of the sentence, "If any man will do His will," and be very careful that we do not mar its usefulness by putting more meaning on it than our Lord intended.

Bishop Hall thus paraphrases the text: "If any man shall, with a simple and honest heart, yield himself over to do the will of my Father, according to the measure of that he knows, God shall encourage and bless that man with further light; so as he shall fully know whether my doctrine be of God, or of myself."

Burgon remarks: "'The perception of truth depends on the

practice of virtue. It is a favourite maxim of the present day, that increased knowledge will bring with it growth in godliness. Scripture at all events entirely reverses the process. The way to know of the doctrine whether it be of God, is to do His will." (See John v. 44 : viii. 12.)

Hengstenberg remarks : "Whosoever would lead souls to Christ, should not tarry long about the specious argument with which the natural man seeks to disguise the hateful perversion of his state of will, but should above all things try to excite willingness to do the will of God."

18.—[*He that speaketh of himself, etc.*] In this verse, as in the preceding verses, "He that speaketh of himself" would be more literally rendered "speaketh from himself." The verse contains a general principle, applicable not only to our Lord's own case, but to teachers of religion in every age. The meaning seems to be as follows: "He that undertakes on his own responsibility, and without being sent by God, to speak to men about religion, will naturally seek to advance his own importance, and get honour for himself. Speaking *from* himself, he will speak *for* himself, and try to exalt himself. He, on the contrary, who is a true messenger of God, and in whom there is no dishonesty or unrighteousness, will always seek first the glory of the God who sent him." In short, it is one mark of a man being a true servant of God, and really commissioned by our Father in heaven, that he ever seeks his Master's glory more than his own.

The principle here laid down is a very valuable one. By it we may test the pretentions of many false teachers of religion, and prove them to be unsound guides. There is a curious tendency in every system of heresy, or unsound religion, to make its ministers magnify themselves, their authority, their importance, and their office. It may be seen in Romanism and Brahminism to a remarkable extent.

Alford's remark, however, is very true : that in the highest and strictest sense, "the latter part of the sentence is only true of the Holy One Himself, and that owing to human infirmity, purity of motive is no sure guarantee for correctness of doctrine ;" and therefore in the end of the verse it is not said, "he who seeketh God's glory," but "he who seeketh His glory that sent Him,"—specially indicating Christ Himself.

Burgon thinks that "true" is a word used intentionally, in contrast with the expression, "He deceiveth the people."

19.—[*Did not Moses give you the law?*] Our Lord here appeals to the well-known reverence with which all Jews regarded Moses and the law. But it is highly probable that He had in view the practice of publicly reading the law of Moses to the people during the seven days of the feast of tabernacles, which was observed once in every seven years at that feast. (Deut. xxxi. 10.) If, as is possible, this was one of ' he seventh years in which the law was so read, there would be a singular significance and aptness in His appeal. "This very day you have been hearing that law, which you profess to honour so much. But do you honour it in your lives?"

[*None of you keepeth the law, etc.*] This would be more literally rendered, "none of you *doeth* the law." It is the same word that is used in the expression, "if any man will do His will." (v. 17.) The meaning seems to be, "You reject Me and my doctrine, and profess to be zealous for the honour of Moses and the law. And yet none of you really obey the law in heart and in spirit. For instance: why do you seek to kill Me? You are full of hatred of Me, and want to put Me to death unjustly, in the face of the sixth commandment. This is not keeping the law."

The Greek word rendered "go about," is the same that is rendered "seek" in v. 1 of this chapter, and ch. v. 16, 18.

20.—[*The people answered and said, etc.*] It seems probable that those who said this were the common people, the multitude of Jews gathered from all parts of the world, to many of whom our Lord was a stranger. We can hardly suppose that the rulers and leaders of Jerusalem would have spoken in this way.

The expression "Thou hast a devil," may possibly be a repetition of the old charge, that our Lord wrought His miracles by Beelzebub, and was in league with the devil, as John viii. 48. In that sense it would be the strongest form of reproach, blasphemy, and contempt. But considering who the speakers were, it is more likely that it simply means, "Thou art beside Thyself, and mad." (So John x. 20.)

The expression, "who goeth about to kill Thee?" can easily be understood, if we suppose the speakers to be the common people and not the rulers. The common people probably knew nothing about the intention of the rulers to put Jesus to death, and would think Him beside himself to say that any one wanted to kill Him.

21.—[*Jesus answered...I have done one work.*] Our Lord can only refer here to the miracle He had wrought on a former occasion at the pool of Bethesda. (Ch. v. 1, etc.) This was at present the only great miracle that had been publicly performed in Jerusalem : **and** from its having led to our Lord being brought before the Sanhedrim, or great Council of the Jews, and to His defence made before them, it would be a miracle that all would know.

[*Ye all marvel.*] This strong present tense seems to mean, " Ye are all still wondering," not only at the greatness of the miracle, but also at my working it on the Sabbath day. Schleusner maintains that the Greek word rendered " marvel " means here, " Ye are indignant, ye take amiss." He thinks the word is used in this sense in Mark vi. 6 : John v. 28 : and Galat. i. 6.

22.—[*Moses therefore gave unto you circumcision.*] There is a difficulty in this verse in the expression we translate " therefore." It is literally, " on this account,—for this reason,—on account of this." It is not easy to say how the expression comes in, and with what it is connected.

(*a*) Some, as Theophylact, Beza, Poole, Whitby, Hammond, Maldonatus, Pearce, Doddridge, Bloomfield, Olshausen, Tholuck, Hengstenberg, and Stier, propose to alter the stopping, and to connect it with the end of the preceding verse : " Ye all marvel because of this one work." (Compare Mark vi. 6.) But it is doubtful whether the Greek language will fairly admit this.

(*b*) Some would connect "therefore" with "are ye angry," in the following verse : " Are you really angry with me on account of this one work, when you yourselves break the Sabbath, in a sense, by circumcising on the Sabbath day ? " But this connection seems very distant indeed.

(*c*) Some, as Grotius, Calovius, Jansenius, and Webster, think the expression altogether elliptical, and would fill up the sense after "therefore" by supposing some such connection as this : " On account of this work and your anger at it, let me remind you of your own practice about circumcision." (See Matt. xviii. 22 : xii. 30 : Luke xii. 22.)

(*d*) Some, as Chemnitius, Musculus and De Dieu, interpret "therefore" as " because," and make the sentence mean, " Because Moses gave you circumcision, you circumcise a man on the Sabbath day," etc. But it seems a violent strain to make the Greek word we render " therefore " mean " because."

(*e*) Some, finally, as Alford, Burgon, Barradius, Toletus, and Lyranus, would connect " therefore " with the middle of this verse, and would have it mean, " For this reason Moses gave you circumcision, viz., not because it was an ordinance appointed first by him, but because it was given to the Fathers,"—*i. e.*, Abraham, Isaac, and Jacob. This last is perhaps as tenable a view as any. But it is undeniably a difficulty, and must remain so. Adopting this view, the whole verse must be paraphrased as follows: " Moses, whose name and law you highly reverence, gave you among other things the ordinance of circumcision. He gave it, remember, for this reason : because it was an old ordinance, handed down to him by your fathers, Abraham, Isaac, and Jacob, and not an ordinance first communicated to him, like the Levitical law. Now you, in obedience to the ordinance of circumcision, which ought to be administered on the eighth day after a child's birth, think it no breach of the fourth commandment to circumcise a child on the Sabbath day. In fact you postpone the law of the Sabbath to the law of circumcision. You admit that a work of piety and necessity may be done on the Sabbath day. You admit that the fourth commandment which was given on Mount Sinai was not so important as the older law of circumcision."

Burgon shows that "therefore" is used just in the same way as here, at the beginning of a sentence, and pointing forward, in John v. 16, 18 ; viii. 47 ; x. 17 ; xii. 18, 39.

We should note how here, as elsewhere, our Lord refers to Moses as a real person, and to the Old Testament history as real true history.

23.—[*If a man, etc.*] The argument in this verse is as follows : " Even among yourselves you circumcise a child on the Sabbath-day, when it happens to be the eighth day after his birth, in order that the law of circumcision, which your great lawgiver, Moses, sanctioned and re-ordained, should not be broken. You thus admit the whole principle that there is some work which may be done on the Sabbath-day. Is it then just and fair to be angry with Me, because I have done a far greater work to a man on the Sabbath, than the work of circumcision? I have not wounded his body by circumcision, but made him perfectly whole. I have not done a purifying work to one particular part of him, but have restored his whole body to health and strength. I have not done a work of necessity to one single member only, but a work of necessity and benefit to the whole man."

I cannot see any ground for the idea suggested by Alford, that our Lord implies in this verse, that the law of the Sabbath is a mere Judaical practice and comparatively a modern ordinance, and that as such it properly gave way to the older and higher law of circumcision, which was " of the Fathers."—It might be replied, firstly, that the Sabbath is so far from being a Judaical institution, that it is actually older than circumcision, and was appointed in Paradise.—It might be replied, secondly, that our Lord seems purposely to guard against the idea by speaking of circumcision as "given by Moses," and as a part of "the law of Moses." In fact, He does this twice, with such curious particularity that one might think He meant to guard against any one wresting this passage into an argument against the perpetual obligation of the Sabbath-day. He is pleased for the occasion to speak both of circumcision and the Sabbath as part of "the law of Moses." He did this purposely, because the minds of His hearers were full of Moses and the law at this particular period. And His argument amounts to this,—that if they themselves allowed the Mosaic law of the Sabbath must give way in a case of necessity to the Mosaic law of circumcision, they admitted that some works might be done on the Sabbath-day ; and therefore His work of healing an entire man on the Sabbath-day could not be condemned as sinful.

The marginal reading "without breaking the law of Moses," instead of, "that the law of Moses should not be broken," appears to me inadmissible and unnecessary. It is inadmissible, because it is a forced and unatural interpretation of the Greeks words. It is unnecessary, because our Lord is evidently speaking of circumcision as part of "the law of Moses."

The idea of some commentators, as Trapp, Rollock, Hutcheson, Beza and Stier, that "every whit whole" means "wholeness" of soul as well as body, and implies conversion of heart as well as restoration to entire health and strength of the physical man, appears to me unlikely and far-fetched. It is a pious thought, but not apparently in our Lord's mind. Moreover, it is not quite certain that the man healed at Bethesda was healed in soul as well as body. There is no clear proof of it.

24.—[*Judge not according to the appearance, etc.*] The sense of this verse must be sought in connection with the subject of which our Lord has just been speaking. The Jews had condemned our Lord and denounced Him as a sinner against the fourth commandment, because He had done a work on the Sabbath-day. Our Lord refers to this, and says, "Judge not the deed I did according to the appearance. I did a work on the Sabbath unquestionably. But what kind of a work was it? It was an act of necessity and mercy, and therefore an act as lawful to be done as circumcision, which you yourselves perform on the Sabbath-day. In appearance the Sabbath was broken. In reality it was not broken at all. Judge fair and just and righteous judgment. Do not hastily condemn an action, such as this, without looking below the surface."

There is perhaps a reference here to Isaiah's prophecy about

Messiah, " He shall not judge after the sight of His eyes." (Isa. xi. 3.)

The principle here laid down is one of vast importance. Nothing is so common as to judge too favourably or too unfavourably of characters and actions, from merely looking at the outward appearance of things. We are apt to form hasty opinions of others, either for good or evil, on very insufficient grounds. We pronounce some men to be good and others to be bad, some to be godly and others to be ungodly, without anything but appearance to aid our decision. We should do well to remember our blindness, and to keep in mind this text. The bad are not always so bad, nor the good so good as they appear. A potsherd may be covered over with gilding and look bright outside. A nugget of gold may be covered with dirt, and look worthless rubbish. One man's work may look good at first, and yet turn out, by and by, to have been done from the basest motives. Another man's work may look very questionable at first, and yet at last may prove Christ-like and truly godly. From rashly "judging by appearances" may the Lord deliver us !

Whether our Lord meant "judge not persons," or "judge not actions," according to appearance, is a point on which commentators do not agree. If we take the application to be to "persons," the sentence means, " Do not hastily suppose that Moses and I are at variance, and that, therefore, I must be wrong, because Moses, the great lawgiver, must be right." But it seems far simpler and more natural to apply the expression to "actions :" "Judge not the thing done by the appearance only. Look below the surface and weigh it justly."

JOHN VII. 25—36.

25 Then said some of them of Jerusalem, Is not this he, whom they seek to kill ?

26 But, lo, he speaketh boldly, and they say nothing unto him. Do the rulers know indeed that this is the very Christ ?

27 Howbeit we know this man whence he is : but when Christ cometh, no man knoweth whence he is.

28 Then cried Jesus in the temple as he taught, saying, Ye both know me, and ye know whence I am : and I am not come of myself, but he that sent me is true, whom ye know not.

29 But I know him : for I am from him, and he hath sent me.

30 Then they sought to take him : but no man laid hands on him, because his hour was not yet come.

31 And many of the people believed on him, and said, When Christ cometh, will he do more miracles than these which this *man* hath done ?

32 ¶ The Pharisees heard that the people murmured such things concerning him ; and the Pharisees and the chief priests sent officers to take him.

33 Then said Jesus unto them, Yet a little while am I with you, and *then* I go unto him that sent me.

34 Ye shall seek me, and shall not find *me* : and where I am, *thither* ye can not come.

35 Then said the Jews among themselves, Whither will he go, that we shall not find him? will he go unto the dispersed among the Gentiles, and teach the Gentiles?

36 What *manner of* saying is this that he said, Ye shall seek me, and shall not find *me:* and where I am, *thither* ye cannot come?

WE see in these verses, *the obstinate blindness of the unbelieving Jews.* We find them defending their denial of our Lord's Messiahship, by saying, "We know this man whence He is: but when Christ cometh no man knoweth whence He is." And yet in both these assertions they were wrong!

They were wrong in saying that they "knew whence our Lord came." They meant no doubt to say that He was born at Nazareth, and belonged to Nazareth, and was therefore a Galilean. Yet the fact was, that our Lord was born at Bethlehem, that He belonged legally to the tribe of Judah, and that His mother and Joseph were of the house and lineage of David. It is incredible to suppose that the Jews could not have found this out, if they had honestly searched and inquired. It is notorious that pedigrees, genealogies, and family histories were most carefully kept by the Jewish nation. Their ignorance was without excuse.

They were wrong again in saying that "no man was to know whence Christ came." There was a well-known prophecy, with which their whole nation was familiar, that Christ was to come out of the town of Bethlehem. (Micah v. 2; Matt. ii. 5; John vii. 42.) It is absurd to suppose that they had forgotten this prophecy. But apparently they found it inconvenient to remember it on this occasion. Men's memories are often sadly dependent on their wills.

The Apostle Peter, in a certain place, speaks of some as "willingly ignorant." (2 Pet. iii. 5.) He had good reason to use the expression. It is a sore spiritual disease, and one most painfully common among men. There are thousands in the present day just as blind in their way as the Jews. They shut their eyes against the plainest facts and doctrines of Christianity. They pretend to say that they do not understand, and cannot therefore believe the things that we press on their attention, as needful to salvation. But, alas, in nineteen cases out of twenty it is a wilful ignorance! They do not believe what they do not like to believe. They will neither read, nor listen, nor search, nor think, nor inquire honestly after truth. Can any one wonder if such persons are ignorant? Faithful and true is that old proverb, "There are none so blind as those who will not see."

We see, for another thing, in these verses, *the overruling hand of God over all His enemies.* We find that the unbelieving Jews "Sought to take our Lord: but no man laid hands on Him, because His hour was not yet come." They had the will to hurt Him, but by an invisible restraint from above, they had not the power.

There is a mine of deep truth in the words before us, which deserves close attention. They show us plainly that all our Lord's sufferings were undergone voluntarily, and of His own free will. He did not go to the cross because He could not help it. He did not die because He could not prevent His death. Neither Jew nor Gen-

tile, Pharisee nor Sadducee, Annas nor Caiaphas, Herod
nor Pontius Pilate, could have injured our Lord, except
power had been given them from above. All that they
did was done under control, and by permission. The
crucifixion was part of the eternal counsels of the Trinity.
The passion of our Lord could not begin until the very
hour which God had appointed. This is a great mystery.
But it is a truth.

The servants of Christ in every age should treasure up
the doctrine before us, and remember it in time of need.
It is "full of sweet, pleasant, and unspeakable comfort to
godly persons." Let such never forget that they live in
a world where God overrules all times and events, and
where nothing can happen but by God's permission.
The very hairs of their heads are all numbered. Sorrow, and sickness, and poverty, and persecution, can
never touch them, unless God sees fit. They may
boldly say to every cross, "Thou couldst have no
power against me, except it were given thee from
above." Then let them work on confidently. They
are immortal, till their work is done. Let them suffer
patiently, if needs be that they suffer. Their "times are
in God's hand." (Psl. xxxi. 15.) That hand guides and
governs all things here below, and makes no mistakes.

We see, lastly, in these verses, the *miserable end to
which unbelievers may one day come.* We find our Lord
saying to His enemies, "Ye shall seek Me, and shall
not find Me; and where I am thither ye cannot come."

We can hardly doubt that these words were meant
to have a prophetical sense. Whether our Lord had in

view individual cases of unbelief among His hearers, or whether He looked forward to the national remorse which many would feel too late in the final siege of Jerusalem, are points which we cannot perhaps decide. But that many Jews did remember Christ's sayings long after He had ascended up into heaven, and did in a way seek Him and wish for Him when it was too late, we may be very sure.

It is far too much forgotten that there is such a thing as finding out truth too late. There may be convictions of sin, discoveries of our own folly, desires after peace, anxieties about heaven, fears of hell,—but all too late. The teaching of Scripture on this point is clear and express. It is written in Proverbs, "Then shall they call upon Me, but I will not answer; they shall seek Me early, but they shall not find me." (Prov. i. 28.) It is written of the foolish virgins in the parable, that when they found the door shut, they knocked in vain, saying, "Lord, Lord, open to us." (Matt. xxv. 11.) Awful as it may seem, it is possible, by continually resisting light and warnings, to sin away our own souls. It sounds terrible, but it is true.

Let us take heed to ourselves lest we sin after the example of the unbelieving Jews, and never seek the Lord Jesus as a Saviour till it is too late. The door of mercy is still open. The throne of grace is still waiting for us. Let us give diligence to make sure our interest in Christ, while it is called to-day. Better never have been born than hear the Son of God say at last, "Where I am, thither ye cannot come."

NOTES. JOHN VII. 25—36.

25.—[*Then said some of...Jerusalem, etc.*] It is likely that these speakers were some of the lower orders who lived at Jerusalem, and knew what the rulers wanted to do to our Lord. They can hardly be the same as "the people" at 20th verse. They, being probably strangers to the plans of the priests and Pharisees, said, "Who goeth about to kill Thee?" These, on the other hand, say, "Is not this He whom they seek to kill?"

Tittman remarks that the argument of the preceding verses "appears to have had great weight in the minds of our Lord's hearers."

26.—[*But, lo, He speaketh boldly, and they say nothing, etc.*] There appears to have been a restraining power put on our Lord's enemies at this juncture. (See verse 30.) It certainly seems to have struck the people before us as a remarkable thing, that our Lord should speak out so boldly, openly, and publicly, and yet no effort be made by the rulers to apprehend Him and stop His teaching. No wonder that they asked the question which immediately follows: "Have our rulers changed their mind? Are they convinced at last? Have they really found out that this is truly the Messiah, the Christ of God."

The Greek words would be more literally rendered, "Have the rulers truly learned that this man is truly the Christ?"

27.—[*Howbeit we know this man whence He is.*] This means that they knew that our Lord was from Nazareth of Galilee. This, we must remember, was the universal belief of all the Jews. When our Lord rode into Jerusalem, just before His crucifixion, the multitude said, "This is Jesus, the prophet of Nazareth of Galilee." (Matt. xxi. 11.) When an inscription was put over His head on the cross, in the letters of the three languages, it was "Jesus of Nazareth the King of the Jews." (John xix. 19. See also Matt. xiii. 55 ; Mark vi. 3 ; Luke iv. 22.) Yet we know all this time that the Jews were mistaken, and that our Lord was in reality born at Bethlehem, according to prophecy. (Micah v. 2.) We can hardly doubt that the Jews might have found out this if they had taken the pains to inquire narrowly into the early history of our Lord's life. In a nation so strict about pedigrees and birth places, such a thing could not be hid. But it seems as if they would not take the pains to inquire, and satisfied themselves with the common story of His origin, as it gave them an additional excuse for not receiving Him as the Messiah.

The entire ignorance which appears to have prevailed among the Jews about all the circumstances of our Lord's miraculous conception and His birth at Bethlehem, is certainly rather remarkable. Yet it should be remembered that thirty years had passed away between our Lord's birth and His public ministry,—that His mother and Joseph were evidently in a very humble position and might easily be overlooked, as well as all that happened to them,—and that living quietly at Nazareth, their journey to Bethlehem at the time of "the taxing" would soon be forgotten by others.

After all we must not forget that it is part of God's dealings with man not to *force* conviction and belief on any one. The obscurity purposely left over our Lord's birth-place was a part of the moral probation of the Jewish nation. If, in their pride and indolence and self-righteousness, they would not receive the abundant evidence which our Lord gave of His Messiahship, it could not be expected that God would make unbelief impossible, by placing His birth of a virgin at Bethlehem beyond the reach of doubt. In this, as in everything else, if the Jews had *honestly* desired to find out the truth they might have found it.

[*When Christ cometh, no man knoweth, etc.*] It is rather difficult to see what the Jews meant by these words. Most writers think that they referred to the mysterious language of Isaiah about Messiah, "Who shall declare His generation" (Isa. liii. 8) ; or to Micah's words, "Whose goings forth have been from of old, from everlasting" (Micah v. 2) ; and that they had in view the Divine and heavenly origin of Messiah, which all Jews allowed would be a mystery. Yet it is hard to understand why they did not say, "When Christ cometh, He shall be born in Bethlehem," and why they should be supposed to speak of our Lord's earthly origin in the beginning of the verse, and of Messiah's Divine origin in the end. There seems no explanation except to suppose that these speakers were singularly ignorant Jews, who did not know that Messiah was to be born at Bethlehem, and only knew that His birth was to be a mysterious thing. This is a possible view, if not a very probable one.—The argument of the speakers before us would then be as follows : "When Messiah comes, He is to come suddenly, as Malachi foretold, saying, 'the Lord shall suddenly come to His temple' (Mal. iii. 1), unexpectedly, mysteriously, and taking people by surprise. This man therefore, who is sitting in the temple among us, cannot be the Messiah, because we know that He came from Nazareth in Galilee, and has been living there for more than thirty years."—The prophecy about Messiah being born at Bethlehem, they conveniently dropped out of sight, and in fact never dreamed that it was fulfilled by our Lord. The only prophecy they choose to look at was the one in Malachi (Mal. iii. 1), and as the Lord did not appear to fulfil that, they concluded that He could not be the Christ.—In religious matters people are easily satisfied with very imperfect and superficial reasoning when they want to be satisfied and to be spared further trouble. Men never want reasons to confirm their will. This seems to have been the case with the Jews.

Rupertus mentions a common tradition of the Jews,—that when Christ came, He would come at midnight, as the angel came at midnight when the first-born were destroyed in Egypt, and he thinks it may have been in their minds here.

Hutcheson observes that "not comparing of Scripture with Scripture, but taking any single sentence that seems to plead for that we would be at, is a very great nursery and cause of error. Such is the Jews' reasoning here. They catch at one thing, speaking of Messiah's Divinity, and take no notice of other places."

Besser quotes a saying of Luther's : "The Jews are poor scholars. They have caught the sound of the prophet's clock (Micah v. 2), but they have not noted the stroke aright. He who does not hear well, imagines well. They heard that Christ was so to come that none should know whence He came. But they understood not right, that coming from God He was to be born of a virgin, and come secretly into the world."

28.—[*Then cried Jesus...temple...taught.*] This is a remarkable expression. We find our Lord departing from His usual practice, when we read that He "cried," or raised His voice to a high pitch. Generally speaking the words in St. Matthew apply strictly, quoted from Isa. xlii. 2: "He shall not strive nor cry, neither shall any man hear His voice in the street." (Matt. xii. 19.) Yet we see there were occasions when He did see it right to cry aloud and lift up His voice, and this is one. The perverse ignorance of the Jews, their persistence in blindness to all evidence, and the great opportunity afforded by the crowds around Him in the temple courts, were probably reasons why He "cried."

Our Lord is only said to have "cried" or lifted up His voice in four other passages in the Gospels: viz., Matt. xxvii. 50 ; Mark xv. 37 ; John vii. 37, and xii. 44. The Greek for "cried" in Matt. xxvii. 46 is even a stronger word than that before us.

[*Ye both know Me, and...whence I am.*] This is an undeniably difficult expression : partly because it is hard to reconcile with

John viii. 14, and partly because it is not clear how the Jews could be said to "know our Lord" and "whence He was." The explanations suggested are various.

(1) Some, as Grotius, Lampe, Doddridge, Bloomfield, Tittman, and A. Clarke, would have the sentence read as a question : "Do you both know Me, and do ye know whence I am? Are you quite sure that you are correct in saying this?"—In this view it would be rather like the mode of expression used by our Lord in John xvi. 31 : "Do ye now believe?" where the interrogative forms the beginning of the sentence.

(2) Some, as Calvin, Ecolampadius, Beza, Flacius, Gualter, Rollock, Toletus, Glassius, Olshausen, Tholuck, Stier, and Webster, think that the sentence is spoken ironically: "Truly you do know Me and whence I am, and poor miserable knowledge it is, worth nothing at all."—Bengel and others object to this view, that our Lord never spoke ironically. Yet it would be hard to show that there is no irony in John x. 32, if not in Matt. xxvi. 45, and Mark vii. 9.

(3) Some think, as Chrysostom, Cocceius, Jansenius, Diodati, Bengel, Henry, Burkitt, Hengstenberg, Alford, Wordsworth, and Burgon, that the sentence is a simple affirmation : "It is true that you know Me and whence I am. I grant that in a certain sense you are right. You know where I have been brought up, and who my relatives according to the flesh are. And yet in reality you know very little of Me. Of my Divine nature and my unity with my Father ye know nothing at all."—On the whole I prefer this last view to either of the other two.

[*And I am not come of myself, etc.*] This sentence and the rest of the verse are evidently elliptical, and must be paraphrased to give a full idea of the sense : "And yet ye do not really and thoroughly know Me ; for I am not come of myself, independent of God the Father, and without commission, but sent by the Father into the world. And He that sent Me has proved Himself true to His promises by sending Me, and is indeed a real true Person, the true and faithful God of Israel, whom ye, with all your profession, do not know."

Here, as elsewhere, our Lord's expression, "not come of myself," points directly to that intimate union between Himself and God the Father which is so constantly referred to in the Gospel of John.

Here too, as elsewhere, our Lord charges on the unbelieving Jews ignorance of the God whom they professed to serve, and for whose honour they professed to be jealous. With all their boasted zeal for true religion and the true God, they did not really know God.

The word "true," here, is of doubtful interpretation. It means "truthful," according to Cyril, Chrysostom, Theophylact, Lampe, Tholuck. But it is not clear that this is so. Alford maintains that it must mean "really existent." Trench takes the same view in his "New Testament Synonyms."

29.—[*But I know Him, etc.*] The knowledge of which our Lord here speaks, is that peculiar and intimate knowledge which is necessarily implied in the unity of the three Persons of the Trinity, in the Godhead. There is a high and deep sense in which the Son knows the Father, and the Father knows the Son, which we cannot pretend to explain, because it is far above our capacities. (John x. 15.) The Jews knew nothing rightly of God the Father. Jesus, on the contrary, could say, "I know Him," as no one else could. "Neither knoweth any man the Father save the Son, and He to whomsoever the Son will reveal Him." (Matt. xi. 27.)

The expression 'I am from Him," must not be confined and cramped down to mean only that our Lord had come like any prophet of old, with a message and commission from God. It declares the relationship between God the Father and God the Son: "I am from Him by eternal generation,—always one with Him,—always equal with Him,—but always a distinct person;— always the only begotten Son,—always from Him."

The expression "He hath sent Me," is, like the preceding one, something far more than the mere assertion of a prophet's commission. It is a declaration that He was the Sent One,—the Messiah, the Prophet greater than Moses, whom the Father had always promised to send: "I am the Seed of the woman sent to bruise the serpent's head. I am He whom the Father covenanted and engaged to send for the redemption of a lost world. I am He whom the Father hath sent to be the Saviour of lost man. I proclaim myself the Sent One,—the Christ of God."

Bishop Hall paraphrases the two verses thus: "Ye mutter secretly that ye know Me, and the place of my birth and parentage; but ye are utterly mistaken, for I have a Father in heaven whom ye know not. I came not of myself, but my Father is He that sent Me, who is the God of truth; of whom ye, after all your pretences of knowledge, are utterly ignorant. But I do perfectly know Him, as I have good reason; for both I am from Him by eternal generation, and am by Him sent into the world to do the great work of redemption."

30.—[*Then they sought to take Him.*] This last declaration seems to have raised the anger of the Jerusalem multitude, who were listen. ing to our Lord. With the characteristic keenness of all Jews, they at once detected in our Lord's language a claim to be received as the Messiah. Just as on a former occassion, they saw, in His "calling God His Father," that He "made Himself equal with God" (John v. 18), so here in His saying "I am from Him : He hath sent Me," they saw an assertion of His right to be received as Messiah.

[*But no man...hour not yet come.*] This restraint on our Lord's enemies can only be accounted for by direct Divine interposition. It is like John viii. 20, and xviii. 6. It is clear that they could do nothing against Him except by God's permission, and when God, in His wisdom, was pleased to let it be done. Our Lord did not fall into His enemies' hands through inability to escape, but be- cause the "hour had come" when He voluntarily undertook to die as a substitute.

The doctrine before us, let us note, is full of comfort to God's people. Nothing can hurt them except and until God permits. We are all immortal till our work is done. To realize that nothing happens in this world except by the eternal counsels of our Father, and according to His eternal plans, is one grand secret of living a calm, peaceful, and contented life.

Besser quotes a saying of Luther's : "God has appointed a nice, easy hour for everything ; and that hour has the whole world for its enemy : it must attack it. The devil shoots and throws at the poor clock-hand, but in vain : for all depends on the hour. Till the hour comes, and the hand has run its course, the devil and the world shall accomplish nothing."

31.—[*Many of the people.*] This means the common people—the lower orders, in contradistinction to the Pharisees and chief priests.

[*Believed on Him.*] There seems no reason to think that this was not a true faith, so far as it went. · But it would not be safe perhaps to conclude that it was more than a general belief that our Lord must be the Messiah, the Christ, and that He deserved to be received as such.

[*When Christ cometh...more miracles...done.*] This language must clearly have been used by people who were familiar with many of our Lord's miracles wrought in Galilee, and knew a good deal about His ministry. So few miracles probably had been wrought as yet in and round Jerusalem that the language would hardly be used by Jerusalem people. The word "more" probably means not only more in number, but "greater" in character.

The question raised by these people was a fair and reasonable one : "What greater evidence could any one give that He is the Christ than this man has given? He could not work greater miracles, even if He worked more numerous ones. What then are we waiting for? Why should we not acknowledge this man as the Christ?"

32.—[*The Pharisees heard that the people murmured...Him.*] This would be more literally translated, "The Pharisees heard the people murmuring:" they actually heard with their own ears the common people, as they walked about the temple courts, and gathered in the streets of Jerusalem at the crowded time of the feast, keeping up their under conversation about our Lord. Here, as at the twelfth verse, the word we render "murmuring" does not necessarily imply any finding fault, but only a dissatisfied and restless state of mind, which found vent in much conversation and whispering among the people.

[*And the Pharisees...sent officers to take Him.*] It would seem that the talk and stir of men's minds about our Lord so alarmed and irritated the rulers of the Jews, that they resolved even now in the midst of the feast to arrest Him, and so stop His preaching. What day of the feast this was, and what interval elapsed between this verse and the thirty-seventh, where we are told of "the last day" of the feast, we are not told. It seems probable that the officers sought an opportunity for taking our Lord, but could find none,—partly because of the crowds that surrounded Him, and partly because of a Divine restraint laid upon them ; and that this was the state of things for three days at least.

Full well did these Pharisees justify our Lord's character of them in another place : "Ye neither go in yourselves into the kingdom : neither suffer ye them that are entering to go in." (Matt. xxiii. 13.)

33.—[*Then said Jesus unto them.*] The officers of the Pharisees and their supporters seem clearly to be the persons whom our Lord here addresses. Not only were they, through Divine restraint, unable to lay hands on Him, but they were obliged to stand by and listen to Him. They dared not seize Him for fear of the people, and yet dared not go away to report their inability to carry out their orders.

[*Yet a little while, etc.*] There is probably an under-tone of sadness and tenderness about this and the following sentences. It is as though our Lord said, "Ye have come to lay hands on Me, and yet ye might well bear with Me. I am only a little time longer with you, and then, when my time is come for leaving the world, I shall go back to my Father who sent Me." Or else it must mean " Ye are sent to lay hands on Me, but it is useless at present? ye cannot do it: because my hour is not yet come. I have yet a little longer time to minister on earth ; and then, and not till then, I go to Him that sent Me." Alford takes this view.

The Jews of course could not understand whom our Lord meant by "Him that sent Me," and this saying must necessarily have seemed dark and mysterious to them.

34.—[*Ye shall seek Me...shall not find Me.*] These words seem addressed both to the officers and to those who sent them,—to the whole body, in fact, of our Lord's unbelieving enemies: "A day will come too late, when you will anxiously seek Me, and bitterly lament your rejection of Me, but too late. The day of your visitation will be past and gone, and you will not find Me."

There is a great Bible truth taught here, as elswhere, which is far too much overlooked by many,—I mean the possibility of men seeking salvation when it is too late, and crying for pardon and heaven when the door is shut for ever. Men may find out their folly and be filled with remorse for their sins, and yet feel that they cannot repent. No doubt true repentance is never too late ; but late repentance is seldom true. Pharaoh, King Saul, and Judas Iscariot, could all say, "I have sinned." Hell itself is truth known too late. God is unspeakably merciful no doubt: but there is a limit even to God's mercy. He can be angry, and may be provoked to leave men alone. People should often study Prov. i. 24—31 ; Job. xxvii. 9 ; Isaiah l. 15 ; Jer. xi. 11 ; xiv. 12 ; Ezek. viii. 18 ; Hosea v. 6 ; Micah iii. 4 ; Zech. vii. 13 ; Matt. xxv. 11, 12.

These words very possibly received a most awful fulfilment during the siege of Jerusalem, forty years after they were spoken. So think Chrysostom, Theophylact, and Euthymius.

But they were probably found true by many of our Lord's hearers long before that time. Their eyes were opened to see their folly and sin, after our Lord had left the world.

Burgon remarks that to this very day the Jews are, in a sense, seeking the Messiah and yet not finding Him.

[*Where I am, thither ye cannot come.*] The place our Lord speaks of here is evidently heaven. Some have thought, as Bengel, that the words, "where I am," should be translated, "where I go." But it is neither a natural nor usual sense to put on the words. Nor is it necessary. There was a sense in which the Son of God could say with perfect truth, "Where I am, thither ye cannot come." As God, he never ceased to be in heaven, even when He was fulfilling His ministry on earth during His incarnation. As God, He could truly say, "Where I am," and not merely where "I was," or where "I shall be." It is like John iii. 13, where our Lord, speaking to Nicodemus, calls Himself the "Son of man which IS in heaven." The expression is one of the many texts proving our Lord's divinity. No mere man, speaking on earth, could speak of heaven as a place " where I am." Augustine strongly maintains this view.

[*Ye cannot come.*] This is one of those expressions which show the impossibility of unconverted and unbelieving men going to heaven. It is a place where they "cannot come." Their own nature unfits them for it. They would not be happy if they were there. Without new hearts, without the Holy Ghost, without the blood of Christ, they could not enjoy heaven. The favourite notion of some modern theologians, that all mankind are finally to go to heaven, cannot possibly be reconciled with this expression. Men may please themselves with thinking it is kind and loving and liberal and large-hearted to teach and believe that all men and women of all sorts will finally be found in heaven. One word of our Lord Jesus Christ's overturns the whole theory.—"Heaven is a place," He says to the wicked, where "ye cannot come."

The word "ye" is emphatical, and in the Greek stands out in strong contrast to the "I" of the sentence.

35.—[*Then said the Jews...themselves.*] The expression "Jews" here can hardly be confined to the Pharisees and rulers. It must mean at any rate those among them who heard our Lord say the words in the preceding verse. Whoever they were, they were probably not friendly to Him.

[*Whither will He go...not find Him.*] This would be more literally rendered, "Whither is this man about to go." They could put no meaning of a spiritual kind on our Lord's words.

[*Will He go...dispersed...Gentiles, etc.*] This would be more literally rendered, "Is He about to go to the dispersion among the Greeks, and to teach the Greeks?" The Greek language, and Greek literature, and Greek philosophy, had so thoroughly leavened Asia Minor and Syria and Palestine, that the expression "Greeks" in the New Testament is often equivalent to Gentiles, and stands for any people who are not Jews. Thus Rom. ii. 9, 10; iii. 9; 1 Cor. x. 32; xii. 13. Yet it is a singular fact that this is the only passage in the New Testament where the word "Greek," standing alone and not in contradistinction to Jews, is rendered "Gentile."

The verse teaches two interesting things. One is the fact that the existence of a large number of Jews scattered all over the Gentile world was acknowledged as notorious in our Lord's time. The other is the impression that it proves to have prevailed among the Jews that a new teacher of religion might be expected to go to the Jews scattered among the Gentiles, and, beginning with them, proceed to teach the Gentiles. This is in fact precisely what the Apostle Paul and his companions afterwards did. They did "go to the dispersed among the Gentiles, and teach the Gentiles." The idea started here of "teaching the Gentiles" was probably the suggestion of those who hated our Lord. How much the Jews detested the opening of the door of salvation to the Gentiles we know from the Acts of the Apostles.

Some, as Chrysostom, Theophylact, Hengstenberg, and many others, think that the words "dispersed among the Gentiles" mean the Gentiles themselves dispersed and scattered all over the world, and not the Jews. But our own version seems far more likely. There is an awkwardness in calling the Gentiles "the dispersion," and it is an expression nowhere else used. James calls the Jews "the twelve tribes scattered abroad." (James i. 1.)

36.—[*What manner of saying, etc.*] This question of the Jews is the language of people who saw that there was probably some deep meaning in our Lord's words, and yet were unable to make out what He meant. Hating our Lord bitterly, as many of them did, —determined to kill Him the first opportunity,—vexed and annoyed at their own inability to answer Him, or to stop His influence with the people,—they suspected everything that fell from His lips.—"Do not these words of His imply some mischief? Is there not some evil at the bottom of them? Do they not indicate that He is going to dishonour the law of Moses by pulling down the wall of partition between Jew and Gentile?"

JOHN VII. 37—39.

37 In the last day, that great *day* of the feast, Jesus stood and cried, saying, If any man thirst, let him come unto me, and drink.

38 He that believeth on me, as the scripture hath said, out of his belly shall flow rivers of living water.

39 (But this spake he of the Spirit, which they that believe on him should receive: for the Holy Ghost was not yet *given*; because that Jesus was not yet glorified.)

IT has been said that there are some passages in Scripture which deserve to be printed in letters of gold.

Of such passages the verses before us form one. They contain one of those wide, full, free invitations to mankind, which make the Gospel of Christ so eminently the " good news of God." Let us see of what it consists.

We have, first, in these verses, *a case supposed.* The Lord Jesus says, " If any man thirst." These words no doubt were meant to have a spiritual meaning. The thirst before us is of a purely spiritual kind. It means anxiety of soul,—conviction of sin,—desire of pardon,— longing after peace of conscience. When a man feels his sins, and wants forgiveness—is deeply sensible of his soul's need, and earnestly desires help and relief— then he is in that state of mind which our Lord had in view, when He said, " If any man thirst." The Jews who heard Peter preach on the day of Pentecost, and were " pricked in their hearts,"—the Philippian jailer who cried to Paυʾ and Silas, " What must I do to be saved?" are both examples of what the expression means. In both cases there was " thirst."

Such thirst as this, unhappily, is known by few. All ought to feel it, and all would feel it if they were wise. Sinful, mortal, dying creatures as we all are, with souls that will one day be judged and spend eternity in heaven or hell, there lives not the man or woman on earth who ought not to "thirst" after salvation. And yet the many thirst after everything almost except salvation. Money, pleasure, honour, rank, self-indulgence,— these are the things which they desire. There is no clearer proof of the fall of man, and the utter corruption of human nature, than the careless indifference or most people about their souls. No wonder the Bible calls the natural man "blind" and "asleep" and "dead," when so few can be found who are awake, alive, and athirst about salvation.

Happy are those who know something by experience of spiritual "thirst." The beginning of all true Christianity is to discover that we are guilty, empty, needy sinners. Till we know that we are lost, we are not in the way to be saved. The very first step toward heaven is to be thoroughly convinced that we deserve hell. That sense of sin which sometimes alarms a man and makes him think his own case desperate, is a good sign. It is in fact a symptom of spiritual life : "Blessed indeed are they which do hunger and thirst after righteousness, for they shall be filled." (Matt. v. 6.)

We have, secondly in these verses, *a remedy proposed.* The Lord Jesus says, "If any man thirst, let him come unto Me and drink." He declares that He is the true fountain of life, the supplier of all spiritual necessities, the reliever of all spiritual wants. He invites all who feel the burden of sin heavy, to apply to Him, and proclaims Himself their helper.

Those words, "Let him come unto Me," are few and very simple. But they settle a mighty question which all the wisdom of Greek and Roman philosophers could never settle : they show how man can have peace with God. They show that peace is to be had in Christ by trusting in Him as our mediator and substitute,—in one word, by believing. To "come" to Christ is to believe on Him, and to "believe" on Him is to come. The remedy

may seem a very simple one, too simple to be true
But there is no other remedy than this; and all the
wisdom of the world can never find a flaw in it, or
devise a better.

To use this grand prescription of Christ, is the secret
of all saving Christianity. The saints of God in every
age have been men and women who drank of this
fountain by faith and were relieved. They felt their
guilt and emptiness, and thirsted for deliverance. They
heard of a full supply of pardon, mercy, and grace in
Christ crucified for all penitent believers. They believed
the good news and acted upon it. They cast aside all
confidence in their own goodness and worthiness, and
came to Christ by faith as sinners. So coming they
found relief. So coming daily they lived. So coming
they died. Really to feel the sinfulness of sin and to
thirst, and really to come to Christ and believe, are the
two steps which lead to heaven. But they are mighty
steps. Thousands are too proud and careless to take
them. Few, alas, think; and still fewer believe!

We have, lastly, in these verses, *a promise held out.*
The Lord Jesus says, "He that believeth on Me, out of
his belly shall flow rivers of living water." These words
of course were meant to have a figurative sense. They
have a double application. They teach, for one thing,
that all who come to Christ by faith shall find in Him
abundant satisfaction. They teach, for another thing,
that believers shall not only have enough for the wants
of their own souls, but shall also become fountains of
blessings to others.

The fulfilment of the first part of the promise could be testified by thousands of living Christians in the present day. They would say, if their evidence could be collected, that when they came to Christ by faith, they found in Him more than they expected. They have tasted peace, and hope, and comfort, since they first believed, which, with all their doubts and fears, they would not exchange for anything in this world. They have found grace according to their need, and strength according to their days. In themselves and their own hearts they have often been disappointed; but they have never been disappointed in Christ.

The fulfilment of the other half of the promise will never be fully known until the judgment-day. That day alone shall reveal the amount of good that every believer is made the instrument of doing to others, from the very day of his conversion. Some do good while they live, by their tongues; like the Apostles and first preachers of the Gospel. Some do good when they are dying; like Stephen and the penitent thief, and our own martyred Reformers at the stake. Some do good long after they are dead, by their writings; like Baxter and Bunyan and M'Cheyne. But in one way or another, probably, almost all believers will be found to have been fountains of blessings. By word or by deed, by precept or by example, directly or indirectly, they are always leaving their marks on others. They know it not now; but they will find at last that it is true. Christ's saying shall be fulfilled.

Do we ourselves know anything of " coming to

Christ"? This is the question that should arise in
our hearts as we leave this passage. The worst of all
states of soul is to be without feeling or concern about
eternity,—to be without "thirst." The greatest of all
mistakes is to try to find relief in any other way than
the one before us,—the way of simply "coming to
Christ." It is one thing to come to Christ's Church,
Christ's ministers, and Christ's ordinances. It is quite
another thing to come to Christ Himself. Happy is he
who not only knows these things, but acts upon them!

NOTES. JOHN VII. 37—39.

37.—[*In...last day...great day...feast.*] There seems to be an interval
of three days between this verse and the preceding one. At any
rate it is certain that our Lord went to the temple and taught "about
the midst of the feast." (v. 14.) There seems no break from that
point, but a continuous narrative of teaching and argument up to
this verse. There is therefore no account of what our Lord did
during the three latter days of the feast. We can only conjecture
that He taught on uninterrupted, and that a restraint was put by
Divine interposition on His enemies, so that they dared not interfere with Him.

Whether this "last day of the feast" means the eighth day or
the seventh, is a question not decided.

(1) Some, as Bengel, and others, think it must be the seventh
day, because in the account of the feast of tabernacles given by
Moses, there is no special mention of anything to be done on the
eighth day (Levit. xxiii. 33—43); while on each of the seven days
of the feast there were special sacrifices appointed, a special reading of the law once every seven years, and also, according to the
Jewish writers, a solemn drawing of water from the pool of
Siloam, to be poured on the altar in the temple.

(2) Others, as Lightfoot, Gill, Alford, Stier, Wordsworth, and
Burgon, think it must be the eighth day, because in reality the
feast could hardly be said to be finished till the end of the
eighth day; and even in the account of the feast in Leviticus,
it is said that the eighth day is to be "a holy convocation" and
a "Sabbath." (Lev. xxiii. 36 and 39.)

The point is of no practical importance; but of the two opinions I incline to prefer the second one. The words seem to me to indicate that all the ceremonial of the feast was over, the last offerings had been made, and the people were on the point of dispersing to their respective homes, when our Lord seized the opportunity, and made the grand proclamation which immediately follows.— It was a peculiarly typical occasion. The last feast of the year was concluding, and before it concluded our Lord proclaimed publicly the great truth which was the commencement of a new dispensation, and Himself as the end of all sacrifices and ceremonies.

The objection that no drawing and pouring of water took place on the eighth day, appears to me of no weight. That our Lord referred to it, is highly probable. But I think He referred to it as a thing which the Jews had seen seven days running, and remembered well. Now on the eighth day, when there was no water drawn, there seemed a peculiar fitness in His crying,— "Come unto Me and drink. The water of life that I give may be drawn, though the feast is over."

[*Jesus stood and cried.*] These words must mean that our Lord chose some high and prominent position, where He could "stand" and be seen and heard by many persons at once. If, as we may suppose, the worshippers at the feast of tabernacles were just turning away from the last of its ceremonies, one can easily imaagine that our Lord "stood" in some commanding position close by the entrance of the temple. When it is said that "He cried," it means that He lifted up His voice in a loud, and, to Him, unusual manner, in order to arrest attention,—like a herald making a public proclamation.

[*If any man thirst...come unto Me and drink.*] These words can have but one meaning.—They are a general invitation to all who are athirst about their souls, to come unto Christ in order to obtain relief. He declares Himself to be the fountain of life,—the reliever of man's spiritual wants,—the giver of satisfaction to weary consciences,—the remover and pardoner of sins. He recommends all who feel their sins and want pardon, to come unto Him, and promises that they shall at once get what they want. The idea is precisely the same as that in Matt. xi. 28, though the image employed is different.

It is probable, as almost all commentators remark, that our Lord chose this figure and imagery, because of the Jewish custom of drawing water from the pool of Siloam during the feast of tabernacles, and carrying it in solemn procession to the temple. And it is thought that our Lord purposely refers to this ceremony, of which the minds of many would doubtless be full : "Does any one want true water of life, better than any water of Siloam ?— Let him come to Me and by faith draw out of Me living waters, —even peace of conscience, and pardon of sins."—But it is fair to remember that this is only conjecture. This custom of drawing water from Siloam at the feast was a human invention, nowhere commanded in the law of Moses, or even mentioned in the Old Testament ; and it admits of doubt whether our Lord would have sanctioned it. Moreover, it is evident from John iv. 10, and vi. 55, that the figures of "water" and "thirst" were not unfrequently used by our Lord.—The figures at any rate were familiar to all Jews, from Isaiah lv. 1.

Some have thought because the feast of tabernacles was specially intended to remind the Jews of their sojourn in the wilderness, that our Lord had in view the miraculous supply of water from the rock, which followed Israel everywhere, and that He wished the Jews to see in Him the fulfilment of that type, the true Rock (1 Cor. x. 4.) The idea is deserving of attention.

The whole sentence is one of those golden sayings which ought to be dear to every true Christian, and is full of wide encouragement to all sinners who hear it. Its words deserve special attention.

We should note *the breadth* of the invitation. It is for "any man." No matter who and what he may have been,—no matter how bad and wicked his former life,—the hand is held out, and the offer made to him : "If any man thirst, let him come." Let no man say that the Gospel is narrow in its offers.

We should note *the persons* invited. They are those who "thirst." That expression is a figurative one, denoting the spiritual distress and anxiety which any one feels when he discovers the value of his soul, and the sinfulness of sin, and his own guilt. Such an one feels a burning desire for relief, of which the distressing sensation of "thirst"—a sensation familiar to all Eastern nations—is a most fitting emblem. No further qualification is named. There is no mention of repentance, amendment, preparation, conditions to fulfil, new heart to be got. One thing alone is named. Does a man "thirst"? Does he feel his sins and want pardon ?—Then the Lord invites him.

We should note *the simplicity* of the course prescribed to a thirsting sinner.—It is simply, "Let him come unto Me." He has only to cast his soul on Christ, trust Him, lean on Him, believe on Him, commit his soul with all its burdens to Him, and that is

enough.   To trust Christ is to "come" to Christ.—So "coming,"
Christ will supply all his need.   So believing, he is at once for-
given, justified, and received into the number of God's children
(See John vi. 35, 37.)

The expression "drink," is of course figurative, answering to
the word "thirst."   It means, "Let him freely take from Me
everything that his soul wants,—mercy, grace, pardon, peace,
strength.   I am the Fountain of Life.   Let him use Me as such,
and I shall be well pleased."

We do not read of any prophet or apostle in the Bible who ever
used such language as this, and said to men, "Come unto me and
drink."   None surely could use it but one who knew that He was
very God.

38.—[*He that believeth on Me, etc.*]   This verse is undoubtedly full of
difficulties, and has received very various interpretations.   Not
the least difficulty is about the connection in which the several
expressions of the verse ought to be taken.

(1) Some, as Stier, would connect "He that believeth on Me"
with the verb "drink" in the preceding verse.   It would then run
thus : "If any man thirst let him come unto Me, and let him
drink that believeth on Me."—I cannot think this is a right view.
For one thing, it would be a violent strain of all grammatical
usage of the Greek language, to interpret the words thus.   For
another thing, it would introduce doctrinal confusion.   Our Lord's
invitation was not made to him "that believeth," but to him that
is "athirst."

(2) Some, as Chrysostom, Theophylact, Pellican, Heinsius,
Gualter, De Dieu, Lightfoot, Trapp, and Henry, would connect
"He that believeth on Me" with the following words : "as the
Scripture hath said."   It would then mean, "He that believeth
on Me after the manner that the Scripture bids him believe."   I
cannot think that this interpretation is correct.   The expression,
"Believeth as the Scripture hath said," is a very strange and vague
one, and unlike anything else in the Bible.

(3) Most commentators think that the word, "as the Scripture
hath said," must be taken in connection with those that follow,
"out of his belly," etc.   They think that our Lord did not mean
to quote precisely any one text of Scripture, but only to give in
His own words the general sense of several well-known texts.
This, in spite of difficulties, I believe is the only satisfactory view.

One difficulty, of a grammatical kind, arises from the expression,

"He that believeth on Me," having no verb with which it is connected in the verse. This cannot be got over. It must be taken
as a nominative absolute, and the sentence must be regarded as an
elliptical sentence, which we must fill up.

Another difficulty arises from the fact, that there is no text in
the Old Testament Scriptures which at all answers to the quotation
apparently given here. This difficulty is undeniable, but not
insuperable. As I have already said, our Lord did not intend to
give an exact quotation, but only the general substance of several
Old Testament promises. Wordsworth thinks Matt. ii. 23 a similar
case. Jerome als-- maintains that frequently the inspired writers
contented themselves with giving the sense and not the precise
words of a quotation. (See also Ephes. v. 14.)

Another difficulty arises as to the application of the words, "Out
of his belly shall flow rivers of living water." Some, as Rupertus,
Bengel, and Stier, would apply this to our Lord Himself, and say
that it means, "Out of Christ's belly shall flow rivers of living
water." But it is a grave objection to this view that it totally
disconnects the beginning of the verse from the end,—makes the
expression "He that believeth on Me" even more elliptical than it
needs be,—and throws the latter part of the verse into the form of
a precise quotation of Scripture.

I venture to think that the true interpretation of the verse is as
follows: "He that believeth on Me, or comes to Me by faith as
his Saviour, is the man out of whose belly shall flow rivers of living
water, as the Scripture hath said it should be." It is a strong
argument in favour of this view that our Lord said to the Samaritan
woman, that the water He could give, would be in him that drank
it "a well of water springing up into everlasting life." (John iv. 14.)
The full meaning of the promise is that every believer in Christ shall
receive abundant satisfaction of his own spiritual wants; and not
only that, but shall also become a source of blessing to others.
From him instrumentally, by his word, work, and example, waters
of life shall flow forth to the everlasting benefit of his fellow-men.
He shall have enough for himself, and shall be a blessing to others.
The imagery of the figure used is still kept up, and "his belly"
must stand for "his inner man." His heart being filled with
Christ's gifts, shall overflow to others, and having received much
shall give and impart much.

The passages to which our Lord referred, and the substance of
which He gives, are probably Isaiah xii. 3; xxxv. 6, 7; xli. 18;
xliv. 3; lv. 1; lviii. 11; Zech. xiv. 8, 16. Of these passages our
Lord gives the general sense, but not the precise words. This is

the view of Calvin, Beza, Grotius, Cocceius, Diodati, Lampe, and Scott. It is a curious, confirmatory fact, that the Arabic and Syriac versions of the text both have the expression "Scripture" in the plural, "As the *Scriptures* have said."

It is a curious fact which Bengel mentions, that the 14th chapter of Zechariah was read in public in the temple on the first day of the feast of tabernacles. If this is correct we can hardly doubt that our Lord must have had this in mind when He used the expression, "As the Scripture hath said." It is as though He said, "As you have heard, for instance, during this very feast, from the book of your prophet Zechariah."

That almost every believer, whose life is spared after he believes, becomes a fountain of blessing and good to others, is a simple matter of fact, which needs no illustration. A truly converted man always desires the conversion of others, and labours to promote it. Even the thief on the cross, short as his life was after he repented, cared for his brother thief; and from the words he spoke have flowed "rivers of living water" over this sinful world for more than eighteen hundred years. He alone has been a fountain of blessing.

Bloomfield quotes a Rabbinical sentence: "When a man turns to the Lord, he is like a fountain filled with living water, and rivers flow from him to men of all nations and tribes."

The favourite notion of some, that our Lord in this place only referred to the miraculous gifts of the Holy Ghost, to be given on the day of Pentecost, is an idea that does not commend itself to me at all. The thing before us is a thing promised to *every believer*.— But the miraculous gifts were certainly not bestowed on *every* believer. Thousands were evidently converted through the Apostles' preaching who did not receive these gifts. Yet all received the Holy Ghost.

Luther paraphrases this verse thus: "He that cometh to Me shall be so furnished with the Holy Ghost, that he shall not only be quickened and refreshed himself and delivered from thirst, but he shall also be a strong stone vessel, from which the Holy Ghost in all His gifts shall flow to others, refreshing, comforting, and strengthening them, even as he was refreshed by Me. So St. Peter on the day of Pentecost, by one sermon, as by a rush of water, delivered three thousand men from the devil's kingdom, washing them in an hour from sin, death, and Satan." Hengstenberg, after quoting this, adds, "That was only the first exhibition of a glorious peculiarity which distinguishes the Church of the

New Testament from the Church of the Old. She has a living impulse which will diffuse the life within her, even to the ends of the earth."

39.—[*But this spake...of the Spirit.*] This verse is one of those explanatory comments which are so common in St. John's Gospel. The opening words would be more literally rendered, "He spake this concerning the Spirit."

Let it be noted that here, at any rate, there can be no doubt that "water" does not mean "baptism," but the Holy Spirit.—St. John himself says so in unmistakable language.

[*Which they...believe...should receive.*] This means, "Which believers in Him were about to receive." There is an inseparable connection between faith in Christ and receiving the Holy Ghost. If any man has faith he has the Spirit. If any man has not the Spirit he has no saving faith in Christ. The effectual work of the Second and Third Persons in the Trinity is never divided.

Rupertus think that our Lord had specially in view that mighty out-pouring of the Spirit on the Gentile world, which was to take place after His own ascension into heaven, and the going forth of the Apostles into the world to preach the Gospel.

[*For the Holy Ghost...not yet given, etc.*] This sentence means that the Holy Ghost was not yet poured on believers in all His fulness, because our Lord had not yet finished His work by dying, rising again, and ascending into heaven for us. It was not till He was "glorified" by going up into heaven and taking His seat at the right hand of God, that the Holy Ghost was sent down in full influence on the Church. Then was fulfilled Psalm lxviii. 18,—"Thou hast ascended on high, Thou hast led captivity captive: Thou hast received gifts for man: yea, for the rebellious also, that the Lord God might dwell among them."—Before our Lord died and rose again and ascended, the Holy Ghost was, and had been from all eternity, one with the Father and the Son, a distinct Person, of equal power and authority, very and eternal God. But He had not revealed Himself so fully to those whose hearts He dwelt in as He did after the ascension ; and He had not come down in person on the Gentile world, or sent forth the Gospel to all mankind with rivers of blessing, as He did when Paul and Barnabas were "sent forth by the Holy Ghost." (Acts xiii. 4.) In a word, the dispensation of the Spirit had not yet begun.

The expression, "the Holy Ghost was not yet given," would be more literally rendered, "the Holy Ghost was not." This cannot of course mean that the Holy Ghost did not exist, and was in no sense present with believers in the Old Testament dispensation. On the contrary, the Spirit strove with the men of Noah's day, —David spake by the Holy Ghost,—Isaiah spake of the Holy Spirit,—and John the Baptist, now dead, was filled with the Holy Ghost from his mother's womb. (Gen. vi. 3 ; Mark xii. 36 ; Isa. lxiii. 10, 11 ; Luke i. 15.)

What the expression does mean is this. The Holy Ghost was not yet with men in such fulness of influence on their minds, hearts, and understandings, as the Spirit of adoption and revelation, as He was after our Lord ascended up into heaven. It is clear as daylight, from our Lord's language about the Spirit, in John xiv. 16, 17, 26 ; xv. 26 ; xvi. 7—15, that believers were meant to receive a far more full and complete outpouring of the Holy Spirit after His ascension than they had received before. It is a simple matter of fact, indeed, that after the ascension the Apostles were quite different men from what they had been before. They both saw, and spoke, and acted like men grown up, while before the ascension they had been like children. It was this increased light and knowledge and decision that made them such a blessing to the world, far more than any miraculous gifts. The possession of the gifts of the Spirit, it is evident, in the early Church was quite compatible with an ungodly heart. A man might speak with tongues and yet be like salt that had lost its savour. The possession of the fulness of the graces of the Spirit, on the contrary, was that which made any man a blessing to the world.

Alford says, "St. John does not say that the words were a prophecy of what happened on the day of Pentecost ; but of the Spirit which the believers were about to receive. Their first reception of Him must not be illogically put in the place of all His indwelling and working, which are here intended."

I am quite aware that most commentators hold that the outpouring of the Spirit at Pentecost was specially meant by St. John in this passage. But after carefully considering the matter, I cannot subscribe to this opinion. To confine this verse to the day of Pentecost appears to me to cramp and narrow its meaning, —to deprive many believers of their interest in a most precious promise,—and to overlook all the special language about the inward teaching of the Comforter as a thing to come on believers, which our Lord used the night before His crucifixion.

Bengel remark that the use of "to be," instead of "to be present," is not uncommon in the Bible. Thus (2 Chron. xv. 3.) When therefore we read "the Holy Ghost was not," we need not be stumbled by the expression. It simply means "He was not fully manifested and poured out on the Church." Peter, and James, and John, no doubt, had the Spirit now, when our Lord was speaking. But they had Him much more fully after our Lord was glorified. This explains the meaning of the passage before us.

We should note, in leaving these three verses, what a striking example they supply to preachers, ministers, and teachers of religion. Let such learn from their Master to offer Christ boldly, freely, fully, broadly, unconditionally to all thirsting souls. The Gospel is too often spoiled in the presentation of it. Some fence it round with conditions, and keep sinners at a distance. Others direct sinners wrongly, and send them to something else beside or instead of Christ. He only copies his Lord who says, "If any one feels his sins, let him come at once, straight, direct; not merely to church, or to the sacrament, or to repentance, or to prayer, but to Christ Himself."

JOHN VII. 40—53.

40 Many of the people therefore, when they heard this saying, said, Of a truth this is the prophet.

41 Others said, This is the Christ. But some said, Shall Christ come out of Galilee?

42 Hath not the scripture said, That Christ cometh of the seed of David, and out of the town of Bethlehem, where David was?

43 So there was a division among the people because of him.

44 And some of them would have taken him; but no man laid hands on him.

45 Then came the officers to the chief priests and Pharisees; and they said unto them, Why have ye not brought him?

46 The officers answered, Never man spake like this man.

47 Then answered them the Pharisees, Are ye also deceived?

48 Have any of the rulers or of the Pharisees believed on him?

49 But this people who knoweth not the law are cursed.

50 Nicodemus saith unto them, (he that came to Jesus by night, being one of them,)

51 Doth our law judge any man, before it hear him, and know what he doeth?

52 They answered and said unto him, Art thou also of Galilee? Search, and look: for out of Galilee ariseth no prophet.

53 And every man went unto his own house.

THESE verses show us, for one thing, *how useless is knowledge in religion, if it is not accompanied by grace in the heart.* We are told that some of our Lord's hearers knew clearly where Christ was to be born. They referred to Scripture, like men familiar with its contents. "Hath not the Scripture said that Christ cometh of the seed of David, and out of the town of Bethlehem, where David was?" And yet the eyes of their understanding were not enlightened. Their own Messiah stood before them, and they neither received, nor believed, nor obeyed Him.

A certain degree of religious knowledge, beyond doubt, is of vast importance. Ignorance is certainly not the mother of true devotion, and helps nobody toward heaven. An "unknown God" can never be the object of a reasonable worship. Happy indeed would it be for Christians if they all knew the Scriptures as well as the Jews seem to have done when our Lord was on earth!

But while we value religious knowledge, we must take care that we do not overvalue it. We must not think it enough to know the facts and doctrines of our faith, unless our hearts and lives are thoroughly influenced by what we know. The very devils know the creed intellectually, and "believe and tremble," but remain devils still. (James ii. 19.) It is quite possible to be familiar with the letter of Scripture, and to be able to quote texts appropriately, and reason about the theory of Christianity, and yet to remain dead in trespasses and sins. Like many of the generation to which our Lord preached, we may know the Bible well, and yet remain faithless and unconverted.

Heart-knowledge, we must always remember, is the one thing needful. It is something which schools and universities cannot confer. It is the gift of God. To find out the plague of our own hearts and hate sin,— to become familiar with the throne of grace and the fountain of Christ's blood,—to sit daily at the feet of

Jesus, and humbly learn of Him,—this is the highest degree of knowledge which mortal man can attain to. Let any one thank God who knows anything of these things. He may be ignorant of Greek, Latin, Hebrew, and mathematics, but he shall be saved.

These verses show us, for another thing, *how eminent must have been our Lord's gifts as a public Teacher of religion.* We are told that even the officers of the chief priests, who were sent to take Him, were struck and amazed. They were, of course, not likely to be prejudiced in His favour. Yet, even they reported, "Never man spake like this man."

Of the *manner* of our Lord's public speaking we can of necessity form little idea. Action, and voice, and delivery are things that must be seen and heard to be appreciated. That our Lord's manner was peculiarly solemn, arresting, and impressive, we need not doubt. It was probably something very unlike what the Jewish officers were accustomed to hear. There is much in what is said in another place: "He taught them as One having authority, and not as the Scribes." (Matt. vii. 29.)

Of the *matter* of our Lord's public speaking we may form some conception from the discourses which are recorded in the four Gospels. The leading features of these discourses are plain and unmistakable. The world has never seen anything like them since the gift of speech was given to man. They often contain deep truths which we have no line to fathom; but they often contain simple things which even a child can understand. They are bold and outspoken in denouncing

national and ecclesiastical sins, and yet they are wise
and discreet in never giving needless offence. They are
faithful and direct in their warnings, and yet loving and
tender in their invitations. For a combination of power
and simplicity, of courage and prudence, of faithfulness
and tenderness, we may well say, " Never man spake like
this Man ! "

It would be well for the Church of Christ if ministers
and teachers of religion would strive more to speak after
their Lord's pattern. Let them remember that fine
bombastic language, and a sensational, theatrical style
of address, are utterly unlike their Master. Let them
realize that an eloquent simplicity is the highest attain-
ment of public speaking. Of this their Master left them
a glorious example. Surely they need never be ashamed
of walking in His steps.

These verses show us, lastly, *how slowly and gradually
the work of grace goes on in some hearts.* We are told
that Nicodemus stood up in the Council of our Lord's
enemies, and mildly pleaded that He deserved fair
dealing. "Doth our law judge any man," he asked,
" before it hear him, and know what he doeth ? "

This very Nicodemus, we must remember, is the man
who, eighteen months before, had come to our Lord by
night as an ignorant inquirer. He evidently knew
little then, and dared not come to Christ in open day.
But now after eighteen months, he has got on so far
that he dares to say something on our Lord's side. It
was but little that he said, no doubt, but it was better
than nothing at all. And a day was yet to come, when

he would go further still. He was to help Joseph of
Arimathæa in doing honour to our Lord's dead body,
when even His chosen Apostles had forsaken Him
and fled.

The case of Nicodemus is full of useful instruction.
It teaches us that there are diversities in the operation
of the Holy Spirit. All are undoubtedly led to the same
Saviour, but all are not led precisely in the same way.
It teaches us that the work of the Spirit does not always
go forward with the same speed in the hearts of men.
In some cases it may go forward very slowly indeed, and
yet may be real and true.

We shall do well to remember these things, in forming
our opinion of other Christians. We are often ready to
condemn some as graceless, because their experience
does not exactly tally with our own, or to set them down
as not in the narrow way at all, because they cannot run
as fast as ourselves. We must beware of hasty judgments. It is not always the fastest runner that wins
the race. It is not always those who begin suddenly in
religion, and profess themselves rejoicing Christians,
who continue steadfast to the end. Slow work is sometimes the surest and most enduring. Nicodemus stood
firm, when Judas Iscariot fell away and went to his own
place. No doubt it would be a pleasant thing, if everybody who was converted came out boldly, took up the
cross, and confessed Christ in the day of his conversion.
But it is not always given to God's children to do so.

Have we any grace in our hearts at all? This, after
all, is the grand question that concerns us. It may be

small,—but have we any? It may grow slowly, as in
the case of Nicodemus,—but does it grow at all? Better
a little grace than none! Better move slowly than
stand still in sin and the world!

Notes John vii. 40—53.

40.—[*Many...people...this saying, said.*] The "people" here evidently
mean the general multitude of common people, who had come together to attend the feast, and not the chief priests and Pharisees.
The "saying" which called forth their remarks, appears to be the
public proclamation that our Lord had just made, inviting all
thirsty souls to come to Him as the Fountain of Life. That any
one person should so boldly announce himself as the reliever of
spiritual thirst, seems to have arrested attention ; and, taken in
connection with the fact of our Lord's public teaching during the
latter half of the feast, which many of the people must have heard,
it induced them to say what immediately follows.

Brentius, Musculus, and others, hold strongly that our Lord's
words in the preceding three verses must have been greatly ampli-
fied, at the time He spoke, and are in fact a sort of text or keynote
to His discourse ; and that this is referred to in the expression,
"this saying." Yet the supposition seems hardly necessary. The
words were a conclusion to three days' teaching and preaching.

[*Oj a truth this man...Prophet.*] This would be more literally
rendered, "This man is truly and really the Prophet." These
speakers meant that He must be "the Prophet" like unto Moses,
foretold in Deuteronomy. (Deut. xviii. 15, 18.)

41.—[*Others said, This is the Christ.*] These speakers saw in our
Lord, the Messiah, or anointed Saviour, whom all pious Jews were
eagerly expecting at this period, and whose appearing the whole
nation were looking for in one way or another, though the most
part expected nothing more than a temporal Redeemer. (Psalm
xlv. 7 ; Isaiah lxi. 1 ; Daniel ix. 25, 26.) Even the Samaritan
woman could say, "I know that Messiah cometh." (John iv. 25.)

[*But some said, Shall Christ...Galilee ?*] This ought to have been
rendered, "But others said." It was not a few exceptional
speakers only, but a party probably as large as any. They raised
the objection, which was not unnatural, that this new teacher and
preacher, however wonderful He might be, was notoriously a
Galilean, of Nazareth, and therefore could not be the promised

Messiah. How utterly ignorant most persons were of our Lord's birth-place, we see here, as elsewhere.

42.—[*Hath not the Scripture said, etc.*] We should note in this verse the clear knowledge which most Jews in our Lord's time had ot Scripture prophecies and promises. Even the common people knew that Messiah was to be of the family of David, and to be born at Bethlehem, the well-known birth-place of David. It may indeed be feared that myriads of Christians know far less of the Bible than the Jews did eighteen hundred years ago.

43.—[*So...division among...people because of Him.*] Here we see our Lord's words literally fulfilled.—He did not bring "peace, but division." (Luke xii. 51.) It will always be so as long as the world stands. So long as human nature is corrupt Christ will be a cause of division and difference among men. To some He is a savour of life, and to others of death. (2 Cor. ii. 16.) Grace and nature never will agree any more than oil and water, acid and alkali. A state of entire quiet, and the absense of any religious division, is often no good sign of the condition of a Church or a parish. It may even be a symptom of spiritual disease and death. The question may possibly be needful in such cases, "Is Christ there?"

44.—[*And some...would...taken Him.*] This would be more satis-factorily rendered, "Some out of those" who made up the crowd "were desirous and wished to take our Lord prisoner."—These were no doubt the friends and adherents of the Pharisees, and very likely were the common people who dwelt at Jerusalem, and knew well what their leaders wanted to do.

[*No man laid hands on Him.*] This must be accounted for primarily by the Divine restraint which was at present laid on our Lord's enemies, because His hour was not yet come; and second-arily by the fear in which the Pharisees' party evidently stood of a rising in our Lord's defence on the part of the Galileans, and others who had come up to the feast. Thus we read that at the last Passover "the priests and Scribes sought how they might kill Him, for they feared the people." (Luke xxii. 2.) Again: "They said, Not on the feast day, lest there be an uproar of the people." (Mark xiv. 2, and Matt. xxvi. 5.)

45.—[*Then came the officers, etc.*] It is not clear what interval of time elapsed between verse 32nd, where we read that the officers were sent by the priests to take our Lord, and the present verse where we are told of their coming back to their masters.—At first sight, of course, it all happened in one day. Yet, if we observe that between the sending them to take our Lord and the present verse, there comes in the remarkable verse, "In the last day, that great day of the feast," it seems impossible to avoid the conclusion that an interval of two or three days must have elapsed.—It seems highly probable that the officers had a general commission and warrant to take our Lord prisoner, whenever they saw a fitting opportunity, about the fourth day of the feast. They found however no opportunity, on account of the temper and spirit of the crowd, and dared not make the attempt. And at last, at the end of the feast, when the multitude was even more aroused than at first by our Lord's open testimony, they were obliged to return to those who sent them, and confess their inability to carry out their orders.

46.—[*The officers answered, etc.*] The answer of the officers has probably a double application. They themselves felt the power of our Lord's speaking. They had never heard any man speak like this man. It tied their hands, and made them feel incapable of doing anything against Him.—They had besides marked the power of His speaking over the minds of the multitude which gathered round Him. They had never seen any one exercise such an influence over His hearers. They felt it useless to attempt arresting one who had such complete command over His audience. We cannot doubt that they had heard much more "speaking" than the few things recorded between verses 32nd and 46th. These are only specimens of what our Lord said, and furnish a keynote to us indicating the general tenor of His teaching.

What it was precisely that the officers meant when they said "Never man spake like this man," we are left to conjecture. They probably meant that they had never heard any one speak such deep and important truths in such simple and yet striking language, and in so solemn, impressive, and yet affectionate style. Above all, they probably meant that He spake with a dignified tone of authority, as a messenger from heaven, to which they were entirely unaccustomed.

47.—[*Then answered them...Pharisees...ye deceived?*] The word rendered "deceived" means, literally, "led astray, or caused to err." Have you too been carried off by this new teaching? The question implies anger, sarcasm, ridicule, and displeasure.

48.—[*Have any...rulers...Pharisees believed on Him?*] This arrogant question was doubtless meant to be an unanswerable proof that our Lord could not possibly be the Messiah: "Can a person be deserving of the least credit, as a teacher of a new religion, if those who are the most learned and highest in position do not

believe Him ? "—This is precisely the common argument of human
nature in every age. The doctrine which the great and learned
do not receive is always assumed to be wrong. And yet St. Paul
says, "Not many wise, not many noble are called." (1 Cor. i. 26.)
The very possession of rank and learning is often a positive
hindrance to a man's soul. The great and the learned are often the
last and most unwilling to receive Christ's truth.—"How hardly
shall a rich man enter the kingdom of God." (Matt. xix. 23.)

It seems clear from this that at present the Pharisees did not
know that one of their own number, Nicodemus, was favourably
disposed to our Lord.

49.—[*But this people...knoweth not law...cursed.*] This sentence is
full of contempt and scorn throughout. "This people,"—a mob,
—a common herd,—"which knoweth not the law," is not deeply
read in the Scriptures, and have no deep Rabbinical learning,—
"are cursed," are under God's curse and given over to a strong
delusion. Their opinion is worthless, and what they think of the
new Galilean teacher is of no moment or value.—Charges like
these have been made in every age, against the adherents of all
reformers and revivers of true religion. The multitude who
followed Luther in Germany, our own Reformers in England, and
the leaders of revived religion in the last century, were always
attacked as ignorant enthusiasts whose opinion was worth
nothing. When the enemies of vital religion cannot prevent people
flocking after the Gospel, and cannot answer the teaching of its
advocates, they often fight with the weapons of the Pharisees in
this verse. They content themselves with the cheap and easy
assertion that those who do not agree with themselves are
ignorant and know nothing, and that therefore it matters nothing
what they think. Yet St. Paul says, "God hath chosen the
foolish things of the world to confound the wise ; and God hath
chosen the weak things of the world to confound the things that
are mighty." (1 Cor. i. 27.) The poorer and humbler classes are
often much better judges of "what is truth" in religion than the
great and learned.

The disposition of the Jews to pronounce those "accursed" who
differed from themselves in religious controversy, is exhibited in
this verse. Jewish converts to Christianity in modern times are
often sadly familiar with cursing from their own relatives.

50.—[*Nicodemus...he.. came to Jesus by night.*] This would be more
literally rendered, "He that came to *Him* by night." The
omission of our Lord's name here is very peculiar.—The fact of

Nicodemus having come to see Jesus "by night" is always mentioned by St. John, where his name occurs. (See John xix. 39.)
It is to my mind a strong proof that he was a coward when he
first came to our Lord, and dared not come openly by day.

[*Being one of them.*] This means that he was a chief man, or
ruler among the Pharisees, and as such was present at all their
deliberations and counsels. His case shows that the grace of God
can reach men in any position, however unfavourable it may be
to true religion. Even a chief Pharisee, one of that company of
men who, as a body, hated our Lord and longed to kill Him,
could believe and speak up for Him. We must never conclude
hastily that there can be no Christians among a body of men,
because the great majority of them hate Christ, and are hardened
in wickedness. There was a Lot in Sodom, an Obadiah in Ahab's
house, a Daniel in Babylon, saints in Nero's palace, and a Nicodemus among the Pharisees. He was "one out of their number,"
but not one of them in spirit.

51.—[*Doth our law judge any man, etc.*] This was undoubtedly
speaking up for our Lord, and pleading for His being treated justly
and fairly, and according to law. At first sight it seems a very
tame and cautious mode of showing his faith, if he had any. But
it is difficult to see what more could have been said in the present
temper of the Pharisees. Nicodemus wisely appealed to law.
"Is it not a great principle of that law of Moses, which we all
profess to honour, that no man should be condemned without first
hearing from him what defence he can make, and without clear
knowledge and evidence as to what he has really done?—Is it fair
and legal to condemn this person before you have heard from His
own lips what He can say in His defence, and before you know from
the testimony of competent witnesses what He has really done?
—Are you not flying in the face of our law by hastily judging His
case, and setting Him down as a malefactor before you have given
Him a chance of clearing Himself?" (See Deut. i. 17, and xvii. 8,
etc., and xix. 15, etc.) Nicodemus, it will be observed, cautiously
takes up his ground on broad general principles of universal application, and does not say a word about our Lord's particular case.

The Greek words would be more literally rendered, "Doth our
law condemn the man unless it hears from him first."

I think there can be no reasonable doubt that these words show
Nicodemus to have become a real, though a slow-growing disciple
of Christ, and a true believer. It required great courage to do even
the little that he did here, and to say what he said.

Let us carefully note that a man may begin very feebly nd grow very slowly, and seem to make very little progress, and yet have the true grace of God in his heart. We must be careful that we do not hastily set down men as unconverted, because they get on slowly in the Christian life. All do not grow equally quick.

Let us learn to believe that even in high places, and most unlikely positions, Christ may have friends of whom we know nothing. Who would have expected a chief ruler among the Pharisees to rise at this juncture, and plead for justice and fair dealing in the case of our Lord.

52.—[*They answered...thou also of Galilee?*] This was the language of rage, scorn, and bitter contempt. "Art thou too, a ruler, a learned man, a Pharisee, one of ourselves, become one of this Galilean party? Hast thou joined the cause of this new Galilean prophet?"

The tone of this bitter question seems to me to prove that Nicodemus had said as much as was possible to be said on this occasion. The temper and spirit of the Pharisees, from disappointment and vexation at our Lord's increasing popularity, and their own utter inability to stop His course, made them furious at a single word being spoken favourably or kindly about Him. They must indeed have been in a violent frame of mind when the mere hint at the desirableness of acting justly, fairly, and legally, made them ask a brother Pharisee whether he was a Galilean!

Musculus remarks that Nicodemus got little favour from the Pharisees, though his favourable feeling towards our Lord was so cautiously expressed. He observes that this is generally the case with those who act timidly as he did. People may just as well be out-spoken and bold.

[*Search and look.*] This seems to be meant sarcastically. "Go and search the Scriptures again, and look at what they say about the Messiah, before thou sayest one word about this new Galilean prophet. Examine the prophets, and see if thou canst find a tittle of evidence in favour of this Galilean, whose cause thou art patronizing."

[*Out of Galilee ariseth no prophet.*] This would be rendered more literally, "a prophet out of Galilee has not been raised." About the meaning of the words there are three very different opinions.

(1) Some think that the words only mean, no "prophet of great note or eminence has ever been raised up in Galilee." This, however, is a tame and unsatisfactory view.

(2) Some, as Bishop Pearce, Burgon, and Sir N. Knatchbull, think that the Pharisees only meant that "THE Prophet like unto Moses, the Messiah has nowhere in the Scripture been foretold as coming out of Galilee." According to this view the Pharisees said what was quite correct.

(3) Others, as Alford, Wordsworth, Tholuck, and most other commentators, think that the Pharisees, in their rage and fury, either forgot, or found it convenient to forget, that prophets had arisen from Galilee. According to this view they made an ignorant assertion, and said what was not true.

I find it very difficult to receive this third opinion. To me it seems quite preposterous to suppose that men so thoroughly familiar with the letter of Scripture as the Pharisees were, would venture on such a monstrous and ignorant assertion, as to say that "no prophet had ever arisen out of Galilee!" Elijah, Elisha, Amos, Jonah, and perhaps Nahum, are all thought by some to have been Galilean prophets. Moreover Isaiah distinctly prophesied that in Messiah's times, Zebulon and Napthali and Galilee of the Gentiles should be a region where "light should spring up." (Matt. iv. 14—16.)

On the other hand, I must frankly admit that the Greek of the sentence must be much strained to make it mean, "the true prophet is not to arise out of Galilee." I do not forget, moreover, that when men lose their tempers and fly into a passion, there is nothing too foolish and ignorant for them to say. Like a drunken man, they may talk nonsense, and say things of which in calm moments they may be ashamed. It may have been so with the Pharisees here. They were no doubt violently enraged, and in this state of mind might say any thing absurd.

The point, happily is not one of first-rate importance, and men may afford to differ about it. Nevertheless if I must give an opinion, I prefer the second of the three views I have given. The improbability of the Pharisees asserting anything flatly contrary to the letter and facts of Scripture, is, to my mind, an insuperable objection to the other views.

53.—[*And every man...his own...house.*] These words seem to indicate that the assembly of Pharisees, before whom the officers had appeared reporting their inability to take our Lord prisoner, broke up at once without taking any further action. They saw they could do nothing. Their design to put our Lord to death at once could not be carried out, and must be deferred. They therefore separated and went to their own houses. We may well believe that they parted in a most bitter and angry frame of mind, boiling over with mortified pride and baulked malice. They had tried hard to stop our Lord's course, and had completely failed. The "Galilean" had proved for the time stronger than the Sanhedrim. Once more, as after the miracle of Bethesda, they had been ignominiously foiled and publicly defeated.

Hutcheson remarks, "There is no council nor understanding against Christ, but when He pleaseth He can dissipate all of it. Here every man went unto his own house, without doing anything."

Maldonatus thinks the verse proves that though the Pharisees sneered at Nicodemus, and reviled him, they could not deny the fairness and justice of what he said. He thinks, therefore, that they dispersed in consequence of Nicodemus' interference. Even one man may do something against many, when God is on his side.

Besser quotes a saying of Luther's: "Much as the Pharisees before had blustered, they dared do nothing to Jesus: they became still and silent. He goes up to the feast meek and silent, and returns home with glory.—They go up with triumph, and come down weak."

Trapp remarks, "See what one man may do against a mischievous multitude. It is good to be doing, though there be few or none to second us."

Baxter remarks, "One man's words may sometimes divert a persecution."

JOHN VIII. 1—11.

1 Jesus went unto the Mount of Olives.

2 And early in the morning he came again into the temple, and all the people came unto him; and he sat down, and taught them.

3 And the scribes and Pharisees brought unto him a woman taken in adultery; and when they had set her in the midst,

4 They say unto him, Master, this woman was taken in adultery, in the very act.

5 Now Moses in the law commanded us, that such should be stoned: but what sayest thou?

6 This they said, tempting him, that they might have to accuse him. But Jesus stooped down, and with *his* finger wrote on the ground, *as though he heard them not.*

7 So when they continued asking him, he lifted up himself, and said unto them, He that is without sin among you, let him first cast a stone at her.

8 And again he stooped down, and wrote on the ground.

9 And they which heard *it*, being convicted by *their own* conscience, went out one by one, beginning at the eldest, *even* unto the last: and Jesus was left alone, and the woman standing in the midst.

10 When Jesus had lifted up himself, and saw none but the woman, he said unto her, Woman, where are those thine accusers? hath no man condemned thee?

11 She said, No man, Lord. And Jesus said unto her, Neither do I condemn thee: go, and sin no more.

THE narrative which begins the eighth chapter of St. John's Gospel is of a rather peculiar character. In some respects it stands alone. There is nothing quite like it in the whole range of the four Gospels. In every age some scrupulous minds have stumbled at the passage, and have doubted whether it was ever written by St. John at all. But the justice of such scruples is a point that cannot easily be proved.

To suppose, as some have thought, that the narrative before us palliates the sin of adultery, and exhibits our Lord as making light of the seventh commandment, is surely a great mistake. There is nothing in the passage to justify such an assertion. There is not a sentence in it to warrant our saying anything of the kind. Let us calmly weigh the matter, and examine the contents of the passage.

Our Lord's enemies brought before Him a woman guilty of adultery, and asked Him to say what punishment she deserved. We are distinctly told that they asked the question, "tempting Him." They hoped to entrap Him into saying something for which they might accuse Him. They fancied perhaps that He who preached pardon and salvation to "publicans and harlots," might be induced to say something which would either contradict the law of Moses, or His own words.

Our Lord knew the hearts of the malicious questioners before Him, and dealt with them with perfect wisdom, as He had done in the case of the "tribute-money." (Matt. xxii. 17.) He refused to be "a judge" and lawgiver among them, and specially in a case which their own law had already decided. He gave them at first no answer at all.

But "when they continued asking," our Lord silenced them with a withering and heart-searching reply.—"He that is without sin among you," He said, "let him first cast a stone at her." He did not say that the woman had not sinned, or that her sin was a trifling and venial one. But he reminded her accusers that they at any rate were not the persons to bring a charge against her. Their own motives and lives were far from pure. They themselves did not come into the case with clean hands. What they really desired was not to vindicate the purity of God's law, and punish a sinner, but to wreak their malice on Himself.

Last of all, when those who had brought the unhappy woman to our Lord had gone out from His presence, "convicted by their own conscience," He dismissed the guilty sinner with the solemn words, "Neither do I condemn thee : go, and sin no more."—That she did not *deserve* punishment He did not say. But He had not come to be a judge. Moreover, in the absence of all witnesses or accusers, there was no case before Him. Let her then depart as one whose guilt was " not proven," even though she was really guilty, and let her "sin no more."

To say in the face of these simple facts that our Lord made light of the sin of adultery is not fair. There is nothing in the passage before us to prove it. Of all whose words are recorded in the Bible there is none who has spoken so strongly about the breach of the seventh commandment as our divine Master. It is He who has taught that it may be broken by a look or a thought, as well as by an open act. (Matt. v. 28.) It is He who has spoken more strongly than any about the sanctity of the marriage relation. (Matt. xix. 5.) In all that is recorded here, we see nothing inconsistent with the rest of His teaching. He simply refused to usurp the office of the judge, and to pronounce condemnation on a guilty woman for the gratification of His deadly enemies.

In leaving this passage, we must not forget that it contains two lessons of great importance. Whatever difficulties the verses before us may present, these two lessons at any rate are clear, plain, and unmistakable.

We learn, for one thing, *the power of conscience.* We read of the woman's accusers, that when they heard our Lord's appeal, " being convicted by their own conscience, they went out one by one, beginning at the eldest, even unto the last." Wicked and hardened as they were, they felt something within which made them cowards. Fallen as human nature is, God has taken care to leave within every man a witness that will be heard.

Conscience is a most important part of our inward man, and plays a most prominent part in our spiritual history. It cannot save us. It never yet led any one to Christ. It is blind, and liable to be misled. It is lame and powerless, and cannot guide us to heaven. Yet conscience is not to be despised. It is the minister's best friend, when he stands up to rebuke sin from the pulpit. It is the mother's best friend, when she tries

to restrain her children from evil and quicken them to
good. It is the teacher's best friend, when he presses
home on boys and girls their moral duties. Happy is
he who never stifles his conscience, but strives to keep
it tender! Still happier is he who prays to have it
enlightened by the Holy Ghost, and sprinkled with
Christ's blood.

We learn, for another thing, *the nature of true repentance.* When our Lord had said to the sinful woman,
"Neither do I condemn thee," He dismissed her with the
solemn words, "Go, and sin no more." He did not
merely say, "Go home and repent." He pointed out
the chief thing which her case required,—the necessity
of immediate breaking off from her sin.

Let us never forget this lesson. It is the very essence
of genuine repentance, as the Church catechism well
teaches, to "forsake sin." That repentance which consists in nothing more than feeling, talking, professing,
wishing, meaning, hoping, and resolving, is worthless in
God's sight. Action is the very life of "repentance unto
salvation not to be repented of." Till a man ceases to
do evil and turns from his sins, he does not really repent.—Would we know whether we are truly converted
to God, and know anything of godly sorrow for sin, and
repentance such as causes "joy in heaven"? Let us
search and see whether we forsake sin. Let us not rest
till we can say, as in God's sight, "I hate all sin, and
desire to sin no more."

NOTES. JOHN VIII. 1—11.

These eleven verses, together with the last verse of the preceding chapter, form perhaps the gravest critical difficulty in the New Testament. Their genuineness is disputed.—It is held by many learned Christian writers, who have an undoubted right to be heard on such matters, that the passage was not written by St. John, that it was written by an uninspired hand, and probably at a later date, and that it has no lawful claim to be regarded as a part of canonical Scripture.—It is held by others, whose opinion, to say the least, is equally entitled to respect, that the passage is a genuine part of St. John's Gospel, and that the arguments against it, however weighty they may appear, are insufficient, and admit of an answer. A summary of the whole case is all that I shall attempt to give.

In the list of those who think the passage either not genuine, or at least *doubtful*, are the following names: "Beza, Grotius, Baxter, Hammond, A. Clark, Tittman, Tholuck, Olshausen, Hengstenberg, Tregelles, Alford, Wordsworth, Scrivener.

In the list of those who think the passage *genuine*, are the following names: Augustine, Ambrose, Euthymius, Rupertus, Zwingle, Calvin, Melancthon, Echolampadius, Brentius, Bucer, Gualter, Musculus, Bullinger, Pellican, Flacius, Diodati, Chemnitius, Aretius, Piscator, Calovius, Cocceius, Toletus, Maldonatus, á Lapide, Ferus, Nifanius, Cartwright, Mayer, Trapp, Poole, Lampe, Whitby, Leigh, Doddridge, Bengel, Stier, Webster, Burgon.

Calvin is sometimes named as one of those who think the passage before us not genuine. But his language about it in his Commentary is certainly not enough to bear out the assertion. He says, "It is plain that this passage was unknown anciently to the Greek Churches; and some conjecture that it has been brought from some other place, and inserted here. But as it has always been received by the Latin Churches, and is found in many old Greek manuscripts, and contains nothing unworthy of an Apostle, there is no reason why we should refuse to apply it to our advantage."

[A.] The arguments against the passage are as follows:—

(1) That it is not found in some of the oldest and best manuscripts, now existing, of the Greek Testament.

(2) That it is not found in some of the earlier versions or translations of the Scriptures.

(3) That it is not commented on by the Greek Fathers, Origen,

Cyril, Chrysostom, and Theophylact, in their exposition of St. John; nor quoted or referred to by Tertullian and Cyprian.

(4) That it differs in style from the rest of St. John's Gospel, and contains several words and forms of expression which are nowhere else used in his writings.

(5) That the moral tendency of the passage is somewhat doubtful, and that it seems to represent our Lord as palliating a heinous sin.

[B.] The arguments in favour of the passage are as follows :—

(1) That it is found in many old manuscripts, if not in the very oldest and best.

(2) That it is found in the Vulgate Latin, and in the Arabic, Coptic, Persian, and Ethiopian versions.

(3) That it is commented on by Augustine in his exposition of this Gospel; while in another of his writings he expressly refers to and explains its omission from some manuscripts; that it is quoted and defended by Ambrose, referred to by Jerome, and treated as genuine in the Apostolical Constitutions.

(4) That there is no proof whatever that there is any immoral tendency in the passage. Our Lord pronounced no opinion on the sin of adultery, but simply declined the office of a judge.

It may seem almost presumptuous to offer any opinion on this very difficult subject. But I venture to make the following remarks, and to invite the reader's candid attention to them. I lean decidedly to the side of those who think the passage is genuine, for the following reasons :—

1. The argument from manuscripts appear to me inconclusive. We possess comparatively few very ancient ones. Even of them, some favour the genuineness of the passage.—The same remark applies to the ancient versions. Testimony of this kind, to be conclusive, should be unanimous.

2. The argument from the Fathers seems to me more in favour of the passage than against it.—On the one side the reasons are simply *negative*. Certain Fathers say nothing about the passage, but at the same time say nothing against it.—On the other side the reasons are *positive*. Men of such high authority as Augustine and Ambrose not only comment on the passage, but defend its genuineness, and assign reasons for its omission by some mistaken transcribers.

Let me add to this, that the negative evidence of the Fathers who are against the passage is not nearly so weighty as it appears at first sight. Cyril of Alexandria is one. But his commentary on the eighth chapter of John is lost, and what we have was supplied by the modern hand of Jodocus Clichtovœus, a Parisian doctor, who lived in the year 1510, A.D. (See Dupin's Eccles. Hist.)—Chrysostom's commentary on John consists of popular public homilies, in which we can easily imagine such a passage as this might possibly be omitted.—Theophylact was notoriously a copier and imitator of Chrysostom.—Origen, the only remaining commentator, is one whose testimony is not of first-rate value, and he has omitted many things in his exposition of St. John.—The silence of Tertullian and Cyprian is perhaps accountable on the same principles by which Augustine explains the omission of the passage in some copies of this Gospel in his own time.

Some, as Calovius, Maldonatus, Flacius, Aretius, and Piscator, think that Chrysostom distinctly refers to this passage in his Sixtieth Homily on John, though he passes it over in exposition.

3. The argument from alleged discrepancies between the style and language of this passage, and the usual style of St. John's writing, is one which should be received with much caution. We are not dealing with an uninspired, but with an inspired writer. Surely it is not too much to say that an inspired writer may occasionally use words and constructions and modes of expression which he generally does not use, and that it is no proof that he did not write a passage because he wrote it in a peculiar way.

I leave the subject here. In cases of doubt like this, it is wise to be on the safe side. On the whole I think it safest to regard this disputed passage as genuine. At any rate I prefer the difficulties on this side to those on the other.

The whole discussion may leave in our minds, at any rate, one comfortable thought. If even in the case of this notoriously disputed passage—more controverted and doubted than any in the New Testament—so much can be said in its favour, how immensely strong is the foundation on which the whole volume of Scripture rests! If even against this passage the arguments of opponents are not conclusive, we have no reason to fear for the rest of the Bible.

After all, there is much ground for thinking that some critical difficulties have been *purposely* left by God's providence in the text of the New Testament, in order to prove the faith and patience of Christian people. They serve to test the humility of those to whom intellectual difficulties are a far greater cross than either doctrinal or practical ones. To such minds it is trying, but useful, discipline to find occasional passages involving knots which they cannot quite untie, and problems which they cannot quite solve. Of such passages the verses before us are a striking instance. That the text of them is "a hard thing" it would be wrong to deny. But I believe our duty is not to reject it hastily, but to sit still and wait. In these matters, "he that believeth shall not make haste."

The following passage from Augustine (De conjug. Adult.) is worth notice. Having argued that it well becomes a Christian husband to be reconciled to his wife, upon her repentance after adultery, because our Lord said, "Neither do I condemn thee: go, and sin no more"—he says, "This, however, rather shocks the minds of some weak believers, or rather unbelievers and enemies of the Christian faith, insomuch that, afraid of its giving their wives impunity of sinning, they struck out of their copies of the Gospel this that our Lord did in pardoning the woman taken in adultery; as if He granted leave of sinning, when He said, "Go, and sin no more." Augustine, be it remembered, lived about 400 A.D.

Those who wish to look further into the subject of this disputed passage will find it fully discussed by Gomarus, Bloomfield, and Wordsworth.

1.—[*Jesus went...mount...Olives.*] The division of the chapter in this place is to be regretted. The last verse of the preceding chapter and the verse before us are evidently intended to be taken together. While the Pharisees and members of the Council "went every man to his own house," our Lord, having no home of His own, retired "to the Mount of Olives," and there spent the night in the open air. In such a climate as that of Judea there was nothing remarkable in His doing this. The garden of Gethsemane, at the foot of the mount, would supply sufficient shelter. That this was our Lord's habitual practice, we are distinctly told in Luke xxi. 37.

Lampe remarks that we never read of our Lord lodging, sleeping, or tarrying a night in Jerusalem.

2.—[*And early in the morning.*] This expression is worth noticing, because, according to some, it explains our Lord's subsequent use of the figure—"I am the light of the world." They think that it refers to the break of day, or rising of the sun.

[*He came again...temple.*] This means the outer courts of the temple, where it was customary for the Jews to assemble and listen to teachers of religion. In eastern countries and in the times when there was no printing, it must be remembered, much instruction was given in this way, by open air addresses or conversations. Thus Socrates taught at Athens.

[*All the people came unto Him.*] "All" here must mean great multitudes of the people. After all that had happened in the last three or four days, we may easily understand that our Lord's appearance would at once attract a crowd. His fame as a teacher and speaker was established.

[*He sat down, and taught.*] That it was common for the teachers to sit, and the hearers to stand, is evident from other texts. "I sat daily with you teaching in the temple." (Matt. xxvi. 55.) In the synagogues of Nazareth, when our Lord began to preach, He first "gave the book to the minister, and sat down." (Luke iv. 20.) "He sat down and taught the people out of the ship." (Luke v. 3.) "We sat down and spake to the women." (Acts xvi. 13.)

3.—[*The Scribes and Pharisees.*] This is the only place in St. John's Gospel where He mentions the " Scribes " at all. He names the Pharisees twenty times,—sixteen times alone, and four times in conjuction with the chief-priests.

This fact is thought by some to be an argument against the genuineness of the passage, but without just cause. St. Mark, in his Gospel, speaks twelve times of the Pharisees, and only twice mentions the Scribes in conjuction with them. Moreover, this is the only occasion recorded in St. John when a formal attempt was made to entrap our Lord by a subtle question. That being so, there may be a good reason why the Scribes should be mentioned as well as the Pharisees, as principal agents in the attempt.

[*Brought unto Him a woman, etc.*] It seems not improbable that this attempt to ensnare our Lord was one result of His enemies' failure to apprehend Him during the feast. Defeated in their effort to meet Him in argument, or to apprehend Him in the absence of any legal charge, they tried next to entrap Him into committing Himself in some way, and so giving them a handle against Him. No time was to be lost. They had failed yesterday, and found their own officers unwilling to apprehend our Lord. They resolved to try another plan to-day. They would ensnare our Lord into doing something illegal or indiscreet, and then get an advantage over Him.

[*Set her in the midst.*] This means in the middle of a ring or circle, composed of themselves and their followers, our Lord and His disciples, and the crowd listening to His teaching.

4.—[*They say…this woman…taken…etc.*] It throws some light on this charge to remember what immense crowds came up to Jerusalem at the great public feasts, and especially at the feast of tabernacles. At such a season, when every house was crowded, as at a fair time, when many consequently slept in the open air, and no small disorder probably ensued, we can well understand that such a sin as a breach of the seventh commandment would be very likely to be committed.

5.—[*Now Moses...law commanded...stoned.*] This is the legitimate conclusion of the two texts, Lev. xx. 10 and Deut. xxii. 22, when compared. There seems no ground for the comment of some writers, that Moses did not command an adulteress to be put to death by stoning.

It is worth notice, that the expression, " Moses in the law," is not used either by Matthew, Mark, or Luke. But it is used by St. John both here and at chap. i. 45.

[*But what sayest Thou ?*] This would be more literally rendered, "What *therefore* sayest Thou ?" The Greek word rendered "but" by our translators, is hardly ever so rendered in the New Testament ; and in most places is either "therefore," "then," "so," "now," or "and." John ix. 18, and Acts xxv. 4, are the only parallel cases.

Ecolampadius thinks the Pharisees were especially sore and irritated because our Lord had said that "publicans and harlots" would enter the kingdom of God before Pharisees. (Matt. xxi. 31.)

6.—[*This they said, tempting...accuse Him.*] In what did this temptation consist ? How did the Jews hope to find ground for an accusation ? The answer seems easy.—If our Lord replied that the woman ought NOT to be stoned, they would have denounced Him to the people as one that poured contempt on the law.—If our Lord, on the contrary, replied that the woman *ought* to be stoned, they would have accused Him to the Romans as one who usurped the prerogative of putting criminals to death. See John xviii. 31 : "It is not lawful for us to put any man to death." Moreover, they would have published everywhere our Lord's inconsistency in offering salvation to publicans and harlots, and yet condemning to death an adulteress for one transgression.

Let it be noticed that subtle ensnaring questions like these, putting the person questioned into an apparent dilemma or difficulty, whatever answer he might give, seem to have been favourite weapons of the Jews. The Pharisees' question about "tribute-money," the lawyer's question about "the great commandment of the law," and the Sadducees' question about "the resurrection, are parallel cases. The question before us is therefore quite in keeping with other places in the Gospels.

Augustine remarks, "They said in themselves, 'Let us put before Him a woman caught in adultery ; let us ask what is ordered in the law concerning her ; if He shall bid stone her, He will not have the repute of gentleness : if He give sentence to let her go, He will not keep righteousness.'" Euthymius says the same.

[*But Jesus stooped down, etc., etc.*] Our Lord's intention in this remarkable sentence can hardly admit of doubt. He declined to answer the subtle question put to Him, partly because He knew the malicious motives of the questioners, partly because He had always announced that He did not come to be "a judge and divider" among men, or to interfere in the slightest degree with the administration of the law. His silence was equivalent to a refusal to answer.

But the peculiar action that our Lord employed, in "writing with His finger on the ground," is undeniably a difficulty. St. John gives no explanation of the action, and we are left to conjecture both *why* our Lord wrote and *what* He wrote.

(1) Some think, as Bede, Rupertus, and Lampe, that our Lord wrote on the ground the texts of Scripture which settled the question brought before Him, as the seventh commandment, and Lev. xx. 10, and Deut. xxii. 22. The action would then imply," "Why do ye ask Me? What is written in the law, that law which God wrote with His own finger as I am writing now?"

(2) Some think, as Lightfoot and Burgon, that our Lord meant to refer to the law of Moses for the trial of jealousy, in which an accused woman was obliged to drink water into which dust from the floor of the tabernacle or temple had been put by the priest. (Num. v. 17.) The action would then imply, "Has the law for trying such an one as this been tried? Look at the dust on which I am writing. Has the woman been placed before the priest, and drank of the dust and water?"

(3) Some think, as Augustine, Melancthon, Brentius, Toletus, and à Lapide, that our Lord's action was a silent reference to the text, Jer. xvii. 13 : "They that depart from Me shall be written in the earth."

(4) One rationalist writer suggests that our Lord "stooped down" from feelings of modesty, as if ashamed of the sight before Him, and of the story told to Him. The idea is preposterous, and entirely out of harmony with our Lord's public demeanour

(5) Some think, as Euthymius, Calvin, Rollock, Chemnitius, Diodati, Flavius, Piscator, Grotius, Poole, and Hutcheson, that our Lord did not mean anything at all by this writing on the ground, and that He only signified that He would give no answer, and would neither listen to nor interfere in such matters as the one brought before Him.

Calvin remarks, "Christ intended, by doing nothing, to show how unworthy they were of being heard ; just as if any one, while another was speaking to him, were to draw lines on the wall, or to turn his back, or to show by any other sign that He was not attending to what was said."

I must leave the reader to choose which solution he prefers. To my eyes, I confess, there are difficulties in each view. If I must select one, I prefer the last of the five, as the simplest.

Quesnell remarks, "We never read that Jesus Christ *wrote* but once in his life. Let men learn from hence never to write but when it it necessary or useful, and to do it with humility and modesty, on a principle of charity, and not of malice."

7.—[*So when they continued...lifted...said unto them.*] The Scribes and Pharisees seem to have been determined to have an answer, and to have made it necessary for our Lord to speak at last. But His first silence and significant refusal to attend, were a plain proof to all around that He did not wish to interfere with the office of the magistrate, and had not come to be a judge of offences against the law. If they got an opinion from Him about this case, they could not say that He gave it willingly, but that it was extorted from Him by much importunity.

[*He that is without sin...first cast a stone at her.*] This solemn and weighty sentence is a striking example of our Lord's perfect wisdom. He referred His questioners to Scripture. Deut. xvii. 7 : "The hands of the witnesses shall be first upon him to put him to death."—It sent their minds home to their own private lives. "Whatever the woman may deserve, are you the people to find fault with her ?"—It neither condemned nor justified the adulteress, and yet showed our Lord's reverence for the law of Moses. " I decline to pronounce sentence on this woman, because I am not the judge. You know yourselves what the law is in such cases as well as I do. You have no right to assume that I do not reverence the law as much as yourselves. But since you profess to honour the law of Moses so much, I remind you that this same law requires the witnesses to be the executioners. Now are you the persons who ought to punish this woman, however guilty she may be ? Do you yourselves come before Me with clear consciences about the seventh commandment ? "

Many think that when our Lord said, " He that is without sin," He meant the expression to be taken in a general sense. I cannot hold this view. It would involve the awkward conclusion that no one could be a judge at all, or punish a criminal, because no one is altogether and absolutely "without sin." I am decidedly of opinion that our Lord referred to sin against the seventh commandment. There is too much reason to think that such sin was very common among the Jews in our Lord's time. The expression " an adulterous generation " (Matt. xii. 39 ; xvi. 4 ; and Mark viii. 38) is full of meaning. (See also Rom. ii. 22 ; Luke xviii. 11 ; and James iv. 4.)

8.—[*And again He stooped down, etc.*] This repeated act would greatly add to the weighty solemnity of the sentence which had just fallen from our Lord's lips. " I have given my opinion ;—now what are you going to do ? I wait for your reply."

9.—[*And they which heard...conscience.*] This sentence seems to me to confirm the opinion, that when our Lord said, " He that is without sin," He referred to sin against the seventh commandment. A general charge would hardly have produced the effect here described. A charge of breaking the seventh commandment, would be just such an one as a man would shrink from, if made publicly. The sin is peculiarly one which brings with it afterwards a certain sense of shame. It is commonly a deed of darkness and done in secret, and the doer of it dreads the light.

The power of conscience stands out here in a very striking manner. It is a part of man's inward nature which is far too little remembered by ministers and teachers. Fallen and corrupt as man is, we must never forget that God has left him a certain sense of right and wrong, called conscience. It has no power to save, or convert, or lead to Christ. But it has a power to accuse, and prick, and witness. Such texts as Rom. ii. 15 and 2 Cor. iv. 2 s'ould be carefully considered.

[*Went out...beginning...eldest...last.*] The words "eldest" and "last" in this sentence are in the plural number, which does not appear in the English version. The oldest would probably have the greatest number of sins on their minds.

[*Jesus was left alone, and the woman...midst.*] This must of course mean that the scribes and Pharisees who accused the woman were all gone away. It does not necessarily follow that the crowd of hearers who were about our Lord when the case was brought to Him, had gone away. They must have stood by, and seen and heard all that passed.

10.—[*When Jesus had lifted up Himself, etc.*] How long the pause must have been during which our Lord stooped down and wrote on the ground a second time, we are not told. But it must probably have been several minutes. When it says that our Lord "saw none but the woman," it must mean "none of the party which came and interrupted His teaching, except the woman." The accusers had disappeared, and the accused alone remained.

The question that our Lord put to the woman must have been for the satisfaction of the crowd around. Let them mark, from the question and answer, that the case had fallen to the ground. No evidence was offered. No accuser appeared. No sentence therefore could be pronounced, and none was needed.

11.—[*She said, No man, Lord.*] We may observe here that our Lord, with merciful consideration, did not ask the woman whether she was guilty or not. Thus she could with truth reply to His question, and yet not criminate herself.

[*Jesus said...Neither do I condemn...sin no more.*] The mingled kindness and perfect wisdom of this sentence deserve special notice. Our Lord says nothing of the question whether the woman deserved punishment, and what kind of punishment. He simply says, "I do not condemn thee. It is not my province or office to judge or pronounce any sentence."—Nor yet does He tell the woman that she may go away without stain or blemish on her character. On the contrary, He implies that she has sinned and was guilty. But in the absence of witnesses she might go away clear of punishment.—Nor yet does He say, "Go in peace," as in Luke vii. 50, and viii. 48.

"Go," He says, "and *sin no more.*" How any one, in the face of this text, can say that our Lord palliates and condones the woman's sin it is rather hard to understand. That He refused to condemn her is clear and plain, because it was not His office. That He ignored or connived at her sin, as Hengstenberg says (in his argument against the genuineness of the whole passage), can never be proved. The very last words show what He thought of her case : "Sin no more." She had sinned, and had only escaped from lack of evidence. Let her remember that, and "sin no more."

Augustine remarks, "How Lord? Dost thou then favour sin? Not so, assuredly. Mark what He says. 'Go: henceforth sin no more.' You see them that the Lord condemned, but He condemned sin, not man. For were He a favourer of sin, He would say, "Neither will I condemn thee. Go : live as thou wilt."

The remark of Euthymius, that our Lord considered the public shame and exposure sufficient punishment for the woman's sin, is thoroughly unsatisfactory, and not warranted by anything in the context. The view of Bullinger and some others, that one principal object of the passage is to teach our Lord's mercy and readiness to pardon great sinners, appears to me quite destitute of foundation. Christ's abounding mercy is a great truth, but not the truth of this passage.—There seems no parallel between this woman and the Samaritan woman in John iv.

Poole observes that our Lord does not merely say, "Commit adultery no more; but, Sin no more. No partial repentance or sorrow for any particular sin will suffice a penitent that hopes for mercy from God; but a leaving off all sin, of what kind soever it is."

JOHN VIII. 12—20.

12 Then spake Jesus again unto them, saying, I am the light of the world : he that followeth me shall not walk in darkness, but shall have the light of life.

13 The Pharisees therefore said unto him, Thou bearest record of thyself, thy record is not true.

14 Jesus answered and said unto them, Though I bear record of myself, yet my record is true: for I know whence I came, and whither I go; but ye cannot tell whence I come, and whither I go.

15 Ye judge after the flesh; I judge no man.

16 And yet if I judge, my judgment is true: for I am not alone, but I and the Father that sent me.

17 It is also written in your law, that 'he testimony of two men is true.

18 I am one that bear witness of myself, and the Father that sent me beareth witness of me.

19 Then said they unto him, Where is thy Father? Jesus answered, Ye neither know me, nor my Father; if ye had known me, ye should have known my Father also.

20 These words spake Jesus in the treasury, as he taught in the temple : and no man laid hands on him; for his hour was not yet come.

THE conversation between our Lord and the Jews which begins with these verses, is full of difficulties. The connection between one part and another, and the precise meaning of some of the expressions which fell from our Lord's lips, are "things hard to be understood." In passages like this it is true wisdom to acknowledge the great imperfection of our spiritual vision, and to be thankful if we can glean a few handfuls of truth.

Let us notice, for one thing, in these verses *what the Lord Jesus says of Himself*. He proclaims, " I am the light of the world."

These words imply that the world needs light, and is naturally in a dark condition. It is so in a moral and spiriturally point of view: and it has been so for nearly 6,000 years. In ancient Egypt, Greece, and Rome, in modern England, France, and Germany, the same report is true. The vast majority of men neither see nor understand the value of their souls, the true nature of God, nor the reality of a world to come! Notwithstanding all the discoveries of art and science, "darkness still covers the earth, and gross darkness the people." (Isa lx. 2.)

For this state of things the Lord Jesus Christ declares Himself to be the only remedy. He has risen, like the sun, to diffuse light, and life, and peace, and salvation, in the midst of a dark world. He invites all who want spiritual help and guidance to turn to Him, and take Him for their leader. What the sun is to the whole solar system—the centre of light, and heat, and life, and fertility,—that He has come into the world to be to sinners.

Let this saying sink down into our hearts. It is weighty, and full of meaning. False lights on every side invite man's attention in the present day. Reason, philosophy, earnestness, liberalism, conscience, and the voice of the Church, are all, in their various ways, crying loudly that they have got " the light " to show

us. Their advocates know not what they say Wretched
are those who believe their high professions! He only
is the true light who came into the world to save
sinners, who died as our substitute on the cross, and
sits at God's right hand to be our Friend. "In His
light we shall see light." (Psalm xxxvi. 9.)

Let us notice, secondly, in these verses, *what the Lord
Jesus says of those that follow Him.* He promises,
"He that followeth Me shall not walk in darkness, but
shall have the light of life."

To follow Christ is to commit ourselves wholly and
entirely to Him as our only leader and Saviour, and
to submit ourselves to Him in every matter both of
doctrine and practice. "Following" is only another
word for "believing." It is the same act of soul, only
seen from a different point of view. As Israel followed
the pillar of cloud and fire in all their journeyings—
moving whenever it moved, stopping whenever it tarried,
asking no questions, marching on in faith,—so must a
man deal with Christ. He must "follow the Lamb
whithersoever He goeth." (Rev. xiv. 4)

He that so follows Christ shall "not walk in darkness." He shall not be left in ignorance, like the many
around him. He shall not grope in doubt and uncertainty, but shall see the way to heaven, and know
where he is going.—He "shall have the light of life."
He shall feel within him the light of God's countenance
shining on him. He shall find in his conscience and
understanding a living light, which nothing can altogether quench. The lights with which many please

themselves shall go out in the valley of the shadow of death, and prove worse than useless. But the light that Christ gives to every one that follows Him shall never fail.

Let us notice, lastly, in these verses, *what the Lord Jesus says of His enemies.* He tells the Pharisees that, with all their pretended wisdom, they were ignorant of God. "Ye neither know Me nor my Father: if ye had known Me, ye should have known my Father also."

Ignorance like this is only too common. There are thousands who are conversant with many branches of human learning, and can even argue and reason about religion, and yet know nothing really about God. That there is such a Being as God they fully admit. But His character and attributes revealed in Scripture, His holiness, His purity, His justice, His perfect knowledge, His unchangeableness, are things with which they are little acquainted. In fact, the subject of God's nature and character makes them uncomfortable, and they do not like to dwell upon it.

The grand secret of knowing God is to draw near to Him through Jesus Christ. Approached from this side, there is nothing that need make us afraid. Viewed from this stand-point, God is the sinner's friend. God, out of Christ, may well fill us with alarm. How shall we dare to look at so high and holy a Being?—God in Christ is full of mercy, grace, and peace. His law's demands are satisfied. His holiness need not make us afraid. Christ, in one word, is the way and door, by which we must ever draw nigh to the Father. If we know Christ, we shall know the Father. It is His own word,—"No man cometh unto the Father but by Me." (John xiv. 6.) Ignorance of Christ is the root of ignorance of God. Wrong at the starting-point, the whole sum of a man's religion is full of error.

And now, where are we ourselves? Do we know? Many are living and dying in a kind of fog.—Where are we going? Can we give a satisfactory answer? Hundreds go out of existence in utter uncertainty.—Let us leave nothing uncertain that concerns our everlasting salvation. Christ, the light of the world, is for us as well as for others, if we humbly follow Him, cast our souls on Him, and become His disciples.—Let us not, like thousands, waste our lives in doubting and arguing and reasoning, but simply *follow*. The child that says, "I will not learn anything till I know something," will never learn at all. The man that says, "I must first understand everything before I become a Christian," will die in his sins. Let us begin by "following," and then we shall find light.

NOTES. JOHN VIII. 12—20.

Before beginning the notes on this section, I will ask any one who doubts the genuineness of the first eleven verses of the chapter, to consider how very awkwardly the twelfth verse would come in, if it immediately followed the 52nd verse of the seventh chapter.—The omission of the disputed passage about the woman taken in adultery, however necessary some may think it, undoubtedly makes a breach in the connection which cannot be reasonably explained.—*Omit* the passage, and our Lord appears to break in upon the angry council of the Pharisees, foiled in their attempt to take Him, and vexed with Nicodemus for pleading for Him. This is surely very improbable, to say the least.—*Retain* the disputed

passage, on the other hand, and the whole connection seems plain.
A night has passed away.   A sunrise is over the whole party
assembled in the temple court.   And our Lord begins again to
teach by proclaiming a beautiful truth, appropriate to the occasion :
"I am the light of the world."

12—[*Then spake Jesus again...them.*] The expression "spake
again" exactly fits in with the preceding narrative.   It carries us
back to the 2nd verse, where we read that our Lord was sitting in
the temple and teaching the people, when the woman taken in
adultery was brought before Him.   This naturally interrupted
and broke off His teaching for a time.   But when the case was
settled, and both accuser and accused had gone away, He resumed
His teaching.   Then the expression comes in most naturally,
"He spake again."   Once admit that the narrative of the woman
is not genuine and must be left out, and there is really nothing
with which to connect the words before us.   We are obliged to
look back as far as the 37th verse of the last chapter.

The same remark applies to the word "them"   The natural
application of it is to "the people" whom our Lord was teaching,
in the 2nd verse, when the Scribes and Pharisees interrupted Him.
Leave out the narrative of the woman, and there is nothing to
which the word "them" can be referred, except the angry council
of the Pharisees at the end of the seventh chapter.

[*I am...light...world.*]   In this glorious expression our Lord, we
cannot doubt, declares Himself to be the promised Messiah or
Saviour of whom the prophets had spoken.   The Jews would
remember the words,   "I will give Thee for a light of the
Gentiles." (Isai. xlii. 6, xlix. 6.)   So also Simeon had said, He
would be "a light to lighten the Gentiles." (Luke ii. 32.)   Why
He used this figure, and what He had in His mind in choosing it,
is a point on which commentators do not agree.   That He referred
to something before His eyes is highly probable, and in keeping
with His usual mode of teaching.

(1) Some think, as Aretius, Musculus, Ecolampadius, Bullinger,
and Bp. Andrews, that He referred to the sun, then rising while
He spoke.   What the sun was to the earth, that He came to be to
mankind.

(2) Some think, as Stier, Olshausen, Besser, D. Brown, and
Alford, that He referred to the great golden lamps which used to
be kept burning in the temple courts.   He was the true light, able
to enlighten men's hearts and minds.   They were nothing but
ornaments, or at most, emblems.

(3) Some think, as Cyril and Lamp, that He referred to the pillar of cloud and fire which gave light to the Israelites, and guided them through the wilderness. He was the true guide to heaven. through the wilderness of this world.

The first of these three views seems to me most probable, and most in harmony with the context.

Rupertus remarks that two grand declarations of Christ followed each other on two successive days at Jerusalem. On the last day of the feast He said, " If any man thirst let him come unto Me and drink." (John vii. 37.) The very next day He said, " I am the light of the world."

[*He that followeth Me.*] This means "following" as a disciple, servant, traveller, soldier, or sheep. What the teacher is to the scholar, the master to the servant, the guide to the traveller, the general to the soldier, the shepherd to the sheep, that is Christ to true Christians. "Following" is the same as "believing." See Matt. xvi. 24, xix. 21. John x. 27, xii. 26. Following here, we must always remember, does not mean copying and imitating, but trusting, putting faith in another.

Musculus and Henry observe, that it is of no use that Christ is the light of the world if we do not follow Him. "Following" is the point on which all turns. It is not enough to gaze upon and admire the light. We must "follow" it.

[*Shall not walk in darkness.*] The expression "darkness" in the New Testament sometimes denotes sin, as 1 John i. 6, and sometimes ignorance and unbelief, as 1 Thess. v. 4. Some have thought that our Lord referred to the woman taken in adultery, and to such deeds of moral darkness as she had been guilty of. The meaning would then be, "He that follows Me and becomes my disciple shall be delivered from the power of darkness and shall no longer commit such sins as you have just heard of."— Others, on the contrary, think that our Lord only referred to the intellectual darkness and ignorance of man's mind, which He had come to illuminate. The meaning would then be, "He that follows Me as my disciple shall no longer live in ignorance and darkness about his soul." I decidedly prefer this second view. The promise seems to me to have a special reference to the ignorance in which the Jews were about everything concerning Christ, as shown in the preceding chapter.

[*Shall have...light of life.*] This expression means, "He shall possess living light. He shall have spiritual light, as much superior to the light of any lamp or even of the sun, as the living water offered to the Samaritan woman was superior to the water of Jacob's well." The spiritual light that Christ gives is independent of time or place,—is not affected by sickness or death,—burns on for ever, and cannot be quenched. He that has it shall feel light within his mind, heart, and conscience,—shall see light before him on the grave, death, and the world to come,—shall have light shining round him, guiding him in his journey through life, and shall reflect light by his conduct, ways and conversation.

Chrysostom thinks that one purpose of this promise was to draw on and encourage Nicodemus, and to remind him of the former saying Jesus had used about light and darkness, John iii. 20, 21.

Augustine remarks on this verse, "What is our duty to do, Christ puts in the present tense: what He promiseth to them that do it, He hath denoted by a future time. He that followeth *now*, shall have *hereafter*,—followeth now by faith, shall have hereafter by sight. When by sight? When we shall have come to the vision yonder, when this night of ours shall have passed away." I should be sorry however to confine the promise to so limited an interpretation as this, and though I have no doubt it will only be completely fulfilled at the second advent, I still think that it is partially and spiritually fulfilled now to every believer.

Calvin remarks, that in this verse "Benefit is offered not only to one person or another, but to the whole world. By this universal statement Christ intended to remove the distinction, not only between Jews and Gentiles, but between learned and ignorant, between persons of distinction and common people." He also says, "In the latter clause of the verse, the perpetuity of light is stated in express terms. We ought not to fear therefore lest it leave us in the middle of our journey."

Brentius remarks, that if a man could continually "follow" the sun, he would always be in broad daylight in every part of the globe. So it is with Christ and believers. Always following Him, they will always have light.

In this most precious and interesting verse there are several things which deserve our special attention.

(a) We should note the great assumed truth which lies underneath the whole verse. That truth is the fall of man. The world is in a state of moral and spiritual darkness. Naturally men know nothing rightly of themselves, God, holiness, or heaven. They need light.

(*b*) We should note the full and bold manner of our Lord's declaration. He proclaims Himself to be "the light of the world." None could truly say this but one, who knew that He was very God. No Prophet or Apostle ever said it.

(*c*) We should note how our Lord says that He is "the light of the world." He is not for a few only, but for all mankind. Like the sun He shines for the benefit of all, though all may not value or use His light.

(*d*) We should note the man to whom the promise is made. It is to him "that followeth Me." To follow a leader if we are blind, or ignorant, or in the dark, or out of the way, requires trust and confidence. This is just what the Lord Jesus requires of sinners who feel their sins and want to be saved. Let them commit themselves to Christ, and He will lead them safe to heaven. If a man can do nothing for himself, he cannot do better than trust another and follow him.

(*e*) We should note the thing promised to him who follows Jesus: viz., deliverance from darkness and possession of light. This is precisely what Christianity brings to a believer. He feels, and sees, and has a sense of possessing something he had not before. God "shines into his heart and gives light." He is "called out of darkness into marvellous light." (2 Co. iv. 4—6 ; 1 Pet. ii. 9.)

Melancthon thinks that this verse is only a brief summary of what our Lord said, and must be regarded as the text or keynote of a long discourse.

Bullinger remarks how useful it is to commit to memory and store up great sentences and maxims of Christ, like this verse.

13.—[*The Pharisees...said unto Him.*] These "Pharisees" were probably some of the multitude who had come together to hear our Lord's teaching, and not those who brought the woman taken in adultery to Him. The Pharisees were a powerful and widely-spread sect, and members of their body would be found in every crowd of hearers, ready to raise objections and find fault with anything our Lord said, wherever they thought there was an opportunity.

[*Thou bearest record of Thyself.*] This would be more literally rendered, "Thou dost witness about Thyself."

[*Thy record is not true.*] This means, "Thy testimony is not trustworthy, and deserving of attention." The Pharisees evidently could not mean "Thy testimony is false." They only meant that it was an acknowledged principle among men that a man's testi-

mony to his own character is comparatively worthless. **Our Lord
Himself** had admitted this on a former occasion, when He said before the Council, "If I bear witness of myself my witness is not
true." (John v. 31.) Solomon had said, "Let another praise
thee, and not thine own mouth; a stranger, and not thine own
lips." (Prov. xxvii. 2.)

14.—[*Jesus answered...though I bear record...true.*] Our Lord meant
by these words that even if He did testify of Himself, and make
assertions about His own office and mission, His testimony ought
not to be despised and disregarded as not trustworthy. Whether
His enemies would hear it or not, what He said deserved credit,
and was worthy of all acceptation.—"The testimony that I bear
is not the testimony of a common witness, but of one who is
thoroughly to be depended on."

[*For I know whence I came, etc.*] Our Lord here gives a solemn
and weighty reason why His testimony to Himself ought to be reverently received by the Jews, and not refused. That reason was His
divine nature and mission. He came to them and stood before them
not as a common prophet and an every-day witness, but as one
who knew the mysterious truth that He was the Divine Messiah
that should come into the world.—"I know whence I came:—I came
forth from the Father, to be His Messenger to a lost world. I know
whither I go:—I am about to return to my Father when I have
finished His work, and to sit down at His right hand after my
ascension. Knowing all this, I have a right to say that my testimony is trustworthy. You, on the other hand, are utterly ignorant about Me. You neither know nor believe my Divine origin
nor mission. Justly, therefore, I may say that it matters little
whether you think my testimony deserving of credit or not. Your
eyes are blinded, and your opinion is worthless."

Chrysostom observes that our Lord "might have said, I am
God. But He ever mingleth lowly words with sublime, and even
these He veileth."

Bucer, Chemnitius, and Quesnel observe that our Lord's argument is like that of an ambassador from a king, who says, "I
know my commission and who sent Me, and therefore I claim
attention to my message."

Webster paraphrases the sentence: "I speak in the full con-
sciousness of my previous and future existence in the glory of the
Father; and I therefore feel and assert my right to be believed on
my own testimony. If you knew whence I came and whither I

go, you would not want any other witness than myself. And this you might know if you were spiritual; but you are carnal and judge after the flesh."

15.—[*Ye judge after the flesh.*] The meaning of this sentence seems to be, "You judge and decide everything on fleshly and worldly principles, according to the outward appearance. You estimate Me and my mission according to what you see with the eye. You presume to despise Me and set light by Me, because there is no outward grandeur and dignity about Me. Judging everything by such a false standard, you see no beauty in Me and my ministry. You have already set Me down in your own minds as an impostor, and worthy to die. Your minds are full of carnal prejudices, and hence my testimony seems worthless to you."

Calvin thinks that "flesh" is here used in opposition to "spirit," and that the meaning is, "You judge on carnal wicked principles;" and not, "You judge after the outward appearance." Most commentators think that the expression refers to our Lord's humble appearance.

[*I judge no man.*] In these words our Lord puts in strong contrast the difference between Himself and His enemies. "Unlike you, I condemn and pass judgment on no man, even on the worst of sinners. It is not my present business and office, though it will be one day. I did not come into the world to condemn, but to save." (John iii. 17.) It is useless, however, to deny that the connection between the beginning and end of the verse is not clear. It seems to turn entirely on the twice-repeated word "judge," and the word appears to be used in two different senses.

Some have thought that our Lord refers to the case of the woman taken in adultery, and contrasts His own refusal to be a judge in her case, with the malicious readiness of the Pharisees to judge Him and condemn Him even when innocent. "I refuse to condemn even a guilty sinner. You, on the contrary, are ready to condemn Me in whom you can find no fault, on carnal and worldly principles."

Some, as Bullinger, Jansenius, Trapp, Stier, Gill, Pearce and Barnes, have thought that the sentence before us means, "I judge no man according to the flesh, as you do." But this view does not seem to harmonize with the following verse.

Bishop Hall paraphrases the verse this: "Ye presume to judge according to your own carnal affections, and follow your outward senses in the judgment ye pass on Me. In the meantime ye will not endure Me, who do not challenge or reconcile that power which I might in judging you."

16.—[*And yet if I judge, my judgment, etc.*] This verse seems to come in parenthetically. It appears intended to remind the Jews that if our Lord did not assume the office of a judge now, it was not because He was not qualified. The sense is as follows : "Do not however suppose, because I say that I judge no man, that I am not qualified to judge. On the contrary, if I do pass judgment on any person's actions or opinions, my judgment is perfectly correct and trustworthy. For I am not alone. There is an inseparable union between Me and the Father that sent Me. When I judge, it is not I alone, but the Father with Me that judges. Hence, therefore, my judgment is and must be trustworthy." The reader should compare John v. 19, and 30. The doctrine is the same. That mighty truth,—the inseparable union of the Father and the Son,—is the only key that unlocks the deep expression before us. Our Lord's frequent reference to that truth, in St. John's Gospel, should be carefully noted.

17.—[*It is also written, etc.*] Our Lord, in this verse, reminds the Jews of an admitted principle of the law of Moses,—that the testimony of two witnesses deserved credit. (Deut xvii. 6 ; xix. 15). "You will admit that the testimony of two witnesses deserves credit at any rate, although one witness alone may prove nothing. Now admitting this, hear what testimony I can adduce to the divine character of my mission."

Let it be noted, that where our Lord says, "in YOUR law," He did not mean that He was above the law and did not recognise its authority. He only intended, by laying stress on the word "your," to remind the Jews that it was their own honoured law of Moses, to which they were continually professing to refer, that laid down the great principle to which He was about to direct their attention. "It is written in the law that YOU speak of so much, and that *you* so often quote."

It admits of consideration whether our Lord did not mean to use the expression "of two men" emphatically. It may be that He would put in strong contrast the testimony of two mere *men*, with the testimony of Himself and His Father in heaven. It is like the expression, "If we receive the witness of men, the witness ot God is greater." (1 John v. 9.) At any rate the word rendered "men" is emphatic in the Greek.

18.—[*I am one, etc.*] The connection and sense of this verse are as follows. "Admitting that the testimony of two witnesses is trust-worthy, I bid you observe that there are two witnesses to my Divine nature and mission. I myself, the Eternal Son, am one of these witnesses : I am ever testifying concerning myself. The Father that sent Me into the world is the other witness : He is ever testifying concerning Me. He has testified by the mouth of the Prophets in the Old Testament. He is testifying now by the miraculous works which He is continually doing by my hands. The reader should compare John v. 31—39.

There is undeniably something very remarkable about this verse. It seems a singular condescension on our Lord's part to use the train of argument that it contains. The true solution probably lies in the very high dignity of the two witnesses, whom He places together before the Jews. The Greek words beginning the verse are peculiar, and can hardly be rendered in English. They will almost bear to be translated, "I, the great I am, am the person witnessing about myself : and the Father," etc.

Chrysostom and Theophylact both remark that our Lord here claims equality of honour with the Father, by putting His testi-mony and the Father's side by side.

Poole remarks, "Our Saviour must not be understood here to distinguish himself from His Father in respect of His Divine being, for so He and His Father are one ; but in respect of His office, as He was sent, and His Father was He who sent Him."

19.—[*Then said they... Where is thy Father ?*] This question of the Jews' was probably not asked in a tone of serious inquiry, or from real desire to know. It was more likely sneering and sarcastic.

Calvin observes, "By these words they meant that they did not so highly value Christ's Father as to ascribe anything to the Son on His account."

Hengstenberg bids us observe that they did not ask, "Who is thy Father?" but, "Where is thy Father?" It sounds as if they looked round in contempt, as if scornfully expecting an earthly father to stand forth and testify to Christ.

[*Jesus answered, Ye neither know Me...Father.*] Our Lord here tells His enemies that they were ignorant both of Himself and of His Father in heaven. With all their pride of knowledge and fancied high attainments they knew nothing rightly either of the Father or the Son. The expression certainly favours the idea that the expression " Ye know Me " (John vii. 28), must be taken as a slight sarcasm.

Let it be noted that great familiarity with the letter of Scripture is perfectly compatible with gross spiritual darkness. The Pharisees knew the old Testament prophecies well; but they neither knew God nor Christ.

[*If ye had known Me...my Father also.*] These words teach plainly that ignorance of Christ and ignorance of God are inseparably connected. The man who thinks he knows anything rightly of God while he is ignorant of Christ, is completely deceived. The God whom he thinks he knows is not the God of the Bible, but a God of his own fancy's invention. At any rate he can have a most imperfect conception of God, and can have but little idea of His perfect holiness, justice and purity. The words teach also that Christ is the way by which we must come to the knowledge of God. In Him, through Him, and by Him, we may come boldly into the Father's presence, and behold His high attributes without fear.

He that would have saving, soul-satisfying religion, and become a friend and servant of God, must begin with Christ. Knowing Him as his Saviour and Advocate, he will find it easy and pleasant to know God the Father. Those that reject Christ, like the Jews, will live and die in ignorance of God, however learned and clever they may be. But the poorest, humblest man, that lays hold on Christ and begins with Him, shall find out enough about God to make him happy for ever. In the matter of becoming acquainted with God, it is the first step to know Jesus Christ, the Mediator, and to believe on Him.

Augustine and others think that the thought here is the same as that in the words spoken to Philip, when in reply to Philip's question, "Lord, show us the Father," Jesus said, "He that hath seen Me hath seen the Father." (John xiv. 8, 9.) I think this is at least doubtful. The thing that Philip needed to know was the precise relation between the Father and the Son. The thing that the Jews needed was a right knowledge of God altogether.

20.—[*These words spake Jesus...treasury...temple.*] This sentence seems meant to mark a pause or break in the discourse, and to show also how publicly and openly our Lord proclaimed His Messiahship. It was in a well known part of the temple called the treasury that He declared Himself to be "the light of the world," and defended His testimony.

Calvin thinks that "the treasury was a part of the temple where the sacred offerings were laid up, and therefore a much frequented place."

[*No man laid hands on Him.*] The remark made on a former occasion applies here. (John vii. 30.) A divine restraint was laid on our Lord's enemies. They felt unable to lift a finger against Him. They had the will to hurt, but not the power.

[*His hour was not yet come.*] The same deep thought that we remarked in ch. vii. 30, comes up here again. There was a certain fixed time during which our Lord's ministry was to last, and till that time was expired His enemies could not touch Him. When the time had expired, our Lord said, " This is your hour, and the power of darkness." (Luke xxii. 53.)

The expression should be carefully noticed, and remembered by all true Christians. It teaches that the wicked can do no harm to Christ and His members until God gives them permission. Not a hair of a believer's head can be touched until God in His sovereign wisdom allows it.—It teaches that all times are in God's hand. There is an allotted "hour" both for doing and for suffering. Till the hour comes for dying no Christian will die. When the hour comes nothing can prevent his death. These are comfortable truths, and deserve attention. Christ's members are safe and immortal till their work is done. When they suffer it is because God wills it and sees it good.

Quesnel remarks, " A man enjoys the greatest peace of mind when he has once settled himself in a firm and steadfast belief of God's providence, and an absolute dependence upon His design and will."

JOHN VIII. 21—30.

21 Then said Jesus again unto them, I go my way, and ye shall seek me, and shall die in your sins: whither I go, ye cannot come.

22 Then said the Jews, Will he kill himself? because he saith, Whither I go, ye cannot come.

23 And he said unto them, Ye are from beneath ; I am from above : ye are of this world; I am not of this world.

24 I said therefore unto you, that ye shall die in your sins: for if ye believe not that I am *he*, ye shall die in your sins.

25 Then said they unto Him, Who art thou? And Jesus saith unto them, Even *the same* that I said unto you from the beginning.

26 I have many things to say and to judge of you: but he that sent me is true ; and I speak to the world those things which I have heard of him

27 They understood not that he spake to them of the Father.

28 Then said Jesus unto them, When ye have lifted up the Son of man, then shall ye know that I am *he*, and *that* I do nothing of myself; but as my Father hath taught me, I speak these things.

29 And he that sent me is with me: the Father hath not left me alone : for I do always those things that please him.

30 As he spake these words, many believed on him.

THIS passage contains deep things, so deep that we have

no line to fathom them. As we read it we should call
to mind the Psalmist's words: "Thy thoughts are very
deep." (Psalm xcii. 5.) But it also contains, in the
opening verses, some things which are clear, plain, and
unmistakable. To these let us give our attention, and
root them firmly in our hearts.

We learn, for one thing, *that it is possible to seek Christ
in vain.* Our Lord says to the unbelieving Jews, "Ye
shall seek Me, and shall die in your sins." He meant,
by these words, that the Jews would one day seek Him
in vain.

The lesson before us is a very painful one. That
such a Saviour as the Lord Jesus, so full of love, so
willing to save, should ever be sought "in vain," is a
sorrowful thought. Yet so it is! A man may have
many religious feelings about Christ, without any saving
religion. Sickness, sudden affliction, the fear of death,
the failure of usual sources of comfort,—all these causes
may draw out of a man a good deal of "religiousness."
Under the immediate pressure of these he may say his
prayers fervently, exhibit strong spiritual feelings, and
profess for a season to "seek Christ," and be a different
man. And yet all this time his heart may never be
touched at all? Take away the peculiar circumstances
that affected him, and he may possibly return at once
to his old ways. He sought Christ "in vain," because
he sought Him from false motives, and not with his
whole heart.

Unhappily this is not all. There is such a thing as
a settled habit of resisting light and knowledge, until we

seek Christ "in vain." Scripture and experience alike prove that men may reject God until God rejects them, and will not hear their prayer. They may go on stifling their convictions, quenching the light of conscience, fighting against their own better knowledge, until God is provoked to give them over, and let them alone. It is not for nothing that these words are written: "Then shall they call upon Me, but I will not answer; they shall seek Me early, but they shall not find Me: for that they hated knowledge, and did not choose the fear of the Lord." (Prov. i. 28, 29.) Such cases may not be common; but they are possible, and they are sometimes seen. Some ministers can testify that they have visited people on their death-beds who seem to seek Christ, and yet to seek in vain.

There is no safety but in seeking Christ while He may be found, and calling on Him while He is near,— seeking Him with a true heart, and calling on Him with an honest spirit. Such seeking, we may be very sure, is never in vain. It will never be recorded of such seekers, that they "died in their sins." He that really comes to Christ shall never be "cast out." The Lord has solemnly declared that " He hath no pleasure in the death of him that dieth,"—and that "He delighteth in mercy." (Ezekiel xviii. 32; Micah vii. 18.)

We learn, for another thing, how *wide is the difference between Christ and the ungodly*. Our Lord says to the unbelieving Jews, "Ye are from beneath; I am from above: ye are of this world; I am not of this world."

These words, no doubt, have a special application to

our Lord Jesus Christ Himself. In the highest and most literal sense there never was but One who could truly say, "I am from above: I am not of this world." That One is He who came forth from the Father, and was before the world,—even the Son of God.

But there is a lower sense, in which these words are applicable to all Christ's living members. Compared to the thoughtless multitude around them, they are "from above," and "not of this world," like their Master. The thoughts of the ungodly are about things beneath; the true Christian's affections are set on things above. The ungodly man is full of this world; its cares and pleasures and profits absorb his whole attention. The true Christian, though in the world, is not of it; his citizenship is in heaven, and his best things are yet to come.

The true Christian will do well never to forget this line of demarcation. If he loves his soul, and desires to serve God, he must be content to find himself separated from many around him by a gulf that cannot be passed. He may not like to seem peculiar and unlike others; but it is the certain consequence of grace reigning within him. He may find it brings on him hatred, ridicule, and hard speeches; but it is the cup which his Master drank, and of which his Master forewarned all His disciples.—" If ye were of the world, the world would love his own, but because ye are not of the world, but I have chosen you out of the world, therefore the world hateth you." (John xv. 19.) Then let the Christian never be ashamed to stand alone and to show his colours.

He must carry the cross if he would wear the crown. If he has within him a new principle " from above," it must be seen.

We learn, lastly, how *awful is the end to which unbelief can bring men*. Our Lord says to His enemies, " If ye believe not that I am He, ye shall die in your sins."

These solemn words are invested with peculiar solemnity when we consider from whose lips they came. Who is this that speaks of men dying " in their sins," unpardoned, unforgiven, unfit to meet God,—of men going into another world with all their sins upon them? He that says this is no other than the Saviour of mankind, who laid down His life for His sheep,—the loving gracious, merciful, compassionate Friend of sinners. It is Christ Himself! Let this simple fact not be overlooked.

They are greatly mistaken who suppose that it is harsh and unkind to speak of hell and future punishment. How can such persons get over such language as that which is before us? How can they account for many a like expression which our Lord used, and specially for such passages as those in which He speaks of the "worm that dieth not, and the fire that is not quenched"? (Mark ix. 46.) They cannot answer these questions. Misled by a false charity and a morbid amiability, they are condemning the plain teaching of Scripture, and are wise above that which is written.

Let us settle it in our minds, as one of the great foundation truths of our faith, that there is a hell. Just as we believe firmly that there is an eternal heaven for the

godly, so let us believe firmly that there is an eternal
hell for the wicked.   Let us never suppose that there is
any want of charity in speaking of hell.   Let us rather
maintain that it is the highest love to warn men plainly
of danger, and to beseech them to " flee from the wrath
to come."   It was Satan, the deceiver, murderer, and
liar, who said to Eve in the beginning, " Ye shall not
surely die."   (Gen. iii. 4.)   To shrink from telling men,
that except they believe they will " die in their sins,"
may please the devil, but surely it cannot please God.

Finally, let us never forget that unbelief is the special
sin that ruins men's souls.   Had the Jews believed on
our Lord, all manner of sin and blasphemy might have
been forgiven them.   But unbelief bars the door in
mercy's face, and cuts off hope.   Let us watch and pray
hard against it.   Immorality slays its thousands, but
unbelief its tens of thousands.   One of the strongest
sayings ever used by our Lord was this,—" He that believeth not shall be damned."   (Mark xvi. 16.)

Notes John viii. 21—30.

21.—[*Then said Jesus again unto them.*] There seems a break or pause
between this verse and the preceding one.   It is as if our Lord resumed discourse with a new leading thought or key-note.   The
other idea, viz., that "again" refers to chap. vii. 34, and means
that our Lord impressed on his hearers a *second time* that He would
soon leave them, does not seem probable.—It seems not unlikely
that in the first instance our Lord spoke of "going" to the officers of the priests and Pharisees, and that here He speaks to
their masters, or at least to a different set of hearers.

[*I go my way.*] This must mean, "I am soon about to leave
this world.   My mission is drawing to a close.   The time of my
decease and sacrifice approaches, and I must depart, and go back
to my Father in heaven. from whence I came."—The leading object

of the sentence appears to be to excite in the minds of the Jews thought and inquiry about His divine nature. "I am one who came from heaven, and am going back to heaven. Ought you not to inquire seriously who I am?"

Chrysostom thinks our Lord said this, partly to shame and terrify the Jews, and partly to show them that His death would not be effected by their violence, but by His own voluntary submission.

[*Ye shall seek Me...die in...sins.*] This means that His hearers would seek Him too late, having discovered too late that He was the Messiah whom they ought to have received. But the door of mercy would then be shut. They would seek in vain, because they had not known the day of their visitation. And the result would be that many of them would die miserably "in their sins"—with their sins upon them unpardoned and unforgiven.

[*Whither I go ye cannot come.*] This must mean heaven, the everlasting abode of glory which the Son had with the Father before He came into the world, which He left for a season when He became incarnate, and to which He returned when He had finished the work of man's redemption. To this a wicked man cannot come. Unbelief shuts him out. It is impossible in the nature of things that an unforgiven, unconverted, unbelieving man can go to heaven. The words in Greek are emphatic: "Ye *cannot* come."

The notion of Augustine and others that "Ye shall seek Me" only means "Ye shall seek Me in order to kill Me, as ye are wishing to do now, but at last I shall be withdrawn from your reach,"—seems to me quite untenable. The "seeking," to my mind, can only be the too late seeking of remorse.—The theory of some, that it refers exclusively to the time of the siege of Jerusalem by the Romans, seems to me equally untenable. My belief is that from the time that our Lord left the world down to this day, the expression has been peculiarly true of the Jewish nation. They have been perpetually, in a sense, "seeking" and hungering after a Messiah, and yet unable to find Him, because they have not sought aright.—In saying this we must carefully remember that our Lord did not mean to say that any of His hearers were too *sinful* and bad to be forgiven. On the contrary, not a few of them that crucified Him found mercy on the day of Pentecost, when Peter preached. (Acts ii. 22—41.) But our Lord did mean to say prophetically that the Jewish nation, as a nation, would be specially hardened and unbelieving, and that many of them, though an elect remnant might be saved, would "die in their sins." In proof of this peculiar blindness and unbelief of the

Jewish nation we should study Acts xxviii. 25—27, Romans xi. 7, and 1 Thes. ii. 15, 16. The Greek expression for "sins" in this verse confirms the view. It is not, literally rendered, "sins," but "sin:" your special sin of unbelief.

Let us note that it is possible to seek Christ too late, or from a wrong motive, and so to seek Him in vain. This is a very important principle of Scripture. True repentance, doubtless, is never too late, but late repentance is seldom true. There is mercy to the uttermost in Christ; but if men wilfully reject Him, turn away from Him, and put off seeking Him in earnest, there is such a thing as "seeking Christ" in vain. Such passages as Proverbs i. 24—32; Matt. xxv. 11—12; Luke xiii. 24—27; Heb. vi. 4—8, and x. 26—31, ought to be carefully studied.

Let us note that our Lord teaches plainly that it is possible for men to "die in their sins," and never come to the heaven where He has gone. This is flatly contrary to the doctrine taught by some in the present day, that there is no hell, and no future punishment, and that all will finally go to heaven.

It is worthy of remark that our Lord's words, "Ye shall seek Me," and "Whither I go ye cannot come," are used three times in this Gospel:—twice to the unbelieving Jews, here and at vii. 34, and once to the disciples, xiii. 33. But the careful reader will observe that in the two first instances the expression is coupled with, "Ye shall not find Me," and "Ye shall die in your sins." In the last, it evidently means the temporary separation between Christ and His disciples which would be caused by His ascension.

Melancthon observes that nothing seems to bring on men such dreadful guilt and punishment as neglect of the Gospel. The Jews had Christ among them and would not believe, and so when afterward they sought they could not find.

Rollock observes that the "seeking" which our Lord here foretells was like that of Esau, when he sought too late for the lost birthright.

Burkitt observes. "Better a thousand times to die in a ditch than to die in our sins! They that die in their sins shall rise in their sins, and stand before Christ in their sins. Such as lie down in sin in the grave shall have sin lie down with them in hell to all eternity. The sins of believers go to the grave before them; sin dieth while they live. The sins of unbelievers go to the grave with them."

22.—[*Then said the Jews, etc.*] It is plain that this last saying of our Lord perplexed His enemies. It evidently implied something which they did not understand. In the preceding chapter (vii. 34) they began speculating whether it meant that our Lord was going forth into the world to teach the Gentiles. Here they start another conjecture, and begin to suspect that our Lord must mean His going into another world by death. But by what death did He think of going! Did He mean to "kill Himself"? It seems strange that they should start such an idea. But may it not be that their minds were occupied with their own plan of putting Him to death? "Will He really anticipate our plan, by committing suicide, and thus escape our hands?"

Origen suggests that the Jews had a tradition about the manner in which Messiah would die: viz. "that He would have power to depart at His own time, and in a way of His own choosing."

Rupertus observes that afterwards at the siege of Jerusalem by Titus, many of the desperate Jews did the very thing they here said of our Lord,—they killed themselves in madness of despair.

Melancthon remarks that nothing seems to anger wicked men so much as to be told they cannot come where Christ is.

23.—[*And He said Ye are from beneath, etc.*] Our Lord's argument in this case appears to be as follows. "There is no union, harmony, or fellowship between you and Me. Your minds are entirely absorbed and buried in earth and objects of a mere earthly kind. You are from beneath, and of this world; while I came from heaven, and my heart is full of the things of heaven and my Father's business. No wonder, therefore, that I said you cannot come where I go, and will die in your sins. Unless your hearts are changed, and you learn to be of one mind with Me, you are totally unmeet for heaven, and must at last die in your sins."

The expressions "from beneath" and "from above" are strong figurative phrases, intended to put in contrast earth and heaven. See Col. iii. 1, 2. The Greek phrases literally rendered would be, "Ye are from the things beneath: I am from the things above."

The expression "of this world" means bound up with, and inseparably connected, by tastes, aims, and affections, with this world, and nothing else but this world. It is the character of one utterly dead and graceless, who looks at nothing but the world, and lives for it. It is a character utterly at variance with that of our Lord, who was eminently "not of this world;" and therefore those who were of this character were incapable of union and friendship with Him."

Let it be noted that what our Lord says of Himself here, is the very same thing that is said of His true disciples elsewhere. If a man has grace he is "not of the world." (See John xv. 19 ; xvii. 16 ; and 1 John iv. 5.) Christ's living members always have more or less of their Master's likeness in this respect. They are always more or less separated from and distinct from this world. He that is thoroughly worldly has the plainest mark of not being a member of Christ and a true Christian.

Theophylact observes that the strange notion of the Apollinarian heretics, that our Lord's body was not a real human body, but came down from heaven, was built on this verse for one of its reasons. But, as he remarks, they might as well say the Apostles had not common human bodies, since the same thing is said of them : "not of this world."

24.—[*I said therefore, etc.*] This verse seems elliptical, and must be filled up in some such manner as this : "It is because you are thoroughly earthly and of this world, that I said, Ye cannot come where I go. You are not heavenly minded, and cannot go to heaven, but must go to your own place. The end will be that you will die in your sins. Not believing in Me as the Messiah, you cut yourselves off from all hope, and must die in your sins. This, in short, is the root of all your misery,—your unbelief."

Let it be noted that unbelief is the thing that specially ruins men. All manner of sin may be forgiven. But unbelief bars the door against mercy. (Mark xvi. 16, and John iii. 36.)

Let it be noted that unbelief was the secret of the Jews being so thoroughly "of the world." If they would only have believed in Christ, they would have been "delivered from this present evil world." The victory that overcomes the world is faith. Once believing on a heavenly Saviour a man has a portion and a heart in heaven. (Gal. i. 4 ; 1 John v. 4, 5.)

Let it be noted that there is nothing hard or uncharitable in warning men plainly of the consequences of unbelief. Never to speak of hell is not acting as Christ did.

The expression "Believe not that I am He" would be more literally rendered "Believe not that I am." Hence some think that our Lord refers to the great name, well known to the Jews, under which God revealed Himself to Israel in Egypt : "Say unto the children of Israel, I AM hath sent you." (Ex. iii. 14.)

Augustine remarks that "the whole unhappiness of the Jews was not that they had sin, but to die in sins." He also observes, "In these words, 'Except ye believe that I am,' Jesus meant nothing short of this, 'Except ye believe that I am God, ye shall die in your sins.' It is well for us, thank God, that He said except ye *believe*, and not except ye *understand*."

Quesnel remarks, "It is a mistaken prudence to hide these dreadful truths from sinners, for fear of casting them into despair by the force of God's judgments. We ought, on the contrary, to force them, by the sight of danger, to throw themselves into the arms of Christ, the only refuge for sinners."

25.—[*Then said they... Who art Thou?*] This question cannot have been an honest inquiry about our Lord's nature and origin. Our Lord had spoken so often of His Father,—for instance, in the fifth chapter, when before the Council,—that the Jews of Jerusalem must have known well enough who and what He claimed to be. It is far more likely that they hoped to elicit from Him some fresh declaration which they could lay hold of, and make the ground of an accusation. Anger and malice seem at the bottom of the question : "Who art Thou that sayest such things of us? Who art Thou that undertakest to pronounce such condemnation on us?"

Ecolampadius thinks the question was asked sarcastically,— "Who art thou, indeed, to talk in this way?"

[*And Jesus saith...even the same ...beginning.*] Our Lord's reply here seems so guarded and cautious, that it increases the probability of the Jews' question being put with a malicious intention. He knew their thoughts and designs, and answered them by re-minding them what He had always said of Himself : "Why ask Me who I am? You know well what I have always said of myself. I am the same that I said to you from the beginning. I have nothing new to say."

Scott thinks it simply means, "I am the same that I told you at the beginning of this discourse,—the Light of the World."

There is an undeniable difficulty and obscurity about the sentence before us, and it has consequently received three different interpretations. The difficulty arises chiefly from the word "beginning."

(*a*) Some think, as our own English version, Chrysostom, Calvin, Bucer, Gualter, Cartwright, Rollock, and Lightfoot, that "beginning" means the beginning of our Lord's ministry. "I am the same person that I told you I was from the very first beginning of my ministry among you." This view is confirmed by the Septuagint rendering of Gen. xliii. 18, 20.

(*b*) Some think, as Theophylact, Melancthon, Aretus, and Musculus, that "beginning" is an adverb. and means simply, "as an

opening or beginning statement." "First of all, as a commencement of my reply, I tell you that I am what I always said I was."

(c)   Some think, as Augustine, Rupertus, Toletus, Ferus, Jansenius, Lampe, and Wordsworth, that "beginning" is a substantive,
and means the Beginning of all things, the personal Beginning, like
"I am the Alpha and the Omega, the Beginning and the end."
(Rev. i. 8 ; xxi. 6; xxii. 13.) It would then mean, "I am the great
beginning of all things, the eternal God, as I always said."

The reader must exercise his own judgment on these three
views.   The extreme brevity and conciseness of the Greek words
make it very hard to give a decided opinion upon them.   On the
whole, I prefer the view taken by our translators.   In three other
places in St. John's Gospel our Lord speaks of His early ministry
as "the beginning."   (John vi. 64 ; xv. 27 ; xvi. 4.)   In no place
in St. John's Gospel does He ever call Himself "the beginning."
As to the second view, that it only means, "First of all, as an
opening statement," it seem to me so meagre, flat and bald, that
I cannot think it is correct.

Rollock, who takes the view of our English version, observes
what a bright example our Lord here sets to all Christians, and
especially to ministers, of always telling the same story, and witnessing one and the same confession without variation.

26.—[*I have many things, etc.*] This verse again is very elliptical.
The meaning seems to be as follows : "You marvel and are angry
at my saying that you are from beneath, and will die in your sin,
and cannot come where I go.   You ask who I am that speak and
judge in this manner.   But I tell you that I have many other
things that I might say, and other judgments that I might pronounce about you.   But I forbear now.   Yet I tell you that He
who sent Me is the one true God ; and I only speak to the world
things which I have heard of Him, and am commissioned by Him
to proclaim.   He that sent Me will prove them to be true one day."

The general idea seems to be that our Lord defends His right to
speak decidedly and pronounce judgment on His enemies' conduct,
on the ground of His divine mission,   "I have a right to say what
I have said ; and I might say much more, because I am not a
common prophet, but am commissioned and sent as the Word of
the Father."

The frequency with which our Lord speaks of Himself as "sent
by the Father," in St John's Gospel, should be carefully noticed.

When our Lord speaks of Himself as "hearing" things from the
Father, we must remember that His language is accommodated to

our understanding. The relation between the Father and the Son in the Trinity is something too mysterious for us fully to comprehend. The Son does not really and literally need the Father to "speak" to Him, and does not himself need to "hear" Him. The first and second Persons in the Trinity are ineffably united, though two distinct Persons.

Lightfoot thinks the latter part of this verse means, "He that sent Me hath of old said and judged of you, and He is true, and they are true things that He said. Of this kind are the passages Isaiah xi. 10. and xxix. 10, and from such predictions Christ concludes thus, 'Ye shall die in your sins.'"

27.—[*They understood not, etc.*] Why the Jews who heard these words did not comprehend that our Lord spoke of the "Father" is not clear. They must have thought that "He that sent Me" meant some earthly sender. The extent to which our Lord's hearers sometimes understood Him, as in John v. 18, and sometimes did not understand Him, as here, is a curious subject.

Alford observes, "There is no accounting for the ignorance of unbelief ; as any minister of Christ knows by painful experience."

28.—[*Then said Jesus, etc.*] This verse is prophetical. Our Lord predicts that after His crucifixion the Jews would know that He was the Messiah, that He had done all He had done not of His own private authority but by God's commission, and that He had spoken to the world only such things as the Father had taught and appointed Him to speak. But whether our Lord meant that His hearers would really believe with the heart and really confess His Messiahship, or that they would know it too late and be convinced when the day of grace was past and gone, is a nice and difficult question.

My own opinion, judging from the context and the analogy of other places, is in favour of the latter view : viz., that our Lord predicted the Jewish nation would know the truth and discover their own mistake too late. I think so because our Lord seems so frequently to allude to the light which would come on the minds of the Jewish nation at large after His death. They would be convinced though not converted.

(1) Chrysostom thinks that our Lord meant, "Do you expect that you shall certainly rid yourselves of Me, and slay Me ? I tell you that then ye shall most surely know that I am, by reason of the miracle of my resurrection, and the destruction of Jerusalem. When ye have been driven away from your place of worship, and

it is not even allowed you to serve God as hitherto, then ye shall know that He doth this to avenge Me, and because He is wroth with those who would not hear Me."

(2) Augustine takes the other side, and says, "Without doubt Jesus saw there some whom He knew, whom in His foreknowledge He had elected together with His other saints before the foundation of the world, that after His passion they should believe."

(3) Euthymius, agreeing with Chrysostom, remarks how the crowds that saw our Lord crucified, and returned home smiting their breasts,—the centurion who superintended His crucifixion,—the chief priests who tried in vain to stifle the report of His resurrection, and Josephus the historian, who attributed the misfortunes of the nation to their murder of Christ,—were all witnesses to the truth of this verse. When too late they knew who our Lord was.

(4) Alford thinks that the words admit of a double fulfilment, and that the Jews were to "know" that Jesus was the Christ, in two different ways. Some would know by being converted, some by being punished and judged.

The expression "lifted up," both here and elsewhere in St. John's Gospel, can mean nothing but our Lord's crucifixion and lifting up on the cross. (John iii. 14, and xii. 32.) It is never used in any other sense, and the modern habit of talking of Christ as "lifted up," when magnified and exalted in the pulpit, is a total misapprehension, and a play upon words.

Rollock and others think that the phrase "lifted up" may fairly include all the consequences and effects of our Lord's crucifixion, such as His second advent to judge the world, and that this will be the time when the unbelieving will at last know and be convinced that Christ is Lord of all. But the idea seems far-fetched.

The expression "then ye shall know" may possibly refer both to our Lord's resurrection as well as His crucifixion. Certainly the rising again from the dead silenced our Lord's enemies in a way that nothing else ever did.

The expression "that I am He," here as elsewhere, might be equally well rendered "that I am:" that I am the great "I AM," the Messiah.

The phrase "that I do nothing of myself" is the same that we have had frequently before, as in John v. 19, 30. It means "that I do nothing of my own independent authority." The reference is to the perfect union between the Son and the Father.

The expression, "as my Father hath taught Me I speak these things," again bears special reference to the divine commission of our Lord and the perfect union between Himself and His Father. "I do not speak the things I speak of myself and by my own authority only. I speak nothing but what my Father has taught, commissioned, and appointed Me to speak." (Compare 7th, 16th, and 26th verses of this chapter.)

Augustine says here, "Do not as it were represent to yourselves two men, the one father, the other son, and the father speaking to the son, as thou doest when thou sayest certain words to thy son, advising and instructing him how to speak, that whatever he has heard from thee he may commit to memory, and having committed to memory utter also with the tongue. Do not so conceive. Stature and motion of the body, the office of the tongue, distinction of sounds, do not go about to conceive them in the Trinity." Again : "Incorporeally the Father spake to the Son, because incorporeally the Father begat the Son. And He taught him not as if He had begotten Him ignorant and in need of teaching; but this 'taught' is the same as begat Him knowing."

29.—[*And He that sent Me, etc.*] This verse contains once more that deep and oft-repeated truth, the entire unity between God the Father and the Lord Jesus Christ, and the consequent entire and complete harmony between the mind of the Father and the mind of the Son. It contains moreover that entire and complete performance of the Father's will by the Son, and that perfect righteousness, obedience, and holiness, wherewith the Father is well-pleased.

When we read such words as "He that sent Me is with Me," and "hath not left Me alone," we must remember that there is much in them which we cannot fully explain. We must be content to believe that the Father was "with" the Son, and never "left" Him during the whole period of His incarnation, in an ineffable and inscrutable manner. Perhaps also there is a reference to Is. l. 7, 8, 9.

Augustine remarks, "Albeit both are together, yet one was sent, and the other did send. The Father sent the Son, yet quitted not the Son."

When we read such words as "I do always those things that please Him," we must see in the expression a description of that spotless perfection with which the Son during His incarnation constantly pleased the eternal Father.

Let Christians never forget the practical lesson that in this verse, as in many other places, Christ is their example and their encouragement. Like Him, however short they may come, let them aim at "always doing what pleases God." Like Him, let them be sure that so doing they will find the Father "with them," and will never be left quite "alone."

Calvin remarks, "This is the courage with which we ought to be animated in the present day, that we may not give way on account of the small number of believers : for though the whole world be opposed to His doctrine, still we are not alone. Hence it is evident how foolish is the boasting of the Papists, who while they neglect God, proudly boast of their vast numbers."

30.—[*As He spake these words, many believed on Him.*] There can be little doubt that "these words" in this place, refer to the whole discourse which was delivered at this time, and not to the single verse which immediately precedes this one. It is possible that the reference to Isa. l. 7, 8, 9, may have brought light to the Jews' minds, and explained our Lord's relation to the Father and His claim to be received as the Messiah.—Otherwise it is not very clear what it was that made "many believe" on Him at this juncture. There is, however, no reason to think that the "belief" here was anything more than a head belief that our Lord was the Messiah. That many did so believe whose hearts remained unchanged, there can be little doubt. The same expression occurs at x. 42, and xi. 45, and xii. 42. The extent to which men may be intellectually convinced of the truth of religion and know their duty, while their hearts are unrenewed and they continue in sin, is one of the most painful phenomena in the history of human nature. Let us never be content with believing things to be true, without a personal laying hold on the living Person, Christ Jesus, and actually following Him.

Chrysostom observes "They believed, yet not as they ought, but carelessly and by chance, being pleased and refreshed by the humility of the words. For that they had not perfect faith the Evangelist shows by their speeches after this, in which they insult Him again. Theophylact, Zwingle, and Calvin take the same view.

JOHN VIII. 31—36.

31 Then said Jesus to those Jews which believed on him, If ye continue in my word, *then* are ye my disciples indeed ;

32 And ye shall know the truth, and the truth shall make you free.

33 They answered him, We be Abraham's seed, and were never in bondage to any man : h w sayest thou. Ye shall

be made free ?

34 Jesus answered them, Verily, verily, I say unto you, Whosoever committeth sin is the servant of sin.

35 And the servant abideth not in the house for ev ⋅ *but* the Son abideth ever.

36 If the Son therefore shall make you free. ye shall be free indeed.

THESE verses show us, for one thing, *the importance of steady perseverance in Christ's service.* There were many, it seems, at this particular period, who professed to believe on our Lord, and expressed a desire to become His disciples. There is nothing to show that they had true faith. They appear to have acted under the influence of temporary excitement, without considering what they were doing. And to them our Lord addresses this instructive warning: " If ye continue in my word, then are ye my disciples indeed."

This sentence contains a mine of wisdom. To make a beginning in religious life is comparatively easy. Not a few mixed motives assist us. The love of novelty, the praise of well-meaning but indiscreet professors, the secret self-satisfaction of feeling " how good I am," the universal excitement attending a new position,—all these things combine to aid the young beginner. Aided by them he begins to run the race that leads to heaven, lays aside many bad habits, takes up many good ones, has many comfortable frames and feelings, and gets on swimmingly for a time. But when the newness of his position is past and gone, when the freshness of his feelings is rubbed off and lost, when the world and the devil begin to pull hard at him, when the weakness of his own heart begins to appear,—then it is that he finds out the real difficulties of vital Christianity. Then it is that he discovers the deep wisdom of our Lord's saying now before us. It is not beginning, but "continuing" a religious profession, that is the test of true grace.

We should remember these things in forming our

estimate of other people's religion. No doubt we ought
to be thankful when we see any one ceasing to do evil
and learning to do well. We must not "despise the day
of small things." (Zech. iv. 10.) But we must not forget
that to begin is one thing, and to go on is quite another.
Patient continuance in well-doing is the only sure evidence of grace. Not he that runs fast and furiously at
first, but he that keeps up his speed, is he that "runs so
as to obtain." By all means let us be hopeful when we
see anything like conversion. But let us not make too
sure that it is real conversion, until time has set its seal
upon it. Time and wear test metals, and prove whether
they are solid or plated. Time and wear, in like manner
are the surest tests of a man's religion. Where there is
spiritual life there will be continuance and steady perseverance. It is the man who goes on as well as begins,
that is "the disciple indeed."

These verses show us, for another thing, *the nature of
true slavery.* The Jews were fond of boasting, though
without any just cause, that they were politically free,
and were not in bondage to any foreign power. Our
Lord reminds them that there was another bondage to
which they were giving no heed, although enslaved by
it.—" He that committeth sin is the servant of sin."

How true that is! How many on every side are
thorough slaves, although they do not acknowledge it.
They are led captive by their besetting corruptions and
infirmities, and seem to have no power to get free. Am-
bition, the love of money, the passion for drink, the
craving for pleasure and excitement, gambling, gluttony,

illicit connections,—all these are so many tyrants among men. Each and all have crowds of unhappy prisoners bound hand and foot in their chains. The wretched prisoners will not allow their bondage. They will even boast sometimes that they are eminently *free*. But many of them know better. There are times when the iron enters into their souls, and they feel bitterly that they are slaves.

There is no slavery like this. Sin is indeed the hardest of all task masters. Misery and disappointment by the way, despair and hell in the end,—these are the only wages that sin pays to its servants. To deliver men from this bondage is the grand object of the Gospel. To awaken people to a sense of their degradation, to show them their chains, to make them arise and struggle to be free,—this is the great end for which Christ sent forth His ministers. Happy is he who has opened his eyes and found out his danger! To know that we are being led captive, is the very first step toward deliverance.

These verses show us, lastly, *the nature of true liberty*. Our Lord declares this to the Jews in one comprehensive sentence. He says, " If the Son shall make you free, ye shall be free indeed."

Liberty, most Englishmen know, is rightly esteemed one of the highest temporal blessings. Freedom from foreign dominion, a free constitution, free trade, a free press, civil and religious liberty,—what a world of meaning lies beneath these phrases ! How many would sacrifice life and fortune to maintain the things which

they represent! Yet, after all our boasting, there are
many so-called freemen who are nothing better than
slaves. There are many who are totally ignorant of the
highest, purest form of liberty. The noblest liberty is
that which is the property of the true Christian. Those
only are perfectly free people whom the Son of God
" makes free." All else will sooner or later be found
slaves.

Wherein does the liberty of true Christians consist?
Of what is their freedom made up?—They are freed
from the guilt and consequences of sin by the blood of
Christ. Justified, pardoned, forgiven, they can look
forward boldly to the day of judgment, and cry " Who
shall lay anything to our charge? Who is he that
condemneth?"—They are freed from the power of sin by
the grace of Christ's Spirit. Sin has no longer dominion
over them. Renewed, converted, sanctified, they mortify and tread down sin, and are no longer led captive
by it.—Liberty, like this, is the portion of all true
Christians in the day that they flee to Christ by faith,
and commit their souls to Him. That day they become
free men. Liberty, like this, is their portion for evermore. Death cannot stop it. The grave cannot even
hold their bodies for more than a little season. Those
whom Christ makes free are free to all eternity.

Let us never rest till we have some personal experience of this freedom ourselves. Without it all other
freedom is a worthless privilege. Free speech, free laws,
political freedom, commercial freedom, national freedom,
all these cannot smooth down a dying pillow, or disarm

death of his sting, or fill our consciences with peace. Nothing can do that but the freedom which Christ alone bestows. He gives it freely to all who seek it humbly. Then let us never rest till it is our own.

NOTES. JOHN VIII. 31—36.

31.—[*Then Jesus said...Jews...believed...Him.*] It is clear, I think, from the tone of the conversation that runs from this verse uninterruptedly to the end of the chapter, that this "believing" was not faith of the heart. These Jews only "believed" that our Lord was One sent from heaven, and deserved attention. But they were the same Jews to whom He says by and by, "Ye are of your father the devil."

[*If ye continue...my word...disciples indeed.*] This sentence does not mean that these Jews had really begun to receive Christ's word into their hearts. Such a sense would be contradictory to the context. It must mean, "If you take up a firm stand on that Gospel and Word of Truth which I have come to proclaim, and go on sticking firmly to it in your hearts and lives, not merely convinced and wishing, but actually following Me, then you are truly my disciples."—The word rendered "indeed" is more literally, "truly." The converse throws light on our Lord's meaning: "You are not truly disciples, unless you continue steadfast in my doctrine."

Our Lord teaches the great principle, that steady continuance is the only real and safe proof of discipleship. No perseverance, no grace! No continuance in the word, no real faith and conversion! This is one of the meeting-points between Calvinist and Arminian. He that has true grace will not fall away. He that falls away has no true grace, and must not flatter himself he is a disciple.

Let us note that it is not the "word continuing in us," but "our continuing in the word," which makes us true disciples. The distinction is very important. The word "might continue in us," and not be seen. If we "continue in the word," our lives will show it. In John xv. 7, we have both expressions together: "If ye abide in Me, and my words abide in you."

32.—[*And ye shall know the truth.*] The expression, "the truth," here cannot, I think, mean the Personal Truth, the Messiah. It must be the whole doctrinal truth concerning myself, my nature,

my mission. and my Gospel. Steady continuance in my Service
shall lead to clear knowledge. It is a parallel saying to the sentence
—"If any man will do His will, he shall know of the doctrine."
(vii. 17.) Honest obedience and steady perseverance in acting up
to our light, and doing what we learn, are one grand secret of
obtaining more knowledge.

Chrysostom, however, thinks that our Lord means by "truth,'
Himself. "Ye shall know Me, for I am the truth." So also
Augustine, Theophylact, Euthymius, and Lampe.

[*The truth shall make you free.*] This freedom can only mean
spiritual freedom,—freedom from the guilt, burden, and dominion
of sin,—freedom from the heavy yoke of Pharisaism, under which
many Jews were labouring and heavy laden. (Matt. xi. 28.) "The
Gospel I preach, and its good news, shall deliver you from spiritual
bondage, and make you feel like men set at liberty."

I think these words must have been spoken with special reference
to the bondage and spiritual slavery in which the Jews were kept
by their principal teachers, when our Lord came among them. In
the synagogue at Nazareth He had said, that He came "to preach
deliverance to the captives." (Luke iv. 18.) This, however, is the
first place in the Gospels where He openly declares that His Gospel
will give men freedom.

Until truth comes into a man's heart, he never really knows
what it is to feel true spiritual liberty.

Augustine says, "To Christ let us all flee. Against sin let us
call on God to interpose as our Liberator. Let us ask to be taken
on sale, that we may be redeemed by His blood."

33.—[*They answered, We be Abraham's seed.*] Here we see the
usual pride of carnal descent coming out in the Jewish mind.
It is just what John the Baptist told them when he preached,
"Think not to say that we have Abraham to our father."
(Matt. iii. 19.)

[*And were never in bondage to any man.*] This is the blindness
of pride in its strongest form. The seed of Abraham were in
bondage to the Egyptians and Babylonians for many years, to say
nothing of the frequent bondages to Philistines, and other nations,
as recorded in the book of Judges. Even now, while they spoke,
they were in subjection to the Romans. The power of self-decep-
tion in unconverted man is infinite. These Jews were not more
unreasonable than many now-a-days, who say, "We are not dead
in sin ; we have grace, we have faith, we are regenerate, we have

the Spirit," while their lives show plainly that they are totally mistaken.

[*How sayest Thou...made free.*] This question was partly asked in anger and resentment, and partly in curiosity. Angry as the Jews were at the idea of being subject to any one, they yet caught at the expression, "be made free." It made them think of the glorious kingdom of Messiah, foretold in the Prophets.—"Art Thou going to restore the kingdom to Israel? Art Thou going to set us free from the Romans?"

We should observe here, as elsewhere, the readiness of our Lord's hearers to put a carnal sense on spiritual language. Nicodemus misunderstanding the new birth, the Samaritan woman and the living waters, the Capernaites and the bread from heaven, are all illustrations of what I mean. (See John iii. 4; iv. 11; vi. 34.)

Pearce thinks the Jews here spoke of themselves individually, and not of the Jewish nation. Yet surely even when they spoke they were subject to the Romans.

Henry observes, "Carnal hearts are sensible of no other grievances than those that molest the body and injure their secular affairs. Talk to them of encroachments on their civil liberty and property, tell of waste committed on their lands or damage done to their houses, and they understand you very well, and can give you a sensible answer: the thing touches and affects them. But discourse to them of the bondage of sin, or captivity to Satan, and a liberty by Christ,—tell them of wrong done to their souls, and you bring strange things to them."

34.—[*Jesus answered, etc.*] In this verse our Lord shows His hearers what kind of freedom He had meant, by showing the kind of slavery from which He wished them to be delivered. Did they ask in what sense He meant they should be made free? Let them know, first of all, that in their present state of mind, wicked, worldly, and unbelieving, they were in a state of bondage. Living in habitual sin they were the "servants of sin." This was a general proposition which they themselves must admit. The man that lived wilfully in habits of sin was acknowledged by all to be the slave of sin. Sin ruled over him, and he was its servant. This was an axiom in religion which they could not dispute, for even heathen philosophers admitted it. See Rom. vi. 16—20; 2 Pet. ii. 19.

"Committeth," we must remember here, does not mean "commits an act of sin," but habitually lives in the commission of sin. It is in this sense that St. John says, "He that committeth sin is of

the devil," and "He that is born of God doth not commit sin."
(1 John iii. 8, 9.)

35.—[*And the servant abideth not, etc.*] This is a difficult, because a
very elliptical, verse. The leading object in our Lord's mind seems
to be to show the Jews the servile and slavish condition in which
they were, so long as they rejected Him, the true Messiah, and the
free and elevated position which they would occupy if they would
believe in Him and become His disciples.—"At present, living
under the bondage of the ceremonial law, and content with it and
Pharisaic traditions, you are no better than slaves and servants,
liable, like Hagar and Ishmael, to be cast out of God's favour and
presence at any moment.—Receiving Me, and believing on Me as
the Messiah, you would at once be lifted to the position of sons,
and would abide for ever in God's favour, as adopted children and
dear sons and daughters.—You know yourselves that the servant
has no certain tenure in the house, and may be cast out at any
time ; while the son is heir to the father, and has a certain tenure
in the house for ever.—Know that I wish you to be raised from the
relation of servants to that of sons. Now, under the bondage you
are in, you are like slaves. Receiving Me and my Gospel you
would become children and free."

Something like this seems the leading idea in our Lord's mind.
But it is vain to deny that it is a dark and difficult sentence, and
requires much filling up and paraphrasing to complete its meaning.
The simplest plan is to take it as a parenthesis. It then becomes
a comment on the word "servant," which to a Jew, familiar with
the story of Hagar and Ishmael, would be very instructive, and
would convey the latent thought that our Lord wished them to be
not servants but sons. I cannot for a moment think that "the
Son" in the last clause means the Son of God, or that the whole
clause was meant to teach His eternity.

It is certainly possible that a deep mystical sense may lie under
the words "servant" and "son" in this verse. "Servant" may
mean the Jew, content with the inferior and servile religion of
Moses. "Son" may mean the believer in Christ, who receives the
adoption and enjoys Gospel liberty. He that is content with
Judaism will find his system and religion soon pass away. He
that enters into Christ's service will find himself a son for ever.
But this is at best only conjectural, and a somewhat questionable
interpretation.

One thing, at any rate, is very clear to my mind. The latent
thought in our Lord's mind is a reference to the story of Hagar

and her son Ishmael being cast out as bondservants, while Isaac the son and heir abode in the house. He wished to impress on His hearers' minds, that He desired them, like Isaac, to have the privilege of sons for ever, and to be free to all eternity. Keeping this thought in view, and regarding the verse as a parenthesis, its difficulties are not insuperable.

Chrysostom says, "'Abideth not' means 'hath not power to grant favours, as not being master of the house;' but the son is master of the house." The Jewish priests were the servants, and Christ was the Son. The priests had no power to set free, the Son of God had. Theophylact and Euthymius take the same view.

Maldonatus calls attention to the expression in Hebrews, where Moses and Christ are put in contrast, and each in connection with the word "house,"—Moses as a servant, Christ as a Son. St. Paul certainly seems there to refer to this passage. (Heb. iii. 2, 5, 6.)

36.—[*If the Son shall make you free, etc.*] In this verse our Lord explains what He had meant by freedom. It was a freedom from sin, its guilt, and power, and consequences, which believers in Him were to receive. "If I, the Son of man make you free, in the sense of delivering you from the burden of sin, then you will be free indeed!" This was the freedom that He wished them to obtain. Here, as elsewhere, our Lord carefully avoids saying anything to bring on Himself the charge of rebelling against constituted authorities, and of heading a popular rise for liberty.

The word rendered "indeed" here is not the word so rendered at the 31st verse. Here it means "really, in reality," from the participle of the verb "to be." There it means "truly."

Let us not forget in these days that the only liberty which is truly valuable in God's sight is that which Christ gives. All political liberty, however useful for many purposes, is worthless, unless we are children of God, and heirs of the kingdom, by faith in Jesus. He only is perfectly free who is free from sin. All beside are slaves. He that would be free in this fashion has only to apply to Christ for freedom. It is the peculiar office and privilege of the Lord Jesus to enfranchise for ever all who come to Him.

Augustine carries the freedom here promised far into the future. He remarks, "When shall there be full and perfect liberty? When there shall be no enemies, when the last enemy shall be destroyed, even death."

JOHN VIII. 37—47.

37 I know that ye are Abraham's seed; but ye seek to kill me, because my word hath no place in you.

38 I speak that which I have seen with my Father: and ye do that which ye have seen with your father.

39 They answered and said unto him, Abraham is our father. Jesus saith unto them, If ye were Abraham's children, ye would do the works of Abraham.

40 But now ye seek to kill me, a man that hath told you the truth, which I have heard of God: this did not Abraham.

41 Ye do the deeds of your father. Then said they to him, We be not born of fornication; we have one father, *even* God.

42 Jesus said unto them, If God were your Father, ye would love me: for I proceeded forth and came from God; neither came I of myself, but he sent me.

43 Why do ye not understand my speech? *even* because ye cannot hear my word.

44 Ye are of *your* father the devil, and the lusts of your father ye will do. He was a murderer from the beginning, and abode not in the truth, because there is no truth in him. When he speaketh a lie, he speaketh of his own: for he is a liar, and the father of it.

45 And because I tell *you* the truth, ye believe me not.

46 Which of you convinceth me of sin? And if I say the truth, why do ye not believe me?

47 He that is of God heareth God's words: ye therefore hear *them* not, because ye are not of God.

THERE are things taught in this passage of Scripture which are peculiarly truth for the times. Well would it be for the Churches if all Christians would ponder carefully the matter which it contains.

We are taught, for one thing, *the ignorant self-righteousness of the natural man.* We find the Jews pluming themselves on their natural descent from Abraham, as if that must needs cover all deficiencies: "Abraham is our father." We find them going even further than this, and claiming to be God's special favourites and God's own family: "We have one Father, even God." They forgot that fleshly relationship to Abraham was useless, unless they shared Abraham's grace. They forgot that God's choice of their father to be head of a favoured nation, was never meant to carry salvation to the children, unless they walked in their father's footsteps. All this in their blind self-conceit they refused to see. "We are Jews. We are God's children. We are the true Church. We are in the covenant. We must be all right." This was their whole argument!

Strange as it may seem, there are multitudes of so-called Christians who are exactly like these Jews. Their whole religion consists of a few notions neither wiser nor better than those propounded by the enemies of our Lord. They will tell you that " they are regular church people; they have been baptized; they go to the Lord's table ; "—but they can tell you no more. Of all the essential doctrines of the Gospel they are totally ignorant. Of faith, and grace, and repentance, and holiness, and spiritual mindedness they know nothing at all. But, forsooth! they are Churchmen, and so they hope to go to heaven! There are myriads in this condition. It sounds sad, but unhappily it is only too true.

Let us settle firmly in our minds that connection with a good Church and good ancestors is no proof whatever that we ourselves are in the way to be saved. We need something more than this. We must be joined to Christ Himself by a living faith. We must know something experimentally of the work of the Spirit in our hearts. " Church principles," and " sound Churchman-ship," are fine words and excellent party cries. But they will not deliver our souls from the "wrath to come," or give us boldness in the day of judgment.

We are taught, for another thing, *the true marks of spiritual sonship.* Our Lord makes this point most plain by two mighty sayings. Did the Jews say, " We have Abraham to our father " ? He replies, " If ye were Abraham's children ye would do the works of Abraham."

—Did the Jews say, " We have one Father, even God " ? He replies, " If God were your Father ye would love Me."

Let these two sayings of Christ sink down into our hearts. They supply an answer to two of the most mischievous, yet most common, errors of the present day. What more common, on one side, then vague talk about the universal Fatherhood of God? " All men," we are told, " are God's children, whatever be their creed or religion: all are finally to have a place in the Father's house, where there are many mansions." —What more common, on another side, than high-sounding statements about the effects of baptism and the privileges of Churchmembership? " By baptism," we are confidently told, "all baptized people are made children of God; all members of the Church, without distinction, have a right to be addressed as sons and daughters of the Lord Almighty."

Statements like these can never be reconciled with the plain language of our Lord in the passage before us. If words mean anything, no man is really a child of God who does not love Jesus Christ. The charitable judgment of a baptismal service, or the hopeful estimate of a catechism, may call him by the name of a son, and reckon him among God's children. But the reality of sonship to God, and all its blessings, no one possesses who does not love the Lord Jesus Christ in sincerity. (Ephes. vi. 24.) In matters like these we need not be shaken by mere assertions. We may well afford to despise the charge of undervaluing the sacraments. We have only to ask one question : " What is written ?

What saith the Lord?" And with this saying before
us, we can only come to one conclusion: "Where there
is no love to Christ, there is no sonship to God."

We are taught, lastly, in these verses, *the reality and
character of the devil.* Our Lord speaks of him as on
whose personality and existence are beyond dispute.
In solemn words of stern rebuke He says to His unbelieving enemies, " Ye are of your father the devil,"—
led by him, doing his will, and showing unhappily that
you are like him. And then He paints His picture in
dark colours, describing him as a "murderer" from the
beginning, as a "liar" and the father of lies.

There is a devil! We have a mighty invisible enemy
always near us,—one who never slumbers and never
sleeps,—one who is about our path and about our bed,
and spies out all our ways, and will never leave us till
we die.—He is a murderer! His great aim and object
is to ruin us for ever and kill our souls. To destroy,
to rob us of eternal life, to bring us down to the second
death in hell, are the things for which he is unceasingly
working. He is ever going about, seeking whom he
may devour.—He is a liar! He is continually trying
to deceive us by false representations, just as he deceived
Eve at the beginning. He is always telling us that
good is evil and evil good,—truth is falsehood and
falsehood truth,—the broad way good and the narrow
way bad. Millions are led captive by his deceit, and
follow him, both rich and poor, both high and low, both
learned and unlearned. Lies are his chosen weapons.
By lies he slays many.

These are awful things; but they are true. Let us live as if we believed them. Let us not be like many who mock, and sneer, and scoff, and deny the existence of the very Being who is invisibly leading them to hell. Let us believe there is a devil, and watch, and pray, and fight hard against his temptations. Strong as he is, there is One stronger than he, who said to Peter, "I have prayed for thee, that thy faith fail not," and who still intercedes at God's right hand. Let us commit our souls to Him. (Luke xxii. 32.) With such a being as the devil going to and fro in the world, we never need wonder to see evil abounding. But with Christ on our side, we need not be afraid. Greater is He that is for us, than he that is against us. It is written, "Resist the devil, and he shall flee from you." —"The God of peace shall bruise Satan under your feet shortly." (James iv. 7; Rom. xvi. 20.)

Notes. John viii. 37—47.

37.—[*I know that ye are Abraham's seed.*] In this verse our Lord takes up the arrogant boast of the Jews, that they were Abraham's seed. He had replied to their assertion, We were never in bondage to any man," by showing the nature of true bondage and true liberty. He now returns to their opening saying, "We be Abraham's seed," and begins by telling them that He knew, and fully admitted, their carnal descent from Abraham.

[*But ye seek to kill Me.*] This must mean, "Your relation to Abraham does you no good, for ye are seeking to murder Me at this very moment, though I have come to fulfil the promises made to Abraham."

Here, as well as at the 40th verse, and chapter vii. 19, our Lord shows His perfect knowledge of all the designs of His enemies. He gives us an example of steady perseverance in God's work, even though we know our lives are in peril.

[*Because my word hath no place in you.*] This means, "Because the Gospel I preach, the message I brought from my Father, makes no way or progress in your hearts, or among you."—The Greek word, which our translators have rendered "hath place," is never so rendered elsewhere. The idea here seems to be that of "going forward, spreading, and marching on."

This describes literally the condition of many who hear Christ's word in every age. It seems to come to a deal stand-still or halt in their hearts, and to make no way with them.

38.—[*I speak that, etc.*] The sense of this verse appears to be filled up thus: "The truth is, that there is an entire gulf and breach between you and Me. I speak and am ever speaking the doctrine which I have seen with my Father, in our eternal councils about mankind, and which I am sent by Him to proclaim to the world. You, on the other hand, do and are always doing the things which your father the devil presents to your minds, and which you have seen and imbibed into your characters, under his influence."

When our Lord speaks of what He has "seen" with His Father, we must remember, as elsewhere, that He uses language accommodated to our weak capacities, to describe the relation between Himself and the first Person in the Trinity. Compare John iii. 32 and v. 19.

There can be no doubt that the "father" of the Jews, to whom our Lord here refers, is "the devil," when we read the verses following. It conveys an awful idea of the state of unbelieving and wicked men, that they are doing what they have seen and learned from the devil. There may, however, be special reference to the design of the Jews to kill Christ. Our Lord's meanings may be, "Ye are doing what ye have seen with the devil your father. He has suggested to you to kill Me, and you are listening to his suggestion."

39.—[*They answered...Abraham is our Father.*] This is a repetition of what the Jews had already said. Startled at what our Lord said about their "father," they re-assert emphatically their relationship to Abraham.—"What do you mean by thus speaking of our father? Abraham is our father."

[*Jesus saith...if Abraham's children...works of Abraham.*] Our Lord here tells them that it is possible to be Abraham's children according to the flesh, and yet not Abraham's children according to the Spirit.—"If ye were true spiritual descendants of Abraham, you would show it by doing such things as Abraham did. Your works would be like his, because springing from a like faith."

The distinction here drawn by our Lord is a very important one for Christians to notice. The utter uselessness of carnal relationship, or formal outward succession, is a truth which man does not like to admit, but one that needs to be constantly taught in the Churches. How common to hear men say, "We belong to the one true Church, we are in the direct succession from the Apostles." Such claims are utterly useless, if not accompanied by "works."

We must never forget the importance of "works," if put in their right place. They cannot justify us. They are at best full of imperfection. But they are useful evidences, and serve to show whose we are, and what our religion is worth.

40.—[*But now ye seek to kill Me, etc.*] Our Lord in this verse confirms the charge made in the preceding one—that His enemies were not Abraham's spiritual children, although carnally descended from Abraham. "At this very moment you are wishing and endeavouring to put Me to death, not for any crime, but simply because I have spoken to you that mighty message of truth which I heard from my Father, and am sent to proclaim to the world as the Messiah. This is the very opposite of what your great forefather Abraham would have done. He longed to see my day. He rejoiced in the prospect of it. He would have hailed my appearance and message with delight. Your conduct, therefore, is an unanswerable proof that you are not Abraham's spiritual children."

Our Lord's argument is the same that St. Paul uses to the Romans. "He is not a Jew which is one outwardly."—"They which are the children of the flesh are not the children of God." (Rom. ii. 28, 29; ix. 8.) The importance of it cannot be overrated. It establishes the great principle that fleshly relationship, or ecclesiastical connection, is nothing without grace in the heart, and indeed only adds to a man's condemnation.

The expression "this did not Abraham" is a Hebraism. Of course literally Abraham could not "seek to kill" Christ, because he never lived with Him on earth. The meaning must be, "Your conduct is the very opposite of what Abraham would have done, and utterly contrary to the general tenor of what he did while he lived." Compare Deut. xvii. 3; Jer. vii. 22—31; xix. 5; xxxii. 35, where the same form of speech is used.

When our Lord calls Himself here simply "a man," He uses an expression which He nowhere else employs in the Gospels. As a rule, He calls Himself "the Son of man," when speaking of His human nature. Here, however, He seems to speak of Himself in the point of view in which His unbelieving enemies ought to have regarded Him, if they could not yet acknowledge His divinity. "I am among you a man speaking the truth : and yet ye seek to kill Me."—The attempt of Jews and Socinians to show that our Lord was not really God, founded on this text, is futile. Our Lord's real and true humanity no sound Trinitarian thinks of denying.

11.—[*Ye do the deeds of your father.*] This means "You are doing the things that your father the devil approves and suggests to you. You are showing yourselves genuine children of the devil, by doing his works." The word " ye " in the Greek is emphatic, and may possibly be intended to contrast with " I," at the beginning of the 35th verse.

[*Then said...not born of fornication.*] These words can hardly be taken literally. Our Lord was speaking to the Jews not as in-dividuals, but as a nation and a class, and was speaking of their descent in a religious point of view. The question was, " Who was their father ? From whom did they get their spiritual character ? To whom were their proclivities and tendencies to be traced ? " This our Lord's hearers understood, and said, " We be not born of fornication, we are not heathens and idolaters at any rate, even if we are not as good as Abraham."—That idolatry was called fornication, because it was unfaithfulness to the covenant God, a forsaking Him for false gods, is I think, clear from many places in the Old Testament. See for instance Jeremiah ii. 1—20, and iii. 1—3. I think this was in the minds of the Jews when they spoke to our Lord here. This is Augustine's view.

The notion of Euthymius, Rupertus, and others, that the Jews refer to other children of Abraham by Hagar and Keturah, and boast themselves his true children by Sarah, is not satisfactory. It is surely too much to charge Abraham with the sin of fornica-tion because he took Hagar to be his wife, at the instance of Sarah, and married Keturah after Sarah's death !

The notion of some, that the Jews refer here to the many mar-riages between Jews and Gentiles in the Old Testament times (as seen in Ezra. x. 1, etc.), and repudiate them, is not probable.

Some have thought that the Jews insinuated wicked doubts of our Lord's legitimate birth in this phrase. But it seems unlikely.

[*We have one Father, even God.*] The Jews here lay claim to be regarded as God's children. That God is called "the Father " of Israel in several places in the Old Testament, is undeniable. See Deut. xxxii. 6; 1 Chron. xxix. 10; Isa. lxiii. 16 and lxiv. 8 ; Mal. i. 6. But it is very clear that these texts specially refer to God's relation to Israel as a nation, and not to Israelites as individuals. The Jews, however, in their pride and self-righteousness, made no such nice distinction. They did not see that national sonship and covenant sonship without spiritual sonship, are nothing worth. Hence they brought on themselves the stern rebuke of the next verse.

42.—[*Jesus said...If God...your Father...love me.*] Our Lord here tells the Jews that although they might be children of God by covenant and nationality, they were evidently not God's children by grace and spiritual birth. If God was really their Father, they would show it by loving the Son of God, even Himself.

Let us note carefully the great principle contained in this sentence. Love to Christ is the infallible mark of all true children of God. Would we know whether we are born again, whether we are children of God? There is one simple way of finding it out. Do we love Christ? If not, it is vain and idle to talk of God as our Father, and ourselves as God's children. No love to Christ, no sonship to God !

The favourite notion of many, that baptism makes us sons and daughters of God, and that all baptized people should be addressed as God's children, is utterly irreconcileable with this sentence. Unless a baptized person loves Christ, he has no right to call God Father, and is not God's child. He has yet to be born again, and brought into God's family. Before the point and edge of these words, the doctrine that spiritual regeneration always accompanies baptism, cannot stand.

The modern notion about God's universal Fatherhood, which finds such favour with many, is no less irreconcileable with this sentence than baptismal regeneration. That God the Father is full of love, mercy, and compassion to all, is no doubt true. But that God is really and truly the spiritual Father of any one who does not love Christ, can never be maintained without contradicting our Lord's words in this place.

The sentence is full of condemnation to all who know nothing experimentally of Christ, and neither think, nor feel, nor care anything about Him. Crowds of so-called Christians are in this unhappy state, and are plainly not God's children, whatever they may think. The sentence is equally full of comfort for all true believers, however weak and feeble. If they feel drawn towards Christ in heart and affection, and can truly say "I do love Him," they have the plainest mark of being God's children, and "if children then heirs." (Rom. viii. 17.)

[*For I proceeded forth, etc.*]   Our Lord here shows the Jews His own divine nature and mission.   He had proceeded forth, and come from God—the eternal Son from the eternal Father.   He had not come of His own independent will and without commission, but specially sent and appointed by the Father, as His last and dearest Messenger to a lost world.   Such was His nature.   Such was His position and relation to the Father.—If therefore they really were children of God the Father, they would love Him as the Father's Son, the Father's Messenger, the Father's promised Messiah.   Not loving Him, they gave the plainest proof that they were not God's children.—A true child of God will love everything belonging to God, and specially he will love God's only begotten and beloved Son.   He can see and find nothing nearer to the Father than the Son, who is the "brightness of His glory and the express image of His person."   (Heb. i. 3.)   If, therefore, he does not love the Son, it is clear that he is no true child of the Father.

Calvin remarks, "Christ's argument is this : whoever is a child of God will acknowledge his first-born Son ; but you hate Me, and therefore you have no reason to boast that you are God's children. We ought carefully to observe in this passage, that there is no piety and no fear of God where Christ is rejected.   Hypocritical religion presumptuously shelters itself under the name of God , but how can they agree with the Father who disagree with His only Son ?"

43.—[*Why do ye not understand? etc.*]   In this verse, our Lord seems to me to draw a distinction between "speech" and "word." The expression "word" is deeper than "speech."   By "speech," He means "my manner of speaking and expressing myself."   By "word," He means generally "my doctrine."—The sense is, "How is it that ye do not understand my manner of expressing myself to you, when I speak of such things as "freedom " and of "your father"?   It is because ye will not receive and attend to my whole message,—the word that I bring to you from my Father."—Lightfoot takes this view.

This explanation seems to me to describe most accurately the state of things between our Lord and His hearers.   They were continually misunderstanding, misinterpreting, and stumbling at the expressions and language that He used in teaching them.   Did He speak of "bread "?   They thought He meant literal bread.— Did He speak of "freedom "?   They thought He meant temporal and political freedom.—Did He speak of "their Father"?   They thought

He meant Abraham.—How was it that they so misunderstood His language and dialect? It was simply because their hearts were utterly hardened and closed against the whole "word of salvation" which He came to proclaim. Having no will to listen to and receive His doctrine, they were ready at every step to misconstrue the words and figures under which it was conveyed and placed before them.

Any one who preaches the Gospel now, must often observe that precisely the same thing happens in the present day. Hearers, who are strongly prejudiced against the Gospel, are constantly perverting, wresting, and misinterpreting the language of the preacher. None are so blind as those who will not see, and none so stupid as those who do not want to understand.

The "cannot" here is a moral inability. It is like "No man can come unto Me," and "His brethren could not speak peaceably unto him." (John vi. 44; Gen. xxxvii. 4.) It means, "Ye have no will to hear with your hearts."

Chrysostom remarks, "Not to be able, here means not to be willing."

44.—[*Ye are of your father the devil, etc.*] This verse deserves special attention, both for the sternness of the rebuke it contains, and the deep subject which it handles. The general sense is as follows: "Ye are so far from being spiritual children of Abraham, or true children of God, that on the contrary ye may be rightly called the children of the devil; and ye show it, by having a will set on doing the evil things which your father suggests to you. He, from the beginning of creation, was a being set on the destruction of man, and abode not in the original truth and righteousness in which he was created; for now truth is not in his nature. When he now speaks and suggests a lie, he speaks out of his own peculiar inward nature, for he is eminently a liar, and the father of a lie."

When our Lord says to the wicked Jews, "Ye are of your father the devil," He does not mean that the wicked are made wicked by the devil in the same sense that the godly are made godly by God, created anew and begotten of God. But He uses a common Hebraism, by which persons who are closely connected with, or entirely under the influence of, another, are called "his children." It is in this sense that the wicked and unbelieving are truly the children of the devil. This must be carefully remembered. The devil has no power to "create" the wicked. He only finds them born in sin, and, working upon their sinful nature, obtains such an influence, that he becomes practically the "father of the wicked."

(See Matt. xiii. 38 and 1 John iii. 10 ; Matt. xiii. 19 ; Luke xvi. 8 ; xx. 34 ; Isai. lvii. 4 ; Numb. xvii. 10.)

Augustine says, "Whence are those Jews sons of the devil ?—By imitation, not by birth." He also refers to Ezek. xvi. 3, as a parallel case.

When our Lord says, "Ye will do the lusts of your father," we must remember that "Ye will" is emphatic in the Greek. "Ye have a will, and mind, and purpose, and disposition."—By "doing the lusts," He means, "Ye follow those evil inclinations and desires" which are peculiarly characteristic of the devil and according to his mind,—such as to commit murder, and to love and tell a lie. The desire of the devil can only be for that which is evil.

When our Lord says the devil was a "murderer from the beginning," I do not think He refers exclusively to Cain's murder of Abel, though I think it was in His mind. (See 1 John iii. 12.) I rather think He means that the devil, from the beginning of creation, was set on bringing death into the world, and murdering man both body and soul.

Origen remarks, "It was not one man only that the devil killed, but the whole human race, inasmuch as in Adam all die. So that he is truly called a murderer."

When our Lord says that the "devil abode not in the truth," I think He teaches that the devil is a fallen spirit, and that he was originally made very good and "perfect," like all other works of God's hands. But he did not continue in that state of truth and righteousness in which he was originally created. He kept not his first estate, but fell away. "Truth" seems to stand for all righteousness and holiness, and conformity to the mind of God, who is "Truth itself." This verse, and Jude 6, are the two clearest proofs in the Bible that the devil fell, and was not created evil at the beginning.

The word "abode" would be more literally rendered, "stood."

When our Lord says, "Because there is no truth in him," He does not mean that this was the reason why the devil "abode not in the truth." If this had been His meaning, He would have said, "Truth *was* not in him." But He says, "is."—His words are meant to describe the present nature of the devil. "He is now a being in whom truth is not."—It seems to me a somewhat similar expression to that of St. Paul, when he says, "I obtained mercy, because I did it ignorantly ; " where "because" does not mean the *reason* why he obtained mercy. (1 Tim. i. 13.) The Greek word for "because" in both cases is the same.

Calvin remarks, "As we are called the children of God, not only because we resemble Him, but because He governs us by His Spirit,—because Christ lives and is vigorous in us so as to conform us to His Father's image; so, on the other hand, the devil is said to be the father of those whose understandings he blinds, whose hearts he moves to commit all unrighteousness, and on whom in short he acts powerfully, and exercises his tyranny."

When our Lord says that "the devil speaketh of his own," He does not mean that he "speaks about his own," but that he speaks "out of his own things." It is like, "Out of the abundance of the heart the mouth speaketh." (Matt. xii. 34.) He speaks out of those things of which he is full.

When our Lord says that the devil "is a liar," I think He refers to the great original lie by which he deceived Eve at the beginning: "Ye shall not surely die." (Gen. iii. 4.)

When our Lord says here of the devil, that "he is a liar and the father of it," I think the most likely and natural meaning is, that "he is the father of every lie." A lie is specially the result and work of the devil. The expression "of it," is undeniably difficult, and is variously interpreted.

(a) Some think that it means "he is the father of him:" viz., of the liar,—of every one that tells a lie. This is the view of Brentius, Bengel, Stier, Hengstenberg, and Alford.

(b) Some think that it means "he is a liar, and his father." This was an error of the Manicheans, and justly reproved by Augustine. Yet Grotius seems to hold this view, and maintains that he who deceived Adam and Eve was not the prince of the devils, but one of his messengers! (See 2 Cor. xii. 7.) This seem an untenable idea.

Neither of these views is at all natural and satisfactory, and the one I have given—"father of a lie"—seems to me much more probable. It is the view of Augustine, Theophylact, Rupertus, Calvin, Bucer, Beza, Bullinger, Rollock, Burgon, Wordsworth, and the great majority of all commentators.

Let us note, in this verse, how strongly and directly our Lord rebukes His enemies. There are times when strong condemnation becomes a positive duty, and we must not refrain from it through fear of being charged with severity, personality, and harshness.

Let us note how clearly this verse establishes the personality of the devil. The expression before us can never be explained by those who think he is only a vague evil influence.

Let us note how the fall of angels is recognised and taught by our Lord, as one of the great truths that we must believe.

Let us note how murder and lying are specially mentioned as characteristics of the devil. They are sins most opposite to the mind of God, however lightly regarded—and lying especially—by man. An indifference to the sin of lying, whether among old or young, rich or poor, is one of the most unmistakable symptoms of an ungodly condition.

Luther says, "The world is a den of murderers, subject to the devil. If we desire to live on earth, we must be content to be guests in it, and to lie in an inn where the host is a rascal, whose house has over the door this sign or shield, 'For murder and lies.' For this sign and escutcheon Christ Himself hung over the door of his house, when He said, He is a murderer and a liar."

45.—[*And because I tell, etc.*] Our Lord in this verse puts in strong contrast His own teaching and the lying suggestions of the devil, and the readiness of the wicked Jews to disbelieve Him and believe the devil.—"The reason why you do not believe Me is, your thorough dislike to the truth of God. You are genuine children of your father the devil. If I told you things that are false, ye would believe Me. But because I tell you things that are true, you believe Me not."

We see here how little cause faithful ministers of Christ have to feel surprise at the unbelief of many of their hearers. If they preach the truth, they must make up their minds not to be believed by many. It is only what happened to their Master. "If they have kept my saying, they will keep your's also." (John xv. 20.)

46.—[*Which of you convinceth me? etc.*] Our Lord in this verse asks two questions, to which it was impossible for them to give an answer: "Which of you can reprove or convince Me as an offender concerning sin of any kind? You know that you cannot lay any offence to my charge. Yet if I am free from any charge, and at the same time speak to you nothing but what is right and true, what is the reason that ye do not believe Me?"

Let us note here the perfect spotlessness and innocence of our Lord's character. None but He could ever say, "I have no sin. I challenge any one to find out any imperfection or fault in Me." Such a complete and perfect Sacrifice and Mediator is just what sinful man needs.

47.—[*He that is of God, etc.*] Our Lord in this verse supplies an answer to His own questions, and conclusively proves the wickedness and ungodliness of His hearers.—"He that is a true child of God hears with pleasure, believes, and obeys God's words, such as I bring to you from my Father. You, by not hearing, believing, and obeying them, prove plainly that you are not God's children. If you were, you would hear gladly, believe, and obey. Your not hearing proves conclusively that you are what I said, —children, not of God, but of the devil."

Let us note here, that the disposition to hear and listen to truth is always a good sign, though not an infallible one, about a person's soul. It is said, in another place, "My sheep hear my voice." (John x. 16, 27.) When we see people obstinately refusing to listen to counsel, and to attend to the Gospel, we are justified in regarding them as not God's children, not born again, without grace, and needing yet to be converted.

Let us note here, as elsewhere, how carefully our Lord speaks of His teaching as "God's words." It consisted of words and truths which God the Father had commissioned Him to preach and proclaim to man. It was not "His own words" only, but His Father's as well as His own.

Rollock observes that there is no surer mark of an unsanctified nature than dislike to God's Word.

Musculus, Bucer, and others maintain here that the phrase, "He that is of God heareth God's words," must be confined to God's election; and means, "He that was chosen of God from all eternity." I cannot, however, see reason for confining the sense so closely. I prefer to consider "of God" as including, not only election, but calling, regeneration, adoption, conversion, and sanctification. This is Rollock's view.

JOHN VIII. 48—59.

48 Then answered the Jews, and said unto him, Say we not well that thou art a Samaritan, and hast a devil?

49 Jesus answered, I have not a devil; but I honour my Father, and ye do dishonour me.

50 And I seek not mine own glory: there is one that seeketh and judgeth.

51 Verily, verily, I say unto you, If a man keep my saying, he shall never see death.

52 Then said the Jews unto him, Now we know that thou hast a devil. Abraham is dead, and the prophets; and thou sayest, If a man keep my saying, he shall never taste of death.

53 Art thou greater than our father Abraham, which is dead? and the prophets are dead: whom makest thou thyself?

54 Jesus answered, If I honour myself, my honour is nothing: it is my Father that honoureth me; of whom ye say, that he is your God:

55 Yet ye have not known him; but I know him: and if I should say, I know him not, I shall be a liar like unto you: but I know him, and keep his saying.

56 Your father Abraham rejoiced to see my day: and he saw it, and was glad.

57 Then said the Jews unto him, Thou art not yet fifty years old, and hast thou seen Abraham?

58 Jesus said unto them, Verily, verily, I say unto you, Before Abraham was, I am.

59 Then took they up stones to cast at him: but Jesus hid himself, and went out of the temple, going through the midst of them, and so passed by.

We should observe, first, in this passage, *what blasphemous and slanderous language* was addressed to our Lord by His enemies. We read that the Jews "said unto Him, Say we not well that Thou art a Samaritan, and hast a devil?" Silenced in argument, these wicked men resorted to personal abuse. To lose temper, and call names, is a common sign of a defeated cause.

Nicknames, insulting epithets, and violent language, are favourite weapons with the devil. When other means of carrying on his warfare fail, he stirs up his servants to smite with the tongue. Grievous indeed are the sufferings which the saints of God have had to endure from the tongue, in every age. Their characters have been slandered. Evil reports have been circulated about them. Lying stories have been diligently invented, and greedily swallowed, about their conduct. No wonder that David said, "Deliver my soul, O Lord, from lying lips, and from a deceitful tongue." (Psalm cxx. 2.)

The true Christian in the present day must never be surprised to find that he has constant trials to endure from this quarter. Human nature never changes. So long as he serves the world, and walks in the broad way, little perhaps will be said against him. Once let him take up the cross and follow Christ, and there is no lie too monstrous, and no story too absurd for some to tell against him, and for others to believe. But let him take comfort in the thought that he is only drinking the cup which his blessed Master drank before him. The lies of his enemies do him no injury in heaven, whatever they may on earth. Let him bear them patiently, and not fret or lose his temper. When Christ was reviled, "He reviled not again." (1 Peter ii. 23.) Let the Christian do likewise.

We should observe, secondly, *what glorious encouragement our Lord holds out to His believing people.* We read that He said, "Verily, verily, I say unto you, If a man keep my saying, he shall never see 'death."

Of course these words do not mean that true Christians shall never die. On the contrary, we all know that they must go down to the grave, and cross the river just like others. But the words do mean that they shall not be hurt by the second death,—that final ruin of the whole man in hell, of which the first death is only a faint type or figure. (Rev. xxi. 8.) And they do mean that the sting of the first death shall be removed from the true Christian. His flesh may fail, and his bones may be racked with strong pain. But the bitter sense of unpardoned sins shall not crush him down. This is the worst part of death,—and in this he shall have the "victory through our Lord Jesus Christ." (1 Cor. xv. 57.)

This blessed promise, we must not forget to notice, is the peculiar property of the man who "keeps Christ's sayings." That expression, it is clear, can never be applicable to the mere outward professing Christian, who neither knows nor cares anything about the Gospel. It belongs to him who receives into his heart, and obeys in his life, the message which the Lord Jesus brought from heaven. It belongs, in short, to those who are Christians, not in name and form only, but in deed and

in truth. It is written, " He that overcometh shall not
be hurt of the second death." (Rev. ii. 11.)

We should observe, thirdly, in this passage, *what
clear knowledge of Christ Abraham possessed.* We read
that our Lord said to the Jews, " Your father Abraham
rejoiced to see my day : and he saw it and was glad."

When our Lord used these remarkable words, Abraham
had been dead and buried at least 1850 years ! And
yet he is said to have seen our Lord's day ! How
wonderful that sounds ! Yet it was quite true. Not
only did Abraham " see " our Lord and talk to Him when
He " appeared unto him in the plains of Mamre," the
night before Sodom was destroyed (Gen. xviii. 1), but
by faith he looked forward to the day of our Lord's
incarnation yet to come, and as he looked he " was glad."
That he saw many things through a glass darkly, we
need not doubt. That he could have explained fully
the whole manner and circumstances of our Lord's
sacrifice on Calvary, we are not obliged to suppose. But
we need not shrink from believing that he saw in
the far distance a Redeemer, whose advent would finally
make all the earth rejoice. And as he saw it, he
" was glad."

The plain truth is, that we are too apt to forget that
there never was but one way of salvation, one Saviour,
and one hope for sinners, and that Abraham and all the
Old Testament saints looked to the same Christ that we
look to ourselves. We shall do well to call to mind the
Seventh Article of the Church of England : " The Old
Testament is not contrary to the New : for both in the

Old and New Testament everlasting life is offered through Christ, who is the only Mediator between God and man, being both God and man. Wherefore they are not to be heard which feign that the old Fathers did look only for transitory promises." This is truth that we must never forget in reading the Old Testament. This is sound speech, that cannot be condemned.

We should observe, lastly, in this prophecy, *how distinctly our Lord declares His own pre-existence.* We read that He said to the Jews, "Before Abraham was, I am."

Without controversy, these remarkable words are a great deep. They contain things which we have no eyes to see through, or mind to fathom. But if language means anything, they teach us that our Lord Jesus Christ existed long before He came into the world. Before the days of Abraham He was. Before man was created He was. In short, they teach us that the Lord Jesus was no mere man, like Moses or David. He was One whose goings forth were from everlasting,—the same yesterday, to-day, and for ever,—very and eternal God.

Deep as these words are, they are full of practical comfort. They show us the length, and breadth, and depth, and height of that great foundation on which sinners are invited to rest their souls. He to whom the Gospel bids us come with our sins, and believe for pardon and peace, is no mere man. He is nothing less than very God, and therefore " able to save to the utter-

most " all who come to Him.   Then let us begin coming
to Him with confidence.   Let us continue leaning on
Him without fear.   The Lord Jesus Christ is the true
God, and our eternal life is secure.

Notes. John viii. 48—59.

48.—[*Then answered the Jews...Samaritan...devil.*] This verse seems
to contain nothing but personal abuse and blasphemous slander.
Unable to answer our Lord's arguments, the unbelieving Jews lost
their temper, and resorted to the last weapon of a disputant,—
senseless invective and calling of names.   The extent to which
calling names is carried by Oriental people, even in the present day,
is something far greater than in this country we can imagine.

When the Jews called our Lord "a Samaritan," they meant
much the same as saying that He was no true Jew, and little
better than a heathen.   "The Jews have no dealings with the
Samaritans." (John iv. 9.)   When they said, "Thou hast a devil,"
I think it meant rather more than "Thou art mad," as in John vii.
20, if we observe the following verse.   It probably implied, "Thou
actest and speakest under the influence of the devil.   The power
Thou hast is from Satan, and not from God."

Let us learn here how little cause Christians have to be surprised
if hard names and insulting epithets are applied to them.   It is
only what was done to their Master, and is no ground for discouragement in doing God's work.

49.—[*Jesus answered, I have not a devil, etc.*]   Our Lord's answer to
the coarse invective of His enemies amounts to this : "In saying
that I have a devil you say that which is not true.   I am simply
honouring my Father in heaven by delivering His message to man,
and you by your violent language are dishonouring Me, and in
effect dishonouring and insulting my Father.   Your insults do not
strike Me only, but my Father also."

Let us note our Lord's calmness and equanimity under insult.
A solemn denial of the blasphemous charge laid against Him,
and an equally solemn reminder that He was honouring the God
whom they themselves professed to worship, are the only reply He
condescends to make.

50.—[*And I seek not mine own glory.*]   This sentence seems to arise
out of the last verse.—"Ye dishonour Me; but you do not move

or hurt Me, for I did not come to seek my own glory, but the glory of Him that sent Me. I receive not honour from men." (See John vii. 18 and v. 41.) Here, as elsewhere, our Lord points to the great principle, " that a true messenger from heaven will never seek his own glory, but his Master's."

[*There is one that seeketh and judgeth.*] There is a very solemn warning in these words. They mean. "There is One, however, even my Father in heaven, who does seek and desire my glory ; and not only seeks, but judges the conduct of all who dishonour Me, with deep displeasure, and will punish it at the last day."

There is comfort here for all Christ's members, as well as for their Head. Though they may not think of it, there is One in heaven who cares deeply for them, sees all they go through, and will one day plead their cause. The latent thought seems the same as in Eccles. v. 8 ; "He that is higher than the highest regardeth." A believer may cheer himself with the thought, "There is One that judgeth. There is One that sees all, that cares for me and will set all right at the last day."

Euthymius remarks on this verse that we should not heed things said against ourselves, but should vindicate the honour of God if things are said against God.

51.—[*Verily...if a man keep my saying...never see death.*] The mighty promise contained in this verse seems intended to wind up the whole conversation. All that our Lord had said had produced no effect. He therefore closes His teaching for the present by one of those mighty sayings which tower above everything near them and of which St. John's Gospel contain so many.—" Whether you will hear or not, whether you choose to know Me or not, I solemnly tell you that if any man receives, believes, and keeps my doctrine, he shall never see death. Despised and rejected as I am by you, life or death, heaven or hell, blessing or cursing, depend and hinge on accepting the message I proclaim to you. I am the way, the truth, and the life."—It is like Moses taking leave of Israel and saying, " I call heaven and earth to record against you, that I have set before you life and death." (Deut. xxx. 15, 19.) Just so our Lord seems to say, "I tell you once more, for the last time, that to keep my saying is the way to escape death."

The expression is parallel to the one our Lord uses in the synagogue of Capernaum. There He says, "He that believeth in Me hath everlasting life." Here it is "shall never see death." (John vi. 47.)

We should notice here, as elsewhere, that when our Lord uses

the expression, "Verily, verily, I say unto you," which is familiar
to all careful readers of St. John's Gospel, He is always about to
say something of peculiar gravity and solemnity.   See John i.
51 ; iii. 3, 5, 11 ; v. 19, 24, 25 ; vi. 26, 32, 47, 53 ; viii. 34, 51, 58 ;
x. 1, 7 ; xii. 24 ; xiii. 16, 20, 21, 38 ; xiv. 12 ; xvi. 20, 23 ; xxi. 18.

The expression "keep my saying," means "receive into his
heart, believe, embrace, obey, and hold fast the doctrine or message
which I am commissioned to teach."—The phrase "my saying,"
means much more than the "words I am speaking at this moment."
It is rather the whole doctrine of my Gospel.

The expression "never see death" cannot be taken literally.
Our Lord did not mean that His disciples would not die and be
buried, like other children of Adam.   We know that they did die.
The meaning is probably three-fold.   (1) "He shall be completely
delivered from that spiritual death of condemnation under which
all mankind are born : his soul is alive and can die no more.   (2)
He shall be delivered from the sting of bodily death : his flesh and
bones may sink under disease and be laid in the grave, but the
worst part of death shall not be able to touch him, and the grave
itself shall give him up one day.   (3) He shall be delivered entirely
from the second death, even eternal punishment in hell : over him
the second death shall have no power."

The width and greatness of this promise are very remarkable.
Ever since the day of Adam's fall death has been man's peculiar
enemy.   Man has found the truth of the sentence, "In the day
thou eatest thou shalt surely die." (Gen. ii. 17.)   But our Lord
boldly, and openly proclaims that in keeping His saying there is
complete deliverance from death.   In fact, He proclaims Himself
the One greater than death.   None could say this but a Redeemer
who was very God.

Augustine says, "The death from which our Lord came to deliver us was the second death, eternal death, the death of hell, the
death of damnation with the devil and his angels.   That is indeed
death ; for this death of ours is only a migration.   What is it but
a putting off a heavy load, provided there be not another load
carried, by which the man shall be cast headlong into hell.   This
is the death of which the Lord says, 'He shall not see death.'"

Let us note the breadth and fulness of this promise.   It is for
any one who keeps Christ's sayings.   "If a man," or rather it
should be rendered, "If any man," etc.

Let us beware of putting a meaning on this promise which it
was not intended to convey.   The idea of some that it means "be-

lievers shall be so completely delivered from death that they shall
neither feel bodily pain nor mental conflict," is one that cannot be
supported.   It is not borne out by other passages of Scripture, and
as a matter of fact it is contradicted by experience.   The Gospel de-
livers believers from that "fear of death" which unbelievers feel,
no doubt.   (Heb. ii. 15.)   But we have no right to expect believers
to have no bodily conflict, no convulsion, no struggle, and no
suffering.   Flesh and blood must and will feel.   "I groan," said
holy Baxter on his deathbed, "but I do not grumble."   Death is
a serious thing, even though the sting is taken away.

Parkhurst thinks the expression here is like Luke ii. 26, where
it was said of Simeon that he should not "see death."   But the
Greek for "see" is there a different word, and the phrase there
seems to mean nothing more than "die," which does not come
up to the full promise here.   He also quotes Psalms xlix. 9 ;
lxxxix. 49.   But neither of these places seem parallel.

The Greek word rendered "see" is so peculiar that one might
almost think the phrase meant, "He shall not gaze upon and
behold death for ever to all eternity, as the wicked shall."   But
I prefer the threefold sense already given.

52.—[*Then said the Jews, etc.*]   The argument of the Jews in this
verse seems to be as follows.   "We know now by Thy own words
that Thou art mad and hast a devil.   Our great father Abraham
and the prophets, holy and good as they all were, are all dead, and
yet Thou presumest to say that if a man keep Thy saying he will
never die.   In short, Thou makest Thyself greater than Abraham,
for Abraham could not escape death, while keeping Thy saying
enables a man to escape death.   To talk in this way is a plain
proof that thou are mad."

The phrase "to have a devil," in this place can hardly mean
anything but "to be mad, or crazy."

The Jews, it will be observed, do not quote our Lord's words
correctly.   He had said, "shall never see death."   They report
Him as saying, "shall never taste of death."   Whether this was a
wilful perversion of His words is rather difficult to decide.   Some
think that the Jews intentionally exaggerated the promise, and put
"taste" for "see," in order to magnify the offence our Lord had
committed.   Others think that the difference means nothing, and
that it only shows how thoroughly the Jews misunderstood our
Lord, and thought that He referred to nothing but bodily death.

Here, as elsewhere, we may remark how ready the Jews were to pervert and warp our Lord's meaning, and to put a carnal and gross sense on spiritual language.

53.—[*Art Thou greater, etc. ?*] The question in this verse shows that our Lord had again succeeded in arousing the curiosity of the Jews, and stirring them to inquire about His nature and person.—" Who art Thou that talkest in this way? Whom dost Thou make Thy-self? To say that those who keep Thy saying shall never die is to make Thyself superior to Abraham and the prophets, who are al! dead. Who and what are Thou? Art Thou really some one greater than Abraham?"

Chrysostom observes that the question of the Jews reminds us of the Samaritan woman's question : " Art thou greater than our father Jacob?" (John iv. 12.)

54.—[*If I honour myself...nothing, etc.*] Our Lord's meaning in this verse seems to be as follows : " If at any time I take to myself and claim honour, such honour would be worthless. He who puts honour on Me, and commissions Me to say that keeping my saying shall deliver a man from death, is my Father in heaven,—that very Being whom you profess to call your God. It is your own God, the God of Abraham, Isaac, and Jacob, who has put such honour on Me, that life or death turn on keeping my sayings, and believing on Me."

Here, as elsewhere, we should mark the carefulness with which our Lord disclaims all self-exaltation, and desire for glory and honour from man. If in claiming for Himself to hold the keys of life and death He seemed to claim honour, He carefully reminds the Jews that it is an honour put on Him by the Father in heaven, even by their own God. He desired no honour independent of Him, or in rivalry to Him.

When our Lord says, " My Father honoureth Me," the expression must include all the works, and signs, and miracles, which the Father gave Him to do ; as well as the words which He gave Him to speak. (John v. 36 ; xiv. 10, 11.)

55.—[*Yet ye have not known Him, etc.*] The meaning of this verse seems to be as follows : " Although you say of my Father in heaven that He is your God, you do not really know Him, and are plainly ignorant of His character, His will, and His purposes. Professing to know Him, in works you deny Him. But I, on the contrary, know Him perfectly ; for I am indeed one with Him from all eternity, and came forth from Him. So perfectly do I know Him, that I should be a liar, and a child of the devil, like yourselves, if I said I did not know Him. But I repeat that I know Him perfectly, and in all my words and works here on earth I carefully keep His sayings, and observe the commission He gave Me."

There is undeniably a great peculiarity in the language of this verse. But it is probably a Hebrew mode of putting in strong contrast the Jews' thorough ignorance of God, notwithstanding their high profession of being His chosen people,—and our Lord's perfect knowledge of God, notwithstanding the repeated assertions that He had a devil, was a Samaritan, and was consequently an enemy to the God of Israel.—The phrase, "I should be a liar, like yourselves, if I said I did not know the Father," was just the phrase to convey the strongest idea to the Jews' minds of our Lord's knowledge. In arguing with some men, nothing but the strongest language, and the most paradoxical expressions, have any effect. Even God himself thinks it good to make such an asseveration as "I swear by myself," and "as I live," in order to command attention. (Jer. xxii. 5; Heb. vi. 13; Ezek. xxxiii. 11.) Those who blame ministers and preachers for using strong language, and say that they should never use any but gentle, tame, and mild phrases, can hardly have studied human nature or the style of Scripture with thorough attention.

56.—[*Your father Abraham, etc.*] Our Lord, in this verse, takes up the question of the Jews, as to His being greater than Abraham, and boldly gives an answer. "You ask Me whether I am greater than Abraham. I tell you in reply that I am He whose coming and whose day of glory Abraham rejoiced to think he should see. Moreover by faith he even saw it, and when he saw it he was glad."

The precise meaning of the words of this verse is rather difficult to discover, though the general idea of it is plain and unmistakable. It is clear that our Lord implies that He is the promised Messiah, the Seed of Abraham, in whom all the generations of the earth should be blessed,—and of whom when Abraham first heard, "he laughed" for joy. (Gen. xvii. 17.)

(*a*) Some think, as most of the Fathers and Reformers, that it means, "Abraham rejoiced in the prospect of seeing, at some future time, my day, the day of Messiah; and by faith he did see it afar off."

(*b*) Some think, as Maldonatus, Lampe, Stier, and Bloomfield, that it means, "Abraham rejoiced when he was told that he should see my day; and he actually has seen it in Paradise, and has been gladdened there in the separate state by the sight."

(c) Some think, as Brown, Olshausen, Alford, Webster, and Hengstenberg, that it means, "Abraham's great desire and joyful expectation was to see my day, and he actually saw Me when I appeared to him and talked with him on earth."

Of these three views the first appears to me the most probable, and most in keeping with the history of Abraham, in Genesis. It should be carefully observed that our Lord does *not* say that "Abraham saw ME," but that "he saw my day."—The cause of Abraham's joy seems to have been, that there was to be of his seed a Messiah, a Saviour ; and that he should see His day,—the day of the Lord, the triumphant day of Messiah's complete victory and restitution of all things. This day he even saw by faith afar off, and was glad at the sight.—Our Lord's object does not seem to me to be to tell the Jews that Abraham had seen Him, but that He was "the Seed," the Messiah who was promised to their father Abraham. The Jews had asked whether he was greater than Abraham ? "Yes !" he replies, "I am. I am that very Messiah whose day Abraham rejoiced to hear of, and saw afar off by faith. If you were like Abraham you would rejoice to see Me."

Chrysostom and Euthymius think that "my day," in this verse, means "the day of the crucifixion, which Abraham foreshowed typically by offering the ram in Isaac's place." This however seems a very cramped and limited view.

Rupertus thinks that Abraham "saw the day of Christ" when he entertained the three angels who came to him.

Augustine thinks it may refer to both the advents of Christ : first in humiliation, and second in glory.

57.—[*Then said the Jews, etc.*] It is plain that the Jews here put a wrong meaning on our Lord's words, and suppose Him to say that Abraham had seen Him, and He had seen Abraham. Yet our Lord had only said, "Abraham saw my day." It is another instance of their readiness to pervert His words.

When the Jews said, "Thou art not yet fifty years old." I believe they only meant, "Thou art not yet a middle-aged man." Fifty years old was the turning point in life, at which the Levites and priests were excused from further active service in the tabernacle. (Numbers iv. 3.) I fancy the reference is to this.—Our Lord was at this time about thirty-three years old, or at most thirty-four. The notion of Irenœus and Papias, that He really was fifty before He was crucified, is utterly without warrant, and absurd.

Some think that our Lord's countenance was so marred and aged by sorrow and care, that He looked much older than He really was. and that hence the Jews supposed Him to be nearly fifty.   But I prefer the former view.

Euthymius thinks that the Jews thought our Lord was fifty years old, on account of His great wisdom and experience.   This, however, seems a weak and untenable view.

58.—[*Jesus said...before Abraham was, I am.*]   This famous verse, I believe, can only receive one honest interpretation.   It is a distinct assertion of our Lord's eternity,—His existence before all creation. "I solemnly declare unto you that before Abraham was and existed I was, the great I AM ; the same yesterday, to-day, and for ever : the eternal God."   All attempts to evade this explanation appear to me so preposterous that it is waste of time to notice them.   The man who can think the words only mean, "I am He who was promised to Adam before Abraham was born," seems past the reach of reasoning.—The name "I AM," we must remember, is the very name by which God revealed Himself to the Jews, when He sent Moses to them : "Say unto the children of Israel, I AM hath sent me." (Exod. iii. 14.)

Let us carefully note what a strong proof we have here of the pre-existence and divinity of our Lord Jesus Christ.   He applies to Himself the very name by which God made Himself known when He undertook to redeem Israel.   It was "I AM " who brought them out of the land of Egypt.   It was "I AM " who died for us upon the cross.   The amazing strength of the foundation of a sinner's hope appears here.   Believing on Jesus we rest on divinity, on One who is God as well as man.

There is a difference in the Greek verbs here employed which we should carefully notice.   The Greek for "was" is quite different from the Greek for "am."   It is as if our Lord said, "Before Abraham was born, I have an existence individual and eternal."

Chrysostom observes, "He said not before Abraham was, I was, but, I am.   As the Father useth this expression I AM, so also doth Christ, for it signifieth continuous being, irrespective of all time. On which account the expression seemed to the Jews blasphemous."

Augustine says, "In these words acknowledge the Creator and discern the creature.   He that spake was made the Seed of Abraham ; and that Abraham might be, He was before Abraham."

Gregory remarks, "Divinity has no past or future, but always the present ; and therefore Jesus does not say, Before Abraham was I *was*, but I *am*."

59.—[*Then took they up stones to cast at Him.*] It is clear that the Jews at any rate had no doubt what our Lord meant in the preceding verse, whatever modern Socinians may think. They saw and knew at once that He who spake to them boldly claimed to be Jehovah, and One far greater than Abraham, being very God. This they did not believe, and therefore regarded Him as a blasphemer who ought at once to be stoned. In their rage and fury they immediately took up stones, which were probably lying about on account of repairs of the temple, in order to stone Him. The whole proceeding appears to have been a tumultuous and disorderly one, not regularly conducted, but sudden and unauthorized, like the stoning of Stephen afterwards. (Acts vii. 58.)

[*But Jesus hid Himself, etc.*] I think this withdrawal can only be regarded as miraculous. The Greek word rendered "hid Himself" is literally "was hid." It seems most improbable that our Lord could "pass by," and "go through the midst" of an angry crowd, whose eyes had for a long time been fixed and concentrated on Him, without being seen and stopped, unless there was a miraculous interposition. I believe that the eyes of His enemies were holden, and that they did not know Him for a season, or that by His own almighty power He rendered Himself temporarily invisible. It is only what He did at Nazareth on a similar occasion (Luke iv. 30) ; and if we once concede that our Lord could work miracles at His will, there seems no reason to suppose that He would not work one on this occasion.

Let us note that our Lord's enemies could do nothing to Him until His hour was come for suffering. When He was at last taken prisoner, brought before Pilate, and crucified, it was not because He could not escape, but because He would not. What He did here He might have done there.

Let us note that it is not always the path of duty and of real obedience to God's will to sit still and submit to sufferings and death. It may be the will of God that we should "flee to some other city" and avoid death. (Matt. x. 23.) To court martyrdom and throw away life, when it might be saved, is not always the duty of a servant of Christ. Some of the martyrs of the primitive Church appear to have forgotten this.

Augustine says, "Jesus did not hide Himself in a corner of the temple as if He were afraid, or take refuge in a house, or run behind a wall or a pillar ; but by His heavenly power He made Himself invisible to His enemies, and went through the midst of them."

The argument of Maldonatus, that this verse proves the possibility of Christ being corporally present in the Lord's Supper in the bread, is so preposterous that it requires no refutation. There is no positive proof that our Lord was actually invisible here. It is quite possible that the eyes of His enemies were "holden that they could not know Him." (Luke xxiv. 16.) If He was invisible, Maldonatus proves too much. The bread in the Lord's Supper is seen, and after consecration the Roman Catholic says its substance is changed. But it is not invisible.

In leaving this remarkable chapter, we should not fail to notice the difficulties under which our Lord's public ministry was carried on. Ten times, between the 12th verse and the 59th, we find His enemies interrupting, contradicting, or reviling Him. Our Master's calm dignity and perfect meekness under all this "contradiction of sinners," ought to be a never-forgotten example to His disciples.

It is a wise remark of Pascal, that our Lord's enemies, by their incessant cavilling and interruption, both here and elsewhere, have supplied us unintentionally with a strong proof of the truth of His teaching. If our Lord's doctrines had only been delivered privately to a prejudiced audience of kind and loving disciples, they would not come down to us with the same weight that they do now. But they were often proclaimed in the midst of bitter enemies, learned Scribes and Pharisees, who were ready to detect any flaw or defect in His reasoning. That the enemies of Christ could never answer or silence Him, is a strong evidence that His doctrine was God's own truth. It was from heaven, and not from men.

JOHN IX. 1—12.

1 And as *Jesus* passed by, he saw a man which was blind from *his* birth.

2 And his disciples asked him, saying, Master, who did sin, this man, or his parents, that he was born blind?

3 Jesus answered, Neither hath this man sinned, nor his parents: but that the works of God should be made manifest in him.

4 I must work the works of him that sent me, while it is day: the night cometh, when no man can work.

5 As long as I am in the world, I am the light of the world.

6 When he had thus spoken he spat on the ground, and made clay of the spittle, and he anointed the eyes of the blind man with the clay.

7 And said unto him, Go wash in the pool of Siloam (which is by interpretation, Sent.) He went his way therefore, and washed, and came seeing.

8 The neighbours therefore, and they which before had seen him that he was blind, said, Is not this he that sat and begged?

9 Some said, This is he; others *said*, He is like him: *but* he said, I am *he.*

10 Therefore said they unto him, How were thine eyes opened?

11 He answered and said, A man that is called Jesus made clay, and anointed mine eyes, and said unto me, Go to the pool of Siloam, and wash: and I went and washed, and I received sight.

1:: Then said they unto him, Where is he? He said, I know not.

THE chapter we now begin records one of the few great works of Christ which St. John has reported. It tells us how our Lord gave sight to a man who had been "blind from his birth." Here, as elsewhere in this Gospel, we find the circumstances of the miracle narrated with peculiar fulness, minuteness, and particularity. Here, too, as elsewhere, we find the narrative rich in spiritual lessons.

We should observe, first, in this passage, *how much sorrow sin has brought into the world.* A sorrowful case is brought before us. We are told of a man "who was blind from his birth." A more serious affliction can hardly be conceived. Of all the bodily crosses that can be laid on man, without taking away life, none perhaps is greater than the loss of sight. It cuts us off from some of the greatest enjoyments of life. It shuts us up within a narrow world of our own. It makes us painfully helpless and dependent on others. In fact, until men lose their eyesight, they never fully realize its value.

Now blindness, like every other bodily infirmity, is one of the fruits of sin. If Adam had never fallen, we cannot doubt that people would never have been blind, or deaf, or dumb. The many ills that flesh is heir to, the countless pains and diseases and physical defects to which we are all liable, came in when the curse came upon the earth. "By one man sin entered into the world, and death by sin." (Rom. v. 12.)

Let us learn to hate sin with a godly hatred, as the root of more than half our cares and sorrows. Let us fight against it, mortify it, crucify it, and abhor it both in ourselves and others. There cannot be a clearer proof that man is a fallen creature, than the fact that he can love sin and take pleasure in it.

We should observe, secondly, in this passage, *what a solemn lesson Christ gives us about the use of opportunities.* He says to the disciples who asked Him about the blind man, "I must work while it is called to-day: the night cometh, when no man can work."

That saying was eminently true when applied to our Lord Himself. He knew well that His own earthly ministry would only last three years altogether, and knowing this He diligently redeemed the time. He let slip no opportunity of doing works of mercy, and attending to His Father's business. Morning, noon, and night He was always carrying on the work which the Father gave Him to do. It was "His meat and drink to do His Father's will, and to finish His work." (John iv. 34.) His whole life breathed one sentiment: "I must work. The night cometh, when no man can work."

The saying is one which should be remembered by all professing Christians. The life that we now live in the flesh is our day. Let us take care that we use it well, for the glory of God and the good of our souls. Let us work out our salvation with fear and trembling, while it is called to-day. There is no work nor labour in the grave, toward which we are all fast hastening. Let us pray, and read, and keep our Sabbaths holy, and hear God's Word, and do good in our generation, like men who never forget that "the night is at hand." Our time is very short. Our daylight will soon be gone. Opportunities once lost can never be retrieved. A second lease of life is granted to no man. Then let us resist procrastination as we would resist the devil. Whatever our hand findeth to do, let us do it with our might. "The night cometh, when no man can work."

We should observe, thirdly, in this passage, *what different means Christ used in working miracles on different occasions.* In healing the blind man He might, if He had thought fit, have merely touched him with His finger, or given command with His tongue. But He did not rest content with doing so. We are told that "He spat on the ground, and made clay of the spittle, and He anointed the eyes of the blind man with the clay." In all these means of course there was no inherent healing virtue. But for wise reasons the Lord was pleased to use them.

We need not doubt that in this, as in every other action of our Lord, there is an instructive lesson. It teaches us, we may well believe, that the Lord of heaven and earth will not be tied down to the use of any one means or instrumentality. In conferring blessings on man, He will work in His own way, and will allow no one to prescribe to Him. Above all, it should teach those who have received anything at Christ's hands, to be careful how they measure other men's experience by their own. Have we been healed by Christ, and made to see and live? Let us thank God for it, and be humbled. But let us beware of saying that no other man has been healed, except he has been brought to spiritual life in precisely the same manner. The great question is, "Are the eyes of our understanding opened? Do we see? Have we spiritual life?" Enough for us if the cure is effected and health restored. If it is, we must leave it to the great Physician to choose the instrument, the means, and the manner,—the clay, the touch, or the command.

We should observe, lastly, in this passage, *the almighty power that Christ holds in His hands.* We see Him doing that which in itself was impossible. Without medicines He cures an incurable case. He actually gives eyesight to one that was born blind.

Such a miracle as this is meant to teach an old truth, which we can never know too well. It shows us that Jesus the Saviour of sinners "has all power in heaven and earth." Such mighty works could never have been done by one that was merely man. In the cure of this blind man we see nothing less than the finger of God.

Such a miracle, above all, is meant to make us hopeful about our own souls and the souls of others. Why should we despair of salvation while we have such a Saviour? Where is the spiritual disease that He cannot take away? He can open the eyes of the most sinful and ignorant, and make them see things they never saw before. He can send light into the darkest heart, and cause blindness and prejudice to pass away.

Surely, if we are not saved, the fault will be all our own. There lives at God's right hand One who can heal us if we apply to Him. Let us take heed lest those solemn words are found true of us, "Light is come into the world: but men loved darkness rather than light because their deeds were evil."—"Ye will not come to Me that ye might have life." (John iii. 19; v. 40.)

Notes. John ix. 1—12.

1.—[*And as Jesus passed by.*] The Greek word rendered "passed by," is the same as the word so rendered in the preceding verse, at the end of the last chapter.—Some think from this repetition, that the miracle recorded here took place immediately after the events of the last chapter, without the least break or interruption; and that it was as our Lord was retiring from the temple, after the attempt of the Jews to stone Him, that He saw the blind man.— Others, however, think that an interval of time must have elapsed, partly because it seems improbable that our Lord and His disciples would all be able to withdraw themselves quietly from an angry mob, and calmly stand still near the scene of attempted violence to attend to a blind man, and partly because it is the manner of St. John's Gospel to pass from one event to another, sometimes without intimating that there is any change of time or place. Thus, John v. 19; vi. 25, 43, 59; vii. 28—33. The point, however, is not one of any practical importance.

Chemnitius holds strongly that an interval of two months comes in here, and that our Lord spent that time in a visitation of the towns and villages of Judæa, as related in Luke xiii. 22. He thinks that He thus occupied the two months after the feast of tabernacles, and that He returned to Jerusalem shortly before the feast of dedication, in winter. The main objection to this theory seems to be, that it is not the natural conclusion we should draw from the text.

Gualter, Ferus, Ecolampadius, and Musculus maintain, on the other hand, that there is a close and intentional connection between this chapter and the preceding one. They think that our Lord desired to show by deed as well as word, that He was "the Light of the world." (John viii. 14.) Bucer says, "This chapter is a sermon in act and deed, on the words, 'I am the Light of the world.'"

In the miracle which occupies the whole of this chapter, the following special circumstances deserve notice:—(1) It is only related by St. John. (2) Like each of the few miracles in St. John, it is described with great minuteness and particularity. (3) It is one of the four miracles wrought in Judæa, or near Jerusalem, mentioned in St. John. He records eight great miracles together : four in Galilee,—turning the water into wine, healing the nobleman's son, feeding the multitude, and walking on the water (chap. ii., iv., and vi.) ; and four in Judæa,—purifying the temple, healing the impotent man, restoring sight to the blind, and raising Lazarus. (Chap. ii., v., vi., and ix.) (4) It is one of those miracles which the Jews were especially taught to expect in Messiah's time : "In that day shall the eyes of the blind see out of obscurity." (Is. xxix. 18.) (5) It is one of those signs of Messiah having come, to which Jesus particularly directed John the Baptist's attention : "The blind receive their sight." (Matt. xi. 5.) (6) It was a miracle worked in so public a place, and on a man so well known, that it was impossible for the Jerusalem Jews to deny it.

It is hardly necessary, perhaps, to bid any well-instructed Christian observe the singularly instructive and typical character of each of the eight miracles which John was inspired to record. Each was a vivid picture of spiritual things.

Hengstenberg observes, that three of the four great miracles wrought by Christ in Judæa, exactly represent the three classes of works referred to in Matt. xi. 5 : "The lame walk, the blind see, the dead are raised up." (John v. ; ix. ; xi.)

[*He saw a man...blind from his birth.*] The man was probably sitting near the temple gateway, to attract the notice of worshippers going to and fro, like the man described in Acts. (Acts iii. 2.) From blindness, he would naturally be dependent on charity. The Jewish law specifies the blind as peculiarly deserving of attention (Levit. xix. 14 ; Deut. xxvii. 18.) To give sight to one who had not lost the use of his eyes by disease or accident, but had never seen at all, was of course a mighty miracle.

Let it be noted, that our Lord "saw" the blind man, and healed him of His own free will, unasked, and unexpectedly. As in the case of the impotent man (John v. 6), He did not wait to be entreated, but was Himself the first to move. Let it however be noted at the same time, that if the man had not been by the wayside our Lord would not have seen him.

Chrysostom observes, that when the Jews "would not receive our Lord's sayings, and tried to kill Him, He went out of the temple, and healed the blind, mitigating their rage by His absence ; and, by working a miracle, both softening their hardness and proving His affections. And it is clear that He proceeded inten-

tionally to this work on leaving the temple, for it was He who saw
the blind man, and not the blind man who came to Him."

Gualter observes, that this passage shows how the eyes of the
Lord are in every place, and how He sees His own people, even
when they think not of Him.

Alford thinks it possible that the blind man was constantly
proclaiming that he had been born blind, to excite pity.

Burgon observes, " More of our Saviour's miracles are recorded
as having been wrought on blindness, than on any other form of
human infirmity. One deaf and dumb man is related to have had
speech and hearing restored to him ; one case of palsy, and one of
dropsy, find special record ; twice was leprosy, and twice was fever
expelled by the Saviour's word; three times were dead persons
raised to life ; but the records of His cures wrought on blindness,
are four in number, at least, if not five." (See Matt. xii. 22.)
Isaiah seems to foretell the recovery of sight by the blind, as "an
act of mercy specially symbolical of Messiah's day." (Isa. xxix.
18 ; xxxii. 3 ; xxxv. 5 ; xlii. 7.)

2.—[*And his disciples asked Him.*] This expression seems to show
that our Lord was surrounded and accompanied by His usual
followers, and favours the idea that there was some break or
interval between the beginning of this chapter and the end of the
last. Though He by Divine power could hide Himself and go
through the midst of His enemies, it is hardly reasonable to suppose
that within a few minutes He would be surrounded again by His
disciples. Yet it is of course possible.

[*Master, who did sin, this man...parents...blind ?*] This curious
question has given rise to much unprofitable discussion. It is
repeatedly asked,—Why did the disciples say this ? What put it
into their minds to start the inquiry ?

(*a*) Some think that the Jews had imbibed the common oriental
notion of the pre-existence and transmigration of souls from one
body to another, and that the disciples supposed that in some
previous state of existence this blind man must have committed
some great sin, for which he was now punished.

(*b*) Some think that the question refers to a strange notion current
among some Jews, that infants might sin before they were born.
In support of this view, they quote Gen. xxv. 22, and Gen.
xxxviii. 28, 29.

(*c*) The most probable view is, that the question arose from a misapplication of such passages of Scripture as the second Command-

ment, where God speaks of "visiting the iniquity of the fathers upon the children" (Exod. xx. 5), and from a forgetfulness of Eze. xviii. 20, etc. There are few notions that men seem to cling to so naturally, as the notion that bodily sufferings, and all afflic-tion, are the direct consequences of sin, and that a diseased or afflicted person must necessarily be a very wicked man. This was precisely the short-sighted view that Job's three friends took up when they came to visit him, and against which Job contended. This was the idea of the people at Melita, when Paul was bitten by a viper, after the shipwreck: "This man is a murderer." (Acts. xxviii. 4.) This appears to have been at the bottom of the question of the disciples: "There is suffering; then there must have been sin. Whose sin was it?"

Chrysostom thinks that the disciples remembered our Lord's words to the paralytic whom He healed (chap. v. 14): "Thou art made whole: sin no more;" and asked now to what sin this man's blindness might be traced. This, however, seems very improbable, considering the length of time between the two miracles.

Hengstenberg observes that the fallacy of supposing that special afflictions are the result of some special sins, "commends itself to low and common spirits by its simplicity and palpableness. It has the advantage of rendering it needless to weep with them that weep. It saves a man from the obligation, when he sees heavy affliction, of smiting on his breast, and saying 'God be merciful to me a sinner.' It gives the natural man the comfortable feeling that he is so much the better than the sufferer, as he is more fortu-nate."

Those who wish to go more deeply into the subject, will find it fully discussed by the great Dutch divine, Gomarus.

It is worth notice that the word here rendered "Master" is the same that is rendered "Rabbi" in five other places in St. John. (i. 38; i. 49; iii. 2; iii. 26; vi. 25.) Why our translators did not observe uniformity in their translation of the word throughout this Gospel is not very clear.

3.—[*Jesus answered, Neither hath this man sinned...parents.*] This first part of our Lord's answer is elliptical. The sense of course must be supplied from the context. Our Lord did not mean that neither this blind man nor his parents had committed any sin at all, but that it was not any special sin of his or theirs which had caused his blindness. Nor yet did our Lord mean that the sins of parents could never entail disease on children; but that the case before Him, at any rate, was not such a case. Of course He did not mean us to forget that sin is the great primeval cause of all the evils that are in the world.

[*But that the works of God...manifest in him.*] The meaning of this must be, that the man's blindness was permitted and over-ruled by God, in order that His works of mercy in healing him might be shown to men. This blindness was allowed and ordained by God, not because he was specially wicked, but in order to furnish a platform for the exhibition of a work of Divine mercy and power.

A deep and instructive principle lies in these words. They surely throw some light on that great question,—the origin of evil. God has thought fit to allow evil to exist, in order that He may have a platform for showing His mercy, grace, and compassion. If man had never fallen, there would have been no opportunity of showing Divine mercy. But by permitting evil, mysterious as it seems, God's works of grace, mercy, and wisdom in saving sinners, have been wonderfully manifested to all His creatures. The redeeming of the Church of elect sinners is the means of "showing to principalities and powers the manifold wisdom of God." (Ephes. iii. 10.) Without the fall we should have known nothing of the cross and the Gospel.

Melancthon, on this verse, suggests no less than ten reasons why God permits evil to come on the Church, which contain much food for thought. Brentius and Chemnitius also say many excellent things on the same theme.

Bucer remarks that this verse should teach us to bear ills patiently and cheerfully, since all that happens to us tends, in some way, to the glory of God.

Gualter remarks, that even wicked men like Pharaoh subserve the glory of God (Rom. ix. 17); much more may men's afflictions and diseases.

Ecolampadius remarks, that God allows nothing whatever to happen without some good reason and cause.

Henry observes, "The intention of Providence often does not appear till a great while after the event, perhaps many years after. The sentences in the book of Providence are sometimes long, and you must read a great way before you understand the meaning."

Jones of Nayland, on this text, remarks, "The best way to answer the great question of the origin of evil, is to consider the end of it, "What good comes out of it?" this makes the subject plain and useful. Why was this man born blind? That the works of God might appear, and Christ might cure him.—Why did man fall? That God might save him.—Why is evil permitted in the world? That God may be glorified in removing it.—Why does the body of man die? That God may raise it up again.—When we philosophize in this manner we find light, certainty, and comfort. We have a memorable example of it in the case before us."

Barnes remarks that, "Those who are afflicted with blindness, deafness, or any deformity, should be submissive to God. It is His appointment, and is right and best. God does no wrong; and when all His works are seen, the universe will see and know that He is just."

4.—[*I must work the works, etc.*] The connection between this verse and the preceding one, seems to be in the word "works." It is as though our Lord said, "Healing the blind man is one of the great 'works' which God has appointed for Me to do, and I must do it during the 'day,' or short period of my ministry. This blindness was ordained by my Father to be a means of showing forth my divine power."

The expression "while it is day," and "the night cometh," must probably be interpreted with special reference to our Lord's ministry upon earth. While He was with His disciples speaking, teaching, and working miracles, it was comparatively "day." His little Church basked in the full sun-light of His Divine presence, and saw and learned countless wonderful things. When He ascended up on high it became comparatively "night." Just as in night "no man can work," so when Christ left the world the visible proof of His Divine mission which the disciples had so long enjoyed and seen, could no longer be given. The proverbial saying, "No man can work in the night," would be verified.

These limits to the application of the figure must be carefully remembered. Of course our Lord did not mean that the Church, after His ascension, would not enjoy far more spiritual light than it did before He came; nor yet that the disciples, after the day of Pentecost, would not see many truths far more clearly even than when Christ was with them. But the words "day and night" here have a special reference to our Lord's bodily presence with His Church. As long as He was visibly with them it was "day." When He left them it was "night." It is well to remark that St. Paul uses the same figures when comparing time present with time to come, at the second advent. He says, "The night is far spent, and the day is at hand." (Rom. xiii. 12.) There the night is Christ's bodily absence, and the day Christ's bodily presence.

Melancthon points out what an example Christ supplies to Christians in this place. The hatred, opposition, and persecution of the world, and the failures and infirmities of professing Christians, must not make us give way to despondency. Like our Master, we must work on.

Calvin observes : " From these words we may deduce the universal rule, that to every man the course of his life may be called his day."

Beza and others think that there is a primary prophecy here of the withdrawal of light and privilege from the Jews, which was in the mind of our Lord, as well as the general principle that to all men day is the time for work and not night.

5.—[*As long as I am in the world, etc.*] This verse seems to be a general broad assertion of our Lord's purpose in coming into the world, and His position while in it. " I came into the world to be its Sun and spiritual Guide, and to deliver men from the natural darkness in which they are ; and so long as I am in the world I wish to be its Light in the fullest sense, the Deliverer of men's souls and the Healer of men's bodies."

Cocceius suggests, that in these words our Lord had respect to the fact that He was going to work a work on the Sabbath, and that it would be disapproved by the Jews, as a breach of the Sabbath. Foreseeing this, He defends what He is about to do, by reminding His disciples that during the short time of His earthly ministry He must seize every opportunity of doing good.

Alford observes, that just as Jesus said before He raised Lazarus, "I am the Resurrection and the Life," so here, before giving sight to the blind, He said, "I am the Light."

6.—[*When...thus spoken...spat.. anointed...clay.*] The action here used by our Lord is the same that we find used on two other occasions,—once when He healed one deaf and dumb (Mark vii. 33) ; once when He healed a blind man. (Mark viii. 23.) The making of the "clay," however, is quite peculiar to this miracle. The reason why our Lord used the action we cannot tell. There is, of course, no special virtue either in spittle, or in clay made from spittle, which could cure a man born blind. Why then did Jesus use this means ? Why did He not heal the man with a word or a touch ?

The only answer to such inquiries is, that our Lord would teach

us, by His peculiar mode of proceeding here, that He is not tied
to any one means of doing good, and that we may expect to find
variety in His methods of dealing with souls as well as with bodies.
May He not also wish to teach us that He can, when He thinks
fit, invest material things with an efficacy which is not inherent in
them ?   We are not to despise Baptism and the Lord's Supper,
because water, bread, and wine are mere material elements.   To
many who use them, no doubt they are nothing more than mere
material things, and never do them the slightest good.   But to
those who use the sacraments rightly, worthily, and with faith,
Christ can make water, bread, and wine, instruments of doing real
good.   He that was pleased to use clay in healing a blind man
may surely use material things, if He thinks fit, in His own ordinances.   The water in Baptism, and the bread and wine in the
Lord's Supper, while they are not to be treated as idols, ought not
to be treated with irreverence and contempt.   It was, of course,
not the clay that healed the blind man, but Christ's word and
power.   Nevertheless the clay was used.   So the brazen serpent
in itself had no medicinal power to cure the bitten Israelites.   But
without it they were not cured.

The selection of clay for anointing the blind man's eyes is thought
by some to be significant, and to contain a possible reference to the
original formation of man out of the dust.   He that formed man
with all his bodily faculties out of the dust could easily restore
one of those lost faculties, even sight, when He thought fit.   He
that healed these blind eyes with clay, was the same Being who
originally formed man out of the clay.

Ecolampadius thinks that the spittle was an emblem of Christ's
Divinity, and the clay of His humanity, and that the union of the
two represented the union of the two natures in Christ's person,
whereby healing came to a sin-sick world.   To say the least, this
seems fanciful.

Barradius suggests that our Lord actually formed new eyes for
the man, as He at first formed man's body out of the dust.   This
however seems needlessly improbable.

Poole thinks that our Lord used spittle to make clay, simply
because there was no water nigh at hand to make it with.

Wordsworth observes that Christ's manner of working the
miracle was "tenderness to the Jews.   They would see the clay
on the man's eyes, and see him going to Siloam."

He also observes, "God loves to effect His greatest works by
means tending under ordinary circumstances to produce the very

opposite of what is to be done. God walls the sea with sand. God clears the air with storms. God warms the earth with snow. So in the world of grace. He brings water in the desert, not from the soft earth, but the flinty rock. He heals the sting of the serpent of fire by the serpent of brass. He overthrows the wall of Jericho by ram's horns. He slays a thousand men with the jaw-bone of an ass. He cures salt water with salt. He fells the giant with a sling and stone. And thus does the Son of God work in the Gospel. He cures the blind man by that which seemed likely to increase his blindness,—by anointing his eyes with clay. He exalts us to heaven by the stumbling-block of the cross."

7.—[*And said...Go, wash...Siloam.*] The direction here given to the blind man would remind any pious Jew of Elisha's directions to Naaman, "Go wash in Jordan." (2 Kings v. 10.) The water of this pool had no inherent healing efficacy any more than other water. But the command was a test of faith, and in obeying the blind man found what he wanted. It is the great principle which runs through Scripture : "Believe and obey, and all will be right."

The pool of Siloam was a well-known reservoir, or artificial pond, in a valley close to Jerusalem, remarkable for a supply of water from an intermittent spring. It is pointed out in the present day, and there seems no reason to doubt that it is the same pool that was so called eighteen hundred years ago. It is first mentioned in Nehemiah iii. 15, and afterwards in Isaiah viii. 6.

Lightfoot asserts that the pool of Bethesda and the pool of Siloam were both supplied from one spring.

[*Which is by interpretation, Sent.*] There is undeniable difficulty about this sentence. It is naturally asked,—Why is this parenthetical explanation inserted by St. John? Why are we specially told that the word Siloam means Sent, or He that was sent?—The most probable answer seems to be, that the name of the fountain was meant to refer the blind man's mind to the Messiah, whom God had "sent." All pious Jews would understand the expression which so frequently occurs in John's Gospel, "He whom God hath sent," to point to Messiah. When therefore Jesus said, "Go wash in Siloam," the naming of that particular fountain would be a silent hint that He who gave the command was the Sent One of God, the great Healer of all diseases. St. John's parenthesis would then mean, when expounded, "This was a most suitable and proper pool for Jesus to name. It was fitting that He who was 'Sent of

God' should work a miracle in the pool called 'Sent.'"—This is the view of Chrysostom and Augustine.

It is impossible to help feeling that the clause looks very much like the insertion of some ignorant early copyist, who wished to show his own knowledge of etymology, and perhaps found it in an old copy as a marginal gloss. The Syriac and Persian versions do not contain the clause. Yet it certainly is found in most manuscripts and versions.

Hutcheson thinks that John inserted this clause for no other end than to remind readers that this fountain was a special gift "sent" by God, among the hills near Jerusalem, for the benefit of the Jews.

Hengstenberg says, "As Jesus represents Himself and His Church as the real Pool of Bethesda, in chap. v., so here He declares Himself the real Sent One, or Siloam, the Fountain of blessings."

[*He went...washed...came seeing.*] The blind man, as is often the case with people born blind, was probably able to find his way about Jerusalem without trouble, and the road from the temple-gate to the pool of Siloam was likely to be much frequented. His implicit faith and obedience contrast favourably with the conduct of Naaman, when told to go and wash in Jordan. (2 Kings v. 14.) The word "came" must either mean "to his own home," or simply "came back to the temple-gate." The miracle of healing seems to have taken place in the act of washing in Siloam.

Let us remember that the blind man's conduct is meant to be a pattern to us. He did not stumble at Christ's command, but simply obeyed; and in obeying he was healed. We must do likewise.

Melancthon thinks it likely that a crowd of curious and jeering spectators accompanied the man to Siloam to see the result of our Lord's prescription.

Scott remarks that the immediate power of using the eyes was no small part of the miracle. When people recover sight now after surgical operations, it requires a considerable time to learn the use of the newly-acquired sense.

8.—[*The neighbours.*] This would seem to show that he "came" to his own house as soon as he was healed of his blindness. The word before us naturally means the people who lived near to him.

[*They which before had seen ..blind.*] This expression includes all persons in Jerusalem who knew the blind man by sight, though

they did not live near him, but had often seen him near the temple
and become familiar with his appearance.   There are generally
blind beggars in the chief thoroughfares of large cities, and near
large public buildings, whom all residents know well by sight.
The slow, uncertain, feeble gait of a blind man always makes him
conspicuous.

[*Is not this he that sat and begged ?*] This question seems to settle
that the blind man was one of the poorest and humblest class of
Jews.   None are so likely to come to poverty and be dependent
on charity as the blind, who of course cannot work for their own
support.

9.—[*Some said, This is he.*] This probably was the saying of the blind
man's neighbours, who naturally knew him best.

[*Others said, He is like him.*] This was probably the saying of
people living in Jerusalem, who knew the blind man by sight, but
did not live near him, and were not therefore so familiar with his
appearance.   The difference between the look and demeanour of the
man before and after his miraculous cure would necessarily be very
great.   One can quite understand that some would hardly know
him again.   Augustine remarks, "The opened eyes had altered
his looks."   Musculus observes how much the expression of a
face depends on the eyes.

[*He said, I am he.*] This was the saying of the man when he
heard people doubting his identity and looking at him with hesita-
tion.   "I assure you," he says, "that I am he who used to sit at
the temple gate and beg."

10.—[*Therefore said they, etc.*] Those who asked this question
appear to have been the people who came together round the blind
man, when he returned from the pool of Siloam with his sight
restored.   Some were his neighbours, and others were inhabitants
of Jerusalem, drawn together by the miracle.   The inquiry was
the natural one that such a wonderful cure would first call forth.

11.— [*He answered and said, etc.*] This verse is a simple unvarnished
account of the facts of the cure.   How the blind man knew that
our Lord's name was "Jesus," does not appear.   It is not unlikely
that some of the bystanders, when our Lord first told him to go
to the pool of Siloam, told him that Jesus of Nazareth, the person
whose preaching was making such stir in Jerusalem, was the
speaker.   We cannot doubt that our Lord was well known by this
time to all dwellers in Jerusalem.   Yet there is no proof that the

beggar recognised Him as anything more than "a man called Jesus." The accuracy with which he recites all the facts of his cure is well worthy of notice. "He first put clay on my eyes; then He bid me go and wash in Siloam. I went: I was cured."

12.—[*Then said they... Where is He?...He...know not.*] The desire to see the worker of this wonderful miracle was natural, but the question, "Where is He?" was probably asked with a mischievous intention. Those who asked it wished to lay hands on our Lord, and bring Him before the rulers. The man's answer certainly seems to show that he did not return to the place where he had sat and begged, but to his house. Had he gone back to the temple gates, he might have replied that Jesus was here only a short time before, and was probably not far off. The questioners seem to suppose that the worker of such a miracle and the subject of it, could not be far apart. They did not understand that our Lord always avoided, rather than courted public notice.

JOHN IX. 13—25.

13 They brought to the Pharisees him that aforetime was blind.

14 And it was the sabbath day when Jesus made the clay, and opened his eyes.

15 Then again the Pharisees also asked him how he had received his sight. He said unto them, He put clay upon mine eyes, and I washed, and do see.

16 Therefore said some of the Pharisees, This man is not of God, because he keepeth not the sabbath day. Others said, How can a man that is a sinner do such miracles? And there was a division among them.

17 They say unto the blind man again, What sayest thou of Him, that hath opened thine eyes? He said, He is a prophet.

18 But the Jews did not believe concerning him, that he had been blind, and received his sight, until they called the parents of him that had received his sight.

19 And they asked them, saying, Is this your son, who ye say was born blind? how then doth he now see?

20 His parents answered them and said, We know that this is our son, and that he was born blind:

21 But by what means he now seeth, we know not; or who hath opened his eyes, we know not: he is of age; ask him; he shall speak for himself.

22 These *words* spake his parents, because they feared the Jews: for the Jews had agreed already, that if any man did confess that he was Christ, he should be put out of the synagogue.

23 Therefore said his parents, He is of age: ask him.

24 Then again called they the man that was blind, and said unto him, Give God the praise: we know that this man is a sinner.

25 He answered and said, Whether he be a sinner *or no*, I know not: one thing I know, that, whereas I was blind, now I see.

THESE verses show us, *how little the Jews of our Lord's time understood the right use of the Sabbath day.* We read that some of the Pharisees found fault because a

blind man was miraculously healed on the Sabbath.
They said, " This man is not of God, because He
keepeth not the Sabbath day." A good work had
manifestly been done to a helpless fellow-creature. A
heavy bodily infirmity had been removed. A mighty
act of mercy had been performed. But the blind-hearted
enemies of Christ could see no beauty in the act. They
called it a breach of the Fourth Commandment !

These would-be wise men completely mistook the
intention of the Sabbath. They did not see that it was
" made for man," and meant for the good of man's body,
mind, and soul. It was a day to be set apart from
others, no doubt, and to be carefully sanctified and kept
holy. But its sanctification was never intended to prevent works of necessity and acts of mercy. To heal a
sick man was no breach of the Sabbath day. In finding
fault with our Lord for so doing, the Jews only exposed
their ignorance of their own law. They had forgotten
that it is as great a sin to add to a commandment, as
to take it away.

Here, as in other places, we must take care that we do
not put a wrong meaning on our Lord's conduct. We
must not for a moment suppose that the Sabbath is no
longer binding on Christians, and that they have nothing
to do with the Fourth Commandment. This is a great
mistake, and the root of great evil. Not one of the ten
commandments has ever been repealed or put aside.
Our Lord never meant the Sabbath to become a day of
pleasure, or a day of business, or a day of travelling and
idle dissipation. He meant it to be "kept holy" as long

as the world stands. It is one thing to employ the
Sabbath in works of mercy, in ministering to the sick,
and doing good to the distressed. It is quite another
thing to spend the day in visiting, feasting, and self-
indulgence. Whatever men may please to say, the way
in which we use the Sabbath is a sure test of the state of
our religion. By the Sabbath may be found out whether
we love communion with God. By the Sabbath may be
found out whether we are in tune for heaven. By the
Sabbath, in short, the secrets of many hearts are revealed.
There are only too many of whom we may say with
sorrow, "These men are not of God, because they keep
not the Sabbath day."

These verses show us, secondly, *the desperate lengths
to which prejudice will sometimes carry wicked men.* We
read that the "Jews agreed that if any man did confess
that Jesus was Christ, he should be put out of the
synagogue." They were determined not to believe. They
were resolved that no evidence should change their minds,
and no proofs influence their will. They were like men
who shut their eyes and tie a bandage over them, and
refuse to have it untied. Just as in after times they
stopped their ears when Stephen preached, and refused
to listen when Paul made his defence, so they behaved
at this period of our Lord's ministry.

Of all states of mind into which unconverted men
can fall, this is by far the most dangerous to the soul.
So long as a person is candid, fair, and honest-minded,
there is hope for him, however ignorant he may be. He
may be much in the dark at present. But is he willing to

follow the light, if set before him? He may be walking
in the broad road with all his might. But is he ready
to listen to any one who will show him a more excellent
way? In a word, is he teachable, childlike, and unfet-
tered by prejudice? If these questions can be answered
satisfactorily, we never need despair about the man's
soul.

The state of mind we should always desire to possess,
is that of the noble-minded Beræans. When they first
heard the Apostle Paul preach they listened with
attention. They received the Word "with all readiness
of mind." They "searched the Scriptures," and compared
what they heard with God's Word. "And therefore," we
are told "many of them believed." Happy are they that
go and do likewise! (Acts xvii. 11, 12.)

These verses show us, lastly, that *nothing convinces a
man so thoroughly as his own senses and feelings.* We read
that the unbelieving Jews tried in vain to persuade the
blind man whom Jesus healed, that nothing had been
done for him. They only got from him one plain answer: "One thing I know, that whereas I was blind,
now I see." How the miracle had been worked he did
not pretend to explain. Whether the person who had
healed him was a sinner, he did not profess to know. But
that something had been done for him he stoutly maintained. He was not to be reasoned out of his senses.
Whatever the Jews might think, there were two distinct
facts of which he was conscious: "I was blind: now
I see."

There is no kind of evidence so satisfactory as this to

the heart of a real Christian. His knowledge may be small. His faith may be feeble. His doctrinal views may be at present confused and indistinct. But if Christ has really wrought a work of grace in his heart by His Spirit, he feels within him something that you cannot overthrow. "I was dark, and now I have light. I was afraid of God, and now I love Him. I was fond of sin, and now I hate it. I was blind, and now I see." Let us never rest till we know and feel within us some real work of the Holy Ghost. Let us not be content with the name and form of Christianity. Let us desire to have true experimental acquaintance with it. Feelings no doubt are deceitful, and are not everything in religion. But if we have no inward feelings about spiritual matters, it is a very bad sign. The hungry man eats, and feels strengthened ; the thirsty man drinks, and feels refreshed. Surely the man who has within him the grace of God, ought to be able to say, "I feel its power."

NOTES. JOHN IX. 13—25.

13.—[*They brought to the Pharisees...blind.*] The prime movers in this matter, seem to have been the neighbours of the blind man. They thought that so marvellous an event as this sudden cure demanded investigation.

The "Pharisees" in this passage, if we may judge by the context, must have been the great council, or Sanhedrim, of the Jewish nation, the same body before whom our Lord made His defence, in the fifth chapter of this Gospel. At any rate, we can hardly imagine any other body at Jerusalem "excommunicating" a man. (See verse 34.)

Whitby observes how wonderfully the providence of God ordered things, that the Pharisees should be put to silence and open shame by a poor blind man !

14 --[*And it was the Sabbath day, etc.*] This seems specially mentioned by the Evangelist parenthetically for two reasons.

(*a*) It proved our Lord's unvarying readiness to do works of mercy on the Sabbath day.

(*b*) It explains the bitter enmity of the Jews against our Lord in this chapter. They regarded Him as a breaker of the Sabbath.

Assuming that there was no interval of time between the end of the last chapter and the beginning of this, it is remarkable how much our Lord did and said on this Sabbath day. From the beginning of the eighth chapter, down to the thirty-fifth verse of the ninth, the narrative at first sight seems to run on without a break. It certainly makes it rather doubtful whether there should not be a break or pause assumed at the end of the eighth chapter.

Burkitt remarks, that one object of our Lord in working so many miracles on the Sabbath, was "to instruct the Jews in the true doctrines and proper duties of the Sabbath, and to let them know that works of necessity and mercy are very consistent with the due sanctification of the Sabbath. It is hard to find any time wherein charity is unseasonable ; for as it is the best of graces, so its works are fittest for the best of days."

Whitby thinks that our Lord frequently did miracles on the Sabbath, to impress on believing Jews the folly of the superstitious observance of it, and to prevent the misery they would run into if they persisted in an extravagant scrupulosity about the Sabbath, when days of vengeance came on Jerusalem.

15.--[*Then again the Pharisees...sight.*] The question asked of the healed man by the council of Pharisees, was precisely the same that had been asked by his neighbours : "Your eyes have been opened suddenly, though you were born blind : tell us how it was done."

It is worthy of remark, that the Greek word which we render here and all through the chapter as "received sight," means literally no more than "looked up, or saw again." This of course could not be precisely true and correct in the case of this man, as he had never seen, or used his eyes at all, and could not therefore see a second time. But it is useful to notice how here and elsewhere in Scripture the Holy Ghost uses the language which is most familiar and easily understood, even when it is not precisely and scientifically correct. And it is what we all do every day. We talk of the sun "rising," though we know well that strictly speaking he does not rise, and that what we see is the effect of the earth moving round the sun.

Barnes observes, "The proper question to have been asked, was whether he had in fact been cured, and not in what way. The question about a sinner's conversion is, whether in fact it has been done, and not about the mode or manner in which it has been effected. Yet no small part of disputes among men are about the *mode* in which the Spirit renews the heart, and not about the *fact* that it is done."

[*He said unto them, etc.*] The answer of the healed man is an honest, bold, plain repetition of the same story he had told already. The only difference is that he does not name "Jesus" here, but says "He" put clay, as if he knew his examiners would understand whom he meant. Or it may be that his mind was so full of his Benefactor that he omits to name Him, and takes for granted that all would know who He was.

The simple straightforward boldness of this man, standing before the most formidable court of the Jews, and telling out his story, is very noteworthy. It is, moreover, a complete statement of facts, and consequences. "He put clay : I washed : I see."

16.—[*Therefore said some, etc.*] This verse brings forward prominently the existence of two classes among the Pharisees. The one was the great majority, consisting of hundreds of bigoted enemies of our Lord, ready to catch at any pretext for injuring His reputation and damaging His character. They said, "This Man is not of God. He is a wicked man, because He keepeth not the Sabbath day. A Prophet sent from God would not have done any work on the Sabbath."—This assertion of course was based on the false and groundless principle that works of mercy to the sick were a violation of the Fourth Commandment. According to Lightfoot, the Rabbins expressly forbid saliva to be applied to the eyelids on the Sabbath day.

The other class, consisting of a small minority, raised the grave question, "How could a man, not sent by God, a wicked man, work such an astonishing miracle as this ? If He were not commissioned and enabled by God, He could not possibly give sight to the blind. Surely He must be from God."—These must have been Nicodemus, Joseph of Arimathæa, Gamaliel, and others. Their line of argument is precisely that of Nicodemus in the famous visit to our Lord by night, when he said, "No man can do these miracles except God be with him." (John iii. 2.)

Three times in John's Gospel we find that expression, "There was a division among them." (Here, and vii. 43, and x. 19.)

The hesitating manner in which the better class of the council raise the question here, "How can a man," etc., is strongly indicative of a timid minority, who felt that the stream of feeling was all against them. It strikingly resembles the question of Nicodemus (John vii. 51), "Doth our law judge any man," etc. One might almost think it was Nicodemus speaking here.

In large assemblies of men convened to consider ecclesiastical and religious questions, we may confidently assume that there are always some present whose hearts are right, and who are willing to support the truth, even though they sit in bad company, and are for the present silenced and overawed. Gamaliel's conduct, in Acts v. 34, is an illustration of this. There is no warrant for staying away from assemblies and councils merely because we happen to be in a minority.

Chrysostom remarks how "none of the assembly dared say what he wished openly, or in the way of assertion, but only in the way of doubt. One party wanted to kill our Lord, and the other to save Him. Neither spoke out."

Bullinger observes, that "all divisions are not necessarily evil, nor all concord and unity necessarily good."

17.—[*They say...blind man again.*] This division among the members of the council had at least this good affect, that they found it necessary to go into the whole case more fully, and ask further questions. These very questions brought the reality of the miracle into fuller light than before.

[*What sayest thou...opened...eyes.*] This question must evidently mean, "What dost thou think about this Person, who, thou sayest, has opened thine eyes? Whom dost thou believe Him to be, seeing that He has wrought this cure?" The question is an inquiry, not about the reality of the miracle, but about the Person who is said to have performed it. It looks, according to some, like an intention to entrap the poor man into saying something about Jesus for which they could condemn Him. On the other hand, Chrysostom, Ferus, and Toletus argue that those who made the inquiry of this text must have been the party which favoured our Lord.

[*He said...a prophet.*] This expression was the beginning of faith in the healed man. It was a declaration of his own belief that the Person who had wrought such a great cure must be a Person specially raised by God to do great works, like Elijah or Elisha. We must not forget that in the present day we are apt to confine the word "prophet" to a man who foretells things to come. But the Bible use of the word is much wider. The "prophets" raised up in the Old Testament were by no means all foretellers of things to come. Preaching, warning, and miracle-working were the whole business of not a few. In this sense the man seems to have called our Lord "a Prophet." It was for what He had *done* rather than for what He had *said*.

We should carefully note that the first idea about our Lord which the Jewish mind seemed ready to embrace, was that He was a "Prophet." Thus the multitude which escorted Him into Jesusalem said, "This is Jesus the Prophet of Nazareth" (Matt. xxi. 11); and again, "The multitude took Him for a Prophet" (Matt. xxi. 46); and again, "Others said it is a Prophet" (Mark vi. 15); and again, "A great Prophet is risen up among us." (Luke vii. 16.) Even the two disciples going to Emmaus were only positive on one point : that Jesus had been "a Prophet mighty in word and deed." (Luke xxiv. 19.) But it was a higher step of faith to say that Jesus was "the Prophet" promised by Moses,—the Messiah. This the healed man did not yet say. As yet he only got so far as "a Prophet," not "the Prophet."

Chemnitius remarks on this poor man's clear view of our Lord's greatness, that "you will often find more solid theological piety among tailors and shoemakers than among cardinals, bishops, and abbots."

Adam Clarke says it was "a Jewish maxim that a prophet might dispense with the observance of the Sabbath." If the healed man referred to this, his answer was a silencing one, and put the Pharisees in a dilemma.

Lampe also remarks that many things were allowed to prophets sent by God on an extraordinary mission, even about the observance of the ceremonial law, as we see in the history of David and Elijah. This gives great weight to the man's reply : "He is a Prophet."

18.—[*But the Jews did not believe, etc.*] Here, as elsewhere, we should mark the extraordinary unbelief of the Jewish people, and their obstinate determination to shut their eyes against light. It teaches the folly of supposing that mere evidence alone will ever make men Christians. It is the want of will to believe, and not the want of reasons for believing, that makes men infidels.

"The Jews" here, as in other places in John's Gospel, mean the teachers of the Jewish nation at Jerusalem, and specially the Pharisees.

The expression, "until they called," deserves special notice. We should remark that it does not mean that "after they called the man's parents they believed,—that they were unbelieving up to the time that they called them, and then began to believe." On the contrary, the context shows that even after they had called them they continued unbelieving. Parkhurst observes that it is a form of speaking, "signifying an interval, but not necessarily excluding the time following." The expression throws light on Matt. i. 25. That well-known text must not be pressed too far. It is no certain proof that Mary had other children after Jesus was born. Compare 1 Sam. xv. 35; 2 Sam. vi. 23; Job xxvii. 5; Isa. xxii. 14; Matt. v. 26; xviii. 34.

The word "called" probably implies the public call or summons of the man's parents to appear before the council, just as witnesses are called aloud by name to appear in our courts of justice.

Gualter observes how close the resemblance was between the conduct of the Pharisees in this case, and that of the Romish Inquisition. The pertinacious, determined effort to condemn the innocent, and to deprive Christ of His glory, is painfully the same.

Besser quotes a saying of the infidel Voltaire: "If in the market of Paris, before the eyes of a thousand men and before my own eyes, a miracle should be performed, I would much rather disbelieve the two thousand eyes and my own two, than believe it!"

19.—[*They asked them, etc.*] The enemies of our Lord over-reached themselves by their summoning the parents of the healed man. They brought publicly forward the two best possible witnesses as to the fact of the man's identity, as to the fact that he was born blind, and as to the fact that he now had his sight. So true is the saying, "He taketh the wise in their own craftiness." (1 Cor. iii. 19.)

Chrysostom thinks that the expression, "whom ye say," insinuated that they supposed the parents to be impostors, and that "they were acting deceitfully, and plotting on behalf of Christ," by spreading a report that their son was born blind.

The language of the verse seems to show that the healed man and his parents were at first confronted, and that the Pharisees pointed to him and asked, "Is this your son?"

20.—[*His parents answered, etc.*] The father and mother of the blind man made a plain statement of facts, that could not be contradicted. They placed it beyond a doubt that the man now standing before the Sanhedrim was one who, from the best possible evidence, they knew had been born blind. The fact of having a blind child is one about which no parent could be mistaken.

21.—[*But by what means...who hath opened...we know not.*] These words of the healed man's parents were probably the simple truth. The time was so short since the cure was wrought, that they might well be ignorant of the manner of it. Hastily summoned before the Sanhedrim, they might well have had no opportunity of conversing with their son, and as yet may have known nothing of the miracle.

[*He is of age, etc.*] These words show the determination of the parents to have nothing more to do with their son's case than they could possibly help. They evidently regarded the council with the same undefined dread with which men at one time regarded the Inquisition in Spain.

The word "age" is the same Greek word that in Matt. vi. 27 is translated "stature." It is highly probable that in that text it would have been better rendered "age," as here.

The words "he," "him," and "himself" in this clause are all emphatic, and all might be rendered "himself."

A man was reckoned "of age" by the Jews when he was thirty.

22.—[*These words spake...feared...Jews.*] This sentence must refer to the latter part of the preceding verse. Fear of the leading Jews in the council of Pharisees made the parents refer their inquirers to their son. Four times in John's Gospel we have special mention made of the "fear of the Jews." Here, and vii. 13 ; xii. 42 ; and xix. 38.

[*The Jews had agreed, etc.*] This is a striking example of the extreme littleness of unbelief, and the lengths to which hatred of Christ will go. To resolve on such a decision as this shows a settled determination not to be convinced.

The punishment of being "put out of the synagogue," was a heavy one to the Jew. It was equivalent to being cut off from all communion with other Jews, and tantamount to excommunication.

Those only who do anything for evangelizing the Jews now, can form any adequate idea of the trials which conversion to Christianity entails on them, and the dread in which they stand of being cut off from Israel.

Trench says, " We must not understand that the Sanhedrim had formally declared Jesus to be an impostor and a false Christ, but only that so long as the truth or falsehood of His claim to be the

Messiah was not clear, and they, the great tribunal, had not given a decision, none were to anticipate that decision, and the penalty of premature confession was to be excommunicated."

23.—[*Therefore said, etc.*] It was the fear of running the slightest risk of excommunication, or being even suspected of favouring the Healer of their son, that made the parents refer all inquiries to him, and refuse to offer any opinion about the means of his cure, whatever they may have felt.

24.—[*Then again.. called...blind.*] This was a second summons into court. Very possibly the healed man had been carefully removed out of court, while his parents were being examined. But when nothing could be got out of them, there was no alternative but to submit him to a second process of cross-examination and intimidation.

[*And said...Give God...praise.*] This sentence admits of two interpretations.

(*a*) Some, as Calvin, Chemnitius, Gualter, Ecolampadius, Beza, Piscator, Diodati, Aretius, Ferus, Maldonatus, Jansenius, Rollock, Alford, and Trench, regard it as a solemn form of adjuration, and think it parallel to Joshua's words to Achan (Joshua vii. 19) : "You stand in God's presence : give glory to Him by speaking the truth." This, however, makes the clause that follows rather unmeaning, and renders it necessary to supply a good deal to fill up the sense.

(*b*) Others, as Chrysostom, Brentius, Musculus, Pellican, Vatablus, and Barradius, regard it as specially referring to the cure which had been performed. "Give God the honour and glory of your healing. He must have wrought the cure, and not this man who anointed your eyes with clay. He could not have wrought this cure, because he is a Sabbath-breaker, and therefore a sinner. A sinner like him could not have healed you." I rather prefer this view.

Gualter and Musculus point out the odious affectation of zeal for God's glory which characterizes the conduct of many wicked persons in every age. Even the Spanish Inquisition professed a zeal for God's glory.

This "we" here is emphatical in the Greek : "We, who are learned men, and ought to know best."

25.—[*He answered... Whether...sinner...know not, etc.*] The healed man's answer is a very simple, and yet very striking one. He tells his inquirers that the question whether Jesus is a sinner, is one he knows nothing about. But he does know the fact, that he himself was blind up to that very day, and that now he can see. He carefully avoids at present saying a word about the character of his Healer. The one point he sticks to is the reality of the miracle. He must believe his own senses. His senses told him that he was cured.

The expression in every age has been regarded as a happy illustration of a true Christian's experience of the work of grace in his heart. There may be much about it that is mysterious and inexplicable to him, and of which he knows nothing. But the result of the Holy Ghost's work he does know and feel. There is a change somewhere. He sees what he did not see before. He feels what he did not feel before. Of that he is quite certain. There is a common and true saying among true Christians of the lower orders : "You may silence me, and beat me out of what I know : but you cannot beat me out of what I feel."

The English translation of the last clause rather misses the brevity and force of the Greek. It would be more literally rendered, "Being blind, now I see."

JOHN IX. 26—41.

26 Then said they to him again, What did he to thee? how opened he thine eyes?

27 He answered them, I have told you already, and ye did not hear : wherefore would ye hear it again? will ye also be his disciples?

28 Then they reviled him, and said, Thou art his disciple ; but we are Moses' disciples.

29 We know that God spake unto Moses : as for this fellow, we know not from whence he is.

30 The man answered and said unto them, Why herein is a marvellous thing, that ye know not from whence he is, and yet he hath opened mine eyes.

31 Now we know that God heareth not sinners ; but if any man be a worshipper of God, and doeth his will, him he heareth.

32 Since the world began was it not heard that any man opened the eyes of one that was born blind.

33 If this man were not of God, he could do nothing.

34 They answered and said unto him, Thou wast altogether born in sins, and dost thou teach us? And they cast him out.

35 Jesus heard that they had cast him out ; and when he had found him, he said unto him, Dost thou believe on the Son of God?

36 He answered and said, Who is he, Lord, that I might believe on him?

37 And Jesus said unto him, Thou hast both seen him, and it is he that talketh with thee.

38 And he said, Lord, I believe. And he worshipped him.

39 ¶ And Jesus said, For judgment I am come into this world, that they which see not might see ; and that they which see might be made blind.

40 And some of the Pharisees which were with him heard these words, and said unto him, Are we blind also?

41 Jesus said unto them. If ye were blind, ye should have no sin : but now ye say, We see ; therefore your sin remaineth.

WE see in these verses *how much wiser the poor some-*

times are than the rich.   The man whom our Lord healed
of his blindness was evidently a person of very humble
condition.   It is written that he was one who "sat and
begged."   (See v. 8.)   Yet he saw things which the
proud rulers of the Jews could not see, and would not
receive.   He saw in our Lord's miracle an unanswerable
proof of our Lord's divine commission.   "If this Man
were not of God," he cries, "He could do nothing."   In
fact from the day of his cure his position was completely
altered.   He had eyes, and the Pharisees were blind.

The same thing may be seen in other places of Scripture.   The servants of Pharaoh saw "the finger of God"
in the plagues of Egypt, when their master's heart was
hardened.   The servants of Naaman saw the wisdom of
Elisha's advice, when their master was turning away in
a rage.   The high, the great, and the noble are often the
last to learn spiritual lessons.   Their possessions and
their position often blind the eyes of their understanding, and keep them back from the kingdom of God.   It
is written that "not many wise men after the flesh, not
many mighty, not many noble, are called." (1 Cor. i. 26.)

The Christian poor man never need be ashamed of
his poverty.   It is a sin to be proud, and worldly-minded,
and unbelieving ; but it is no sin to be poor.   The very
riches which many long to possess are often veils over
the eyes of men's souls, and prevent their seeing Christ.
The teaching of the Holy Ghost is more frequently to
be seen among men of low degree, than among men of
rank and education.   The words of our Lord are continually proved most true: "How hardly shall they that

have riches enter into the kingdom of God."—"Thou hast hid these things from the wise and prudent, and hast revealed them unto babes." (Mark x. 23. Matt. xi. 25.)

We see, secondly, in these verses, *how cruelly and unjustly unconverted men will sometimes treat those who disagree with them.* When the Pharisees could not frighten the blind man who had been cured, they expelled him from the Jewish Church. Because he manfully refused to deny the evidence of his own senses, they excommunicated him and put him to an open shame. They cast him out " as a heathen man and a publican."

The temporal injury that such treatment did to a poor Jew was very great indeed. It cut him off from the outward privileges of the Jewish Church. It made him an object of scorn and suspicion among all true Israelites. But it could do no harm to his soul. That which wicked men bind on earth is not bound in heaven. " The curse causeless shall not come." (Prov. xxvi. 2.)

The children of God in every age have only too frequently met with like treatment. Excommunication, persecution, and imprisonment have generally been favourite weapons with ecclesiastical tyrants. Unable, like the Pharisees, to answer arguments, they have resorted to violence and injustice. Let the child of God console himself with the thought that there is a true Church out of which no man can cast him, and a Church-membership which no earthly power can take away. He only is blessed whom Christ calls blessed ; and he only is accursed whom Christ shall pronounce accursed at the last day.

We see, thirdly, in these verses, *how great is the kind-ness and condescension of Christ*. No sooner was this poor blind man cast out of the Jewish Church than Jesus finds him and speaks words of comfort. He knew full well how heavy an affliction excommunication was to an Israelite, and at once cheered him with kind words. He now revealed Himself more fully to this man than He did to any one except the Samaritan woman. In reply to the question, "Who is the Son of God?" He says plainly, "Thou hast both seen Him, and it is He that talketh with thee."

We have here one among many beautiful illustrations of the mind of Christ. He sees all that His people go through for His sake, and feels for all, from the highest to the lowest. He keeps account of all their losses, crosses, and persecutions. "Are they not all written in His book?" (Psal. lvi. 8.) He knows how to come to their hearts with consolation in their time of need, and to speak peace to them when all men seem to hate them. The time when men forsake us is often the very time when Christ draws near, saying, "Fear thou not; for I am with thee: be not dismayed; for I am thy God: I will strengthen thee: yea, I will help thee; yea, I will uphold thee with the right hand of my righteousness." (Isai. xli. 10.)

We see, lastly, in these verses, *how dangerous it is to possess knowledge, if we do not make a good use of it*. The rulers of the Jews were fully persuaded that they knew all religious truth. They were indignant at the very idea of being ignorant and devoid of spiritual eyesight. "Are we blind also?" they cried. And then came the solemn sentence, "If ye were blind, ye should have no sin: but now ye say, We see; therefore your sin remaineth."

Knowledge undoubtedly is a very great blessing. The man who cannot read, and is utterly ignorant of Scripture, is in a pitiable condition. He is at the mercy of any false teacher who comes across him, and may be taught to take up any absurd creed, or to follow any vicious practice. Almost any education is better than no education at all.

But when knowledge only sticks in a man's head, and has no influence over his heart and life, it becomes a most perilous possession. And when, in addition to this, its possessor is self-conceited and self-satisfied, and fancies he knows everything, the result is one of the worst states of soul into which man can fall. There is far more hope about him who says, "I am a poor blind sinner and want God to teach me," than about him who is ever saying, "I know it, I know it, I am not ignorant," and yet cleaves to his sins.—The sin of that man "remaineth."

Let us use diligently whatever religous knowledge we possess, and ask continually that God would give us more. Let us never forget that the devil himself is a creature of vast head-knowledge, and yet none the better for it, because it is not rightly used. Let our constant prayer be that which David so often sent up in the hundred and nineteenth Psalm, "Lord, teach me Thy statutes:—give me understanding:—unite my heart to fear Thy name."

26.—[*Then said they...How opened...eyes.*] The enemies of our Lord renewed their examination of the healed man, by inquiries into the manner in which our Lord had opened his eyes. Their previous inquiry had been directed to the point, "Who had done the miracle?" They now ask "How it was done?"

The folly of wicked men comes out remarkably in this renewed examination. Had they let the matter drop at this point, they would not have exposed their own malevolent and unreasoning spirit. They madly rush on headlong, and are put to open shame by a poor and humble Jew.

Let it be noted, that the word we have translated "then," is not so strong in the Greek, and does not mark time, but simply connects the verse with the preceding one. "And they said to him again."

Let it be noted, that faith only looks to the *result*, and does not trouble itself about the *manner* in which it is brought about. Unbelief, on the contrary, refuses to look at the *result*, and excuses itself by raising difficulties about the *manner*.

Let it be noted that in every age Satan never so completely outwits himself and defeats his own purpose, as when he presses persecution and annoyance against weak Christians. Hundreds learn lessons under the pressure of incessant attacks, which otherwise they would never learn at all. The very fact of being attacked calls out latent thought, energy, and courage.

27.—*He answered them, etc.*] The patience of the healed man evidently began to be exhausted at this stage of the proceedings. This senseless repetition of questions, this redoubled effort to make him disbelieve his own senses, became more than he could bear. He seems to say, "I have told the whole story once, and I have nothing to add to it. Yet when I told it, you evidently did not listen to me. What is the use of telling it again? Why do you want to hear it a second time?"—"Ye would not hear," is of course equivalent to "ye would not believe."

The expressions "would ye" and "will ye," are both the same verb in the Greek, and would be more literally rendered as a distinct verb, "do ye will."

The last clause can hardly be taken in any other sense than a sarcastic one. It could hardly be a grave question. It was the natural sarcastic remark of a man wearied, irritated, and provoked by a long-drawn teazing repetition of questions. "One might almost think, from your repeated anxious questions, that you yourselves want to be Christ's disciples."

Chrysostom remarks, "How strong is truth, and how weak is falsehood! Truth, though she take hold only of ordinary men, maketh them appear glorious; falsehood, even with the strong, makes them appear weak."

28.—[*Then they reviled him, etc.*] Here we see how one sharp word leads to another. Sarcasm from the lips of the healed man, produces abuse and reviling from his examiners. They were evidently indignant at the very idea of such wise men as they becoming disciples of Jesus. "Thou, poor ignorant creature, and such as thou, art disciples of Jesus. But we are not such fools. We are disciples of Moses, and want no other teacher." And yet in their blindness they did not see, and would not understand, that Jesus was the very Saviour of whom Moses had written, and that every true disciple of Moses must necessarily be a disciple of Jesus. So easy it is to talk high-sounding ignorant phrases in religion, and yet be utterly in the dark!

Brentius remarks how ready men are to maintain that they hold the old religion of their fathers, while in reality they do not know what it was. Thus the Pharisees talked of Moses, as if Moses was contrary to Christ. The Romanist does just the same when he talks of the "old religion." He knows not what the old religion was.

Ferus points out how many of the words of Moses' law these men forgot and despised, even while they boasted of being his "disciples;" as Levit. xix. 14; Exod. xxiii. 7.

29.—[*We know that God spake, etc.*] The meaning of this sentence seems to be, "We know that God commissioned Moses to be a lawgiver and teacher, and that, in following Moses, we are pleasing God. But as for this Jesus, we know not who has commissioned Him, or who sent Him to teach, or by what authority He preaches and works miracles. In a word, we see no proof that He has come from God. We are not satisfied that He has any Divine commission."

The expression "from whence He is," in this place cannot be interpreted as meaning "from what place." It must signify our Lord's commission,—who sent Him, and by whose authority He acts. So in another place, "the baptism of John, whence was it?" (Luke xx. 4), means "whence had it authority?"

We should note here, how firmly implanted it was in the Jewish mind that Moses had received a revelation from God. "God spake unto Moses."

30.—[*The man answered, etc.*] In this verse the healed man begins a simple, yet unanswerable argument, which completely silenced his examiners.—"There is something very wonderful in this. It is an unmistakable fact that this Person has opened my eyes. He has, in short, worked an astonishing miracle; and yet, in the face of this miracle, you say that you do not know whence He is, or who gave Him His power."

The word "ye," is here emphatical. "You, who are learned men, and rulers, and teachers, might have been expected to know whence this man comes."

31.—[*Now we know that, etc.*] In this verse the healed man continues his chain of reasoning.—"We all know, and it is an admitted principle among us, that God does not hear the prayer of wicked people, and give wicked people power to work miracles. The only people whom He hears and enables to do great works, are people who fear God, and habitually do God's will."

The expression "now," in this verse, perhaps conveys too strong an idea of the meaning of the Greek word. The sentence would be more literally rendered, "and we know;" and would thus simply carry on one unbroken chain of argument.

The principle that "God heareth not sinners," is here stated by the man as a great incontrovertible doctrine, which all Jews knew and admitted. It is hardly necessary to say that it did not mean that God is unwilling to hear the prayers of sinners who feel their sins, and cry to Him for pardon. It applies to sinners who do not feel their sins, and are living in sin, and are impenitent. Such persons God does not look on with favour, and will not enable to do miracles. That God will not hear impenitent sinners, is taught in such texts as Job xxxvii. 9; xxxv. 12; Psalm xviii. 41; xxxiv. 15; lxvi. 18; Prov. i. 28; xv. 29; xxviii. 9; Isa. l. 15; Jer. xi. 11; xiv. 12; Ezek. viii. 18; Micah iii. 4; Zech. vii. 13. The Pharisees knew this, and could not possibly deny it.

The expression "a worshipper of God," means something far more than mere outward worship. It is equivalent to a God-fearing man,—one who really honours and reverences God.

The expression "doeth His will," means one who habitually lives in the practice of God's preceptive will,—the things that God commands.

Brentius illustrates this verse by contrasting God's readiness to hear Elijah when he worked a miracle on Carmel, with the useless cries of the worshippers of Baal on the same occasion.

Ecolampadius observes, that hitherto the healed man evidently saw nothing higher in our Lord than a very good man, whose prayers God would hear. He did not yet see in Him one who wrought miracles by His own Divine power.

Musculus observes, that it is the man who not only "knows" God's will, but practically "does" it, and obeys it, whom God hears.

32, 33.—[*Since the world began, etc.*] These two verses contain the conclusion of the healed man's argument. The sense is as follows . "To open the eyes of one born blind, is a work so entirely beyond the power of man, that no man has ever done it since the world began. Divine power alone could effect it. But this Man has done this work, and therefore must evidently be one sent and commissioned by God. If He were not of God He could do nothing miraculous, and at any rate nothing so miraculous as my cure."

The expression "since the world began," would be more literally rendered, "from the age of the world:" *i.e.*, from the beginning of. It is like Acts iii. 21, and xv. 18, and Ephes. iii. 9.

The concluding argument of the healed man is precisely that of Nicodemus, when he came to our Lord by night. "No man can do these miracles except God be with him." (John iii. 2.)

Augustine remarks, "This was frankly, firmly, and truly spoken. These things that were done by the Lord, how should they be done by any but God?"

Brentius shows here the value of miracles as an evidence of Christ's Divine mission. He also shows that the miracles so-called, said to be worked by magicians and false teachers, are either impositions, or else are wrought in support of something contrary to Scripture, and are therefore not worthy of attention. He finally remarks, that if we are not to believe an angel speaking against the Gospel, much less should we believe a miracle, if worked to confirm something contrary to Scripture.

Toletus remarks that at any rate there is no case in Scripture of any open sinner procuring a miracle to be worked in reply to his prayer.

Whitby remarks, "We see here a blind man and unlearned, judging more rightly of Divine things than the whole learned Council of the Pharisees! Hence we learn that we are not always to be led by the authority of councils, popes, or bishops, and that it is not absurd for laymen sometimes to vary from their opinions, these great overseers being sometimes guilty of great over-sights."

There is no weight in the objection raised by some modern German critics, that eminent surgeons have effected the restoration of sight to people born blind. If they have, it has certainly never been done instantaneously, and without the use of outward means, as in this man's case.

34.—[*They answered, etc.*] The argument of the healed man was one which the Pharisees felt to be unanswerable. Silenced before the whole Council they turn on the speaker with anger and abuse. "Thou art a miserable wicked creature, entirely born in sin, and dost thou pretend to know better than us, and to teach us?" They then proceeded at once to excommunicate him. The expression "they cast him out," must surely mean much more than merely turning him out of the room or place where they were assembled. To my mind it means nothing less than a formal expulsion from the commonwealth of Israel, and the consequent degradation of the man. It must be admitted that Maldonatus and some others think it only means that "they turned him out of the room" where they were. But this does not agree with the context, and almost all commentators think "excommunication" is meant.

It is held by many that the expression, "born in sin," was used with special reference to the healed man's old infirmity of blindness. "Thy very blindness shows thee to have been a very wicked man. It is God's stamp on thy wickedness. Body and soul are both polluted by sin." There may be a latent reference to the vulgar error referred to at verse 2, that blindness was an evidence of God's special displeasure.

The expression, "Dost thou teach us?" is precisely one of those which wicked people in possession of place, rank, dignity, and income, are fond of using about Reformers of the Church and independent thinkers.—"How can such an ignorant person as you pretend to know better than us, and teach us. We are high in office, and must know better than you!"

Let us note that this resort to personal abuse and violent language is often a sure mark of a failing cause in religion. Inability to reply to argument is often the true cause of ill-temper and personalities. Truth can afford to be patient; error cannot.

Let us note that persecution and excommunication are common weapons with the enemies of spiritual religion. When men cannot answer arguments they often try to silence and intimidate those who use them.

The dread of excommunication with a Jew was second only to the dread of death.

Calvin remarks, "It is certain that those who are not subject to Christ are deprived of the lawful power of excommunicating. Nor ought we to dread being excluded from their assemblies, since Christ, our Life and Salvation, was banished from them."

Musculus observes that this excommunication could not have been without the vote of the majority of the Council. Truth is too often with minorities.

Pellican remarks that "to be shut out from the communion of the wicked is no dishonour or loss."

Ferus, a Romanist, says that this verse should teach the leaders of Churches not to be hasty in excommunicating people, lest they commit as great mistake as the Pharisees.

Barradius, a Portuguese Romanist, makes strong remarks here on the great sin of unjust excommunication. He quotes the text in Samuel which says that the sons of Eli made men "abhor the offering of the Lord;" and applies to the same point the text in Canticles where the bride complains that the keeper and watchmen who ought to have helped, "smote and wounded her."

Quesnel remarks that wicked pastors are always impatient that any one should remind them of their duty.

Lightfoot observes that this man was the first confessor who suffered for Christ's sake, as John the Baptist was the first martyr.

Trench observes that the Pharisees in their rage forgot "that the two charges,—one, that the man had not been born blind and was an impostor; the other, that he bore the mark of God's anger in blindness reaching back to his birth,—will not agree together."

35.—[*Jesus heard...cast him out.*] An interval of time most probably elapsed between the last verse and the present one. Where our Lord was, at Jerusalem or elsewhere, and what He was doing during the interval, we are not told. We can hardly suppose that the events related in the present and following verses, and the former part of the tenth chapter, took place on the same day that the blind man was cured. There must have been a break. Moreover the very expression before us shows that the excommunication had had time to be reported and known in Jerusalem. Making every allowance for the public notoriety of everything done by the Sanhedrim, we can hardly suppose that in a day when there was no newspaper, the treatment of the blind man would be public news and reported without some interval of time.

As God, our Lord doubtless knew all that happened to the sufferer, but He did nothing till his excommunication was publicly reported.

Burkitt observes, "O happy man! Having lost the synagogue, he finds heaven."

Wordsworth observes, "If those who sit in Moses' seat teach things contrary to the law of Moses, and proceed to impose their false doctrines as terms of communion, if they will not receive Him of whom Moses wrote, and threaten with excommunication those who confess Jesus to be the Christ, then no desire of unity, no love of enemies, no fear of separation from parents and spiritual superiors, no dread of spiritual censures and penalties, must deter the disciples of Christ from confessing Him. Our Lord Himself has set the seal of His divine sanction on these principles."

[*And when He had found, etc.*] We should note in this sentence our Lord's kindness and compassion. As soon as His people suffer for His name's sake He is ready to visit them and speak words of comfort and give special consolation. We see too an example of His zeal to turn temporal trials to spiritual gain. Like Him, we should be ready to say to sufferers, "Dost thou believe on the Son of God? The world fails thee. Turn to Christ, and seek rest."

Chrysostom remarks, "They who for the sake of the truth and confession of Christ suffer anything and are insulted, these are especially honoured. So it was here with the blind man. The Jews cast him out of the temple, and the Lord of the temple found him. He was dishonoured by those who dishonoured Christ, and was honoured by the Lord of angels."

We should note that this is one of the very few occasions on which our Lord called Himself directly "the Son of God." (See John iii. 18; v. 25; x. 36; xi. 4.)

The word "thou" here is emphatic. "Others are unbelieving. Dost thou believe?"

36.—[*He answered and said, etc.*] This is the language of a mind ignorant of many things, yet willing to be instructed. It is like Saul crying, "Who art Thou, Lord?" and the jailer saying, "What must I do?" When a man begins to inquire about Christ, and ask who He is, it is always a hopeful symptom of his state of soul.

It may be doubted whether "Lord" here would not have been better rendered "Sir."

Chrysostom says, "The expression is that of a longing, inquiring soul."

37.—[*And Jesus said, etc.*] We should carefully notice the extraordinary fulness of the revelation which our Lord here made of Himself. In no case but this, and that of the Samaritan woman, do we find Him so unreservedly declaring His own Divinity and Messiahship. So true is it that "the meek He will guide in judgment," and that things "hid to the wise and prudent are revealed to babes." The poor and despised and friendless among mankind are often those whom He favours with special revelations of His kindness and mercy. (John iv. 26. Matt. v. 10—12.)

38.—[*And he said, Lord, I believe.*] This immediate profession of faith seems to indicate that the man's mind had been somewhat prepared by the Holy Ghost during the interval of time since his cure. The more he thought over his miraculous healing, and the Person who had wrought it, the more ready he was to believe in Him as the Messiah.

We must not, however, estimate too highly the extent of this man's faith. At any rate it had the germ and nucleus of all justifying faith about it,—a belief in our Lord as the Messiah.

[*And he worshipped Him.*] This seems to have been something more than an action of respect and reverence to a man. It looks like the worship given to One who was felt to be very God. Our Lord accepts it, and says not one word to check it. We cannot suppose that Paul or Peter or John would have allowed a fellowman to give them "worship." (See Acts x. 25, 26, and xiv. 14, 15 ; Rev. xix. 10, and xxii. 9.)

Chrysostom remarks how few of those whom our Lord miraculously healed, worshipped Him as this man did.

Cocceius remarks that when we consider that this act of worship follows immediately on a full profession of faith in Jesus as the "Son of God," it cannot be lightly passed over as a mere mark of respect.

Ferus observes that there is a thing said of this worshipper which is said of no one else who "worshipped" Christ. He said, "I believe," before he did it, and I believe in the "Son of God."

Poole observes that "although the word 'worshipped' in the Greek be a word used sometimes to signify that civil respect which men show to their superiors, yet it cannot be so interpreted in this place, considering what went before."

39.—[*And Jesus said, For judgment, etc.*] We must not suppose that there is any contradiction between these words and those in John iii. 17, and xii. 47. It was quite true that our Lord had not come into the world to be a Judge, but a Saviour. Yet He had come to produce a judgment, or distinction, or division between class and class of characters, and to be the cause of light breaking in on some minds which before His coming could not see, and of blindness covering other minds which before His coming flattered themselves that they were full of light. In this the expression is very parallel to that of Simeon (Luke ii. 35), "The thoughts of many hearts were revealed by His coming." Humble-minded ignorant people had light revealed to them. Proud self-righteous people were given over to judicial blindness. (See Matt. xi. 25.)

And is not this judgment a common consequence of Christ's Gospel coming to a place or a people for the first time ? Minds previously quite dead receive sight. Minds previously self-satisfied and proud of their own light are given over to utter darkness and left behind. Those who once saw not, see. Those who fancied themselves clear-sighted are found blind. The same fire which melts wax hardens the clay.

Let it be noted that the Greek word rendered "might be made" would be more literally translated "might become." I do not mean to say that in no case does God ever give over people to blindness, by a kind of judgment, on account of their hardness and impenitence. But we should carefully observe how rarely Scripture speaks of it as God's act. Thus here it is not literally true that He "*makes*" them blind, but that they "*became*" blind.

Augustine remarks, "Who are those that see ? Those who think they see, who believe they see." He also says, "The judgment which Christ hath brought into the world is not that wherewith He shall judge the quick and the dead in the end of the world. It is a work of discrimination rather, by which He discerneth the cause of them which believe from that of ᵗʰᵉ ...d who think they see, and therefore are worse blinded."

Zwingle remarks, "Judgment is here taken for discrimination, or separation into classes." Ferus says much the same.

Chemnitius thinks that our Lord spoke these words with special reference to the false and unjust judgment of excommunication, which the Pharisees had just passed. It is as though He would say, "True judgment, a right discrimination into classes, is my prerogative. The excommunication of a Pharisee is worthless."

Musculus and Gualter think that "judgment" here means the

eternal decree of God.   "I came into the world to carry out God's
eternal purposes, which are that the wise and prudent should
remain in darkness, truth should be revealed to babes."   But this
seems far-fetched.

Poole says, "The best notion of 'judgment' here is their's who
interpret it of the spiritual government of the world, committed
to Christ, and managed by Him with perfect rectitude and equity.
One eminent part of this was His publishing the Gospels, the law
of faith.   The result of which is, that many spiritually blind, and
wholly unable to see the way to eternal life, might be enlightened
with saving knowledge, and that many who think they see should
by their obstinate infidelity become more blind than they were
from their birth.   Not that I cast any such evil influence on them,
but this happeneth through their own sore eyes."

Whitby remarks that the Greek conjunction here rendered
"that" is not causal, but only consequential; as when Christ
said, "I came not to send peace, but a sword," meaning, the consequence and result of my coming will be to send a sword, and
not the object of my coming.   He also thinks that the verse
has a wide application to the Gentiles sitting in darkness being
enlightened by Christ's coming, while the Jews were blinded.

Hengstenberg says, "Those that see are the Jews, in contradistinction to the Gentiles."

Burgon remarks, "Judgment is not used here in an active sense.
It is the condemnation implied by severing men into good and bad,
which was one consequence (not the purpose) of Christ's coming
into the world.—When Christ came into the world, men promptly
showed themselves to belong to the state of darkness or of light,
and by their arranging themselves in two great classes, anticipated
their own final sentence."—"The blind (that is, simple and ignorant, yet meek and faithful men) saw; while the seeing (that is,
vain pretenders to discernment, proud presumptuous persons)
were made blind."

40.—[*And some.. Pharisees...heard words.*]   This sentence literally
rendered would be, "Those of the Pharisees who were with Him
heard."   It seems to show that here, as on all other occasions,
some of the party of the Pharisees were in the crowd which hung
round our Lord, narrowly watching all He said and did, and
eagerly catching at anything which might give them an advantage
against Him.   It ought to make us feel the immense difficulty of
our Lord's position.   He was always attended by enemies, and

spoke and acted under the eyes of people desiring to do Him harm. It also teaches us that we must not cease from efforts to do good, because many of our hearers are unbelieving.

[*And said...Are we blind also?*] This question cannot possibly be taken as a humble, anxious inquiry. It is rather the sarcastic, sneering inquiry of men whose consciences were pricked by our Lord's words, and who felt that He was condemning them : "And in what class do you place us? Are we among those whom you call blind? Do you mean to say that we, who are Doctors of the Law, see and understand nothing?"—St. Paul's words to the un-believing Jew should be remembered here : "Thou art confident that thou art a guide of the blind, a light of them which are in darkness." (Rom. ii. 17.) Blindness was probably the last thing which the Pharisees would allow could be predicated of them.

Augustine remarks, "There are many, who according to common usage, are called good people, good men, good women, harmless, honouring their parents, not committing adultery, doing no murder, not stealing, not bearing false witness, and in a sort observing the other duties commanded in the law, and yet are not Christians. And these commonly give themselves airs like the Pharisees here, saying, 'Are we blind also?'"

Ferus observes, "This is just the ancient arrogance of the Jews."

Jones of Nayland makes the pious remark, "Give us, O Lord, the sight of this man who had been blind from birth, and deliver us from the blindness of his judges, who had been learning all their lives, and yet knew nothing. And if the world should cast us out, let us be found of Thee, whom the world crucified."

41.—[*Jesus said unto them, etc.*] Our Lord's answer to the Pharisees is a very remarkable and elliptical one. It may be thus para-phrased : "Well would it be for you, if you were really blind and ignorant. If you were really ignorant, you would be far less blameworthy than you are now. If you were really blind, you would not be guilty of the sin of wilful unbelief, as you are now. But unhappily, you say that you know the truth, and see the light, and are not ignorant, even while you are rejecting Me. This self-satisfied state of mind is the very thing which is ruining you. It makes your sin abide heavily on you."

It is almost needless to say that our Lord did not mean that ignor-ance makes a man entirely free from guilt. He only meant that a really ignorant man is much less guilty than one who has light and knowledge, but does not improve and use them. No man's case is so hopeless as that of the self-confident man, who says that he knows everything, and wants no light. Such a man's sin abides on him, and, unless repented of, will sink him into the pit.

Let us note what a heavy condemnation this text contains for those professing Christians who are constantly comforting themselves by saying, "We know," "We are not ignorant," "We see the truth," while yet they lazily sit still in irreligion, and make no attempt to obey. Such persons, however little they think it, are far more guilty before God than the poor heathen who never hear truth at all. The more light a man has, the more sin, if he does not believe.

To infer the salvation of all the unconverted heathen from this text would be unwarrantable, and going much too far. The worst heathen man has sufficient light to judge and condemn him at last, and far more than he lives up to. But it is not too much to say that an ignorant heathen is in a far more hopeful condition than a proud, self-satisfied, self-righteous, unconverted Christian.

Brentius thinks that the expression, "if ye were blind," means "if ye would confess your blindness," and that "to say we see," is equivalent to a "refusal to acknowledge ignorance and need."

Chemnitius observes that the expression of this verse teaches that there are two sorts of sinners in this world,—those who sin from ignorance and infirmity, and those who sin against light and knowledge, and that they must be regarded and dealt with accordingly.

Musculus remarks, that nothing seems to gall men so much as the imputation of ignorance and want of knowledge of the truth. The very men who are unmoved if charged with immoral actions, such as simony, adultery, gluttony, or misuse of ecclesiastical property, are furious if told that they are dark and blind about *doctrine*.

The expression "your sin remaineth," is very worthy of notice. It teaches the solemn truth that the sins of impenitent and unconverted people are upon them, unforgiven, and not taken away. It condemns the modern idea that all sins are already forgiven and pardoned on account of Christ's death, and all men justified, and that the only thing required is to believe it and know it. On the contrary our sins are upon us, and remain upon us until we believe. Ferus calls it "a terrible saying."

Tholuck remarks on the whole chapter, "The narrative of this miracle has a special value in apologetics. How often do we hear the wish expressed, that Christ's miracles had been put on documentary record, and had been subjected to a thorough judicial investigation. Here we have the very thing that is desired : judicial personages, and these, too, the avowed enemies of Christ, investigate a miracle in repeated hearings, and yet it holds its ground. A man blind from his birth was made to see ! "—No wonder that German sceptics, like Strauss and Bauer, are driven to assert that the whole narrative is a fabrication.

In leaving this chapter, it is worth remembering that this is that one of our Lord's miracles about which nearly all commentators have agreed that it has a spiritual signification, and is emblematic of spiritual truth. Lampe remarks, that even those writers who are ordinarily most averse to spiritualizing and accommodating, admit that the healing of this blind man is a picture of the illumination of a sinner's soul. His healing is a lively figure of conversion.

It is curious that we hear no more of this man who was healed. It is pleasant, however, to bear in mind the thought that there were many who believed in Christ and were true disciples, whose names and lives have never come down to us. We must not suppose that there were none saved but those whose histories are recorded in the New Testament.—The last day, we may well believe, will show that this man was only a type of a large class, whose names were written in the Book of Life, though not recorded for our learning by the inspired writers.

JOHN X. 1—9.

1 Verily, verily, I say unto you, He that entereth not by the door into the sheepfold, but climbeth up some other way, the same is a thief and a robber.

2 But he that entereth in by the door is the shepherd of the sheep.

3 To him the porter openeth ; and the sheep hear his voice : and he calleth his own sheep by name, and leadeth them out.

4 And when he putteth forth his own sheep, he goeth before them, and the sheep follow him : for they know his voice.

5 And a stranger will they not follow, but will flee from him : for they know not the voice of strangers.

6 This parable spake Jesus unto them : but they understood not what things they were which he spake unto them.

7 Then said Jesus unto them again, Verily, verily, I say unto you, I am the door of the sheep.

8 All that ever came before me are thieves and robbers : but the sheep did not hear them.

9 I am the door : by me if any man enter in, he shall be saved, and shall go in and out, and find pasture.

THE chapter we have now begun is closely connected with the preceding one. The parable before us was

spoken with direct reference to the blind teachers of
the Jewish Church. The Scribes and Pharisees were
the persons our Lord had in view, when He described
the false shepherd. The very men who had just said
"We see," were denounced with holy boldness, as
"thieves and robbers."

We have, for one thing, in these verses, *a vivid picture
of a false teacher of religion.* Our Lord says that he is
one who "enters not by the door into the sheepfold, but
climbs up some other way."

The "door," in this sentence, must evidently mean
something far more than outward calling and commission.
The Jewish teachers, at any rate, were not deficient in
this point: they could probably trace up their orders
in direct succession to Aaron himself. Ordination is no
proof whatever that a man is fit to show others the way
to heaven. He may have been regularly set apart by
those who have authority to call ministers, and yet all
his life may never come near the door, and at last may
die nothing better than "a thief and a robber."

The true sense of the "door," must be sought in our
Lord's own interpretation. It is Christ Himself who
is "the door." The true shepherd of souls is he who
enters the ministry with a single eye to Christ, desiring
to glorify Christ, doing all in the strength of Christ,
preaching Christ's doctrine, walking in Christ's steps,
and labouring to bring men and women to Christ. The
false shepherd of souls is he who enters the ministerial
office with little or no thought about Christ, from worldly
and self-exalting motives, but from no desire to exalt

Jesus, and the great salvation that is in Him. Christ, in one word, is the grand touchstone of the minister of religion. The man who makes much of Christ is a pastor after God's own heart, whom God delights to honour. The minister who makes little of Christ is one whom God regards as an impostor,—as one who has climbed up to his holy office not by the door, but by "some other way."

The sentence before us is a sorrowful and humbling one. That it condemns the Jewish teachers of our Lord's time, all men can see. There was no "door" in their ministry. They taught nothing rightly about Messiah. They rejected Christ Himself when He appeared.—But all men do not see that the sentence condemns thousands of so-called Christian teachers, quite as much as the leaders and teachers of the Jews. Thousands of ordained men in the present day know nothing whatever about Christ, except His name. They have not entered "the door" themselves, and they are unable to show it to others. Well would it be for Christendom if this were more widely known, and more seriously considered! Unconverted ministers are the dry-rot of the Church. When "the blind lead the blind," both must fall into the ditch. If we would know the value of a man's ministry, we must never fail to ask, Where is the Lamb? Where is the Door? Does he bring forward Christ, and give Him his rightful place?

We have, for another thing, in these verses, a *peculiar picture of true Christians.* Our Lord describes them as sheep who "hear the voice of a true Shepherd, and know His voice;" and as "sheep who will not follow a stranger, but will flee from him, for they know not the voice of strangers."

The thing taught in these words is a very curious one, and may seem "foolishness" to the world. There is a spiritual instinct in most true believers, which generally enables them to distinguish between true and false teaching. When they hear unsound religious instruction, there is something within them which says, "This is wrong." When they hear the real truth as it is in Jesus, there is something in their hearts which responds, "This is right." The careless man of the world may see no difference whatever between minister and minister, sermon and sermon. The poorest sheep of Christ, as a general rule, will "distinguish things that differ," though he may sometimes be unable to explain why.

Let us beware of despising this spiritual instinct. Whatever a sneering world may please to say, it is one of the peculiar marks of the indwelling of the Holy Ghost. As such, it is specially mentioned by St. John, when he says, " Ye have an unction from the Holy One, and ye know all things." (1 John ii. 20.) Let us rather pray for it daily, in order that we may be kept from the influence of false shepherds. To lose all power of distinguishing between bitter and sweet, is one of the worst symptoms of bodily disease. To be unable to see any difference between law and gospel, truth and error, Protestantism and Popery, the doctrine of Christ and the doctrine of man, is a sure proof that we are yet dead in heart, and need conversion.

We have, lastly, in these verses, *a most instructive picture of Christ Himself.* He utters one of those golden sayings which ought to be dear to all true Christians. They apply to people as well as to ministers. " I am the door: by Me if any man enter in, he shall be saved, and shall go in and out, and find pasture."

We are all by nature separate and far off from God. Sin, like a great barrier-wall, rises between us and our Maker. The sense of guilt makes us afraid of Him. The sense of His holiness keeps us at a distance from Him. Born with a heart at enmity with God, we become more and more alienated from Him by practice, the longer we live. The very first questions in religion that must be answered, are these: " How can I draw near to God? How can I be justified? How can a sinner like me be reconciled to my Maker?"

The Lord Jesus Christ has provided an answer to these mighty questions. By His sacrifice for us on the cross, He has opened a way through the great barrier, and provided pardon and peace for sinners. He has "suffered for sin, the just for the unjust, to bring us to God." (1 Pet. iii. 18.) He has opened a way into the holiest, through His blood, by which we may draw near to God with boldness, and approach God without fear. And now He is able to save to the uttermost all who come unto God by Him. In the highest sense He is "the door." No one can " come to the Father " but by Him.

Let us take heed that we use this door, and do not

merely stand outside looking at it. It is a door free and open to the chief of sinners :—" If any man enter in by it, he shall be saved." It is a door within which we shall find a full and constant supply for every want of our souls. We shall find that we can " go in and out," and enjoy liberty and peace. The day comes when this door will be shut for ever, and men shall strive to enter in, but not be able. Then let us make sure work of our own salvation. Let us not stand tarrying without, and halting between two opinions. Let us enter in and be saved.

NOTES. JOHN x. 1—9.

1.—[*Verily...I say...you.*] Three things must be carefully remembered, if we would rightly understand the first nine verses of this chapter. Inattention to them has caused much confused and inconsistent interpretation.

(*a*) For one thing, the passage is closely connected with the last chapter. The opening sentence should be read on, without break or separation between, together with the forty-first verse of the ninth chapter. Our Lord is still speaking to the hostile Pharisees who asked, " Are we blind also ? " and got the answer, " Ye say, We see ; therefore your sin remaineth."—It is to them that He goes on to say, " I say unto *you*, He that entereth not in by the door, is a thief and a robber." He is not so much comforting His disciples now, as rebuking and exposing His enemies.

(*b*) For another thing, the passage is entirely a parable, or allegory. (See sixth verse.) In interpreting it, like almost all our Lord's parables, the one great lesson should be kept in view, which is the key-note to the whole. We must not press every detail and little point too far, and try to attach a spiritual meaning to the lesser parts of the picture. Those who do so always run aground in their exposition, and get into difficulties. To this parable, if any, the old quaint sayings are applicable : " No parable stands on four legs."—" Squeeze parables too far, and you will draw blood from them, and not milk."

Calvin remarks wisely, " It is useless to scrutinize too closely

every part of this parable.   Let us rest satisfied with this general
view, that as Christ states a resemblance between the Church and
a fold (a sheephold, in which God assembles all His people), so He
compares Himself to a door, because there is no other entrance
into the Church but by Himself.   Then it follows that they are
good shepherds, who lead men straight to Christ ; and that they
are truly gathered into Christ's fold, so as to belong to His flock,
who devote themselves to Christ alone."

(c) For another thing, the object that our Lord had in view, in
speaking this parable, must be kept steadily before our eyes.   That
object was to show the entire unfitness of the Pharisees to be pastors and teachers of the Jews, because they had not taken up their
office in the right spirit, and with a right understanding of the
work they had to do.   He is not in this part speaking of Himself
as "the Shepherd," but as "the Door :" only as the Door.
What Christ is as a "Shepherd," comes afterward ; what Christ is
as "the Door," is the one point of the first nine verses.

The "progressive" character of our Lord's discourses recorded in
St. John, is strikingly illustrated in this chapter.   Starting from a
very simple statement, our Lord goes on to speak of the highest
truths.   We see the same in the fourth, fifth, and sixth chapters.

This is one of the twenty-four places in St. John's Gospel, where
the double "verily" comes in.   Here, as elsewhere, it always
prefaces some statement of more than ordinary importance and
solemnity.

[*He that entereth not, etc.*]   Our Lord here appeals to the
common experience of His hearers.   They all knew well that any
one who was seen entering a sheepfold by climbing over the wall
or fence of enclosure, and not by going through the door, would
be justly suspected of being a thief.   Every true shepherd, as a
matter of course, makes use of the door.

The "door" He afterwards interprets to mean Himself.   The
latent thought evidently is, that any teacher of religion who does
not take up and discharge his office with faith in Christ and His
atonement, and with an aim to glorify Christ, is unfit for his
business, and unable to do any good.   Instead of being a shepherd
who helps and feeds, he is no better than a "robber," who does
harm.   Instead of saving souls, he kills them.   Instead of bringing
life, he brings death to his hearers.

Some, as Chrysostom, Euthymius, Theophylact, Maldonatus,
think the "door" means the Scriptures.   Others, as Tholuck and

Hengstenberg, think the "door" means a proper divine call to office. Both views seem to me unnatural and incorrect.

Augustine observes, "Christ's fold is the Catholic Church. Whoso would enter the fold, let him enter in by the door: let him preach very Christ. Let him not only preach very Christ, but seek Christ's glory, not his own."—He says, again, "I, seeking to enter into your hearts, preach Christ: if I preach other than that, I shall be striving to climb in some other way. Christ is my Door: through Christ I win your hearts."

Language borrowed from the care of sheep and sheepfolds, would be much more intelligible in Palestine than it is in England. Keeping sheep was much more common there than in our climate. Folds, doors, shepherds, thieves climbing over some other way, would be points familiar to most Jews. Moreover, the use of such language in speaking of spiritual things, would be peculiarly intelligible to all who had read Jer. xxiii., Ezek. xxxiv., and Zech. xi.

Brentius remarks on the condescension of our Lord in borrowing spiritual lessons from such humble sources: "What is more low than a shepherd's condition? Every shepherd is an abomination to the Egyptians. What more dull and stupid than a sheep? Yet here is a picture of Christ and believers!

Sir Isaac Newton, in his book on Daniel, supposes that our Lord, in choosing the subject of this parable, had before His eyes the many sheepfolds near the temple and about Jerusalem, where sheep were kept ready to be sold for sacrifice.

The expression, "some other way," seems to me purposely very wide. Men may become teachers of the Church from many different motives, and in many different frames of mind. Some may be sceptical, some formalists, some worldly; but all alike are wrong, if they do not enter office "through the Door:" viz., by Christ.

The word rendered "the same," would be more literally translated, "that man."

The expression, "thief and robber," is very strong, and supplies a striking instance of the use of a parable to convey indirectly a sharp and severe rebuke. Of course our Lord could hardly have said to the Pharisees, "You are thieves and robbers." Yet by use of a parable, He says what is tantamount to it.

Let it be noted that these strong epithets show plainly that there are times when it is right to rebuke sharply. Flattering everybody, and complimenting all teachers who are zealous and earnest, without reference to their soundness in the faith, is not according to Scripture. Nothing seems so offensive to Christ as a false teacher of religion, a false prophet, or a false shepherd. Nothing ought to be so much dreaded in the Church, and if needful, to be so plainly rebuked, opposed, and exposed. The strong language of our Reformers, when writing against Romish teachers, is often blamed more than it ought to be.

The Greek word rendered "thief," implies secret fraud and dishonesty. The word rendered "robber," implies more open violence. There are false teachers of both sorts: open Papists and open Sceptics, semi-Papists and semi-Sceptics. All are alike dangerous.

Augustine observes, "Let the Pagans, the Jews, the heretics say, 'We lead a good life.' If they enter not by the door, what availeth it? A good life only profiteth if it lead to life eternal. Indeed, those cannot be said to lead a good life, who are either blindly ignorant of, or wilfully despise the end of good living. No one can hope for eternal life who knows not Christ, who is the life, and by that door enters the fold."

Hammond alone among commentators applies this verse and the four following entirely to Christ Himself, and considers "the door" to mean the proper evidence of miracles and doctrine. I cannot see this at all.

Bishop Burnet remarks that this parable is the passage above all others which both Fathers and modern writers have chiefly used, in order to show the difference between good and bad ministers. Wordsworth calls the whole chapter "a divine pastoral to Bishops, priests, and deacons."

2.—[*He that entereth in by the door, etc.*] This verse contains the converse of the preceding verse. He that is seen entering the sheepfold by the one proper entrance, the door, may be set down as a true shepherd. Such a man, being duly commissioned by the owner of the flock, and recognized by the sheep as their pastor and friend, has no need to enter clandestinely, like a thief, or by violence, as a robber.

The word "the" before shepherd, is not in the Greek. It should be simply, "a shepherd." The omission of the article seems intentional, to show that our Lord is describing true "shepherds of sheep" generally, and not Himself.

3.—[*To him...porter openeth, etc.*] The whole of this verse is meant to show the character of a true shepherd of sheep, in four respects. (a) The porter opens the gate to him, knowing by his step and manner of approach, that he is a friend, and not an enemy. (b) The sheep recognise his voice, and attend to what he says. (c) He, knowing all his flock individually, calls each sheep by his own peculiar name. (d) He leads them out to feed, desiring daily to promote their health and well-being. In all these four points, he is unlike the thief and robber.

The different customs of Eastern countries, as compared to our own, must be carefully kept in mind, to understand the expressions of this verse. A fold in Palestine was a space enclosed by high walls, not by low hurdles. It had a gate guarded by a porter at night, as the sheep could not be safely left alone. An Eastern shepherd knows each sheep in his flock, and often has a name for each one. The sheep are led, and not driven.

About "the porter who opens," in this verse, opinions differ. Most commentators hold that the "porter" means the Holy Ghost, who calls true ministers into the Church, and "opens hearts ; and that the sense is, "to a true pastor the Holy Ghost gives a call to his office, and makes a way into the hearts of hearers." This no doubt is excellent divinity, but I cannot think our Lord meant anything of the kind. The "porter" here is not said to call the pastor, but to open when the pastor comes ; nor yet to open hearts, but the door of the fold, through which the true pastor enters.—The view of Wordsworth, also held by Augustine, Rupertus, Bullinger, and Flacius,—that the "porter" is Christ Himself, who is not only "Door," but "Porter" also,— does not appear to me necessary. I prefer, with Glassius, Grotius, Hutcheson, and Bloomfield, regarding the whole sentence as a subordinate feature in the parable, signifying that a true shepherd of sheep not only enters by the lawful door, but that every facility is made for his entrance.

Some, as Chrysostom, Euthymius, and Theophylact, think the "porter" may mean "Moses."

Others, as Ecolampadius, Lampe, Webster, think the "porter" means the ministers and teachers of the Church, who have the power of the keys, and the right to admit pastors.

Others, as Gomarus, Brentius, Maldonatus, Hall, Whitby, Bengel, and Hengstenberg, think the "porter" is God the Father.

The expression "his own sheep," must not be pressed too far. It simply means that a real shepherd, according to Eastern custom, knowing *his own flock* individually by name, calls them at once by their names, and proves his relation to them by so doing. If not his own, he could not do so.

4.—[*And when he putteth forth, etc.*]   This verse is simply a continuation of the description of a true and faithful shepherd of sheep.   Whenever such an one takes his flock out to pasture, he walks before them, as an Eastern shepherd always does, never requiring them to go where he does not first go himself.   Such a shepherd the sheep follow with implicit confidence, and knowing his voice, go wherever he calls them.

The words of Moses should be read : "Let the Lord set a man over the congregation, which may go out before them, and which may go in before them, and which may lead them out, and which may bring them in ; that the congregation of the Lord be not as sheep which have no shepherd." (Num. xxvii. 16, 17.)

That Eastern shepherds "lead" their sheep, is clear from Exod. iii. 1 : "He led the flock ;" and Psalm xxiii. 2 : "He leadeth me."

5 —[*And a stranger will they not follow, etc.*]   This verse concludes the picture of a true shepherd and his flock.   It was a fact well-known to all our Lord's hearers, that sheep accustomed to one shepherd's voice would not obey a stranger's voice, but would rather be frightened at it.   Just so true Christians have a spiritual taste and discernment by which they distinguish a false teacher, and will not hear him.   "Ye have an unction from the Holy One, and know all things." (1 John ii. 20.)   The poor and illiterate believers often illustrate this in a very extraordinary way.

Brentius observes here the singular faculty which sheep possess of always knowing and recognizing the voice of their own shepherd. He also notices the extraordinary knowledge that the lamb has of its own mother's bleat among a thousand others, as a curious characteristic of an animal in many respects dull and stupid.

Scott observes that this verse justifies true Christians in not listening to false teachers.   For leaving their parish church perhaps, under these circumstances, many reproach them.   Yet the very men who reproach them would not trust their worldly affairs to an ignorant and dishonest lawyer, or their bodies to an incompetent doctor !   Can it be wrong to act on the same principles for our souls ?

Besser observes, "Sheep flee from a false shepherd.   They will not say, it is enough if we do not follow this strange preacher in those points in which he holds forth unsound teaching.   They will have nothing at all to do with him. They will flee from him as from a contagious disease." (2 Tim. ii. 17.)

Bickersteth observes that this verse, and the third, throw light on the pastoral office of ministers. "How much of ministerial influence depends on personal knowledge. Great is the hindrance to the influence when an overgrown population renders it impossible."

6.—[*This parable...Jesus...them.*] The word rendered "parable" here hardly bears the sense of the expression. It is rather "allegory," or figurative picture. However, it clearly settles that the whole passage must be taken as a picture of spiritual things, and must be carefully handled, and not interpreted too literally. The Greek word used by John for "parable" is not used in any other Gospel.

[*But they understood not...unto them.*] The Pharisees appear to have failed in seeing the application of the parable. This is curious, when we remember how quickly they saw the application to themselves of the parable of the husbandmen who killed the heir of the vineyard. But nothing seems to blind men's eyes so much as pride of office. Wrapped up in their conceit of their own knowledge and dignity, they did not see that they themselves who pretended to be leaders and teachers of the Jewish flocks were not shepherds, but "thieves and robbers," doing more harm than good. They did not see that the fatal defect in their own qualification for office was ignorance of Christ and want of faith in Him. They did not see that no true sheep of Christ could be expected to hear, follow, or obey their teaching. Above all, they did not see that in excommunicating the poor blind man whom our Lord had healed, they were just proving themselves to be "thieves and robbers," and injuring one whom they ought to have helped.

If even One who "spake as never man spake" was not always understood, ministers cannot be surprised if they find they are often not understood now. How little of a sermon is understood, few preachers have the least idea!

Ferus remarks that our Lord's hearers must have been blind not to see that their own prophet Ezekiel had already shown the application of the parable. (Chap. xxxiv.)

Lampe thinks they knew that our Lord was speaking of them, but could not fully comprehend the application of the parable.

7.—[*Then said Jesus...again.*] Here we see the condescension and patience of our Lord. Seeing His hearers not able to understand Him, He proceeds to explain His meaning more fully. This is an example for all teachers of religion. Without frequent repetition and simplification spiritual lessons can never be taught.

[*Verily verily...you.*] Once more this solemn expression is used, and again to the same hearers, the Pharisees.

[*I am the door of the sheep.*] Here is plain exposition. Jesus here declares that He Himself is the Door through whom, and by faith in whom, both shepherd and sheep must pass, if they would go inside God's fold. "Every single sheep must enter through Me, if he would join God's flock. Every teacher who wishes to be a shepherd over God's flock, must enter his office looking to Me."

This high claim of dignity must have sounded startling to the Pharisees ! A higher claim we can hardly conceive. None but One, even the Divine Messiah, could have used such an expression. No prophet or apostle ever did.

At first sight it seems strange that our Lord says, "I am the Door of the sheep," and not simply "the Door." But I think it is meant to teach that the Door is for the benefit of the sheep more than the shepherd, and that He Himself is given more particularly for all His people than for His ministers. Ministers are only servants. The flock might possibly do without them, but they could not do without the flock.

Bullinger calls attention to the many beautiful figures under which our Lord represented Himself and His office to the Jews, in St. John's writings. The Bread, the Living Water, the Light of the World, the Door, the Shepherd, are all in five chapters of this Gospel.

Musculus observes that the simple view of Christ being "the Door," is that He is the Mediator between God and man.

Webster observes, "It is worthy of remark that in the Sermon on the Mount (Matt. vii. 13—17), the description of the strait gate and narrow way immediately precedes the warning against false prophets and ravening wolves." The same also may be seen here.

8.—[*All that ever came before Me, etc.*] These words, "All, before Me," must evidently be limited or qualified. They cannot be taken in their fullest sense. The prophets and John the Baptist were not thieves and robbers. It cannot well be taken to mean, "All who have claimed to be the Messiah." There is no evidence that many claimants did appear before our Lord, if any. Besides, the word "are," in the present tense, seems to exclude those who lived before our Lord's time.

The great knot of the difficulty lies in the words, "came before Me." The Greek word rendered "before," has only four meanings: (1) before in point of time ; (2) before in point of place ; (3) before in point of dignity and honour ; (4) before in the way of substitution. Of these, the two first seem out of the question, and we are shut up to the two last. I can only conjecture that the sentence must be paraphrased in this way : "All who have come into the Church professing to be teachers, claiming honour for themselves instead of Me, or honouring anything in preference to Me, such as you Pharisees,—all such are not true shepherds, but thieves and robbers." I can see no better solution, and I admit that the sentence is a difficulty.

Some, as Chrysostom and Theophylact, think "thieves and robbers" mean Theudas, Judas of Galilee (Acts v. 36, 37), and others like them.

Euthymius remarks that "all" here must not be taken literally, but is a Hebraism meaning, "Anyone who does not come by Me is a thief," etc.

Theophylact observes that the Manichean heretics wrested this text into a proof of their fanatical view, that the Old Testament prophets were not sent by God !

Luther says, "These thieves and robbers form at all times the great majority in the world, and nothing better can they be as long as they are not in Christ. In fact the world will have such wolf's preaching, and indeed desires no better, because it hears not Christ nor regards Christ. It is no wonder that true Christians and their pastors are so few."

Calvin remarks, "That no man may be moved by the consideration that there have been teachers in all ages who gave themselves no concern whatever about directing men to Christ, Christ expressly states that it is no matter how many there may have been of this description, or how early they began to appear. There is but *one Door*, and all who leave it, and make openings or breaches in the walls, are thieves."

Lightfoot thinks that our Lord refers to the Pharisees, Sadducees, and Essenes, who had long misled the Jews before Christ came, and that they were the three false shepherds whose final casting off is foretold in Zechariah xi. 8.

The expression, "The sheep did not hear them," must mean, that true believers, when our Lord came on earth, such as Simeon, Anna, and others, had ceased to put any confidence in the commissioned teachers of the Jews, and were like sheep without a shepherd.

The word "sheep," in this explanatory verse, must evidently be taken in a spiritual sense, and can only mean true believers. Mere outward members of the Church, without faith and grace, are not "sheep."

"Sheep," says Hengstenberg, "in the discourses of Christ, are always the faithful members of God's kingdom, the company of believers."

Alford says, "The sheep throughout this parable are not the mixed multitude of good and bad ; but the real sheep, the faithful, who are what all in the fold should be. The false sheep, the goats, do not appear."

Brentius remarks that we must not hastily assume, from our Lord's saying "the sheep did not hear them," that godly people will never be led away temporarily by false teachers. They may be deceived and seduced, but will return to the truth at last.

9 —[*I am the door, etc.*] This verse is one of those wide, broad, grand statements which our Lord sometimes makes, stretching far beyond the subject of which He is immediately speaking. It is like, "I am the Bread,—I am the Light,—I am the Way."—The primary meaning is, "I am He through whom and by whom alone true pastors must enter the Church. All such pastors, entering by Me, shall find themselves at home in the fold, and enjoy the confidence of my flock, and find food for the souls of my sheep, their hearers."—The secondary or fuller meaning is, "I am the Way of access to God. All who come to the Father by Me, whether pastors or hearers, shall find through Me safety and liberty, and possess continual food for their souls." Strictly speaking the sentence appears to belong specially to the true ministers of the flock of Christ. But I dare not confine it to them alone. It is a grand, wide promise to all who enter in.

Melancthon sees in this verse a most excellent picture of a true pastor, in four respects. (1) He shall be saved personally. (2) He shall go in to close and intimate communion with God. (3) He shall go forth furnished with gifts, and be useful to the Church. (4) He shall find food and refreshment for his own soul.

Musculus observes that our Lord does not say, "If any learned, or righteous, or noble, or rich, or Jewish man enters by Me," but, "any man,"—no matter who, great or small, however wicked in times past,—"any man" that enters by Me shall be saved.

The expression, "go in and out," implies a habit of using familiarly a dwelling, and treating it as a home. It is a Hebraism. It expresses beautifully the habitual communion and happy intercourse with Christ which a true believer enjoys. (See Acts i. 21, ix. 28 ; John xiv. 23 ; Rev. iii. 20.)

Augustine suggests that "go in" means entering by faith, and "going out," dying in faith, and the result of it having life in glory. He says, "We come in by believing : we go out by dying." But this seems far-fetched.

Euthymius thinks that "going out" refers to the Apostles going out into the world to preach the Gospel.

The "finding pasture" implies the satisfaction, comfort, and refreshment of soul which every one who uses Christ as his Door into heaven shall experience. The latent thought is evidently Psalm xxiii. 1, 2, etc.

Burgon remarks, "The concluding words describe the security and enjoyment which are the privilege of God's people. To go in and out is to transact the business of each day's life : its rest and labour, the beginning and end of every work. The Hebrew phrase denotes a man's whole life and conversation. The promises connected therewith seem to imply that in their daily walk, it may be in the world's dusky lane and crowded mart, the people of God will find spiritual support and consolation, even meat for their souls, which the world knows not of. Elsewhere the phrase is often, 'go out and come in.' Here, not without meaning, the expressions are transposed. The former is the order of nature, the latter the order of grace."

In leaving this difficult passage, it is well to remember that though our Lord is not speaking of Himself as a Shepherd here, and is only giving a descriptive picture of a good shepherd, there is a latent application to Himself. There is no one to whom the various features of the picture apply so literally, clearly, and exactly, as they do to the great Shepherd of believers. "Every expression," says Burgon, "has a marked reference to Christ ; yet it is plain that it is not of Himself that He is primarily speaking."

Throughout the passage it is noteworthy how much stress is laid on the "voice" of the shepherd, and on hearing his voice. I cannot but regard this as intentional. It is the "voice in teaching" which makes the great difference between one earthly pastor and another. "The shepherd," says Burgon, "must not be silent while among his sheep." It is hearing the voice of the Chief Shepherd which is one great mark of all true believers.

JOHN X. 10—18.

10 The thief cometh not, but for to steal, and to kill, and to destroy: I am come that they might have life, and that they might have *it* more abundantly.

11 I am the good shepherd: the good shepherd giveth his life for the sheep.

12 But he that is an hireling, and not the shepherd, whose own the sheep are not, seeth the wolf coming, and leaveth the sheep, and fleeth: and the wolf catcheth them, and scattereth the sheep.

13 The hireling fleeth, because he is an hireling, and careth not for the sheep.

14 I am the good shepherd, and know my *sheep*, and am known of mine.

15 As the Father knoweth me, even so know I the Father: and I lay down my life for the sheep.

16 And other sheep I have, which are not of this fold: them also I must bring, and they shall hear my voice; and there shall be one fold, *and* one shepherd.

17 Therefore doth my Father love me, because I lay down my life, that I might take it again.

18 No man taketh it from me, but I lay it down of myself. I have power to lay it down, and I have power to take it again. This commandment have I received of my Father.

THESE verses show us, for one thing, *the great object for which Christ came into the world.* He says, I am come that men "might have life, and that they might have it more abundantly."

The truth contained in these words is of vast importance. They supply an antidote to many crude and unsound notions which are abroad in the world. Christ did not come to be only a teacher of new morality, or an example of holiness and self-denial, or a founder of new ceremonies, as some have vainly asserted. He left heaven, and dwelt for thirty-three years on earth for far higher ends than these. He came to procure eternal life for man, by the price of His own vicarious death. He came to be a mighty fountain of spiritual life for all mankind, to which sinners coming by faith might drink; and, drinking, might live for evermore. By Moses came laws, rules, ordinances, ceremonies. By Christ came grace, truth, and eternal life.

Important as this doctrine is, it requires to be fenced with one word of caution. We must not overstrain the meaning of our Lord Jesus Christ's words. We must not suppose that eternal life was a thing entirely unknown until Christ came, or that the Old Testament saints were in utter darkness about the world to come. The way of life by faith in a Saviour was a way well known to Abraham and Moses and David. A Redeemer and a Sacrifice was the hope of all God's children from Abel down to John the Baptist: but their vision of these things was necessarily imperfect. They saw them afar off, and not distinctly. They saw them in outline only, and not completely. It was the coming of Christ which made all things plain, and caused the shadows to pass away. Life and immortality were brought into full light by the Gospel. In short, to use our Lord's own words, even those who had life had it "more abundantly," when Christ came into the world.

These verses show us, for another thing, *one of the principal offices which Jesus Christ fills for true Christians.* Twice over our Lord uses an expression which, to an Eastern hearer, would be singularly full of meaning. Twice over He says emphatically, " I am the Good Shepherd." It is a saying rich in consolation and instruction.

Like a good shepherd, Christ knows all His believing people. Their names, their families, their dwelling-places, their circumstances, their private history, their experience, their trials,—with all these things Jesus is perfectly acquainted. There is not a thing about the least and lowest of them with which He is not familiar. The children of this world may not know Christians, and may count their lives folly: but the Good Shepherd knows them thoroughly, and, wonderful to say, though He knows them, does not despise them.

Like a good shepherd, Christ cares tenderly for all His believing people. He provides for all their wants in the wilderness of this world, and leads them by the right way to a city of habitation. He bears patiently with their many weaknesses and infirmities, and does not cast them off because they are wayward, erring, sick, footsore, or lame. He guards and protects them against all their enemies, as Jacob did the flock of Laban; and of those that the Father has given Him He will be found at last to have lost none.

Like a good shepherd, Christ lays down His life for the sheep. He did it once for all, when He was crucified for them. When He saw that nothing could deliver them from hell and the devil but His blood, He willingly made His soul an offering for their sins. The merit of that death He is now presenting before the Father's throne. The sheep are saved for evermore, because the Good Shepherd died for them. This is indeed a love that passeth knowledge! "Greater love hath no man than this, that a man lay down his life for his friends." (John xv. 13.)

Let us only take heed that this office of Christ is not set before us in vain. It will profit us nothing at the last day that Jesus was a Shepherd, if during our lifetime, we never heard His voice and followed Him.

If we love life, let us join His flock without delay. Except we do this, we shall be found at the left hand in the day of judgment, and lost for evermore.

These verses show us, lastly, that *when Christ died, He died of His own voluntary free will.* He uses a remarkable expression to teach this: "I lay down my life that I might take it again. No man taketh it from Me, but I lay it down of myself. I have power to lay it down, and I have power to take it again."

The point before us is of no mean importance. We must never suppose for a moment that our Lord had no power to prevent His sufferings, and that He was delivered up to His enemies and crucified because He could not help it. Nothing could be further from the truth than such an idea. The treachery of Judas, the armed band of priests' servants, the enmity of Scribes and Pharisees, the injustice of Pontius Pilate, the rude hands of Roman soldiers, the scourge, the nails, and the spear,—all these could not have harmed a hair of our Lord's head, unless He had allowed them. Well might He say those remarkable words, "Thinkest thou that I cannot now pray to my Father, and He shall presently give Me more than twelve legions of angels. But how, then, shall the Scripture be fulfilled?" (Matt xxvi. 53.)

The plain truth is, that our Lord submitted to death of His own free will, because He knew that His death was the only way of making atonement for man's sins. He poured out His soul unto death with all the desire of His heart, because He had determined to pay our

debt to God, and redeem us from hell. For the joy
set before Him He willingly endured the cross, and
laid down His life, in order that we, through His death,
might have eternal life. His death was not the death
of a martyr, who sinks at last overwhelmed by enemies,
but the death of a triumphant conqueror, who knows
that even in dying He wins for Himself and His people
a kingdom and a crown of glory.

Let us lean back our souls on these mighty truths,
and be thankful. A willing Saviour, a loving Saviour,
a Saviour who came specially into the world to bring
life to man, is just the Saviour that we need. If we
hear His voice, repent and believe, He is our own.

NOTES. JOHN X. 10—18.

10.—[*The thief...destroy.*] In this passage our Lord entirely drops
the figure of "the door," and presents Himself under a new aspect,
as "the Shepherd." And the first thing He does is to show the
amazing difference between Himself and the false teachers who
bore rule among the Jews. He had already told the Pharisees
that they were no better than "thieves and robbers." He now
contrasts their objects with His own. A thief does not come to
the fold to do good to the flock, but harm ; for his own selfish
advantage, and for the injury of the sheep. Just so the Pharisees
only became teachers of the Jewish Church for their own advantage
and interest, and taught doctrine which was only calculated to ruin
and destroy souls.

A. Clarke observes, "How can worldly-minded hirelings, fox-
hunting, card-playing priests, read these words without trembling
to the centre of their souls !"

Bickersteth suggests, that "the thief in the singular number
may remind us of the prince of darkness, the great chief robber
and thief of souls."

[*I am come.. life.. abundantly.*] Our Lord here puts in strong
contrast with the false teachers of the Jews, His own purpose and
object in coming into the world. He drops the figure of "the

door," and says plainly and distinctly, stating it in the widest, broadest way, that, as a personal Saviour, He came that men might have life. The thief came to take life : He came to give it. He came that the way to eternal life might be laid open, the life of justification purchased by His blood, the life of sanctification provided by the grace of His Spirit. He came to buy this life by His sacrifice on the cross. He came to proclaim this life and offer it to a lost world. To bring life and hope to a lost, dead, perishing world, was the grand object of His incarnation. The ministry of the Pharisees was death, but that of Christ was life. The word "they" before "might have," must be taken generally here for "men." There is nothing else to which it can apply.

But this was not all. Our Lord came that men who had life already "might have it more abundantly :" that is that they might see the way of life more clearly, and have no uncertainty about the way of justification before God ; and that they might feel the possession of life more sensibly, and have more conscious enjoyment of pardon, peace, and acceptance. This seems to me by far the simplest view of the text. Of course there were millions in the world who before Christ came knew nothing of life for their souls : to them Christ's coming brought "life."—But there were also many believing Jews who had life already when Christ came, and were walking in the steps of Abraham : to them Christ's coming brought "life more abundantly." It enlarged their vision and increased their comfort. So Paul tells Titus that "Christ's appearing brought life and immortality to light." (2 Tim. i. 10.)

Most commentators do not admit the comparative idea in "more abundantly," but interpret it as simply meaning the abundance of grace and mercy which Christ brings into the world : as Rom. v. 20, 21. This is true, but I venture to think it is not all the truth.

Chemnitius, following Augustine, thinks that "more abundantly" may refer to the life of glory hereafter, which saints will have after the life of faith here. But I cannot see this.

11.—[*I am the Good Shepherd.*] Here our Lord declares that He Himself is the great Head Shepherd of God's people, of whom all ministers, even the best, are only faint imitators. It is as if He said, "I am towards all who believe in Me, what a good shepherd is to his sheep, careful, watchful, and loving." The article in the Greek is twice used to increase the emphasis : "I am the Shepherd, the good or excellent One." In the second verse of the chapter, before the word "Shepherd," in the Greek, we may remember, there is no article at all.

It is probable that the name "shepherd," in Jewish ears, would convey, mnch more clearly than it does in ours, a claim to be regarded as the Messiah or Shepherd of souls. (See Gen. xlix. 24 ; Psalm xxiii. ; Ezek. xxxiv.)

[*The good shepherd giveth his life for the sheep.*] Our Lord here shows the distinguishing mark of a good shepherd. Such an one will lay down his life for his sheep, to save, protect, and defend them. He will die rather than lose one. He will peril his life, like David attacking the lion and the bear, rather than let one be taken from him. "All this," our Lord implies, "I have come to do for my spiritual sheep. I have come to shed my life-blood to save their souls : to die that they may live." The word "giveth" here should have been translated "layeth down." It is so rendered in the 15th verse.

Flacius observes how our Lord here, as elsewhere, always brings round His discourse to His own atoning death.

Hengstenberg observes, "This expression, 'laying down the soul or life' for any one, does not occur anywhere else independently in the New Testament. It is never found in profane writers. It must be referred back to the Old Testament, and specially to Isa. liii. 10, where it is said of Messiah, 'He shall make, or place, His soul an offering for sin.'"

Tittman says, "Those who maintain that Christ died only to confirm the truth of His doctrine, or to confirm the certainty of the promises of pardon and acceptance with God, are under a mistake. The death of Christ was not necessary for either of those purposes. The truth of His doctrine and the certainty of His promises must be established by other evidence. Neither does our Lord say, that He laid down life for His *doctrines*, but for His sheep."

12, 13. —[*But he that is an hireling, etc.*] Our Lord in these two verses illustrates the subject He has taken up, by showing the wide difference between a mere hired shepherd, and one who feels a special interest in his sheep because they are his own. A mere hired servant, who has not spent his money in buying the sheep, but only takes charge of a flock for pay, and cares little so long as he gets his money, such an one, as a general rule, will make no sacrifice and run no risk for the sheep. If he sees a wolf coming he will not meet him and fight, but will run away, and leave the flock to be scattered and devoured. He acts in this way because his whole heart is not in his work. He feeds the flock for money and not for love,—for what he can get by it, and not because he really cares for the sheep. Of course the picture must be taken as *generally* true : we cannot suppose our Lord meant that no paid servant was trustworthy. Jacob was a hired shepherd, yet trustworthy. But doubtless His Jewish hearers knew many such "hirelings" as He here describes. The picture of a faithless shepherd in Ezekiel xxxiv. would also occur to those who were familiar with Old Testament Scripture.

It is worth remembering that St. Paul specially warns the Ephesian elders, in Acts xx. 29, that "grievous wolves" would enter in among them, not sparing the flock. Our Lord also in the Sermon on the Mount compares false prophets to "ravening wolves." (Matt. vii. 15.)

Musculus observes how great a misfortune it is to Christ's sheep when they are deserted by ministers, and left without regular means of grace. It has a scattering weakening effect. The best of ministers are poor weak creatures. But Churches cannot keep together, as a rule, without pastors : the wolf scatters them. The ministry no doubt may be overvalued, but it may also be undervalued.

We cannot doubt that the latent thought of our Lord's language here was as follows. The Pharisees and other false teachers were no better than hireling shepherds. They cared for nothing but themselves, and their own honour or profit. They cared nothing for souls. They were willing to have the name and profession of shepherds, but they had no heart in their work. They had neither will nor power to protect their hearers against any assault which that wolf, the devil, might make against them. Hence the Jews, when our Lord came on earth, were without help for their souls, fainting, and scattered like sheep without a shepherd, a prey to every device of the devil.

Let it be noted that the great secret of a useful and Christlike ministry is to love men's souls. He that is a minister merely to get a living, or to have an honourable position, is "the hireling" of these verses. The true pastor's first care is for his sheep. The false pastor's first thought is for himself.

Our Lord's strong language about the false teachers of the Jews ends here. Those who think that unsound ministers ought never to be exposed and held up to notice, and men ought never to be warned against them, would do well to study this passage. No class of character throughout our Lord's ministry seems to call forth such severe denunciation as that of false pastors. The reason is obvious. Other men ruin themselves alone: false pastors ruin their flocks as well as themselves. To flatter all ordained men, and say they never should be called unsound and dangerous guides, is the surest way to injure the Church and offend Christ.

Chrysostom, Theophylact, and most commentators think that the "wolf" here means the devil, even as he is called elsewhere a roaring lion, a serpent, and a dragon.

Lampe, on the other hand, thinks that the wolf signifies the same as the thief and robber, and that it must mean the false prophet, the wolf in sheep's clothing. (See Zeph. iii. 3 ; Matt. vii. 15.)

In interpreting this whole passage we must be careful not to strain it too far. Our Lord did not mean that in no case is flight from danger lawful in a pastor. He Himself says elsewhere, "When they persecute you in one city, flee ye to another." (Matt. x. 23.) So Paul left Damascus by stealth to escape the Jews. (Acts ix. 25.)

Calvin remarks, "Ought we to reckon that man an hireling who for any reasons whatever shrinks from encountering the wolves ? This was anciently debated as a practical question, when tyrants raged cruelly against the Church. Tertullian and others were, in my opinion, too rigid on this point. I prefer greatly the moderation of Augustine, who allows pastors to flee on certain conditions."

No unbending rule can be laid down. Each case must be decided by circumstances. There are times when, like St. Paul or Jewell, a man may see it a duty to flee, and await better days ; and times when, like Hooper, he may feel called to decline flight and to die with his sheep. Barnabas and Paul were specially commended to the Church at Antioch (Acts xv. 25), as those who had "hazarded their lives for the name of the Lord Jesus." St. Paul tells the Ephesian elders, "I count not my life dear unto myself so that I may finish my course with joy." (Acts xx. 24.) Again he says, "I am ready to die at Jerusalem for the name of the Lord Jesus." (Acts xxi. 13.)

14.—[*I am the Good Shepherd.*] These words are repeated to show the importance of the office our Lord fills as the Good Shepherd, and to bring into stronger light the wide difference between Him and the Pharisees.

[*And know my sheep, and am known of mine.*] These words express the close and intimate union there is between Christ and all His believing people, an union understood fully by those alone who feel it, but to the world foolishness. Our Lord, like a good earthly shepherd, knows every one of His people,—knows them with a special knowledge of love and approval ; knows where they dwell and all about them, their weaknesses, trials, and temptations, and knows exactly what each one needs from day to day. His people, on the other hand, know Him with the knowledge of faith and confidence, and feel in Him a loving trust of which an unbeliever can form no idea. They know Him as their own sure Friend and Saviour, and rest on the knowledge. The devils know that Christ is *a* Saviour. The sheep know and feel that He is *their* Saviour.

The fulness of this verse would be far more plain to Jews accustomed to Oriental shepherds and their flocks, to the care of a good shepherd and the confidence of a flock, than it is to us in this Northern climate. At any rate it teaches indirectly the duty of every Christlike pastor to be personally acquainted with all his people, just as a good shepherd knows each one of his sheep.

Musculus points out the strong contrast between "I know my sheep," and the solemn saying to the virgins, "I know you not," and to the false professors, "I never knew you," in Matt. xxv. 7 ; vii. 23.

Besser remarks that "I am known of mine" is a sharp rebuke to those doubters who in voluntary humility refuse to be sure of their salvation.

15.—[*As the Father...me...I the Father.*]   I believe this sentence ought to be read in close connection with the last verse, and without any full stop between. There is nothing in the Greek against this view. The sense would then be, "I know my sheep and am known of mine, even as the Father knoweth Me and I know the Father." The meaning will then be that the mutual knowledge of Christ and His sheep is like the mutual knowledge of the Father and the Son,—a knowledge so high, so deep, so intimate, so ineffable, that no words can fully convey it. The full nature of that knowledge which the First Person of the Trinity has of the Second and the Second has of the First, is something far beyond finite man's understanding. It is in short a deep mystery. Yet the mutual knowledge and communion of Christ and believers is something so deep and wonderful that it can only be compared, though at a vast distance, to that which exists between the Father and the Son.

To understand this knowledge a little, we should read carefully the language used in Proverbs viii. 22—30.

[*And I lay down my life for the sheep.*] Our Lord, to show how truly He is the Good Shepherd, declares that like a good shepherd He not only knows all His sheep, but lays down His life for them. By using the present tense, He seems to say, "I am doing it. I am just about to do it. I came into the world to do it." This can only refer to His own atoning death on the cross : the great propitiation He was about to make by shedding His life-blood. It was the highest proof of love. "Greater love hath no man than this, that a man lay down his life for his friends." (John xv. 13.)

Taken alone and by itself this sentence undoubtedly contains the doctrine of particular redemption. It declares that Christ "lays down His life for the sheep." That He does so in a special sense I think none can deny. The "sheep" alone, or true believers, obtain any saving benefit from His death. But to argue from this text, that in no sense and in no way did Christ die for any beside His "sheep," is to say what seems to me to contradict Scripture. The plain truth is that the extent of redemption is not the leading subject of this verse. Our Lord is saying what He does for His sheep : He loves them so that He dies for them. But it does not follow that we are to conclude that His death was not meant to influence and affect the position of all mankind. I venture to refer the reader to my own notes, in this commentary, on John i. 28 ; iii. 16 ; and vi. 32, for a full discussion of the subject.

Both here and in the 11th verse, I do not think the Greek word translated "for" should be pressed too far, as if it necessarily implied the doctrine of substitution, or the vicariousness of Christ's death. That doctrine is a blessed and glorious truth, and is taught plainly and unmistakably elsewhere. Here, however, we are reading parabolic figurative language, and I doubt whether it is quite fair to explain it as meaning more than "on account of," or "in behalf of," the sheep. Of course it comes to the same thing at last : if the Shepherd did not die, the sheep would die. But I do not quite think "vicariousness," at any rate, is the primary idea of the sentence.

I fully agree with Parkhurst, at the same time, that the Greek expression for "dying for any one," in Rom. v. 6—8, never has any signification other than that of "rescuing the life of another at the expense of our own."

16.—[*And other sheep I have...fold.*] In this sentence, our Lord declares plainly the approaching conversion of the Gentiles. The sheep He specially died for were not merely the few believing Jews, but the elect Gentiles also   They are the "other sheep :"

"this fold" means the Jewish Church. It reads as though He would show the real measure and size of His flock. It was one much larger than the Jewish nation, of which the scribes and Pharisees were so proud.

Let it be noted here that our Lord uses the present tense. The heathen sheep were as yet heathen, and not brought in : yet He says, "I have them." They were already given to Him in the eternal counsels, and foreknown from the beginning of the world. So it was with the Corinthians before their conversion : "I have much people in this city." (Acts xviii. 10.)

Augustine remarks : "They were yet without, among the Gentiles, predestinated, not yet gathered in. These He knew who had predestinated them : He knew who had come to redeem them with the shedding of His own blood. He saw them who did not yet see Him : He knew them who yet believed not in Him."

[*Them also...bring.*] Our Lord here declares that it is necessary for Him, in order to fulfil the prophecies of the Old Testament, and to carry out the great purpose of His coming, to bring in and add to His flock other believers beside the Jewish sheep : "It is part of my work, office, and mission, to gather them out from the heathen by the preaching of my Apostles."

The prediction here made was contrary to Jewish prejudices The Jews thought they alone were God's flock and favoured people. Even the Apostles afterwards were slow to remember these words.

Hutcheson observes, "Christ Himself is chief in bringing in His elect, whatever instruments He employs ; and He is at pains to seek them, and gain their consent, as being bound in the covenant of redemption to present all that are given Him blameless before the Father." Saints are "the called of Jesus Christ." (Rom. i. 6.)

[*They shall hear my voice.*] This is a prophecy and a promise combined. It was a prophecy that the elect among the heathen, however unlikely it might appear, would hear Christ's voice speaking to them in the Gospel preached ; and hearing, would believe and obey.—It was a promise that would encourage His Apostles to preach to the heathen : "They will listen, and be converted, and follow Me."—It is a saying that was wonderfully forgotten by the Apostles afterwards. They were backward to bring in the other sheep, after their Master left the world.—It is a sentence that should nerve and cheer the missionary. Christ has said it: "The sheep who are scattered among the heathen will hear."

The text, "He that heareth you heareth Me" (Luke x. 16), is the Divine explanation of the expression, "hear my voice."

[*And there shall be one fold...shepherd.*] This sentence contains one word which ought to have been differently translated. It ought to be, as Tyndale renders it, "one *flock* and one shepherd." There is an evident difference. Christ's universal Church is a mighty company, of which the members may be found in many different visible Churches, or ecclesiastical "folds:" but it composes only one "flock." There is only "one Holy Catholic Church," which is the blessed company of all faithful people; but there are many various visible Churches.

The sentence is true of all believers now. Though differing in various points, such as government or ceremonies, true believers are all sheep of one flock, and all look up to one Saviour and Shepherd. It will be more completely fulfilled at Christ's second coming. Then shall be exhibited to the world one glorious Church under one glorious Head. In the view of this promise unity with all true Christians should be sought and striven for by every true sheep.

Gualter remarks that there never has been, or can be, more than one Holy Catholic Church, and unless we belong to it we cannot be saved, and he warns us against the pernicious error that all men shall get to heaven if sincere, whether they belong to the Holy Catholic Church or not.

Chemnitius observes that we must be careful not to make this one Church either too narrow or too broad. We make it too narrow when, like the Jews and the Papists, we exclude any believer who does not belong to our particular fold. We make it too broad when we include every professing Christian, whether he hears Christ's voice or not. It is a flock of "sheep."

In every other place in the New Testament the word here wrongly translated "fold," is rendered "flock." (Matt. xxvi. 31; Luke ii. 8; 1 Cor. ix. 7.) The word "fold," before us, is evidently an oversight of our translators.

17.—[*Therefore...my Father love Me because, etc.*] This is a deep and mysterious verse, like all verses which speak of the relation between the First and Second Persons of the Trinity. We must be content to admire and believe what we cannot fully understand.

When, as in John v. 20, and here, our Lord speaks of "the Father loving the Son," we must remember that He is using language borrowed from earthly affection, to express the mind of one Person of the Trinity towards another, and accordingly we must interpret it reverently.—Yet we may surely gather from this verse that our Lord's coming into this world to lay down His life for the sheep by dying on the cross, and to take it again for their justification by rising again from the dead, was a transaction viewed with infinite complacency and approbation by God the Father.—"I am about to die, and after death to rise again. My so doing, however strange it may seem to you Pharisees, is the very thing which my Father in heaven approves, and for which He specially loves Me." It is like the Father's words, "In whom I am well pleased;" and St. Paul's, "Wherefore God hath highly exalted Him" (Matt. iii. 17; Phil. ii. 9); and Isaiah's, "I will divide Him a portion with the great, because He hath poured out His soul unto death." (Is. liii. 12.)

Our Lord, by mentioning His resurrection, seems to remind His hearers that in one respect He was different from the best of shepherds. They might lay down their lives; but then there would be an end of them. He meant to lay down His life, but after that to take it again. He would not only die for His people, but also rise again.

Guyse thinks the true meaning is, "I cheerfully lay down my life for the expiation of my sheep's offences, in order that I may rise again for their justification."

Let it be noted here, that there is no part of Christ's work for His people that God the Father is said to regard with such special complacency as His dying for them. No wonder that ministers ought to make Christ crucified the principal subject of their teaching.

Gualter thinks these words were specially meant to prevent the offence of the ignominious death of Christ on the cross. That death, whatever the Jews might think, was part of Christ's plan and commission, and one reason why the Father loved Him.

Brentius thinks that there is here a reference to the story of Abraham offering Isaac, when the words were used, "Because thou hast done this thing, and not withheld thy son, therefore blessing I will bless thee." (Gen. xxii.)

Hengstenberg remarks that the Father's love "was the very opposite of that wrath of God, of which the Jews regarded

Christ's death as a proof and sign." They thought that God had forsaken Him, and given Him up to be crucified in displeasure, when in reality God was well pleased.

18.—*[No man taketh...of myself.]* In this sentence our Lord teaches that His own death was entirely voluntary. An earthly shepherd may die for his flock, but against his own will. The great Shepherd of believers made His soul an offering for sin of His own free will. He was not obliged or compelled to do it by superior force. No one could have taken away His life had He not been willing to lay it down : but He laid it down "of Himself," because He had covenanted to offer Himself as a propitiation for our sins. His own love to sinners, and not the power of the Jews or Pontius Pilate's soldiers, was the cause of His death.

The word "I" is inserted emphatically in the Greek. "I myself" lay down my life "of myself."

Henry observes, "Christ could, when He pleased, slip the knot of union between body and soul, and without any act of violence done to Himself, could disengage them from each other. Having voluntarily taken up a body, He could voluntarily lay it down again. This appeared when He cried with a loud voice, and 'gave up' the ghost."

[I have power...down...take it up.] Our Lord here amplifies His last statement, and magnifies His own Divine nature, by declaring that He has full power to lay down His life when He pleases, and to take it again when He pleases. This last point deserves special notice. Our Lord teaches that His resurrection, as well as His death, was in His own power. When our Lord rose again, He was not passive, and raised by the power of another only, but rose by His own Divine power. It is noteworthy that the resurrection of our Lord in some places is attributed to His Father's act, as Acts ii. 24—32 ; once, at least, to the Holy Spirit, as 1 Pet. iii. 18 ; and here, and in John ii. 19, to Christ Himself. All leads to the same great conclusion,—that the resurrection of our Lord, as well as every part of His mediatorial work, was an act in which all three Persons of the Trinity concurred and co-operated.

Hutcheson observes that if Christ had power to take life again, when He pleased, "so He can put a period to the sufferings of His own when He pleaseth, without any help of their crooked ways."

[This commandment received.. Father.] Chrysostom, and most

other commentators, apply these words strictly to the great work which our Lord has just declared He had power to do : viz., to lay down His life and to take it again. "This is part of the commission I received from my Father on coming into the world, and one of the works He gave Me to do."

No doubt this is good exposition and good divinity. Yet I am rather inclined to think that our Lord's words refer to the whole doctrine which He had just been declaring to the Jews : viz., His office as a Shepherd, His being the true Shepherd, His laying down His life for the sheep, and taking it again, His having other sheep who were to be brought into the fold, His final purpose to exhibit to the world one flock and one Shepherd. Of all this truth, He says, "I received this doctrine in charge from my Father, to proclaim to the world, and I now declare it to you Pharisees." I suspect that both here and elsewhere the word "commandment" has a wide, deep meaning, and points to that solemn and mysterious truth, the entire unity of the Father and the Son in the work of redemption, to which John frequently refers : "I am in the Father, and the Father in Me. The *words* that I speak unto you, I speak not of myself, but the Father that dwelleth in Me, He doeth the works." (John xiv. 10.) "The Father gave Me a commandment what I should speak." (John xii. 49.) Our Lord's object in these often repeated expressions seems to be to keep the Jews in mind that He was not a mere human Prophet, but one who was God as well as man, and in whom, both speaking and working, the Father always dwelt.

When our Lord speaks of "receiving a commandment," we must take care that we do not suppose the expression implies any inferiority of the Second Person of the Trinity to the First. We must reverently remember the everlasting covenant between Father, Son, and Holy Ghost, for the salvation of man, and interpret "commandment" as meaning a part of the charge or commission with which the Second Person, Christ, was sent into the world, to carry out the purposes of the Eternal Trinity.

JOHN X. 19—30.

19 There was a division therefore again among the Jews for these sayings.

20 And many of them said, He hath a devil, and is mad; why hear ye him?

21 Others said, These are not the words of him that hath a devil. Can a devil open the eyes of the blind?

22 And it was at Jerusalem the feast of the dedication, and it was winter.

23 And Jesus walked in the temple in Solomon's porch.

24 Then came the Jews round about him, and said unto him, How long dost thou make us to doubt? If thou be the Christ, tell us plainly.

25 Jesus answered them, I told you, and ye believed not · the works that I do in my Father's name, they bear witness of me.

26 But ye believe not, because ye are not of my sheep, as I said unto you.

27 My sheep hear my voice, and I know them, and they follow me:

28 And I give unto them eternal life; and they shall never perish, neither shall any *man* pluck them out of my hand.

29 My Father, which gave *them* me, is greater than all; and no *man* is able to pluck *them* out of my Father's hand.

30 I and *my* Father are one.

WE should notice, first, in this passage, *what strifes and controversies our Lord occasioned when He was on earth.* We read that "there was a division among the Jews for His sayings,"—and that "many of them said He hath a devil, and is mad," while others took an opposite view. It may seem strange, at first sight, that He who came to preach peace between God and man, should be the cause of contention. But herein were His own words literally fulfilled : "I came not to send peace, but a sword." (Matt. x. 34.) The fault was not in Christ or His doctrine, but in the carnal mind of His Jewish hearers.

Let us never be surprised if we see the same thing in our own day. Human nature never changes. So long as the heart of man is without grace, so long we must expect to see it dislike the Gospel of Christ. Just as oil and water, acids and alkalies cannot combine, so in the same way unconverted people cannot really like the people of God.—"The carnal mind is enmity against God."—"The natural man receiveth not the things of the Spirit of God." (Rom viii. 7; 1 Cor. ii. 14.)

The servant of Christ must think it no strange thing if he goes through the same experience as his Master. He will often find his ways and opinions in religion the cause of strife in his own family. He will have to endure ridicule, hard words, and petty persecution, from

the children of this world. He may even discover that
he is thought a fool or a madman on account of his
Christianity. Let none of these things move him. The
thought that he is a partaker of the afflictions of Christ
ought to steel him against every trial. "If they have
called the Master of the house Beelzebub, how much
more shall they call them of His household." (Matt.
x. 25.)

One thing, at any rate, should never be forgotten. We
must not allow ourselves to think the worse of religion
because of the strifes and dissensions to which it gives
rise. Whatever men may please to say, it is human
nature, and not religion, which is to blame. We do not
blame the glorious sun because its rays draw forth
noxious vapours from the marsh. We must not find
fault with the glorious Gospel if it stirs up men's corruptions, and causes the "thoughts of many hearts to
be revealed." (Luke ii. 35.)

We should notice, secondly, *the name which Christ
gives to true Christians.* He uses a figurative expression
which, like all His language, is full of deep meaning.
He calls them, " My sheep."

The word "sheep," no doubt, points to something in
the character and ways of true Christians. It would be
easy to show that weakness, helplessness, harmlessness,
usefulness, are all points of resemblance between the
sheep and the believer. But the leading idea in our
Lord's mind was the entire dependence of the sheep upon
its shepherd. Just as sheep hear the voice of their own
shepherd, and follow him, so do believers follow Christ.

By faith they listen to His call. By faith they submit
themselves to His guidance.   By faith they lean on
Him, and commit their souls implicity to His direction.
The ways of a shepherd and his sheep, are a most
useful illustration of the relation between Christ and
the true Christian.

The expression, " My sheep," points to the close connection that exists between Christ and believers.   They
are His by gift from the Father, His by purchase, His
by calling and choice, and His by their own consent and
heart-submission.   In the highest sense they are Christ's
property ; and just as a man feels a special interest in
that which he has bought at a great price and made his
own, so does the Lord Jesus feel a peculiar interest in
His people.

Expressions like these should be carefully treasured
up in the memories of true Christians.   They will be
found cheering and heart-strengthening in days of trial.
The world may see no beauty in the ways of a godly
man, and may often pour contempt on him.   But he
who knows that he is one of Christ's sheep has no cause
to be ashamed.   He has within him a " well of water
springing up into everlasting life."   (John iv. 14.)

We should notice, lastly, in this passage, *the vast
privileges which the Lord Jesus Christ bestows on true
Christians.*   He uses words about them of singular
richness and strength.   " I know them.—I give unto
them eternal life.—They shall never perish,—neither
shall any man pluck them out of my hand."   This
sentence is like the cluster of grapes which came from

Eshcol. A stronger form of speech perhaps can hardly be found in the whole range of the Bible.

Christ "knows" His people with a special knowledge of approbation, interest, and affection. By the world around them they are comparatively unknown, uncared for, or despised. But they are never forgotten or overlooked by Christ.

Christ "gives" His people "eternal life." He bestows on them freely a right and title to heaven, pardoning their many sins, and clothing them with a perfect righteousness. Money, and health, and worldly prosperity He often wisely withholds from them. But He never fails to give them grace, peace, and glory.

Christ declares that His people "shall never perish." Weak as they are, they shall all be saved. Not one of them shall be lost and cast away: not one of them shall miss heaven. If they err, they shall be brought back: if they fall, they shall be raised. The enemies of their souls may be strong and mighty, but their Saviour is mightier; and none shall pluck them out of their Saviour's hands.

A promise like this deserves the closest attention. If words mean anything, it contains that great doctrine, the perseverance, or continuance in grace, of true believers. That doctrine is literally hated by worldly people. No doubt, like every other truth of Scripture, it is liable to be abused. But the words of Christ are too plain to be evaded. He has said it, and He will make it good : " My sheep shall never perish."

Whatever men may please to say against this doctrine,

it is one which God's children ought to hold fast, and defend with all their might. To all who feel within them the workings of the Holy Spirit, it is a doctrine full of encouragement and consolation. Once inside the ark, they shall never be cast out. Once converted and joined to Christ, they shall never be cut off from His mystical body. Hypocrites and false professors shall doubtless make shipwreck for ever, unless they repent. But true "sheep" shall never be confounded. Christ has said it, and Christ cannot lie: "they shall never perish."

Would we get the benefit of this glorious promise? Let us take care that we belong to Christ's flock. Let us hear His voice and follow Him. The man who, under a real sense of sin, flees to Christ and trusts in Him, is one of those who shall never be plucked out of Christ's hand.

NOTES. JOHN x. 19—30.

19.—[*There was a division, etc.*] This is the third time that we find our Lord's words causing a division, or schism, among His hearers. Each time it occurred at Jerusalem. At chap. vii. 43, it was among "the people;" at ix. 16, among the "Pharisees." Here it was among the "Jews," an expression in St. John's Gospel generally applied to our Lord's enemies among the Pharisees.

The special "sayings" which caused the division were probably our Lord's words about His Father, His claim to have power to lay down His life and take it again, and His proclamation of Himself as "the Good Shepherd." Words like these from a Galilean teacher of humble appearance, were likely to offend the proud Pharisees of Jerusalem.

That our Lord would be a cause of division,—a stone of stumbling to some, and set for the rise and fall of many in Israel,—had been foretold by Isaiah viii. 14, and by Simeon, Luke ii. 34. Divisions among His hearers are therefore no proof that He was not the Messiah, and divisions among hearers of the Gospel in the present day are no argument against the truth of the Gospel. Even now the same Gospel is a savour of death to some, and of life to others, calls forth love in some, and hatred in others. The same fire which melts wax, hardens clay.

20.—[*And many of them said, etc.*] This is the sort of profane remark which we can well imagine many unconverted hearers of our Lord making : "What! a humble Galilæan like this man call Himself the only good Shepherd, and talk of having power to lay down His life and take it again, and of having a special commission from His Father in heaven. He must surely have a devil, or be out of his senses. He must be mad. Why do you waste your time in listening to Him?" Thousands talk in this way now against Christ's servants. They would probably have talked in the same way against their Master!

Let us note what blasphemous and slanderous things were said against our Lord. True Christians, and specially ministers, must never wonder if they are treated in the same manner.

21 —[*Others said, These are not, etc.*] Here we see that there were some among the Pharisees who took our Lord's part, and were disposed to believe on Him. Such probably were Gamaliel, Nicodemus, and Joseph of Arimathæa. They defend Him on the score both of His words and works.—As to His words, they argue that no one of common sense could call such words as our Lord had just spoken, the words of a man possessed with a devil. The devil and his agents, do not desire to do good to man, or to glorify God. The calm, solemn, loving, God-glorifying language just used, was the very opposite to that which might be expected from a demoniac.—As to His works, they argue that no devil, however powerful, could work such a miracle as to open the eyes of the blind. Some wonderful works the devil might do, but no such work as that of giving sight. It is worth noticing that the Jews held that to give sight to the blind was one of the special miracles which Messiah would work. "Then the eyes of the blind shall be opened." (Isaiah xxxv. 5.)

The Greek word here rendered "words," is not the same as that rendered "sayings," in verse 19. Webster says it is a stronger expression, and means, "the whole transaction," as well as the things said. The word "blind" here in the Greek is plural, and would be more accurately translated, "of blind persons."

22.—[*And it was at Jerusalem.*] Many think that an interval of time comes in between this verse and the preceding one. I doubt it. From chap. vii. 2, where we are told it was the feast of taber-

nacles, the narrative runs on at first sight continuously : yet if we
look at John ix. 35, there must have been one break of time.—If
there was any interval before the verse we are now considering,
I think it must have been very short. The following verses show
that the discourse about "the sheep" must have been fresh in
the minds of the Jews, as our Lord refers to it as a thing they
could remember : He would hardly have done so if the interval
had been very long. At any rate, I can see no proof that our Lord
left Jerusalem between the discourse about "the sheep" and the
verse before us.

[*The feast of the dedication.*] This Jewish festival is one which
is nowhere else mentioned in the Bible. It is however a matter of
history, according to most commentators, that it was first appointed
by Judas Maccabeus to commemorate the purging of the temple,
and the rebuilding of the altar, after the Syrians were driven out.
Its appointment is recorded in the Apocrypha, in 1 Maccabees iv.
52—59. The Apocryphal books are, no doubt, uninspired. But
there is no reason to question the accuracy of their historical
statements. The passage before us is often referred to, as proving
that our Lord recognized, and tacitly sanctioned, a man-made and
man-appointed festival. "The Church has power to decree rites
and ceremonies," and so long as it ordains nothing against God's
Word, its appointments deserve respect. At any rate our Lord did
not denounce the feast of dedication, or refuse to be present at it.

Chrysostom and others think that the feast of dedication was
appointed to commemorate the rebuilding of the temple after the
Babylonian captivity, in Ezra's time. (Ezra vi. 16.)

Some think that it was to commemorate the dedication of Solomon's temple. (2 Chron. vii. 9.) There is, however, no warrant
for this view.

Pearce remarks, that John alone of all the evangelists records
our Lord's attendance at four of the great feasts of the Jews : viz.,
passover (John ii. 13), pentecost (v. 1), tabernacles (vii. 2), and
dedication here.

[*It was winter.*] This shows that three months had passed
since the miracle of healing the blind man, which was worked at
the feast of tabernacles. That was about Michaelmas, by our
reckoning. The season of winter is here mentioned to explain why
our Lord walked under cover, "in a porch."

The mention of winter goes far to prove that the feast of dedi-

cation must have been appointed in commemoration of the work
of Judas Maccabeus.   Solomon's dedication was at Michaelmas,
in the seventh month ; Ezra's about Easter, in the first month.

23.—[*And Jesus walked.*]   This must either mean that "it was the
habit" of our Lord to walk, or else that "one day Jesus was
walking :" the latter seems the more likely sense.

[*In the temple.*]   This means in the outer court, or area around
the temple, which was a common place of resort for the Jews, and
specially upon festivals.   Here teachers expounded, and discussions
on religious questions seem to have taken place.   Here probably
our Lord was found "among the doctors," hearing and asking
questions, when he was twelve years old.   (Luke ii. 4—6.)

[*In Solomon's porch.*]   The word "porch" rather means what we
should call a verandah, or colonnade.   It was one of those long
covered walks under a roof supported by columns, on one side at
least, which the inhabitants of hot countries appear to find absolutely needful.   Singularly enough, one sect of heathen philosophers
at Athens were called "Stoics," from its meeting in a place called
"Stoa," here rendered a porch ; while another was called "Peri-
patetics," from its habit of "walking about" during its discussions,
just as our Lord did in this verse.   The cloisters of a cathedral or
abbey, perhaps, are most like the building called a "porch" here.

Josephus says this porch was one of the buildings which remained
partly undestroyed from Solomon's temple.

Tacitus expressly mentions it as one of the defences of the temple
at the siege of Jerusalem.

24.—[*Then came...Jews round...said...Him.*]   This would be more
literally rendered, "encircled Him," or surrounded Him in a
circle.

[*How long...make...doubt.*]   This would be more literally rendered,
"Until what time dost Thou lift up our souls?   How long dost
Thou keep us in a state of suspense and excitement?"

Elsner thinks it means, "How long dost Thou take away our
life (as at verse eighteen), or kill us with doubt and perplexity?"
Suicer, Schleusner, and Parkhurst, however, prefer, "hold us in
suspense."   (See marginal reading in Luke xii. 29.)

[*If...Christ, tell us plainly.*]   The Jews had no right to say they
had not sufficient evidence that our Lord was the Christ.   But
nothing is more common with hardened and wicked men than to

allege a want of evidence, and to pretend willingness to believe, if only more evidence was supplied.

"Plainly" here does not mean in plain language, and easily understood, but openly, boldly, unreservedly, and without mystery.

25.—[*Jesus answered...I told...ye believed not.*] To what does our Lord refer here? I believe He refers to what He had said in the fifth chapter before the Sanhedrim, and in the eighth chapter in the discourse beginning, "I am the Light," etc. The words would be more literally rendered, "I have told you, and ye do not believe."

Henry observes, "The Jews pretended that they only *doubted*, but Christ tells them that they did not believe. Scepticism in religion is no better than downright infidelity."

Hengstenberg thinks that "I have told you," specially refers to our Lord's recent proclamation of Himself as "the Good Shepherd." To a Jewish ear it would sound like a claim to be the Messiah.

[*The works...Father's name...witness of Me.*] Here, as in other places, our Lord appeals to His miracles as the grand proof that He was the Christ. (Compare iii. 2, and v. 36, and vii. 31, and ix. 33, 34, and Acts ii. 22.) It is as though our Lord said, "The miracles I have done are more than sufficient proof that I am the Messiah. Nothing can account for them but the fact that I am the promised Messiah."

We should observe how our Lord says, "The works which I do in my Father's name;" that is, by my Father's commission and appointment, and as His Messenger. Here, as elsewhere, He carefully reminds the Jews that He does not act independently of His Father, but in entire harmony and unity with Him. His works were works which "the Father gave Him to finish."

We should observe how our Lord always and confidently appeals to the evidence of His miracles. Those who try to depreciate and sneer at miracles, seem to forget how often they are brought forward as good witnesses in the Bible. This, in fact, is their great object and purpose. They were not so much meant to convert, as to, prove that He who did them was from God, and deserved attention.

"Of Me," would be more literally rendered, "concerning or about Me."

26.—[*But ye believe not, because...not ..sheep.*] I doubt whether the word "because" does not put a meaning on this verse which it

hardly bears in the Greek. It should rather be, "Ye neither believe my words nor my works, FOR ye are not in the number of
my sheep. If ye were my sheep ye would believe : faith is one
of their marks." Not being Christ's sheep was not the CAUSE of
the unbelief of the Jews ; but their unbelief was the EVIDENCE
that they were not Christ's sheep.

Tyndale and others think that the full stop should be after the
word "sheep," and that "as I said unto you," should be taken
with the following verse ; but I see no necessity for this.

[*As I said unto you.*] I think these words refer to two sayings
of our Lord, which He had used in speaking to the Jews, one in
chap. viii. 47 : "He that is of God heareth God's words : ye therefore hear them not, because ye are not of God ; " and the other at
the third and fourth verses of this chapter : "The sheep hear His
voice"—"the sheep follow Him, for they know His voice."

27.—*My sheep hear my voice, etc.*] Having told the Pharisees that
they were not His sheep, our Lord goes on to describe the character
of those who were His sheep ; that is, of His own true people and
servants. This He does in a verse of singular richness and fulness. Every word is instructive.

Christ calls His people "sheep." He does so because they are
in themselves singularly helpless and dependent on their Shepherd ;
because comparatively they are the most harmless and helpless of
animals ; because even at their best they are weak, foolish, and
liable to go astray.

Chemnitius gives thirteen distinct reasons why believers are
called sheep. They are too long to quote here, but will repay the
examination of any one who has access to his commentary.

He calls them, "My sheep." They are His by God the Father's
gift,—His by redemption and purchase,—His by calling and choosing,—His by feeding, keeping, and preserving,—and His by their
own consent and will. They are His peculiar property.

He says, "They hear my voice." By this He means that they
listen to His invitation, when He calls them to repent, believe,
and come to Him. This supposes that Christ first speaks, and then
they hear. Grace begins the work : they, through grace, obey His
calling, and willingly do as He bids them. The ears of unconverted people are deaf to Christ's call, but true Christians hear
and obey.

He says, "I know them." This means that He knows them

with a special knowledge of approbation, complacency, love, and interest. (See the word "know" in Psalm i. 6, xxxi. 8, Amos iii. 2.) Of course He knows the secrets of all men's hearts, and all about all wicked people. But He knows with a peculiar knowledge those who are His people. The world knows them not, but Christ knows and cares for them. (1 John iii. 1.)

He says, "They follow Me." This means that His people, like sheep, obey, trust, and walk in the steps of their Divine Master. They follow Him in holy obed'ence to His commandments; they follow Him in striving to copy His example; and they follow Him in trusting implicitly His providential leadings,—going where He would have them go, and taking cheerfully all He appoints for them.

It is almost needless to remark that this description belongs to none but true Christians. It did not belong to the Pharisees to whom our Lord spoke. It does not belong to multitudes of baptized people in our own day.

Luther says: "The sheep, though the most simple creature, is superior to all animals in this, that he soon hears his shepherd's voice, and will follow no other. Also he is clever enough to hang entirely on his shepherd, and to seek help from him alone. He cannot help himself, nor find pasture for himself, nor heal himself, nor guard against wolves, but depends wholly and solely on the help of another."

In the Greek of this verse, there is a nice distinction between the number of the verb "hear" and the verb "follow," which the English language cannot convey. It is as though our Lord had said, my sheep are a body, which "*hears*" my voice, in the singular; and of which the individual members "*follow*" Me, in the plural.

28.—[*And I give, etc.*] From the character of Christ's sheep the Good Shepherd goes on to describe their privileges. He gives to them eternal life; the precious gift of pardon and grace in this world, and a life of glory in the world to come.—He says, "I give," in the present tense. Eternal life is the present possession of every believer.—He declares that they shall never perish or be lost, unto all eternity; and that no one shall ever pluck them out of His hand.

We have here the divinity and dignity of our Lord Jesus Christ. None but one who was very God could say, "I give eternal life." No Apostle ever said so.

We have here the perpetuity of grace in believers, and the certainty that they shall never be cast away. How any one can deny this doctrine, as the Arminians do, and say that a true believer may fall away and be lost, in the face of this text, it is hard to understand. It is my own deliberate opinion that it would be almost impossible to imagine words in which a saint's "perseverance" could be more strongly asserted.

We have here a distinct promise, that "no one," man, angel, devil, or spirit, shall be able to tear from Christ His sheep. The Greek literally is not "any man," but "any person, or any one."

The doctrine plainly taught in this text may be called "Calvinism" by some, and "of dangerous tendency" by others. The only question we ought to ask is, whether it is scriptural. The simplest answer to that question is, that the words of the text, in their plain and obvious meaning, cannot be honestly interpreted in any other way. To thrust in, as some enemies of perseverance do, the qualifying clause, "They shall never perish *so long as they continue my sheep*," is adding to Scripture, and taking unwarrantable liberties with Christ's words.

So, again, Whitby's interpretation, "They shall never perish through any defect on my part," though they may fall away by their own fault, is a sad instance of unfair handling of Scripture.

Let it only be remembered that the character of those who shall never perish is most distinctly and carefully laid down in this place. It is those who hear Christ's voice and follow Him, who alone are "sheep:" it is "His sheep," and His sheep alone, who shall never perish. The man who boasts that he shall never be cast away, and never perish, while he is living in sin, is a miserable self-deceiver. It is the perseverance of *saints*, and not of sinners and wicked people, that is promised here. Doubtless the doctrine of the text may be misused and abused, like every other good thing. But to the humble penitent believer, who puts his trust in Christ, it is one of the most glorious and comfortable truths of the Gospel. Those who dislike it would do well to study the 17th Article of the Church of England, and Hooker's sermon on the "Perpetuity of Faith in the Elect."

Let it be noted that the last clause of the text plainly implies that many will try to pluck away Christians from Christ, and draw them back to sin. To feel that something is always "plucking" and "pulling" at us must never surprise believers. There is a devil, and saints will always feel and find his presence.

Let it be noted, that to *be* safe in Christ's hand, and so never to perish, is one thing; but to *feel* that we are safe is quite another. Many true believers *are* safe, who do not realize and *feel* it.

Musculus observes that our Lord does not say in this verse that His sheep shall lose nothing in this world. They may lose property, liberty, and life, for Christ's sake. But their souls cannot be lost. He also observes that all Christ's sheep are in Christ's hand. *His* hand holding them, and not *their* hand holding Him, is the true secret of their safety and perseverance.

The importance of the doctrine contained in this text cannot, in my judgment, be overrated. The Christian who does not hold it is a great loser. It is one of the grand elements of the good news of the Gospel. It is a safeguard against much unsound doctrine. Perseverance can never be reconciled with baptismal regeneration. The advocates of an extravagant view of baptismal grace, it may be observed, always have a special dislike to the doctrine of this text.

Hengstenberg wisely remarks, " It is cold consolation to say, if and so long as they remain my sheep they are secure, and shall never perish. The whole strength of our soul's desire is for a guarantee against *ourselves*. That there is such a guarantee is here assured to us."

29.—[*My Father who gave, etc., etc.*] Our Lord here strengthens the mighty promise just made, by declaring that His sheep are not His only, but His Father's : His Father gave them to Him. "My Father, He declares, is 'almighty,' or greater than all ; the possessor of all power. No one is able to pluck *anything* out of my Father's hand, so that my sheep's safety is doubly secured." Let it be noted that the word "them," in the last clause of our English version, is not in the Greek.

It is probable that both in this verse and the preceding one, there is a latent reference to the case of the man whom the Pharisees had lately "cast out " of the Church, or excommunicated. Our Lord seems to say, "You may cut off and tear away from your outward Church-membership whom you will ; but you can never pluck away any of my people from Me."

Let it be noted here that the Father is just as much interested in the safety of believers as the Son. To leave out of sight the Father's love, in our zeal for the glory of Christ, is very poor theology.

Melancthon dwells on this promise in a passage of singular beauty. He specially dwells on it as a ground of comfort against the invasion of Europe by the Turks, the persecution of truth by so-called Christian princes, and the furious strifes and controversies of teachers of the Church. There is a Church which nothing can harm.

Calvin remarks, "Our salvation is certain, because it is in the hand of God. Our faith is weak, and we are prone to waver: but God, who hath taken us under His protection is sufficiently powerful to scatter with a breath all the power of our adversaries. It is of great importance to turn our eyes to this."

Musculus observes that it is said the Father "gave" the sheep to Me, in the past tense. Believers were given to Christ before the foundation of the world.

30.—*I and the Father are one*] In order to explain how it is that the Father should take as much interest in the sheep as the Son, our Lord here declares in the plainest and most explicit terms, the deep truth of the essential unity between Himself and His Father. Literally translated, the sentence is, "I and my Father are one thing." By this, of course, He did not mean that His Father and He were one Person. This would overthrow the doctrine of the Trinity. But He did mean, "I and my eternal Father, though two distinct Persons, and not to be confounded, are yet one in essence, nature, dignity, power, will, and operation. Hence, in the matter of securing the safety of my sheep, what I do, my Father does likewise. I do not act independently of Him."

This is one of those deep and mysterious texts which we must be content to receive and believe, without attempting to pry too curiously into its contents. The cautious and exact words of the Athanasian Creed should be often remembered: "Neither confounding the Persons, nor dividing the substance. There is one Person of the Father, another of the Son, and another of the Holy Ghost: but the Godhead of the Father, of the Son, and of the Holy Ghost is all one, the glory equal, the majesty co-eternal."

Augustine remarks that this text alone overthrows both the doctrine of the Sabellians and the Arians. It silences the Sabellians, who say there is only one Person in the Godhead, by speaking of two distinct Persons. It silences the Arians, who say the Son is inferior to the Father, by saying that Father and Son are "one."

Let it be noted that the doctrine of this verse is precisely the same that our Lord had maintained on a former occasion (in the fifth chapter) before the Sanhedrim.   There it was expounded fully : here it is briefly asserted.   And the interpretation put on His meaning, in both cases, by the Jews, was exactly the same. They regarded it as a claim to be regarded as "God."

The practical use of the text to a believer in Christ is far too much overlooked.   It shows the entire childlike confidence with which such an one may look at the Father.   "He who hath the Son hath the Father."   The remark is only too true that while some ignorantly talk of the Father, as if there was no Christ crucified, others with no less ignorance talk of Christ crucified as if there was no God and Father of Christ, who loved the world !

Chrysostom observes, "That thou mayest not suppose that Christ is weak, and the sheep are in safety through the Father's power, He addeth, 'I and the Father are one.'   As though He had said, I did not assert that on account of the Father no man plucketh them away, as though I were too weak to keep the sheep.   For I and the Father are one.   He speaks here with reference to power, for concerning this was all His discourse ; and if the power be the same, it is clear that the essence is also."

Ecolampadius remarks, "He does not say we are one in the masculine gender,—that is one person ; but one in the neuter gender,—that is one in nature, power, and majesty.   If you were to say one Person, you would take away both, and leave neither Father nor Son."

Maldonatus quotes a saying of Augustine's, "that it is invariably found in Scripture that things called 'one' are things of the same nature."

It is fair to admit that Erasmus, Calvin, and a few others, think the "oneness" here only means unity of consent and will. But the vast majority of commentators think otherwise, and the Jews evidently thought so also.

JOHN X. 31—42.

31 Then the Jews took up stones again to stone him.

32 Jesus answered them, Many good works have I shewed you from my Father; for which of those works do ye stone me?

33 The Jews answered him, saying, For a good work we stone thee not; but for blasphemy : and because that thou, being a man, makest thyself God.

34 Jesus answered them, Is it not written in your law, I said, Ye are gods?

35 If he called them gods, unto whom the word of God came, and the scripture cannot be broken ;

36 Say ye of him, whom the Father hath sanctified, and sent into the world, Thou blasphemest; because I said, I am the Son of God?

37 If I do not the works of my Father, believe me not.

38 But if I do, though ye believe not me, believe the works: that ye may know, and believe, that the Father is in me, and I in him.

39 Therefore they sought again to take him: but he escaped out of their hand,

40 And went away again beyond Jordan into the place where John at first baptized; and there he abode.

41 And many resorted unto him, and said, John did no miracle: but all things that John spake of this man were true.

42 And many believed on him there

WE should observe, in these verses, *the extreme wickedness of human nature.* The unbelieving Jews at Jerusalem were neither moved by our Lord's miracles nor by His preaching. They were determined not to receive Him as their Messiah. Once more it is written that "they took up stones to stone Him."

Our Lord had done the Jews no injury. He was no robber, murderer, or rebel against the law of the land. He was one whose whole life was love, and who "went about doing good." (Acts x. 38.) There was no fault or inconsistency in His character. There was no crime that could be laid to His charge. So perfect and spotless a Being had never walked on the face of this earth. But yet the Jews hated Him, and thirsted for His blood. How true are the words of Scripture: "They hated Him without a cause." (John xv. 25.) How just the remark of an old divine: "Unconverted men would kill God Himself if they could only get at Him."

The true Christian has surely no right to wonder if he meets with the same kind of treatment as our blessed Lord. In fact, the more like he is to his Master, and the more holy and spiritual his life, the more probable is it that he will have to endure hatred and persecution. Let him not suppose that any degree of consistency will deliver him from this cross. It is not his faults, but his graces, which call forth the enmity of men. The world hates to see anything of God's image. The children of the world are vexed and pricked in conscience when they see others better than themselves. Why did Cain hate his brother Abel, and slay him? "Because," says St. John, "his own works were evil, and his brother's righteous." (1 John iii. 12.) Why did the Jews hate Christ? Because He exposed their sins and false doctrines; and they knew in their own hearts that He was right and they were wrong. "The world," said our Lord, "hateth Me, because I testify of it, that the works thereof are evil." (John vii. 7.) Let Christians make up their minds to drink the same cup, and let them drink it patiently and without surprise. There is One in heaven who said, "If the world hate you, ye know that it hated Me before it hated you." (John xv. 18.) Let them remember this and take courage. The time is short. We are travelling on towards a day when all shall be set right, and every man shall receive according to his works. "There is an end: and our expectation shall not be cut off." (Prov. xxiii. 18.)

We should observe, secondly, in these verses, *the high honour that Jesus Christ puts on the Holy Scriptures.* We find Him using a text out of the Psalms as an argument against His enemies, in which the whole point lies in the single word "gods." And then having quoted the text, He lays down the great principle, "the Scripture cannot be broken." It is as though He said, " Wherever the Scripture speaks plainly on any subject, there can be no more question about it. The case is settled and decided. Every jot and tittle of Scripture is true, and must be received as conclusive."

The principle here laid down by our Lord is one of vast importance. Let us grasp it firmly, and never let it go. Let us maintain boldly the complete inspiration of every word of the original Hebrew and Greek Scriptures. Let us believe that not only every book of the Bible, but every chapter,—and not only every chapter, but every verse,—and not only every verse, but every word, was originally given by inspiration of God. Inspiration, we must never shrink from asserting, extends not only to the thoughts and ideas of Scripture, but to the least words.

The principle before us, no doubt, is rudely assaulted in the present day. Let no Christian's heart fail because of these assaults. Let us stand our ground manfully, and defend the principle of plenary inspiration as we would the apple of our eye. There are difficulties in Scripture, we need not shrink from conceding; things hard to explain, hard to reconcile, and hard to understand. But in almost all these difficulties, the fault, we may justly suspect, is not so much in Scripture as in our own weak minds. In all cases we may well be content to wait for more light, and to believe that all shall be made clear at last. One thing we may rest assured is very certain,—if the difficulties of plenary inspiration are to be numbered by thousands, the difficulties of any other view of inspiration are to be numbered by tens of thousands. The wisest course is to walk in the old path,

—the path of faith and humility ; and say, " I cannot give up a single word of my Bible. All Scripture is given by inspiration of God. The Scripture cannot be broken."

We should observe, lastly, in these verses, *the impor-tance which our Lord Jesus Christ attaches to His miracles.* He appeals to them as the best evidence of His own Divine mission. He bids the Jews look at them, and deny them if they can. " If I do not the works of my Father, believe Me not. But if I do, though ye believe not Me, believe the works."

The mighty miracles which our Lord performed during the three years of His earthly ministry, are probably not considered as much as they ought to be in the present day. These miracles were not few in number. Forty times and more we read in the Gospels of His doing things entirely out of the ordinary course of nature,—healing sick people in a moment, raising the dead with a word, casting out devils, calming winds and waves in an instant, walking on the water as on solid ground. These miracles were not all done in private among friends. Many of them were wrought in the most public manner, under the eyes of unfriendly wit-nesses. We are so familiar with these things that we are apt to forget the mighty lesson they teach. They teach that He who worked these miracles must be no-thing less than very God. They stamp His doctrines and precepts with the mark of Divine authority. He only who created all things at the beginning, could sus-pend the laws of creation at His will. He who could suspend the laws of creation, must be One who ought to be thoroughly believed and implicitly obeyed. To reject One who confirmed His mission by such mighty works, is the height of madness and folly

Hundreds of unbelieving men, no doubt, in every age, have tried to pour contempt on Christ's miracles, and to deny that they were ever worked at all. But they labour in vain. Proofs upon proofs exist that our Lord's ministry was accompanied by miracles; and that this was acknowledged by those who lived in our Lord's time. Objectors of this sort would do well to take up the one single miracle of our Lord's resurrection from the dead, and disprove it if they can. If they cannot disprove that, they ought, as honest men, to confess that miracles are possible. And then, if their hearts are truly humble, they ought to admit that He whose mission was confirmed by such evidence must have been the Son of God.

Let us thank God, as we turn from this passage, that Christianity has such abundant evidence that it is a religion from God. Whether we appeal to the internal evidence of the Bible, or to the lives of the first Christians, or to prophecy, or to miracles, or to history, we get one and the same answer.—All say with one voice, "Jesus is the Son of God, and believers have life through His name."

NOTES. JOHN x. 31—42.

31.—[*Then the Jews took up stones, etc.*] The conduct of the Jews is just the same as it was when our Lord said, "Before Abraham was I am." (John viii. 59.) They regarded His words as blasphemy, and proceeded to take the law in their own hands, as they did in Stephen's case, and to inflict the punishment due to blas-phemy. (See Lev. xxiv. 14—16.) "He that blasphemeth the name of the Lord, he shall surely be put to death, and all the congrega-tion shall certainly stone him." (So Num. xv. 36 ; 1 Kings xxi. 13.) The Jews of course had no power to put any man to death, being under the dominion of the Romans, and if they did stone any one it would have been a sudden tumultuary proceeding, or act of what is called in America Lynch-law.

Let it be noted that the Greek word for "took up" here, is not the same that is used at viii. 59. Here it rather means "they carried." Parkhurst thinks this implies the great size of the stones they brought. No doubt the stones used in stoning to death, were not pebbles, but large stones. Yet I rather incline to think that it shows that they had to carry stones from some little distance for their murderous purpose. We can hardly sup-pose there were suitable stones lying about within an old finished building like Solomon's porch, though there might be stones at a little distance on account of the repairs of the temple.

Augustine remarks, "Behold the Jews understood what Arians do not understand."

Maldonatus observes that "these stones cry out against the Arians."

32.—[*Jesus...many good works...shewed.. Father, etc.*] Our Lord here appeals to the many miracles He had publicly wrought before the Jews, in discharging His commission as sent by the Father to be the Messiah, all good and excellent works, in which none could find any fault, and He asks whether they proposed to stone Him for any of them. They had often asked for signs and proofs of His being the Messiah. Well, He had wrought many such signs. Did they really mean to kill Him for His works? He had gone about only doing good. Did they intend to stone Him for this?

The expression "I have shewed" is curious, and we should have expected rather "I have worked." It probably means, "I have publicly exhibited before your eyes, and not in a corner, but in such a manner as to court the fullest public observation, many wonderful proofs of my Messiahship." (Compare John ii. 18 : "What sign shewest Thou.") So St. Paul says that "God shall in His own time shew the appearing of Jesus Christ." (1 Tim. vi. 15.) The expression is probably a Hebraism. (Compare Psalm iv. 6 ; lx. 3 ; lxxi. 20. Exod. vii. 9.)

The expression "from my Father" points to the great truth continually brought forward by our Lord in this Gospel : viz., that all His works as well as words were given to Him by the Father, to be worked and spoken in the world, and ought therefore to be held in special reverence.

Hengstenberg observes, that the expression "many good works," evidently supposes that John knew of many other miracles, which he does not record, and that many had been done at Jerusalem beside the few that are recorded.

[*For which...works...stone Me ?*] This could be literally rendered, "On account of which work of all these are you stoning Me?" Some, as Gualter and Tholuck, have thought that there is a slight tinge of sarcasm about the question. "Is it so that you are actually going to stone Me for good actions? Are not men generally stoned for evil doings?" Yet this seems an unlikely idea, and is needless. Is not the meaning made clear by simply inverting the order of words? "For what work or action are you going to stone Me? Justice requires that criminals should be punished for doing evil works : but all the many wonderful works I have done among you have been good and not evil. You surely will not stone Me for any of these : reason and your laws teach that this would be wrong. It is not therefore for my works and life that you are going to stone Me. I challenge you to prove that I have done evil. Which of you convicteth Me of sin?"

Taken in this view, the verse is simply a strong assertion made by our Lord, of His own entire innocence of any crime for which He could be stoned.

Hutcheson thinks that "some stones were already cast at Christ, and therefore He says, Do you stone Me?" Yet this seems needless. The present tense here implies only, Are ye on the point of stoning Me?

33.—[*The Jews answered, etc.*] Our Lord's confident challenge, as in chap. viii. 46, seems to have been found unanswerable by the Jews. They could not prove any evil work against Him. They therefore reply that they do not propose to stone Him for His *works*, but for having spoken blasphemous *words*. The precise nature of the blasphemy they say is, that "being nothing but a mere man, He made Himself God, or spoke of Himself in such a way as showed that He claimed to be God."

This is a very remarkable verse. It is like chap. v. 18 : "The Jews sought to kill Him, because He said that God was His Father, making Himself equal with God." It shows clearly that the Jews in our Lord's time attached a much higher and deeper sense to our Lord's frequently used language about God being His Father than modern readers are apt to do. In fact they regarded it as nothing less than a claim to equality with God.—Modern Arians and Socinians, who profess to see nothing in our Lord's Sonship but a higher degree of that relationship which exists between all believers and God, would do well to mark this verse. What they say they cannot see, the Jews who hated Christ could see. This "cotemporaneous exposition," to use a legal phrase, of our Lord's words, deserves great respect, and carries with it great weight and authority. As a man, our Lord was a Jew, educated and trained among Jews. Common sense points out that the Jews who lived in His times were more likely to put a correct sense on His words than modern Socinians.

Gualter observes, how frequently wicked men and persecutors of Christ's people have affected a zeal for God's glory, and pretended a horror of blasphemy. The accusers of Naboth and Stephen are examples : so also the Spanish Inquisition.

A. Clarke observes, "that had the Jews, as many called Christians do, understood our Lord only to mean, by being 'one with the Father,' that He had unity of *sentiment* with the Father, they would not have attempted to treat Him as a blasphemer. In this sense Abraham, Isaac, Moses, David, and all the prophets were one with God. But what irritated them was that they understood him to speak of unity of *nature*. Therefore they say, "Thou makest Thyself God."

34.—[*Jesus answered them, etc.*] Our Lord's defence of His own language against the charge of blasphemy is very remarkable. It is an argument from a lesser to a greater. If princes, who are merely men, are called gods, He who was the eternal Son of the Father could surely not be justly chargeable with blasphemy for calling Himself the "Son of God."

The expression "your law," means the Scriptures. Sometimes our Lord speaks of two great divisions into which the Jews divided the Old Testament : viz., the law and the prophets. (As Matt. xxii. 40.) The "law" then included not the books of Moses only, but everything down to the end of the Song of Solomon. Sometimes He distributes the Scriptures into three parts : the law, the psalms, and the prophets. (As in Luke xxii. 44.) Here He uses one word for all the Old Testament, and calls it "the law." By saying "your law," our Lord reminds His hearers that He appeals to *their own* honoured sacred writings.

The expression, "I said ye are gods," is drawn from the 82nd Psalm, in which Asaph is speaking of princes and rulers, and their position and duties. Their elevation above other men was so great, and their consequent responsibility for the state of nations so great, that compared to other men, it might be said, "You are as gods." A King is called "the Lord's anointed." (2 Sam. i. 14.) So "Ye judge not for man, but for the Lord." (2 Chron. xix. 6.) Princes and magistrates are ordained of God, derive their power from God, act for God, and stand between the people and God. Hence, in a sense, they are called "gods." Those who wish to see this subject fully worked out, will see it in Hall and Swinnock's Exposition of the 82nd Psalm.

We should observe how our Lord appeals to Scripture as the judge of controversy : "Is it not written?" A plain text ought to settle every disputed point. He might have argued : He simply quotes a text. By so doing He puts peculiar honour on Scripture.

It is worth noticing that the Hebrew word rendered "judges" in our version of Exodus xxii. 8, 9, might have been rendered "gods." (Compare Exodus xxii. 28 ; xxi. 6.)

35.—[*If he called them gods.*] Here our Lord proceeds to show what was the edge and point of His argument. All turned on the use of the single word "gods" in one single verse of a Psalm.

It is not very clear what governs the word we render "called" in this sentence. Our translators evidently thought it meant "God." But why should it not refer direct to "your law" in the last verse ? "If your own book of the law in a Psalm has called certain persons gods."

Chrysostom observes, "What He saith is of this kind : 'If those who have received this honour by grace, are not found fault with for calling themselves gods, how can He deserve to be rebuked who hath this by nature.'" Theophylact says the same.

[*To whom the Word of God came.*] This is a rather difficult expression. Some, as Bullinger and Burgon, think that it refers to the commission from God which rulers receive : "they are persons to whom God has spoken, and commanded them to rule for Him." Some, as Alford, think it simply means, "if He called them gods, to whom God spake in these passages." But it may justly be replied that it does not say "God spake ;" but, "There was the Word of God."—Of the two views the former seems best. The Greek is almost the same as that of Luke iii. 2 : "The word of God came to John,"—meaning a special commission.

Heinsius suggests that the sentence means "*against* whom the word of God was" spoken in the 82nd Psalm : that Psalm containing a rebuke of princes. But this seems doubtful.

Pearce thinks that it means "with whom was the word of judgment?" and refers to the Septuagint version of 2 Chron. xix. 6.

It deserves notice that it is never said of Christ Himself, that the "Word of God came to Him." He was above all other commissioned judges.

[*And the Scripture cannot be broken.*] In this remarkable parenthesis our Lord reminds His Jewish hearers of their own acknowledged principle, that the "Scripture cannot be annulled or broken:" that is, that everything which it says must be received reverently and unhesitatingly, and that not one jot or tittle of it ought to be disregarded. Every word of Scripture must be allowed its full weight, and must neither be clipped, passed over, nor evaded. If the 82nd Psalm calls princes who are mere men "gods," there cannot be any impropriety in applying the expression to persons commissioned by God. The expression may seem strange at first. Never mind, it is in the Scripture and it must be right.

Few passages appear to me to prove so incontrovertibly, the plenary inspiration and divine authority of every word in the original text of the Bible. The whole point of our Lord's argument hinges on the divine authority of a single word. Was that word in the Psalms? Then it justified the application of the expression "gods" to men. Scripture cannot be broken. The theories of those who say that the writers of the Bible were inspired, but not all their writings,—or the ideas of the Bible inspired, but not all the language in which these ideas are conveyed,—appear to be totally irreconcilable with our Lord's use of the sentence before us. There is no other standing ground I believe, about inspiration, excepting the principle that it is plenary, and reaches to every syllable. Once leaving that ground, we are plunged in a sea of uncertainties. Like the careful composed language of wills, settlements, and conveyances, every word of the Bible must be held sacred, and not a single flaw or slip of the pen admitted.

Let it be noted that the literal meaning of the word rendered "broken," is loosed or untied.

Gill observes, "This is a Jewish way of speaking, much used in the Talmud. When one doctor has produced an argument, another says, 'It may be broken,' or objected to, or refuted. But the Scripture cannot be broken."

Hengstenberg says, "It cannot be doubted that the Scripture is broken by those who assert that the Psalms breathe a spirit of revenge, that Solomon's song is a common Oriental love song, that there are in the Prophets predictions never to be fulfilled,—or by those who deny the Mosaic authorship of the Pentateuch."

36.—[*Say ye of Him, etc.*] Our Lord in this verse presses home on the Jews the force of the expression in the 82nd Psalm. "If princes are called gods, do you mean to call Me, whom the Father sanctified from eternity to be Messiah, and sent into the world in due time, a blasphemer, because I have said I am the Son of God"?

"Say ye of *Him*" would have been better rendered, "Say ye of *Me*." The Greek leaves it open.

The expression "whom the Father hath sanctified," must mean, "whom the Father hath set apart, and appointed from all eternity in the covenant of grace, as a priest is sanctified and set apart for the service of the temple." It cannot mean literally "made holy." It implies eternal dedication and appointment to a certain office. This is one of the places which teach the eternal generation of Christ. Long before He came into the world, "the Father" (not *God*, observe) had sanctified and appointed the Son. He did not become the Son when He entered the world : He was the Son from all eternity.

The expression, "sent into the world," means that *mission* of Christ's to be the Saviour, which took place when He became incarnate, and came among us in the form of a man. He was the Father's "sent One," the "Apostle" of our profession. (See Heb. iii. 1. John iii. 17, and 1 John iv. 14.) He that was so "sanctified" and "sent," might well speak of Himself as the Son of God, and equal with God.

Calvin remarks, "There is a sanctification that is common to all believers. But here Christ claims for Himself something far more excellent : namely, that He alone was separated from all others, that the grace of the Spirit and majesty of God might be displayed in Him ; as He said formerly, "Him hath God the Father sealed." (John vi. 27.)

37.—[*If I do not the works, etc.*] Here our Lord once more appeals to the evidence of His miracles, and challenges attention to them. "I do not ask you to believe that I am the Son of God and the Messiah, if I do not prove it by my works. If I did no miracles, you might be justified in not believing Me to be the Messiah, and in calling Me a blasphemer."

Here, again, we should observe how our Lord calls His miracles the "works of His Father." They were works given to Him by His Father to do. They were such works as none but God the Father could possibly perform.

Gualter observes, what a proof this verse indirectly supplies of the nullity of the Pope's claim to be God's vice-gerent and head of the Church. What are his works? What evidence of a divine mission does he give?

Musculus also remarks that the Pope's high claims and great sounding titles are useless, so long as his works contradict his words.

38.—[*But if I do, though, etc.*] Our Lord here concludes His reply to the Jews : "If I do the works of my Father, then, though ye may not be convinced by what I say, be convinced by what I do. Though ye resist the evidence of my words, yield to the evidence of my works. In this way learn to know and believe that I and my Father are indeed one, He in Me and I in Him, and that in claiming to be His Son, I speak no blasphemy."

We should note here, as elsewhere, our Lord's strong and repeated appeals to the evidence of His miracles. He sent to John the Baptist, and desired him to mark His works, if he would know whether He was "the coming One,"—"Go and tell John what ye have seen and heard, the blind receive their sight," etc. Just so He argues here. (Matt. xi. 4.)

Let us note the close and intimate union that exists between the First and Second Persons of the Trinity : "The Father is in Me, and I in Him." Such language can never be reconciled with the views of Socinians.

"By these words," says Bloomfield, "our Lord meant communion of mind and equality of power. It is plain that the Jews clearly understood that He claimed and ascribed to Himself the attributes of Godhead, and made Himself equal with the Father."

Chrysostom remarks, that our Lord seems to say, "I am nothing different from what the Father is, so however as that I remain Son ; and the Father is nothing different from what I am, so however as that He remains Father. He that knows Me has known the Father, and learned the Son."

39.—[*Therefore...sought...take Him.*] Here we see the utter insensibility of our Lord's hardened enemies to any argument or appeal to their reason. In spite of what He had now said, they showed a determination to go on with their wicked designs, and tried again to lay violent hands on Him. Nothing seems to harden the heart and take away the reasoning faculty, so completely as obstinate resistance to plain evidence.

[*But He escaped...hand.*] This would be literally rendered, "And He came forth out of their hand," as in Luke iv. 30 ; and at viii. 59 of this Gospel. The escape seems to have been effected by miracle. A restraint was put on the hands of His enemies, and their eyes were temporarily blinded.

40.—[*And went...again...Jordan...John...baptized.*] I know not to what the expression "again" can refer here, except to the time when our Lord began His ministry by coming to be baptized by John at Bethabara, beyond Jordan. (See John i. 28.) I do not find that He had been there again during the three years of His ministry. There is something touching and instructive in the choice of this place. Where our Lord began His ministry, there He resolved to end it. It would remind His Jewish hearers that John the Baptist had repeatedly proclaimed Him as "the Lamb of God," and they could not deny John's divine mission. It would remind His own disciples of the first lessons which they learned under their Master's teaching, and recall old things to their minds. It is good to revisit old scenes sometimes. The flesh needs many helps to memory.

Henry makes the quaint remark, "The Bishop of our souls came not to be fixed in one See, but to go about from place to place doing good."

[*And there He abode.*] Our Lord must evidently have remained here between three and four months,—from the feast of dedication to the last passover, when He was crucified ; that is from winter to Easter. Where precisely, and with whom He stayed, we do not know. It must have been a solemn and quiet season to Himself and His disciples.

Musculus observes that this verse teaches us that it is lawful to regard localities in which great spiritual works have been done with more than ordinary reverence and affection.

41.—[*And many resorted, etc.*] Our Lord's choice of an abode seems to have had an excellent effect. It was not so far from Jerusalem but that "many" could come to hear Him, as they did to hear John the Baptist. There, on the very spot where John, now no longer living, used to preach to enormous crowds, and baptize, they could not help being reminded of John's repeated testimony to Christ. And the consequence was, that they said, "John, whom we believe to have been a prophet, certainly did no miracles, but everything that he said of this Jesus as the coming One, whose shoes he was not worthy to wear, was true. We believed John to be a prophet sent of God. Much more ought this man to be believed."

Let us observe that John's preaching was not forgotten after his death, though it seemed to produce little effect during his life. Herod could cut short his ministry, put him in prison, and have him beheaded ; but he could not prevent his words being remembered. Sermons never die. The Word of God is not bound. (2 Tim. ii. 9.)

We never read of any miracle or mighty work being performed by John. He was only "a voice." Like all other ministers, he had one great work,—to preach, and prepare the way for Christ. To do this is more lasting work than to perform miracles, though it does not make so much outward show.

Besser remarks, "John is a type of every servant of Christ. The gift of working miracles, imparted but to few, we can do without, if only one hearer testify of us, 'All things that they spake of Christ are true.' If only our preaching, though it may last longer than three years, is sealed as the true witness of Christ, through the experience of those who believe and are saved, then we shall have done miracles enough."

42.—[*And many believed—there.*] Whether this was head belief, the faith of intellectual conviction,—or heart belief, the faith of reception of Christ as a Saviour,—we are left in doubt. We have the same expression in viii. 30 and xi. 45. Yet we need not doubt that very many Jews, both here and elsewhere, were secretly convinced of our Lord's Messiahship. and after His resurrection came forward and confessed their faith, and were baptized. It seems highly probable that this accounts for the great number converted at once on the day of Pentecost and at other times. (See Acts iv. 4; vi. 7; and xxi. 20.) The way had been prepared in their hearts long before, by our Lord's own preaching, though at the time they had not courage to avow it.

The good that is done by preaching is not always seen immediately. Our Lord sowed, and His Apostles reaped, all over Palestine.

Chrysostom has a long and curious comment on this verse. He draws from it the great advantage of privacy and quiet to the soul, and the benefit that women especially derive from living a retired life at home, compared to men. His exhortation to wives to use their advantages in this respect, and to help their husbands' souls, is very singular, when we consider the times he wrote in, and the state of society at Constantinople. "Nothing," he says, "is more powerful than a pious and sensible woman, to bring a man into proper order, and to mould his soul as she will."

Henry observes, "Where the preaching of repentance has had success, there the preaching of reconciliation and Gospel grace is most likely to be prosperous. Where John has been acceptable, Jesus will not be unacceptable. The jubilee trumpet sounds sweetest in the ears of those who, in the day of atonement have afflicted their souls for sin."

JOHN XI. 1—6.

1 Now a certain *man* was sick, *named* Lazarus, of Bethany, the town of Mary and her sister Martha.

2 (It was *that* Mary which anointed the Lord with ointment, and wiped his feet with her hair, whose brother Lazarus was sick.)

3 Therefore his sisters sent unto him, saying, Lord, behold, he whom thou lovest is sick.

4 When Jesus heard *that*, he said, This sickness is not unto death, but for the glory of God, that the Son of God might be glorified thereby.

5 Now Jesus loved Martha, and her sister, and Lazarus.

6 When he had heard therefore that he was sick, he abode two days still in the same place where he was.

THE chapter we have now begun is one of the most remarkable in the New Testament. For grandeur and simplicity, for pathos and solemnity, nothing was ever written like it. It describes a miracle which is not recorded in the other Gospels,—the raising of Lazarus from the dead. Nowhere shall we find such convincing proofs of our Lord's Divine power. As God, He makes the grave itself yield up its tenants.—Nowhere shall we find such striking illustrations of our Lord's ability to sympathize with his people. As man, He can be touched with the feeling of our infirmities.—Such a miracle well became the end of such a ministry. It was meet and right that the victory of Bethany should closely precede the crucifixion at Calvary.

These verses teach us that *true Christians may be sick and ill as well as others*. We read that Lazarus of Bethany was one "whom Jesus loved," and a brother of two well-known holy women. Yet Lazarus was sick, even unto death! The Lord Jesus, who had power over all diseases, could no doubt have prevented this illness, if He had thought fit. But He did not do so. He allowed Lazarus to be sick, and in pain, and weary, and to languish, and suffer, like any other man.

The lesson is one which ought to be deeply graven in our memories. Living in a world full of disease and death, we are sure to need it some day. Sickness, in the very nature of things, can never be anything but trying to flesh and blood. Our bodies and souls are strangely linked together, and that which vexes and weakens the body can hardly fail to vex the mind and soul. But sickness, we must always remember, is no sign that God is displeased with us: nay, more, it is generally sent for the good of our souls. It tends to draw our affections away from this world, and to direct them to things above. It sends us to our Bibles, and teaches us to pray better. It helps to prove our faith and patience, and shows us the real value of our hope in Christ. It reminds us betimes that we are not to live always, and tunes and trains our hearts for our great change Then let us be patient and cheerful when we are laid aside by illness. Let us believe that the Lord Jesus loves us when we are sick no less than when we are well.

These verses teach us, secondly, that *Jesus Christ is the Christian's best Friend in the time of need.* We read that when Lazarus was sick, his sisters at once sent to Jesus, and laid the matter before Him. Beautiful, touching, and simple was the message they sent. They did not ask Him to come at once, or to work a miracle, and command the disease to depart. They only said, " Lord, he whom Thou lovest is sick," and left the matter there, in the full belief that He would do what was best. Here was the true faith and humility of saints! Here was gracious submission of will!

The servants of Christ, in every age and climate, will do well to follow this excellent example. No doubt when those whom we love are sick, we are to use diligently every reasonable means for their recovery. We must spare no pains to obtain the best medical advice. We must assist nature in every possible manner to fight a good fight against its enemy. But in all our doing, we must never forget that the best and ablest and wisest Helper is in heaven, at God's right hand. Like afflicted Job, our first action must be to fall on our knees and worship. Like Hezekiah, we must spread our matters before the Lord. Like the holy sisters at Bethany, we must send up a prayer to Christ. Let us not forget, in the hurry and excitement of our feelings, that none can help like Him, and that He is merciful, loving, and gracious.

These verses teach us, thirdly, that *Christ loves all who are true Christians.* We read that "Jesus loved Martha, and her sister, and Lazarus." The characters of these three good people seem to have been somewhat different. Of Martha, we are told in a certain place, that she was "careful and troubled about many things," while Mary "sat at Jesus' feet, and heard His word." Of Lazarus, we are told nothing distinctive at all. Yet all these were loved by the Lord Jesus. They all belonged to His family, and He loved them all.

We must carefully bear this in mind in forming our estimate of Christians. We must never forget that there are varieties in character, and that the grace of God does not cast all believers into one and the same mould. Admitting fully that the foundations of Christian character are always the same, and that all God's children repent, believe, are holy, prayerful, and Scripture-loving, we must make allowances for wide varieties in their temperaments and habits of mind. We must not undervalue others because they are not exactly like ourselves. The flowers in a garden may differ widely, and yet the gardener feels interest in all. The children of a family may be curiously unlike one another, and yet the parents care for all. It is even so with the Church of Christ. There are degrees of grace, and varieties of grace ; but the least, the weakest. the feeblest disciples, are all loved by the Lord Jesus. Then let no believer's heart fail because of his infirmities and, above all, let no believer dare to despise and undervalue a brother.

These verses teach us, lastly, that *Christ knows best at what time to do anything for His people.* We read that "when He had heard that Lazarus was sick, He abode two days still in the same place where He was." In fact, He purposely delayed His journey, and did not come to Bethany till Lazarus had been four days in the grave. No doubt He knew well what was going on : but He never moved till the time came which He saw was best. For the sake of the Church and the world, for the good of friends and enemies, He kept away.

The children of God must constantly school their minds to learn the great lesson now before us. Nothing so helps us to bear patiently the trials of life as an abiding conviction of the perfect wisdom by which everything around us is managed. Let us try to believe not only that all that happens to us is well done, but that it is done in the best manner, by the right instrument, and at the right time. We are all naturally impatient in the day of trial. We are apt to say, like Moses, when beloved ones are sick, "Heal her *now*, Lord, we beseech Thee." (Num. xii. 13.) We forget that Christ is too wise a Physician to make any mistakes. It is the duty of faith to say, "My times are in Thy hand. Do with me as Thou wilt, how Thou wilt, what Thou wilt, and when Thou wilt. Not my will, but Thine be done." The highest degree of faith is to be able to wait, sit still, and not complain.

Let us turn from the passage with a settled determination to trust Christ entirely with all the concerns

of this world, both public and private. Let us believe
that He by whom all things were made at first is He
who is managing all with perfect wisdom. The affairs
of kingdoms, families, and private individuals, are all
alike overruled by Him. He chooses all the portions
of His people. When we are sick, it is because He
knows it to be for our good : when He delays coming
to help us, it is for some wise reason. The hand that
was nailed to the cross is too wise and loving to smite
without a needs-be, or to keep us waiting for relief
without a cause.

NOTES. JOHN XI. 1—6.

The raising of Lazarus, described in this chapter, is one of the
most wonderful events recorded in the Gospels, and demands more
than ordinary attention. In no part of our Lord's history do we
see Him so distinctly both man and God at the same time : man
in sympathy, and God in power. Like each of the few incidents
in our Lord's ministry related by St. John, it is placed before us
with peculiar minuteness and particularity. The story is singularly
rich in delicate, tender, and beautiful expressions. Before entering
upon it, I venture to offer the following preliminary remarks.

(a) The raising of Lazarus was manifestly intended to supply
the Jews with one more incontrovertible proof that Jesus was the
Christ of God, the promised Messiah. In the tenth chapter, at the
Feast of Dedication, our Lord had been asked, "If Thou be the
Christ, tell us plainly." (John x. 24.) In reply He had distinctly
appealed to His "works," as the best evidence of His Messiahship.
He had deliberately challenged attention to those works as witnesses
to His commission. And now, after a short interval, we find Him
for the last time, within two miles of Jerusalem, before many eye-
witnesses, doing such a stupendous work of Divine power that a
man might have thought any sceptic would have been silenced for
ever. After the raising of Lazarus, the Jews of Jerusalem at any
rate could never say that they were left destitute of proofs of
Christ's Messiahship.

(b) The raising of Lazarus was meant to prepare the minds of the Jews for our Lord's own resurrection. It took place between Christmas and Easter, and probably within two months of His own crucifixion. It proved incontrovertibly that a person dead four days could be raised again by Divine power, and that the restoration to life of a corpse was not an impossibility with God. I think it impossible not to see in this a latent design to prepare the minds of the Jews for our Lord's own resurrection. At any rate it paved the way for men believing the event to be not incredible. No one could say on Easter Sunday, when the grave of Jesus was found empty, and the body of Jesus was gone, that His resurrection was an impossibility. The mere fact that between winter and Easter in that very year a man dead four days had been restored to life within two miles of Jerusalem, would silence such remarks. Though improbable, it could not be called impossible.

(c) The raising of Lazarus is of all our Lord's miracles the one which is most thoroughly credible, and supported by most incontrovertible evidence. The man who disbelieves it may as well say plainly that he does not believe anything in the New Testament, and does not allow that a miracle is possible. Of course there is no standing-ground between denying the possibility of miracles, and denying the existence of a creating God. If God made the world, He can surely change the course of nature at any time, if He thinks fit.

The famous sceptic, Spinosa, declared that if he could be persuaded of the truth of the miracle before us, he would forsake his own system, and embrace Christianity. Yet it is extremely difficult to see what evidence of a fact a man can desire, if he is not satisfied with the evidence that Lazarus really was raised from the dead. But, unhappily, none are so blind as those who will not see.

The following passage from Tittman, the German Commentator, is so sensible that I make no apology for giving it at length, though somewhat condensed. "The whole story," he says, "is of a nature calculated to exclude all suspicion of imposture, and to confirm the truth of the miracle. A well-known person of Bethany, named Lazarus, falls sick in the absence of Jesus. His sisters send a message to Jesus, announcing it; but while He is yet absent Lazarus dies, is buried, and kept in the tomb for four days, during which Jesus is still absent. Martha, Mary, and all his friends are convinced of his death. Our Lord, while yet remaining in the place where He had been staying, tells His disciples in plain terms that He means to go to Bethany, to

raise Lazarus from the dead, that the glory of God may be illustrated, and their faith confirmed. At our Lord's approach, Martha
goes to meet Him, and announces her brother's death, laments
the absence of Jesus before the event took place, and yet expresses
a faint hope that by some means Jesus might yet render help. Our
Lord declares that her brother shall be raised again, and assures
her that He has the power of granting life to the dead. Mary
approaches, accompanied by weeping friends from Jerusalem. Our
Lord Himself is moved, and weeps, and goes to the sepulchre,
attended by a crowd. The stone is removed. The stench of the
corpse is perceived. Our Lord, after pouring forth audible prayer
to His Father, calls forth Lazarus from the grave, in the hearing of
all. The dead man obeys the call, comes forth to public view in the
same dress that he was buried in, alive and well, and returns home
without assistance. All persons present agree that Lazarus is raised
to life, and that a great miracle has been worked, though not all
believe the person who worked it to be the Messiah. Some
go away and tell the rulers at Jerusalem what Jesus has done.
Even these do not doubt the truth of the fact ; on the contrary,
they confess that our Lord by His works is becoming every day
more famous, and that He would probably be soon received as
Messiah by the whole nation. And *therefore* the rulers at once
take counsel how they may put to death both Jesus and Lazarus.
The people, in the mean-time hearing of this prodigious transaction,
flock in multitudes to Bethany, partly to see Jesus, and partly to
view Lazarus. And the consequence is that by and by, when our
Lord comes to Jerusalem, the population goes forth in crowds to
meet Him and show Him honour, and chiefly because of His work
at Bethany. Now if all these circumstances do not establish the
truth of the miracle, there is no truth in history." I only add the
remark, that when we consider the place, the time, the circumstances, and the singular publicity of the raising of Lazarus, it
really seems to require more credulity to deny it than to believe
it. It is the unbeliever, and not the believer of this miracle,
who seems to me the credulous man. The difficulties of disbe-
lieving it are far greater than those of believing it.

(d) The raising of Lazarus is not mentioned by Matthew,
Mark, and Luke. This has stumbled many persons. Yet the
omission of the story is not hard to explain. Some have said
that Matthew, Mark, and Luke purposely confine themselves to
miracles done in Galilee.—Some have said that when they wrote
their Gospels Lazarus was yet alive, and the mention of his
name would have endangered his safety.—Some have said that

it was thought better for the soul of Lazarus not to draw attention to him and surround him with an unhealthy celebrity till after he had left the world.—In each and all of these reasons there is some weight. But the best and simplest explanation probably is, that each Evangelist was inspired to record what God saw to be best and most suitable. No one, I suppose, imagines that the Evangelists record a tenth part of our Lord's miracles, or that there were not other dead persons raised to life, of whom we know nothing at all. "The dead are raised up," was our Lord's own message, at an early period of His ministry, to John the Baptist. (Matt. xi. 5.) "If the works that Jesus did should be written every one," says John, "the world itself could not contain the books that should be written." (John xxi. 25.) Let it suffice us to believe that each Evangelist was inspired to record exactly those events which were most likely to be profitable for the Church in studying his Gospel. Our Lord's ministry and sayings at Jerusalem were specially assigned to John. What wonder then that he was appointed to record the mighty miracle which took place within two miles of Jerusalem, and proved incontrovertibly the guilt of the Jerusalem Jews in not receiving Jesus as the Messiah ?

Bucer remarks, that there is a continually ascending greatness and splendour in those miracles which John was inspired to record in his Gospel, and that the raising of Lazarus was the most illustrious of all. He also observes that our Lord specially chose the great feasts at Jerusalem as occasions of working miracles.

Chemnitius remarks. "There is not in the whole Evangelical narrative a more delightful history, and one more abundant both in doctrine and consolation, than this of the raising of Lazarus. It therefore ought to be studied most closely and minutely by all pious minds.

1.—[*Now a certain man...sick...Lazarus.*] These simple words are the keynote to the whole chapter. All turns on the bodily illness of an obscure disciple of Christ. How much in the history of our lives hinges on little events, and specially on illnesses ! Sickness is a sacred thing, and one of God's great ordinances.

This illness took place between winter and Easter, during the time that our Lord was at Bethabara, beyond Jordan. The nature of the disease we are not told ; but from its rapid course, it is not unlikely it was a fever, such as is common even now in Palestine.

This is the first time that Lazarus is mentioned in the New Testament, and we know nothing certain of his history. Some have conjectured that he was the young ruler who came to our Lord, asking what he must do to obtain eternal life, and went away sorrowful at the time, but was afterwards converted.—Some have conjectured that he is the young man who followed our Lord when he was taken prisoner, mentioned by St. Mark, and fled away naked.—But these are mere guesses, and there is really no solid foundation for them. That he was not a poor man, but comparatively rich, seems highly probable from the "feast" in John xii., the number of friends who came to mourn him, the alabaster box of precious ointment used by his sister, and the sepulchre hewn out of rock. But even this is only a conjecture.

The name "Lazarus" no doubt is a Greek form of the Hebrew name "Eleazar." It is worth noticing, that it survives to this day in the modern name of Bethany : "El-Azarizeh." (*See Smith's Biblical Dictionary.*)

[*Of Bethany...town...Mary...Martha.*] The word "town" in this sentence would have been better translated "village," as it is in sixteen other texts in the New Testament. Bethany, in truth, was only a small village, a short two miles from Jerusalem, on the east side ; and its situation is perfectly known now. It lies on the eastern slope of the Mount of Olives, on the road to Jericho. It is not once mentioned in the Old Testament, and owes its fame to its being the place where Lazarus was raised,—the place where our Lord rested at night just before the passion,—the place from which He commenced His triumphant entry into Jerusalem,—the place from which He finally ascended into heaven (Luke xxiv. 10), and the dwelling-place of Mary and Martha.

Let it be noted that the presence of God's elect children is the one thing which makes towns and countries famous in God's sight. The village of Martha and Mary is noticed, while Memphis and Thebes are not named in the New Testament. A cottage where there is grace, is more pleasant in God's sight than a cathedral town where there is none.

Let it be noted that this verse supplies internal evidence that St. John's Gospel was written long after the other historical parts of the New Testament. He speaks of Martha and Mary as persons whose names and history would be familiar to all Christian readers.

There is a peculiarity in the Greek of this verse, which is hardly

conveyed in our English translation. Literally it would be rendered, "Lazarus *from* Bethany, *out of* the town of Mary," etc.
That "from" Bethany means exactly what we render it, is clear
from Acts xvii. 13 ; Heb. xiii. 24. But why "out of the village, or
town of Mary," is said, is not quite so clear. It is open to the
conjecture that it may mean "Lazarus was now a man of Bethany,
but was originally out of the town of Mary and Martha :" viz.,
some other place. But this seems unlikely.—Webster suggests
that "out of " is added by way of emphasis, to show that Lazarus
not only lived there, but that it was also the place of his nativity.
Greswell says much the same. It is noteworthy that John i. 44
contains exactly the same form of expression about Philip and
Bethsaida.

It is noteworthy that Mary is named before Martha, though
Martha was evidenty the older sister, and head of the house. The
reason, I suppose, is that Mary's name and character were better
known of the two.

Chemnitius thinks it possible that all Bethany belonged to
Martha and Mary, and that this accounts for the consideration in
which they were held, and the number of mourners, etc. It is
worth remembering that Bethany was a very small place. Yet
Bethsaida was called the "town of Andrew and Peter" (John i. 44),
and clearly did not belong to two poor fishermen.

2.—[*It was that Mary, etc.*] This verse is a parenthetical explanation
inserted by St. John after his manner, to make it certain what
Mary he refers to, as the sister of Lazarus. Christians knew there
were in our Lord's time, no less than four Maries : (1) The Virgin
Mother of our Lord, (2) the wife of Cleophas, (3) Mary Magdalene,
(4) Mary the sister of Martha. To prevent, therefore, any mistake, John says, " It was that Mary who anointed our Lord, whose
brother Lazarus was dead."

Simple as these words seem, there is a singular diversity of
opinion as to the question who Mary the sister of Martha and
Lazarus was, and how many times our Lord was anointed.

(*a*) Some, as Chrysostom, Origen, and Chemnitius, maintain that
the anointing took place three times : once, in Luke vii., at the
house of Simon the Pharisee ; once in Bethany, at the house of
Simon the leper ; and once in Bethany, at the house of Martha
and Mary. Others, as Ferus, while agreeing with Chrysostom
that our Lord was anointed three times, think Mary was the
woman who twice did it.

(*b*) Some maintain that our Lord was anointed twice : once at the Pharisee's house (in Luke vii.), and once at Bethany, at the house of Simon the leper, where Martha and Mary and Lazarus lived, for some cause which we do not know.

(*c*) Some, as Augustine, Bede, Toletus, Lightfoot, Maldonatus, Cornelius à Lapide, and Hengstenberg, maintain that our Lord was only once anointed,—that the narrative in Luke vii. was inserted out of chronological order,—that Simon the Pharisee and Simon the leper were the same person, and that the one anointing took place at Bethany. Hengstenberg supports his theory very ingeniously, and boldly suggests that Simon the Pharisee was also called Simon the leper, was the husband of Martha, and not friendly to Christ; that this accounts for Martha being more "careful and troubled" (in Luke x. 41) than Mary, and for unfriendly Pharisees being present at the raising of Lazarus; that Mary Magdalene was the same as Mary of Bethany,—and that Mary of Bethany was the "sinner," in Luke vii.

Toletus frankly admits that the Romish Church holds that there was only one anointing by one person, as it is plainly declared in one of her formularies : viz., the Breviary.

My own opinion is decidedly against the last of these views. I hold that there were *at least* two anointings ; one at a comparatively early period of our Lord's ministry, and another at the close of it,—one in the house of an unfriendly Pharisee named Simon, and another at the house of Simon the leper, in Bethany, —one by a woman who had been pre-eminently a sinner, another by Mary the sister of Martha, against whose moral character we know nothing.—Why the house of Martha and Mary at Bethany is called the house of Simon the leper, I admit I cannot explain. I can only surmise that there was some relationship of which we know nothing. But this difficulty is nothing in my eyes, compared to that of supposing, with Augustine and his followers, that the event described in Luke vii., took place just at the end of our Lord's ministry. There is strong internal evidence that it did not, to my mind. Surely at the end of our Lord's ministry, people would not have said with wonder, "Who is this that forgiveth sins?" Surely Mary would not be spoken of as a notorious "sinner."

On the other hand, if we hold the view that our Lord was only anointed twice,—once at the house of Simon the Pharisee, and once at Bethany,—it must be frankly admitted that there is a very grave difficulty to be got over. That difficulty is that St. Mark says that a woman anointed our Lord "two days" before the Passover, and poured the ointment on His "head," while John says He was anointed "six days before the passover," and the ointment poured on His "feet."—I do not see how this difficulty can be got over. If however we hold that our Lord was anointed twice in the last week before He was crucified, once "six days" before, and once "two days" before, and on each occasion by a woman, the whole thing is clear. That such a thing should be done more than once, in those days, does not strike me as any objection, considering the customs of the age. That our Lord's language in defence of the woman should on each occasion be the same is somewhat remarkable. But it is only a minor difficulty. On the whole therefore, if I must give an opinion, I incline to agree with Chrysostom, that there were three anointings. I also think there is something in the view of Ferus, that Mary, sister of Lazarus, anointed our Lord twice,—once six days before the passover, and once again two days before.

The use of the past participle in the verse before us, seems to me no difficulty at all. It is of course true that at this time Mary had not anointed our Lord. But it is no less true that John evidently mentions it by anticipation, as an historical fact long-past and well known in the Church when he wrote his Gospel, which his readers would understand. "It was that Mary which afterwards anointed Christ's feet."

Let us note in this verse, that the good deeds of all Christ's saints are carefully recorded in God's book of remembrance. Men are forgetful and ungrateful. Nothing done for Christ is ever forgotten.

Let us note that sickness comes to Christ's people as well as to the wicked and worldly. Grace does not exempt us from trial. Sickness, on the contrary, is one of God's most useful instruments for sanctifying His saints, and making them bear fruit of patience, and for showing the world that His people do not serve Him merely for what they get of bodily ease and comfort in this life. "Job does not serve God for nought," was the devil's sneer, in the days when Job prospered. "Lazarus and his sisters make a good thing of their religion,"—might have been said if they had had no trials.

Brentius remarks, "God does not go away when bodily health goes away. Christ does not depart when life departs."

3.—[*Therefore his sisters sent...saying.*] This is an example of what all Christians should do in trouble. Like Mary and Martha, we should first send a message to Christ. By prayer we can do it as really as they did. This is what Job did in his trouble: he first of all "worshipped," and said, "Blessed be the name of the Lord." This is what Asa did not do: "He sought not to the Lord, but to the physicians." (Job i. 20; 2 Chron. xv. 12.)

Let it be noted that the Greek would be more literally rendered "the sisters," and not "his." This message, from the expression in next verse, "heard," would seem to have been a verbal and not a written one.

[*Lord...he whom thou lovest is sick.*] This is a very touching and beautiful little message.—Its humble and respectful confidence is noteworthy: "He whom Thou lovest is sick." They do not say, "Do something," or "Heal him," or "Come at once." They simply spread the case before the Lord, and leave Him to do what He thinks wisest and best. It is like Hezekiah spreading Sennacherib's letter before God. (2 Kings xix. 14)—The name given to Lazarus is noteworthy: they do not say "our brother," or "Thy disciple," or even "one who loves Thee," but simply "he whom Thou lovest;" one whom Thou hast been pleased to treat graciously and kindly as a beloved friend. Christ's love to us, and not our love to Christ is the blessed truth which we ought continually to keep before our minds. His love never changes: ours is wavering and uncertain.

The idea of some, that sending a message to Christ was a mark of weak faith in the two sisters, as if it showed doubt of Christ's omniscience, is absurd. At this rate we might never pray, and might say there is no need, because God knows all!

The world "behold" seems either to indicate something "sudden" in the illness of Lazarus, like Mark ii. 21, and to be used adverbially; or else we must take it as an imperative verb. "Behold a case of great affliction: look upon it and see. He whom Thou lovest is sick." This would be like Hezekiah's prayer: "Open Thine eyes and see." (2 Kings xix. 16.) We can hardly suppose that such disciples as Martha and Mary would think it a strange or surprising thing that a disciple of Christ should be ill; yet it is possible they did. However, Theophylact and Ferus suppose that "Behold" implies a degree of wonder and surprise.

Rupertus remarks, on the message containing no request: "To a loving friend it was quite enough to announce the fact that Lazarus was sick." Affectionate friends are not verbose or lengthy in descriptions.

Brentius remarks that the message is like all true prayer : it does not consist in much speaking, and fine long sentences.

Musculus and Chemnitius both remark, that when a man's child falls into a well or pit, it is enough to tell a loving father the simple fact, in the shortest manner possible, without dwelling on it verbosely and rhetorically.

Rollock observes how useful it is to have praying sisters.

Let us note that Christ's friends may be sick and ill, just like other people. It is no proof that they are not beloved, and specially preserved and cared for by God. "Whom the Lord loveth He chasteneth." The purest gold is most in the fire ; the most useful tools are oftenest ground. Epaphroditus and Timothy were both of weak health, and Paul could not prevent it.

4.—[*When Jesus heard that, He said.*] This verse seems to contain the reply which our Lord gave to the messenger. It was to him probably, though in the hearing of all His disciples, that He addressed the words which follow. It is as though He said, "Go, return to thy mistress, and say as follows."

[*This sickness is not unto death, etc.*] The meaning of this sentence must evidently be taken with qualification. Our Lord did not mean that Lazarus would not in any sense die. It is as though He said, "The end of this sickness is not Lazarus's death and entire removal from this world, but generally the glory of God, and specially the glorifying of Me, His Son, which will be effected by my raising him again." Death's temporary victory over us is not complete till our bodies perish and return to dust. This was not allowed in the case of Lazarus, and hence death had not full dominion over him, though he ceased to breathe and became unconscious.

It is undeniable that there was something dark and mysterious about our Lord's message. He might of course have said plainly, "Lazarus will die, and then I will raise him again." Yet there is a wonderful likeness between the style of His message and many an unfulfilled prophecy. He said enough to excite hope, and encourage faith and patience and prayer, but not enough to make Mary and Martha leave off praying and seeking God. And is not this exactly what we should feel about many an unfulfilled prediction of things to come ? Men complain that prophecies are not so literally fulfilled as to exclude doubt and uncertainty. But they forget that God wisely permits a degree of uncertainty in order to keep us watching and praying.   It is just what He did with Martha and Mary here.

Let us remember that the final result of Lazarus' sickness is what we should desire as the result of any sickness that comes on us and our families : viz., that God and Christ may be glorified in us.   We cannot say, "It shall not end in death ; " but we can say, "By God's help, it shall be for God's glory."

Chrysostom observes, "The expression *that* in this passage denotes not cause but consequence.   The sickness happened from other causes.   Christ used it for the glory of God."

Calvin remarks, that God wishes to be honoured by Christ being glorified.   "He who does not honour the Son does not honour the Father."   (John v. 23.)

5.—[*Now Jesus loved Martha, etc.*] This verse is meant to show that all the members of the family at Bethany were disciples of Jesus and beloved by Him, the brother as well as the sisters, and one sister as well as the other.   A happy family, Lampe remarks, in which all the members were objects of Christ's special love !

We know not where Lazarus was at the time when Jesus stopped at Martha's house, in Luke x. 38 ; perhaps he was not converted at that time.   But this is only conjecture.

We are generally apt to undervalue the grace of Martha and overvalue that of Mary, because of what happened when Jesus was at Martha's house before.   Many foolish things are sometimes lightly said against mothers and mistresses as being Marthas, "careful and troubled about many things."   Yet people should remember that different positions call out different phases of character.   Mary certainly shines more brightly than Martha in the 10th of Luke ; but it is a grave question whether Martha did not outshine her in the 11th of John.   Active-minded Christians come out better under some circumstances ; quiet-minded Christians, in others.   Our Lord teaches us here that He loves all who have grace, though their temperaments differ.   Let us learn not to judge others rashly, and not to form hasty estimates of Christians, until we have seen them under every sort of circumstances, in winter as well as summer, in dark days as well as bright.

Let it be noted that the Greek word here rendered "loved," is not the same that is rendered "lovest," in the 3rd verse.   The word describing the love of Jesus to the three in this verse is a word expressing a high, deep, excellent, and noble affection.   It is

the same as Mark x. 21, and John iii. 16.—The word used in the
message of the sisters, is a lower word, such as is used to describe
the affection between a parent and child, or husband and wife. It
is the word used for "kiss" in Matt. xxvi. 48 ; Mark xiv. 44; and
Luke xxii. 47. It is very noticeable that this word is carefully
avoided here, when the two sisters are mentioned.   The Holy
Ghost inspired John to abstain even from the appearance of evil.
What a lesson this ought to be to us !

Let it be noted that we see here an example of the broad distinction that ought to be drawn between Christ's general love of
compassion which He feels towards all mankind, and His special
love of election which He feels towards His own members.   He
loved all sinners to whom He came to preach the Gospel, and He
wept over unbelieving Jerusalem.   But He specially loved those
who believed on Him.

6.—[*When He had heard therefore, etc.*] It is impossible not to remark an intentional and most instructive connection between this
verse and the preceding one. Our Lord loved the family of Bethany,
all three of them ; and yet when He heard Lazarus was sick, instead
of hastening at once to Bethany to heal him, He quietly remained
at Bethabara for two days, without moving.

We cannot doubt that this delay was intentional and of purpose,
and it throws immense light on many of God's providential
dealings with His people.   We know that the delay caused immense mental pain and suffering to Martha and Mary, and obliged
Lazarus to go through all the agony of death, and the sorrow of
parting.   We can easily imagine the grief and suspense and perplexity in which the household at Bethany must have been kept
for four days, when their loving Master did not appear ; and we
know that our Lord could have prevented it all, but did not.
But we know also that if He had at once hurried to Bethany and
healed Lazarus, or spoken a word from a distance at Bethabara
and commanded his healing, as in John iv. 50, the mighty miracle
of raising him would never have been wrought, and the wonderful
sayings of Bethany would never have been spoken. In short the
pain of a few was permitted for the benefit of the whole Church
of Christ.

We have here the simplest and best account of the permission
of evil and suffering.   God could prevent it.   God does not love
to make His creatures suffer.   But God sees there are lessons which
mankind could not learn unless evil was permitted : therefore

God permits it. The suffering of some tends to the good of many. "He that believeth shall not make haste." (Isa. xxviii. 16.) We shall see at the last day that all was well done. Even the delays and long intervals which puzzle us in God's dealings, are wisely ordered, and are working for good. Like children, we are poor judges of half-finished work.

Chrysostom says, "Christ tarried that none might be able to assert that He restored Lazarus when not yet dead, saying it was a lethargy, a fainting, a fit, but not death. He therefore tarried so long that corruption began."

Calvin observes, "Let believers learn to suspend their desires, if God does not stretch out His hand to help as soon as they think necessity requires. Whatever may be His delays, He never sleeps, and never forgets His people.

Quesnel remarks, "God permits evil, that He may make the power of His grace and the might of His love more conspicuous in the conversion of a sinner."

Poole remarks, "We must not judge of Christ's love to us by His mere external dispensations of providence, nor judge that He doth not love us, because He doth not presently come in to our help at our time, and in such ways and methods as we think reasonable."

JOHN XI. 7—16.

7 Then after that saith he to *his* disciples, Let us go into Judæa again.

8 *His* disciples say unto him, Master, the Jews of late sought to stone thee; and goest thou thither again?

9 Jesus answered, Are there not twelve hours in the day? If any man walk in the day, he stumbleth not, because he seeth the light of this world.

10 But if a man walk in the night, he stumbleth, because there is no light in him.

11 These things said he: and after that he saith unto them, Our friend Lazarus sleepeth; but I go, that I may awake him out of sleep.

12 Then said his disciples, Lord, if he sleep, he shall do well.

13 Howbeit Jesus spake of his death: but they thought that he had spoken of taking of rest in sleep.

14 Then said Jesus unto them plainly, Lazarus is dead.

15 And I am glad for your sakes that I was not there, to the intent ye may believe; nevertheless let us go unto him.

16 Then said Thomas, which is called Didymus, unto his fellow-disciples, Let us also go, that we may die with him.

WE should notice, in this passage, *how mysterious are the ways in which Christ sometimes leads His people.* We are told that when He talked of going back to

Judæa, His disciples were perplexed. It was the very place where the Jews had lately tried to stone their Master. To return thither was to plunge into the midst of danger. These timid Galilæans could not see the necessity or prudence of such a step. "Goest Thou thither again?" they cried.

Things such as these are often going on around us. The servants of Christ are often placed in circumstances just as puzzling and perplexing as those of the disciples. They are led in ways of which they cannot see the purpose and object; they are called to fill positions from which they naturally shrink, and which they would never have chosen for themselves. Thousands in every age are continually learning this by their own experience. The path they are obliged to walk in is not the path of their own choice. At present they cannot see its usefulness or wisdom.

At times like these, a Christian must call into exercise his faith and patience. He must believe that his Master knows best by what road His servant ought to travel, and that he is leading him, by the right way, to a city of habitation. He may rest assured that the circumstances in which he is placed are precisely those which are most likely to promote his graces and to check his besetting sins. He need not doubt that what he cannot see now he will understand hereafter. He will find one day that there was wisdom in every step of his journey, though flesh and blood could not see it at the time. If the twelve disciples had not been taken back into Judæa, they would not have seen the glorious miracle of Bethany. If Christians were allowed to choose their own course through life, they would never learn hundreds of lessons about Christ and His grace, which they are now taught in God's ways. Let us remember these things. The time may come when we shall be called to take some journey in life which we greatly dislike. When that time comes, let us set out cheerfully, and believe that all is right.

We should notice, secondly, in this passage, *how tenderly Christ speaks of the death of believers.* He announces the fact of Lazarus being dead in language of singular beauty and gentleness : " Our friend Lazarus sleepeth."

Every true Christian has a Friend in heaven, of almighty power and boundless love. He is thought of, cared for, provided for, defended by God's eternal Son. He has an unfailing Protector, who never slumbers or sleeps, and watches continually over his interests. The world may despise him, but he has no cause to be ashamed. Father and mother even may cast him out, but Christ having once taken him up will never let him go. He is the "friend of Christ" even after he is dead ! The friendships of this world are often fair-weather friendships, and fail us like summer-dried fountains, when our need is the sorest ; but the friendship of the Son of God is stronger than death, and goes beyond the grave. The Friend of sinners is a Friend that sticketh closer than a brother.

The death of true Christians is "sleep," and not

annihilation. It is a solemn and miraculous change, no doubt, but not a change to be regarded with alarm. They have nothing to fear for their souls in the change, for their sins are washed away in Christ's blood. The sharpest sting of death is the sense of unpardoned sin. Christians have nothing to fear for their bodies in the change : they will rise again by and by, refreshed and renewed, after the image of the Lord. The grave itself is a conquered enemy. It must render back its tenants safe and sound, the very moment that Christ calls for them at the last day.

Let us remember these things when those whom we love fall asleep in Christ, or when we ourselves receive our notice to quit this world. Let us call to mind in such an hour, that our great Friend takes thought for our bodies as well as for our souls, and that He will not allow one hair of our heads to perish. Let us never forget that the grave is the place where the Lord Himself lay, and that as He rose again triumphant from that cold bed, so also shall all His people. To a mere worldly man death must needs be a terrible thing; but he that has Christian faith, may boldly say, as he lays down life, " I will lay me down in peace, and take my rest: for it is Thou, Lord, that makest me dwell in safety." (Psalm. iv. 8.)

We should notice, lastly, in this passage, *how much of natural temperament clings to a believer even after conversion.* We read that when Thomas saw that Lazarus was dead, and that Jesus was determined, in spite of all danger, to return into Judæa, he said, " Let us

also go, that we may die with Him." There can only
be one meaning in that expression: it was the language of a despairing and desponding mind, which
could see nothing but dark clouds in the picture. The
very man who afterwards could not believe that his
Master had risen again, and thought the news too good
to be true, is just the one of the twelve who thinks that
if they go back to Judæa they must all die!

Things such as these are deeply instructive, and are
doubtless recorded for our learning. They show us that
the grace of God in conversion does not so re-mould
a man as to leave no trace of his natural bent of character. The sanguine do not altogether cease to be sanguine,
nor the desponding to be desponding, when they pass
from death to life, and become true Christians. They
show us that we must make large allowances for natural
temperament, in forming our estimate of individual
Christians. We must not expect all God's children
to be exactly one and the same. Each tree in a forest
has its own peculiarities of shape and growth, and yet
all at a distance look one mass of leaves and verdure.
Each member of Christ's body has his own distinctive
bias, and yet all in the main are led by one Spirit, and
love one Lord. The two sisters Martha and Mary, the
Apostles Peter and John and Thomas, were certainly
very unlike one another in many respects. But they
had all one point in common: they loved Christ, and
were His friends.

Let us take heed that we really belong to Christ.
This is the one thing needful. If this is made sure.

we shall be led by the right way, and end well at last.
We may not have the cheerfulness of one brother, or
the fiery zeal of another, or the gentleness of another.
But if grace reigns within us, and we know what repentance and faith are by experience, we shall stand
on the right hand in the great day.   Happy is the
man of whom, with all his defects, Christ says to
saints and angels, "This is our friend."

NOTES. JOHN XI. 7—16.

7.—[*Then after that saith...disciples.*]   The Greek words which
begin this sentence, mark an interval of time even more emphatically than our English version does.   They would be literally
rendered, "Afterwards, after this."   The word translated "then"
is the same that is translated "after that" in 1 Cor. xv. 6, 7.

[*Let us go...Judœa again.*]   This is the language of the kind
and loving Head of a family, and the Chief in a party of friends.
Our Lord does not say, "I shall go to," or, "Follow Me to Judæa,
but, "Let us go."   It is the voice of a kind Master and Shepherd
proposing a thing to His pupils and followers, as though He would
allow them to express their opinions about it.   How much depends
on the manner and language of a leader !

The familiar, easy manner in which our Lord is said here to tell
His disciples what He proposes to do, gives a pleasant idea of the
terms on which they lived with Him.

8.—[*His disciples say...Master.*]   The answer of the disciples is an
interesting illustration of the easy terms on which they were with
their Master.   They tell Him frankly and unreservedly their feelings
and fears.

Let it be noted that the word rendered "Master" here is the
well known word "Rabbi."   The use of it shows that there is
nothing necessarily insulting, sneering, or discourteous about the
term.   It was the title of honour and respect given by all Jews to
their teachers.   Thus John the Baptist's disciples said to him,
when jealous for is honour, "Rabbi, he that was with thee," etc.
(John iii. 26.)

[*The Jews of late sought to stone Thee.*]   The "Jews" here mean especially the leaders or principal persons among the Scribes and Pharisees at Jerusalem, as it generally does in St. John's Gospel. The word rendered "of late" is generally translated "now," or "at this time." There is not another instance of its being translated "of late" in the New Testament. Hence the sentence would be more literally rendered, "The Jews even now were seeking to stone Thee." They allude to the attempt made at the Feast of Dedication a few weeks before. The attempt was so recent that it seemed "even now."

[*And goest Thou thither again ?*] This question indicates surprise and fear.—"Do we hear aright ? Dost Thou really talk of going back again to Judæa ? Dost Thou not fear another assault on Thy life ?"—We can easily detect fear for their own safety, as well as their Master's, in the question of the disciples : yet they put it on "Thee," and not on "us."

Let us note how strange and unwise our Lord's plans sometimes appear to His short-sighted people. How little the best can understand His ways !

9, 10.—[*Jesus answered, Are there not twelve hours, etc.*] The answer which our Lord makes to the remonstrance of His timid disciples is somewhat remarkable. Instead of giving them a direct reply, bidding them not to be afraid, He first quotes a proverbial saying, and then draws from that saying general lessons about the time which any one who is on a journey will choose for journeying. He draws no conclusion, and leaves the application to be made by the disciples themselves. To an English ear the answer seems far more strange than it would to an Eastern one. To quote a proverb is, even now, a common reply among Orientals. To fill up the sense of our Lord's elliptical reply, and draw the conclusions He meant to be drawn, but did not express, is, however, not very easy. The following may be taken as a paraphrase of it :—

"Are not the working hours of the day twelve ? You know they are, speaking generally. If a man on a journey walks during these twelve daylight hours, he sees his road, and does not stumble or fall, because the sun, which is the light of the world, shines on his path. If, on the contrary, a man on a journey chooses to walk in the unreasonable hour of night, he is likely to stumble or fall, for want of light to guide his feet. It is even so with Me. My twelve hours of ministry, my day of work, is not yet over. There is no fear of my life being cut off before the time : I shall not be slain till my work is done. Till mine hour is come, 1 am safe, and not a hair of my head can be touched. I am like one walking in the full light of the sun, and cannot fall. The night will soon be here when I shall walk on earth no longer : but the night has not yet come. There are twelve hours in my day of earthly ministry, and the twelfth with Me has not arrived."

This seems to me substantially the correct explanation of our Lord's meaning. The idea of ancient writers, as Hugo and Lyranus, that our Lord meant, by mentioning the twelve hours of the day, that men often change their minds as the day goes on, and that the Jews, perhaps, no longer wished to kill Him, is very improbable and unsatisfactory.

I grant that the conclusion of the tenth verse, "there is no light in him," presents some difficulty. The simplest explanation is, that it only means, "because he has no light."

Pearce conjectures that the clause should be rendered, "Because there is no light in it : viz., the world." The Greek will perhaps bear this interpretation.

Let us note that the great principle underlying the two verses is the old saying in another form, "Every man is immortal till his work is done." A recollection of that saying is an excellent antidote against fears of danger. The missionary in heathen lands, and the minister at home, pressed down by unhealthy climate, or over-abundant work, may take comfort in it, after their Lord's example. Let us only, by way of caution, make sure that our dangers meet us in the path of duty, and that we do not go out of the way to seek them.

Rupertus suggests that our Lord had in His mind His own doctrine, that He was the Light and Sun of the world. Now as the sun continues shining all the twelve hours of the day, and no mortal power can stop it, so He would have the disciples know that until the evening of His own course arrived, no power of the Jews could possibly check, arrest, or do Him harm. As to the disciples, He seems to add, "So long as I am shining on you with my bodily presence, you have nothing to fear, you will not fall into trouble. When I am taken from you, and not till then, you will be in danger of falling into the hands of perse-cutors, and even of being put to death." Ecolampadius takes the same view.

Melancthon thinks that our Lord uses a proverbial mode of speech, in order to teach us the great broad lesson that we must attend to the duties of our day, station, and calling, and then leave the event to God. In the path of duty all will turn out right. Calvin, Bullinger, Gualter, and Brentius, take much the same view.

Leigh remarks, "Christ comforts from God's providence. God made the day twelve hours. Who can make it shorter? Who can shorten man's life?"

Does it not come to this, that our Lord would have the disciples know that He Himself could not take harm till His day of work was over, and that they could take no harm while He was with them? (Compare Luke xiii. 32, 33.) Bishop Ellicot suggests that this was the very time in our Lord's ministry when He said to the Pharisee, "I do cures to-day and to-morrow, and the third day I shall be perfected. Nevertheless I must walk to-day and to-morrow and the day following." But I doubt this.

It is certain that there came a time when our Lord said, "This is your hour, and the power of darkness," to His enemies. Then He was taken, and His disciples fled.

11.—[*These things...our friend Lazarus...sleepeth.*] In this verse our Lord breaks the fact that Lazarus is dead, to His disciples. He does it in words of matchless beauty and tenderness. After saying "these things" about the twelve hours of the day, which we have considered in the last verse, He seems to make a slight pause. Then, "after that," comes the announcement, which would be more literally rendered, "Lazarus, the friend of us, has been laid asleep."

The word "sleepeth" means, "is dead." It is a gentle and pathetic way of expressing the most painful of events that can befall man, and a most suitable one, when we remember that after death comes resurrection. In dying we are not annihilated. Like sleepers, we lie down, to rise again. Estius well remarks, "Sleeping, in the sense of dying, is only applied to men, because of the hope of the resurrection. We read no such thing of brutes."

The use of the figure is so common in Scripture, that it is almost needless to give references. (See Deut. xxxi. 16; Daniel xii. 2; Matt. xxvii. 52; Acts vii. 60; xiii. 36: 1 Cor. vii. 39; xi. 30; xv. 6—18; 1 Thess. iv. 13, 14.) But it is a striking fact that the figure is frequently used by great heathen writers, showing clearly that the tradition of a life after death existed even among the heathen. Homer, Sophocles, Virgil, Catullus, supply instances. However, the Christian believer is the only one who can truly regard death as sleep,—that is, as a healthy, refreshing thing, which can do him no harm. Many among ourselves, perhaps, are not aware that the figure of speech exists among us in full force in the word "cemetery," applied to burial ground. That word is drawn from the very Greek verb which our Lord uses here. It is literally a "sleeping place."

The word "friend," applied to Lazarus, gives a beautiful idea of the relation between the Lord Jesus and all His believing people. Each one is His "friend,"—not servant, or subject only, but "friend." A poor believer has no cause to be ashamed. He has a Friend greater than kings and nobles, who will show Himself friendly to all eternity. A dead saint lying in the grave is not cut off from Christ's love: even in his grave, he is still the friend of Christ.

The expression "our," attached to friend, teaches the beautiful lesson that every friend of Christ is or should be the friend of all Christians. Believers are all one family of brothers and sisters, and members of one body. Lazarus was not "my" friend, but "our" friend. If any one is a friend of Christ, every other believer should be ready and willing to hold out his hand to him, and say, "You are my friend."

When our Lord says, "I go that I may awaken him out of sleep," He proclaims His deliberate intention and purpose to raise Lazarus from the dead. He boldly challenges the attention of the disciples, and declares that He is going to Bethany, to restore a dead man to life. Never was bolder declaration made. None surely would make it but One who knew that He was very God.

"I go," is equivalent to saying, "I am at once setting forth on a journey to Bethany." The expression that "I may awake him out of sleep," is one word in Greek, and is equivalent to "that I may unsleep him." What our Lord went to do at Bethany, He is soon coming to do for all our friends who are asleep in Christ. He is coming to awaken them.

Some commentators have thought that Lazaaus died in the very moment that our Lord said, "Our friend sleepeth," and that it means, "Lazarus has just fallen asleep and died." But this is only conjecture, though doubtless our Lord knew the moment of his decease.

Let it be noted that our Lord says, "I go," in the singular number, and not "Let us go." Does it not look as if He meant, "Whether you like to go or not, I intend to go"?

Hall remarks, " None can awaken Lazarus out of this sleep, but He that made Lazarus.   Every mouse or gnat can raise us up from that other sleep ; none but an omnipotent power from this."

-12.—[*Then said...disciples...sleep...well.*]   It seems strange that the disciples should misunderstand our Lord's words, considering how commonly death was called sleep.   But their unwillingness to go into Judæa probably made them shut their eyes to our Lord's real meaning.

Most writers think that the disciples referred to the general opinion, that sleep in a sickness is a sign of amendment.   Some, however, suggest that they had gathered from the messenger sent by Martha and Mary what was the precise nature of Lazarus' illness, and therefore knew that it was one in which sleep was a favourable symptom.

The Greek word for " he shall do well," is curious.   It is the same that is often rendered, " shall be made whole."   Sometimes it is " healed," and generally " saved."

The latent thought is manifest : " If Lazarus sleeps, he is getting better, and there is no need of our going to Judæa."

13.—[*Howbeit Jesus spake, etc.*]   This verse is one of those explanatory glosses which St. John frequently puts into his narrative parenthetically.   The three first words of the verse would be more literally rendered, " But Jesus had spoken."

How the disciples could have " thought " or " supposed " that our Lord meant literal sleep, and not death, seems strange, when we remember that Peter, James, and John, had heard Him use the same expression after the death of the ruler's daughter : "The maid sleepeth." (Matt. ix. 24.)   Two probable reasons may be assigned :—one is that they had heard from the messenger that Lazarus' recovery turned on his getting sleep, and that if he only got some sleep he might do well ; the other is that they were so afraid of returning to Judæa, that they determined to believe Lazarus was getting better, and to construe our Lord's words in the way most agreeable to their fears.   It is common to observe that men will not understand what they do not want to understand.

Quesnel remarks here, " The misunderstanding of the Apostles was a great instance of stupidity, and shows plainly how sensual and carnal their minds still were.   The knowledge of this is useful in order to convince incredulous persons that the Apostles were

not of themselves capable either of converting the world, or of in-
venting the wonderful things and sublime discourses which they
relate."

The readiness of the disciples to misunderstand figurative language is curiously shown in two other places, where our Lord
spoke of "leaven" and "meat." (Matt. xvi. 6; John iv. 32.)

14.—[*Then said...plainly...Lazarus...dead.*] Here at last our Lord
breaks the fact of Lazarus' death to His disciples openly, and
without any further reserve.   He had approached the subject
gently and delicately, and thus prepared their minds for something
painful, by steps.   First He said simply, "Let us go into Judæa,"
without assigning a reason.   Secondly He said, "Lazarus sleepeth."
Lastly He says, "Lazarus is dead."   There is a beautiful consideration for feelings in these three steps.   It is a comfortable
thought that our mighty Saviour is so tender-hearted and gentle.
It is an instructive lesson to us on the duty of dealing gently with
others, and specially in announcing afflictions.

The word rendered "plainly" is the same as in John x. 24.
Here, as there, it does not mean "in plain, intelligible language,"
so much as "openly, unreservedly, and without mystery."

15.—[*And I am glad...not there...believe.*] This sentence would be
more literally rendered, "And I rejoice on account of you, in
order that ye may believe, that I was not there."   Our Lord evidently means that He was glad that He was not at Bethany when
Lazarus became ill, and had not healed him before his death, as
in all probability He would have done.   The result now would be
most advantageous to the disciples.   Their faith would receive an
immense confirmation, by witnessing the stupendous miracle of
Lazarus being raised from the dead.   Thus great good, in one respect,
would come out of great evil.   The announcement they had just
heard might be very painful and distressing, but He, as their
Master, could not but be glad to think how mightily their faith
would be strengthened in the end.

Let us note that our Lord does not say, "I am glad Lazarus is
dead, but I am glad I was not there."   Had He been there, He
seems to say, He could not have refused the prayer of Martha
and Mary, to heal His friend.   We are not intended to be so unfeeling as to rejoice in the death of Christian friends : but we
may rejoice in the circumstances attending their deaths, and the
glory redounding to Christ, and the benefit accruing to saints
from them.

Let us note that our Lord does not say, "I am glad for the sake of Martha and Mary and Lazarus that I was not there, but for your sakes." It is no pleasure to Him to see His individual members suffering, weeping, and dying ; but He does rejoice to see the good of many spring out of the suffering of a few. Hence He permits some to be afflicted, in order that many may be instructed through their afflictions. This is the key to the permission of evil in the world : it is for the good of the many. When we ourselves are allowed of God to suffer, we must remember this. We must believe there are wise reasons why God does not come to our help at once and take the suffering away.

Let us note our Lord's desire that His disciples "may believe." He did not mean that they might believe now for the first time, but that they might believe more firmly, heartily, and unhesitatingly ; that their faith in short might receive a great increase by seeing Lazarus raised. We see here the immense importance of faith. To believe on Christ, and trust God's word, is the first step towards heaven. To believe more and trust more, is the real secret of Christian growth, progress, and prosperity. To make us believe more is the end of all Christ's dealings with us. (See John xiv. 1.)

[*Nevertheless let us go unto him.*] The first word here would be more literally rendered "But." It is as though our Lord said, "But let us delay no longer : let us cast aside all fears of danger ; let us go to our friend."

It is noteworthy that our Lord says, "Let us go to Lazarus," though he was dead, and would be buried by the time they reached Bethany. Can be it that the disciples thought He had David's words about his dead child in His mind, "I shall go to him"? The words of Thomas, in the next verse, seem to make it possible.

We may notice three gradations in our Lord's language about going to Bethany. The first, in the 7th verse : there He says in the plural, "Let us all go into Judæa." The second, in verse 11 : there He says in the singular, "I go to awake him :" as though He was ready to go alone.—The third is here in the plural, "Let us all go."

Toletus thinks that by these words our Lord meant to hint His intention of raising Lazarus.

Burkitt remarks, "O love, stronger than death ! The grave cannot separate Christ and His friends. Other friends accompany us to the brink of the grave, and then they leave us.—Neither life nor death can separate from the love of Christ."

Bengel remarks, "It is beautifully consonant with divine propriety, that no one is ever read of as having died while the Prince of Life was present."

16.—[*Then said Thomas...go...die with Him.*] The disciple here named is also mentioned in John xvi. 5, and John xx. 24—26, 27. On each occasion he appears in the same state of mind,—ready to look at the black side of everything,—taking the worst view of the position, and raising doubts and fears. In John xiv. 5, he does not know where our Lord is going. In John xx. 25, he cannot believe our Lord has risen. Here he sees nothing but danger and death, if his Master returns to Judæa. Yet He is true and faithful nevertheless. He will not forsake Christ, even if death is in the way. "Let us go," he says to his fellow-disciples, "and die with our Master. He is sure to be killed if He does go ; but we cannot do better than be killed with Him."

Some, as Brentius, Grotius, Leigh, Poole, and Hammond, think that "with him," refers to Lazarus. But most commentators think that Thomas refers to our Lord : with them I entirely agree.

Let it be noted that a man may have notable weaknesses and infirmities of Christian character, and yet be a disciple of Christ. There is no more common fault among believers, perhaps, than despondency and unbelief. A reckless readiness to die and make an end of our troubles is not grace but impatience.

Let us observe how extremely unlike one another Christ's disciples were. Peter, for instance, overrunning with zeal and confidence, was the very opposite of desponding Thomas. Yet both had grace, and both loved Christ. We must not foolishly assume that all Christians are exactly like one another in details of character. We must make large allowances, when the main features are right.

Let us remember that this same Thomas, so desponding in our Lord's lifetime, was afterwards the very Apostle who first preached the Gospel in India, according to ecclesiastical history, and penetrated further East than any whose name is recorded. Chrysostom says, "The very man who dared not go to Bethany in Christ's company, afterwards ran alone through the world, and dwelt in the midst of nations full of murder and ready to kill him."

Some have thought that his Greek name "Didymus," signifying

"two" or "double," was given him because of his character being double : viz., part faith and part weakness. But this is very doubt-ful. In the first three Gospels, in the catalogue of the twelve, he is always named together with Matthew the publican. But why we do not know.

The Greek word for "fellow-disciple" is never used in the New Testament excepting here.

JOHN XI. 17—29.

17 Then when Jesus came, he found that he had *lain* in the grave four days already.

18 Now Bethany was nigh unto Jeru-salem, about fifteen furlongs off :

19 And many of the Jews came to Martha and Mary, to comfort them con-cerning their brother.

20 Then Martha, as soon as she heard that Jesus was coming, went and met him : but Mary sat *still* in the house.

21 Then said Martha unto Jesus, Lord, if thou hadst been here, my brother had not died.

22 But I know, that even now, what-soever thou wilt ask of God, God will give *it* thee.

23 Jesus saith unto her, Thy brother shall rise again.

24 Martha saith unto him, I know that he shall rise again in the resur-rection at the last day.

25 Jesus said unto her, I am the resurrection, and the life : he that be-lieveth in me, though he were dead, yet shall he live :

26 And whosoever liveth and believeth in me shall never die. Believest thou this ?

27 She saith unto him, Yea, Lord : I believe that thou art the Christ, the Son of God, which should come into the world.

28 And when she had so said, she went her way, and called Mary her sister secretly, saying, The Master is come, and calleth for thee.

29 As soon as she heard *that*, she arose quickly, and came unto him.

THERE is a grand simplicity about this passage, which is almost spoilt by any human exposition. To comment on it seems like gilding gold or painting lilies. Yet it throws much light on a subject which we can never understand too well : that is, the true character of Christ's people. The portraits of Christians in the Bible are faithful likenesses. They show us saints just as they are.

We learn, firstly, *what a strange mixture of grace and weakness is to be found even in the hearts of true believers.*

We see this strikingly illustrated in the language used by Martha and Mary. Both these holy women

had faith enough to say, "Lord, if Thou hadst been
here, my brother had not died." Yet neither of them
seems to have remembered that the death of Lazarus
did not depend on Christ's absence, and that our Lord,
had He thought fit, could have prevented his death
with a word, without coming to Bethany.—Martha had
knowledge enough to say, "I know, that even now,
whatsoever Thou wilt ask of God, God will give it
Thee. I know that my brother shall rise again at the
last day; I believe that Thou art the Christ, the Son
of God:" but even she could get no further. Her dim
eyes and trembling hands could not grasp the grand
truth that He who stood before her had the keys of life
and death, and that in her Master dwelt "all the fulness
of the Godhead bodily." (Colos. ii. 9.) She saw indeed, but through a glass darkly. She knew, but only
in part. She believed, but her faith was mingled with
much unbelief. Yet both Martha and Mary were
genuine children of God, and true Christians.

These things are graciously written for our learning.
It is good to remember what true Christians really are.
Many and great are the mistakes into which people
fall, by forming a false estimate of the Christian's
character. Many are the bitter things which people
write against themselves, by expecting to find in their
hearts what cannot be found on this side of heaven.
Let us settle it in our minds that saints on earth are
not perfect angels, but only converted sinners. They
are sinners renewed, changed, sanctified, no doubt; but
they are yet sinners, and will be till they die. Like

Martha and Mary, their faith is often entangled with much unbelief, and their grace compassed round with much infirmity. Happy is that child of God who understands these things, and has learned to judge rightly both of himself and others. Rarely indeed shall we find the saint who does not often need that prayer, "Lord, I believe: help Thou mine unbelief." (Mark ix. 24.)

We learn, secondly, what need many believers have of *clear views of Christ's person, office, and power.* This is a point which is forcibly brought out in the well-known sentence which our Lord addressed to Martha In reply to her vague and faltering expression of belief in the resurrection at the last day, He proclaims the glorious truth, "I am the resurrection and the life;"— "I, even I, thy Master, am He that has the keys of life and death in His hands." And then He presses on her once more that old lesson, which she had doubtless often heard, but never fully realized:—"He that believeth in Me, though he were dead, yet shall he live; and whosoever liveth and believeth in Me shall never die."

There is matter here which deserves the close consideration of all true Christians. Many of them complain of want of sensible comfort in their religion. They do not feel the inward peace which they desire. Let them know that vague and indefinite views of Christ are too often the cause of all their perplexities. They must try to see more clearly the great object on which their faith rests. They must grasp more firmly His love and power toward them that believe, and the riches He has laid up for them even now in this world. We are

many of us sadly like Martha. A little general knowledge of Christ as the only Saviour, is often all that we
possess. But of the fulness that dwells in Him, of His
resurrection, His priesthood, His intercession, His unfailing compassion, we have tasted little or nothing at all.
They are things of which our Lord might well say to
many, as He did to Martha, "Believest thou this?"

Let us take shame to ourselves that we have named
the name of Christ so long, and yet know so little about
Him. What right have we to wonder that we feel so
little sensible comfort in our Christianity? Our slight
and imperfect knowledge of Christ is the true reason of
our discomfort. Let the time past suffice us to have
been lazy students in Christ's school: let the time to
come find us more diligent in trying to "know Him
and the power of His resurrection." (Philip. iii. 10.)
If true Christians would only strive, as St. Paul says,
to "comprehend what is the breadth, and length, and
depth, and height, and to know the love of Christ, which
passeth knowledge," they would be amazed at the discoveries they would make. (Eph. iii. 18, 19.) They
would soon find, like Hagar, that there are wells of water
near them of which they had no knowledge. They would
soon discover that there is more of heaven to be enjoyed
on earth than they had ever thought possible. The root
of a happy religion is clear, distinct, well-defined knowledge of Jesus Christ. More knowledge would have
saved Martha many sighs and tears. Knowledge alone,
no doubt, if unsanctified, only "puffeth up." (1 Cor.
viii. 1.) Yet without clear knowledge of Christ in all

His offices we cannot expect to be established in the faith, and steady and unmoved in the time of need.

17.—[*Then when Jesus came.*] We are left entirely to conjecture as to the time spent by our Lord in His journey from Bethabara to Bethany. We do not know anything certain of the place where He was abiding, except that it was beyond Jordan. Probably it was between twenty and thirty miles from Bethany, and this distance, to those who travelled on foot, would be at least a day's journey.

[*He found...lain...grave...four days already.*] The Greek form of language here is peculiar, and a literal translation would be impossible. It would be, "He found him being already four days in the grave." It is highly probable that Lazarus was buried the same day that he died. In a country like Palestine, with a hot climate, it is quite impossible to keep corpses long unburied, without danger and discomfort to the living. A man may talk to his friend one day, and find him buried the next day.

One thing is abundantly proved by this verse. Lazarus must certainly have been dead, and not in a trance or swoon. A person lying in a grave for four days, all reasonable people would admit, must have been a dead man.

The various forms of death which our Lord is recorded to have triumphed over should not be forgotten. Jairus' daughter was just dead ; the son of the widow of Nain was being carried to the grave ; Lazarus, the most extraordinary case of all, had been four days in the tomb.

The expression, "He found," in this verse, must not be thought to imply any surprise. We know that our Lord began His journey from Bethabara with a full knowledge that Lazarus was dead. What "He found" applies to Lazarus therefore, and to the precise length of time that he had been in the grave. He was not only dead, but buried.

We can well imagine what a sorrowful time those four days must have been to Martha and Mary, and how many thoughts must have crossed their minds as to the reason of our Lord's delay, as to the day He would come, and the like. Nothing so wears us down as suspense and uncertainty. Yet of all graces there is none so glorifying to God and sanctifying to the heart as that of patience or quietly waiting. How long Abraham, Jacob, Joseph, Moses, and David were kept waiting. Jesus loves to show the world that His people can wait. Martha and Mary had to exemplify this. Well if we can do likewise!

Gomarus discusses at length the curious question, where the soul of Lazarus was during those four days. He dismisses as unscriptural the idea that it was yet in the body, and seems to hold that it was in Paradise.

The "four days" are easily accounted for, if we remember the time occupied by the messenger from Bethany, the two days' delay at Bethabara, and the journey to Bethany.

18.—[*Now Bethany...nigh...Jerusalem, about fifteen furlongs off.*] This verse shows that John wrote for readers who were not acquainted with Palestine. According to his manner he gives a parenthetical description of the situation of Bethany, partly to show how very near to Jerusalem the wonderful miracle he relates was worked,—within a walk of the temple, and almost within view; and partly to account for the number of the Jews who came from Jerusalem to comfort Martha and Mary.

The distance, fifteen furlongs, is rather less than two miles. The use of the expression, "about," shows that the Holy Ghost condescends to use man's common form of language in describing things, and that such expressions are not inconsistent with inspiration. (See John ii. 6, and vi. 19.)

19.—[*And many Jews...came...Mary.*] This sentence would be more literally rendered, "Many from among the Jews had come to those around Martha and Mary." Who these Jews were it is impossible to say, except that they evidently came from Jerusalem. One can hardly suppose that they were the leaders and rulers of the Pharisees. Such men would not be likely to care for friends of Jesus, and would hardly have condescended to visit Martha and Mary, who were doubtless known to be His disciples. Of course it is possible that Simon the leper, in whose house Lazarus died, may have been a man of consideration, and that the Jews may have come out of respect to him. At any rate it is clear that those who saw the stupendous miracle of this chapter were Jerusalem Jews, and were "many," and not few.—The expression, "Those around Martha and Mary," is a form of language not uncommon in Greek, and is probably rightly translated in our version. It can hardly mean, "the women who had come to mourn with Martha and Mary," though it is well known that women were the chief mourners at funerals. It is, however, only fair to say that Beza decidedly holds that the women and female friends who had come to mourn with Mary and Martha are meant in this verse.

[*To comfort them concerning their brother.*] This appears to have been a common practice among the Jews. When any one died, friends and neighbours assembled for several days at the house of the deceased, to mourn with and comfort the relatives. Lightfoot specially mentions it. The same custom prevails in many parts of the world at the present day : Hindostan and Ireland are instances.

We cannot doubt that many of these Jews came to Martha and Mary from form and custom, and not from any genuine sympathy or kind feeling, much less from any unity of spiritual taste. Yet it is striking to observe how God blesses even the semblance of sympathy. By coming they saw Christ's greatest miracle. If unbelief can sympathize, how much more should grace.

One thing at any rate seems very clearly proved by this verse. Whatever was the rank or position of Martha, Mary, and Lazarus, they were well-known people, and anything that happened in their house at Bethany was soon public news in Jerusalem. Had they been strangers from Galilee, the thing named in this verse would not have been written.

Chrysostom thinks the Evangelist mentioned the Jews coming to comfort Martha and Mary, as one of the many circumstances proving that Lazarus was really dead. They evidently thought him dead, or they would not have come.

Lightfoot gives a long and curious account of the customs of the Jews about comforting mourners. He says that "thirty days were allotted for the time of mourning. The three first days were for weeping ; seven days for lamentation ; and thirty days for intermission from washing or shaving. The beds in the house of mourning were all taken down and laid on the ground, as soon as the coffin left the house. The comforter sat on the floor ; the bereaved sat chief. The comforter might not say a word till the chief mourner broke silence."

Poole observes that the mourning for Jacob was forty days, for Aaron and Moses, thirty days. (Gen. l. 3 ; Num. xx. 29 ; Deut. xxxiv. 8.)

20.—[*Then Martha. .heard…Jesus…coming.. met Him.*] The Greek word for "was coming," would have been more literally translated, "is coming," or, "comes," in the present tense. It then gives the idea that Martha received from some friend, servant, or watchman, who was on the look out on the road from Jordan, the message long looked for, "Jesus is in sight:" "He is coming." She then hurried out, and met our Lord outside the village. The Greek is simply, "met Him;" and "went" is needless.

Bullinger thinks that Martha, with characteristic activity, was bustling after domestic duties, and heard from some one that Jesus was coming, and ran to meet Him, without going to tell Mary.

[*But Mary sat still . house.*] While Martha hurried out to meet Jesus, Mary continued sitting in the house. Martha's "met" is a perfect tense; Mary's "sat" is an imperfect. It is impossible not to see the characteristic temperament of each sister coming out here, and doubtless it is written for our learning. Martha—active, stirring, busy, demonstrative—cannot wait, but runs impulsively to meet Jesus. Mary—quiet, gentle, pensive, meditative, contemplative, meek,—sits passively at home. Yet I venture to think that of the two sisters, Martha here appears to most advantage. There is such a thing as being so crushed and stunned by our affliction that we do not adorn our profession under it. Is there not something of this in Mary's conduct throughout this chapter? There is a time to stir, as well as to sit still; and here, by not stirring, Mary certainly missed hearing our Lord's glorious declaration about Himself. I would not be mistaken in saying this. Both these holy women were true disciples; yet if Mary showed more grace on a former occasion than Martha, I think Martha here showed more than Mary.

Let us never forget that there are differences of temperament among believers, and let us make due allowance for others if they are not quite like ourselves. There are believers who are quiet, passive, silent, and meditative; and believers who are active, stirring, and demonstrative. The well-ordered Church must find room, place, and work for all. We need Marys as well as Marthas, and Marthas as well as Marys.

Nothing brings out character so much as sickness and affliction. If we would know how much grace believers have, we should see them in trouble.

Let us remember that "sitting" was the attitude of a mourner, among the Jews. Thus Job's friends "sat down with him on the ground." (Job ii. 13.)

Henry remarks, "In the day of affliction Mary's contemplative and reserved temper proved a snare to her, made her less able to grapple with grief, and disposed her to melancholy. It will be our wisdom to watch against the temptations, and improve the advantages of our natural temper."

21.—[*Then said Martha...if Thou...not died.*] This is the first account of Martha's feelings. It was the uppermost thought in her mind, and with honest impulsiveness she brings it out at once. It is easy to detect in it a strange mixture of emotions.

Here is passion, not unmixed with a tinge of reproach. "I wish you had been here: why did you not come sooner? You might have prevented my brother's death."

Here is love, confidence, and devotion creeping out. "I wish you had been here. We loved you so much. We depended so entirely on your love. We felt if you had been here all would be ordered well."

Here is faith. "I wish you had been here. I believe you could have healed my brother, and kept death from him."

Nevertheless there is something of unbelief at bottom. Martha forgets that the bodily presence of Jesus was not necessary in order to cure her brother, or to prevent his death. She must have known what our Lord did for the Centurion's servant, and the ruler of Capernaum. He had but to speak the word anywhere and Lazarus would have recovered. But memories often fail in time of trouble.

Ferus remarks how apt we all are to say, as Martha, "If God had been here, if Christ had been present, this would not have happened ; as if Christ was not always present, and everywhere near His people ! "

Henry remarks that in cases like Martha's, "we are apt to add to our trouble by fancying what might have been. If such a method had been taken, such a physician employed, my friend had not died ! which is more than we know. And what good does it do? When God's will is done, our business is to submit."

22.—[*But I know...even now...ask ..give it thee.*] In these words poor Martha's faith and hope shine clearly and unmistakably, though not without serious blemishes. "Even now," she says, "though my brother is dead and lying in the grave, I know, and feel confident, from the many proofs I have seen of Thy power, that whatsoever things Thou mayest ask of God, God will give them to Thee.   I must therefore even now cling to the hope that in some way or other Thou wilt help us."

The faith of these words is plain and unmistakable.   Martha hopes desperately against hope, that somehow all will be right, though she knows not how.   She has strong confidence in the efficacy of our Lord's prayers.

The presence of dim views and indistinct apprehensions of Christ in Martha's mind, is as evident as her faith.   She speaks as if our Lord was a human prophet only, and had no independent power of His own, as God, to work a miracle, and as if He could not command a cure, but must ask God for it, as Elisha did.   She must have strangely forgotten the manner in which our Lord had often worked His miracles.   Chrysostom remarks, that she speaks as if Christ was only "some virtuous and approved mortal."

Let us note here that there may be true faith and love toward Christ in a person, and yet much dimness and ignorance mixed up with it. Love to Christ, in Christian women especially, is often much clearer than faith and knowledge. Hence women are more easily led astray by false doctrine than men. It is of the utmost importance to remember that there are degrees of faith and knowledge. How small a degree of faith may save, and how much of ignorance may be found even in one who is on the way to heaven, are deep points which probably the last day alone will fully disclose.

Let us do Martha the justice to observe that she shows great confidence in the value and efficacy of prayer.

23.—[*Jesus saith...brother...rise again.*] These words, the first spoken by our Lord after arriving at Bethany, are very remarkable. They sound as if He saw the vague nature of Martha's faith, and would gradually lead her on to clearer and more distinct views of Himself, His office, and Person. He therefore begins by the broad, general promise, "Thy brother shall be raised up." He does not say when or how. If His disciples heard him say this, they might have some clue to His meaning, as He had said, "I go that I may awake him out of sleep." But Martha had not heard that.

Let us note that our Lord loves to draw out the faith and knowledge of His people by degrees. If He told us everything at once, plainly, and without any room for misunderstanding, it would not be good for us. Exercise is useful for all our graces.

Rollock sees in this verse a signal example of our Lord's unwillingness to "break the bruised reed, or quench the smoking flax."

He nourishes and encourages the little spark of faith which Martha had.

24.—[*Martha.. I know...resurrection...last day.*] Martha here reveals the extent of her faith and knowledge. She knows and feels sure that her brother will be raised again from the dead in the last day, when the resurrection takes place. This, as a pious Jewess, she had learned from the old Testament Scriptures, and as a Christian believer, she had gathered even more distinctly from the teaching of Jesus. But she does not say, "I know and feel confident" of anything more. She may perhaps have had some glimmering of hope that Jesus would do something, but she does not say, "I know that He will." General faith is easier than particular.

We see from this verse that the resurrection of the body formed part of the creed of the Jewish Church, and of the faith of our Lord's disciples. Martha's "*I know*," sounds as if she remembered the words of Job, "I know that my Redeemer liveth." What she did not understand, or had failed to remember, was our Lord's peculiar office as Lord of the resurrection. We cannot now understand how she can have failed to hear what our Lord had said before the Sanhedrim. (John v. 25 —29.) Very probably she was not at Jerusalem at the time. If she did hear it, she evidently had not comprehended it. Even our Lord's teaching was often not taken in by His people! How much less must His ministers expect all their sermons to be understood.

To my eyes there is an evident tone of disappointment about Martha's speech. It is as though she said, "I know, of course, that he will rise again at last; but that is cold comfort. It is a far distant event. I want nearer and better consolation."

Hutcheson remarks, "It is no uncommon thing to see men believing great things that are far off, and about which they have no present exercise, when yet their faith proves weak in the matter of a present trial, though less difficult than that which they profess to believe."

25.—[*Jesus said...I am...resurrection...life.*] In this and the following verses, our Lord corrects Martha's feeble and inadequate notions, and sets before her more exalted views of Himself. As Chrysostom says, "He shows her that He needed none to help Him." He tells her that He is not merely a human teacher of the resurrection, but the Divine Author of all resurrection, whether spiritual or physical, and the Root and Fountain of all life. "I am that high and holy One who by taking man's nature upon Me, have ennobled his body, and made 'ts resurrection possible. I am the great

First Cause and Procurer of man's resurrection, the Conqueror of death, and the Saviour of the body. I am the great Spring and Source of all life, and whatever life any one has, eternal, spiritual, physical, is all owing to me. All that are raised from the grave will be raised by Me. All that are spiritually quickened are quickened by Me. Separate from Me there is no life at all. Death came by Adam : life comes by Me."

All must feel that this is a deep saying, so deep that we see but a little of it. One thing only is very clear and plain : none could use this language but one who knew and felt that He was very God. No prophet or Apostle ever spoke in this way.

I do not feel sure that the two first words of this verse do not contain a latent reference to the great title of Jehovah, "I am." The Greek quite permits it.

[*He that believeth...Me...dead...live.*] This sentence receives two interpretations. Some, as Calvin and Hutcheson, hold that "dead" here means *spiritually* dead.—Others, as Bullinger, Gualter, Brentius, Musculus, hold that " dead " means *bodily* dead.— With these last I entirely agree, partly because of the point that our Lord is pressing on Martha, partly because of the awkwardness of speaking of a believer as "dead." Moreover, the expression is a verb,— " though he has died," and not an adjective,—" is a dead person." The sense I believe to be this : " He that believes in Me, even if he has died, and been laid in the grave, like thy brother, shall yet live, and be raised again through my power. Faith in Me unites such an one to the Fountain of all life, and death can only hold him for a short time. As surely as I, the Head, have life, and cannot be kept a prisoner by the grave, so surely all my members, believing in Me, shall live also."

26.—[*And whosoever liveth...believeth...never die.*] In this verse our Lord seems to me to speak of living believers, as in the last verse He had spoken of dead ones. Here, then, He makes the sweeping declaration, that "every one who believes in Him shall never die : " that is, " he shall not die eternally," as the Burial Service of the Church of England has it. The second death shall have no power over him. The sting of bodily death shall be taken away. He partakes of a life that never ends, from the moment that he believes in Christ. His body may be laid in the grave for a little season, but only to be raised after a while to glory ; and his soul lives on uninterruptedly for evermore, and, like the great risen Head, dieth no more.

That there are great depths in this and the preceding sentence, every reverent believer will always admit. We feel that we do not see the bottom. The difficulty probably arises from the utter inability of our gross, carnal natures to comprehend the mysteries of life, death, and resurrection of any kind. One thing is abundantly clear, and that is the importance of faith in Christ. "He that believeth" is the man who though dead shall live, and shall never die. Let us take care that we believe, and then all shall one day be plain. The simple questions, "What is life, and what is death?" contain enough to silence the wisest philosopher.

[*Believest thou this?*] This searching question is the application to Martha of the great doctrines just laid down. "Thou believest that the dead will rise. It is well. But dost thou believe that I am the Author of resurrection, and the source of life? Dost thou realize that I, thy Teacher and Friend, am very God, and have the keys of death and the grave in my hands? Hast thou yet got hold of this? If thou hast not, and only knowest me as a prophet sent to teach good and comfortable things, thou hast only received half the truth."

Home questions like these are very useful. How little we most of us know what we really believe, and what we do not; what we have grasped and made our own, and what we hold loosely. Above all, how little we know what we really believe about Christ.

Melancthon points out how immensely important it is to know whether we really have faith, and believe what we hold.

27.—[*She saith... Yea, Lord: I believe.*] Poor Martha, pressed home with the mighty question of the last verse, seems hardly able to give any but a vague answer. In truth, we cannot expect that she would speak distinctly about that which she only understood imperfectly. She therefore falls back on a general answer, in which she states simply, yet decidedly, what was the extent of her creed.

Our English word, "I believe," hardly gives the full sense of the Greek. It would be literally, "I have believed, and do believe." This is my faith, and has been for a long time.

Augustine, Bede, Bullinger, Chemnitius, Gualter, Maldonatus, Quesnel, and Henry, think that the first word of Martha's reply is a full and explicit declaration of faith in everything our Lord had just said. "Yes, Lord, I do believe Thou art the resurrection and the life," etc. I cannot see this myself. The idea seems contradicted by Martha's subsequent conduct at the grave.

Musculus strongly maintains that Martha's confession, good as it was, was vague and imperfect. Lampe takes much the same view.

[*Thou art the Christ...Son of God...come...world.*] Here is Martha's statement of her belief. It contains three great points : (1) that Jesus was the Christ, the anointed One, the Messiah ; (2) that He was the Son of God ; (3) that He was the promised Redeemer, who was to come into the world. She goes no further, and probably she could not. Yet considering the time she lived in, the universal unbelief of the Jewish nation, and the wonderful difference in the views of believers before the crucifixion and after, I regard it as a noble and glorious confession, and even fuller than Peter's, in Matthew xvi. 16. Melancthon points out the great superiority of Martha's faith to that of the most intellectual heathen, in a long and interesting passage.

It is easy to say that Martha's faith was rather vague, and that she ought to have seen everything more clearly. But we at this period of time, and with all our advantages, are very poor judges of such a matter. Dark and dim as her views were, it was a great thing for a solitary Jewish woman to have got hold of so much truth, when, within two miles, in Jerusalem, all who held such a creed as her's were excommunicated and persecuted.

Let us note that people's views of truth may be very defective on some points, and yet they may have the root of the matter in them. Martha evidently did not yet fully realize that Christ was the resurrection and the life : but she had learned the alphabet of Christianity,—Christ's Messiahship and Divinity, and doubtless learned more in time. We must not condemn people hastily or harshly, because they do not see all at once.

Chrysostom says, "Martha seems to me not to understand Christ's saying. She was conscious it was some great thing, but did not perceive the whole meaning, so that when asked one thing she answered another."

Toletus remarks, " Martha thought she believed everything Christ said, while she believed Him to be the true promised Messiah. And she did truly believe, but her faith was implicit and general. It is just as if some rustic, being questioned about some proposition of faith which he does not quite comprehend, replies, 'I believe in the Holy Church.' So here Martha said, 'I believe Lord, that Thou art the true Christ, and that all things

Thou sayest are true;' and yet she did not distinctly perceive them." This is a remarkable testimony from a Romanist.

Ought we not, perhaps, to make some allowance for the distress and affliction in which Martha was when she made her confession? Is it fair to expect a person in her position to speak as distinctly and precisely as one not in trouble?

28.—[*And when she had said this, etc.*] The affection of Martha for her sister appears here. Once assured that her Master was come, and perhaps somewhat cheered by the few words He spoke, she hastens home to tell Mary that Jesus was come, and had called for her. We are not told expressly that Jesus had mentioned Mary, but we may suppose that He did, and had asked where she was.

The word "secretly" may be applied to the word which follows, if we like, and it would then mean that "Martha called Mary, saying secretly." This is probably the correct rendering.

The words rendered, "is come" would be more literally translated, "is present: is actually here."

The expression, "the Master," is probably the name by which our Lord was familiarly known by the family at Bethany. It is literally, "the Teacher."

Bullinger remarks that the word "secretly" is purposely inserted, to show that the Jews who followed Mary had no idea that Jesus was come. Had they known it, he thinks, they would not have followed her, and so would not have seen the miracle.

Hall evidently thinks that Martha told Mary "secretly," for fear of the unbelieving Jews who were among the comforters. He remarks, "Christianity doth not bid us abate anything of our wariness and honest policy: yea, it requires us to have no less of the serpent than of the dove."

29.—[*As soon as she heard, etc.*] The two last words in this sentence are both in the present tense. It would be more literally rendered, "She, when she heard, arises quickly and comes to Him." It is evident, I think, that the sudden movement of Mary was not caused by hearing that Jesus was come, but that Jesus called for her.

It is not unlikely, from the word "arose," that Mary was lying or sitting prostrate on the ground, under the pressure of grief. We may also well suppose that our Lord, who doubtless knew her state, asked for her, in order to rouse her to exertion. When David heard that his child was dead, and nothing left for him to do but to be resigned, he "arose from off the earth." (2 Sam. xii. 20.)

JOHN XI. 30—37.

30 Now Jesus was not yet come into the town, but was in that place where Martha met him.

31 The Jews then which were with ner in the house, and comforted her, when they saw Mary, that she rose up hastily and went out, followed her, saying, She goeth unto the grave to weep there.

32 Then when Mary was come where Jesus was, and saw him, she fell down at his feet, saying unto him, Lord, if thou hadst been here, my brother had not died.

33 When Jesus therefore saw her weeping, and the Jews also weeping which came with her, he groaned in the spirit, and was troubled,

34 And said, Where have ye laid him? They said unto him, Lord, come and see.

35 Jesus wept.

36 Then said the Jews, Behold how he loved him!

37 And some of them said, Could not this man, which opened the eyes of the blind, have caused that even this man should not have died?

Not many passages in the new Testament are more wonderful than the simple narrative contained in these eight verses. It brings out, in a most beautiful light, the sympathizing character of our Lord Jesus Christ. It shows us Him who is "able to save to the uttermost them that come to God by Him," (Heb. vii. 25,) as able to feel as He is to save. It shows us Him who is one with the Father, and the Maker of all things, entering into human sorrows, and shedding human tears.

We learn, for one thing, in these verses, *how great a blessing God sometimes bestows on actions of kindness and sympathy.*

It seems that the house of Martha and Mary at Bethany was filled with mourners when Jesus arrived. Many of these mourners, no doubt, knew nothing of the inner life of these holy women. Their faith, their hope, their love to Christ. their discipleship, were things

of which they were wholly ignorant. But they felt for
them in their heavy bereavement, and kindly came to
offer what comfort they could. By so doing they reaped
a rich and unexpected reward. They beheld the greatest
miracle that Jesus ever wrought. They were eye witnesses when Lazarus came forth from the tomb. To
many of them, we may well believe, that day was a
spiritual birth. The raising of Lazarus led to a resurrection in their souls. How small sometimes are the
hinges on which eternal life appears to depend! If these
people had not sympathized they might never have been
saved.

We need not doubt that these things were written
for our learning. To show sympathy and kindness to
the sorrowful is good for our own souls, whether we know
it or not. To visit the fatherless and widows in their
affliction, to weep with them that weep, to try to bear
one another's burdens, and lighten one another's cares,
—all this will make no atonement for sin, and will
not take us to heaven. Yet it is healthy employment
for our hearts, and employment which none ought to
despise. Few perhaps are aware that one secret of being
miserable is to live only for ourselves, and one secret of
being happy is to try to make others happy, and to do a
little good in the world. It is not for nothing that these
words were written by Solomon, " It is better to go to the
house of mourning than to the house of feasting : "—
" The heart of the wise is in the house of mourning,
but the heart of fools is in the house of mirth." (Eccl.
vii. 2, 4.) The saying of our Lord is too much over-

looked: "Whosoever shall give to drink to one of these little ones a cup of cold water only in the name of a disciple, verily I say unto you he shall in no wise lose his reward." (Matt. x. 42.) The friends of Martha and Mary found that promise wonderfully verified. In an age of peculiar selfishness and self-indulgence, it would be well if they had more imitators.

We learn, for another thing, *what a depth of tender sympathy there is in Christ's heart towards His people.* We read that when our Lord saw Mary weeping, and the Jews also weeping with her, "He groaned in the spirit and was troubled." We read even more than this. He gave outward expression to His feelings: He "wept." He knew perfectly well that the sorrow of the family of Bethany would soon be turned into joy, and that Lazarus in a few minutes would be restored to his sisters. But though He knew all this, He "wept."

This weeping of Christ is deeply instructive. It shows us that it is not sinful to sorrow. Weeping and mourning are sadly trying to flesh and blood, and make us feel the weakness of our mortal nature. But they are not in themselves wrong. Even the Son of God wept.—It shows us that deep feeling is not a thing of which we need be ashamed. To be cold and stoical and unmoved in the sight of sorrow is no sign of grace. There is nothing unworthy of a child of God in tears. Even the Son of God could weep.—It shows us, above all, that the Saviour in whom believers trust is a most tender and feeling Saviour. He is one who can be touched with sympathy for our infirmities.   When we turn to Him in the hour of trouble, and pour out our hearts before Him, He knows what we go through, and can pity.   And He is One who never changes.   Though He now sits at God's right hand in heaven, His heart is still the same that it was upon earth.   We have an Advocate with the Father, who, when He was upon earth, could weep.

Let us remember these things in daily life, and never be ashamed of walking in our Master's footsteps.   Let us strive to be men and women of a tender heart and a sympathising spirit.   Let us never be ashamed to weep with them that weep, and rejoice with them that rejoice.   Well would it be for the Church and the world if there were more Christians of this stamp and character!   The Church would be far more beautiful, and the world would be far more happy.

Notes.   John xi. 30—37.

30.—[*Now Jesus was not yet come, etc.*]   The Greek word for "come" is in the preterperfect tense.   The sentence, translated literally, would be, "Jesus had not yet come into the town" when Martha left Him to tell Mary, but was still waiting or remaining in the place outside Bethany, where Martha at first met Him.   The word "town" would be more correctly rendered "village," according to our present acceptation of the word.   Yet it is fair to remember that words change their meaning with lapse of time.   Even at this day a little Suffolk village of 1,400 people, is called a "town" by many of its inhabitants.

Calvin thinks that Jesus remained outside Bethany by Martha's request, that His life might not be endangered.

31.—[*The Jews then...comforted her...saw Mary...followed her.*]   It is probable that the persons here mentioned formed a considerable number,—as many as could crowd into the house.   "Comforted" in the Greek is the present participle, and implies that they were actually employed in comforting Mary.   Concerning the manner of

comforting on such occasions, we know nothing certain. People
who only talk common places are miserable comforters, and far
worse than Job's friends, who sat for seven days saying nothing
at all.   It may be that among the Jews the mere presence of
courteous and sympathizing people was thought a kind attention,
and soothed the feelings of the bereaved. The customs of nations
differ widely in such matters.

It is evident these Jews did not hear Martha's message, and
knew nothing of Jesus being near. Some of them perhaps, had
they known it, would not have followed Mary; not knowing, they
all followed without exception, and unexpectedly became eye-
witnesses of a stupendous miracle. All they knew was that Mary
went out hastily. They followed in a spirit of kind sympathy,
and by so doing reaped a great blessing.

Rupertus shrewdly remarks that the Jews did not follow Martha,
when she ran to meet Jesus, but did follow Mary. He conjectures
that Mary's affliction was deeper and more overwhelming than
Martha's, and her friends devoted themselves more to comfort her,
as needing most consolation. Yet the simpler reason seems to be
that when *both* sisters had left the house, the friends could hardly
do anything else but go out and follow.

[*She goeth...grave...weep there.*] We must suppose from this
sentence, that weeping at the grave of dead friends was a custom
among the Jews in our Lord's time. In estimating such a custom,
which to most thinking persons may seem as useless as rubbing a
wound, and very likely to keep up pain without healing, it is only
fair to remember that Old Testament views of the state after death
were not nearly so well lighted and comfortable as ours. The removal of death's sting, the resurrection and paradise, were things
not nearly so well understood even by the best saints before Christ,
as they were after Christ rose again. To most of the Jews in our
Lord's time, we can well believe that death was regarded as the
end of all happiness and comfort, and the state after death as a
dreary blank. When Sadducees, who said there was "no resurrection," were chief rulers and high priests, we may well suppose
that the sorrow of many Jews over the death of friends, was a
"sorrow without hope." Even at this day, "the place of wailing"
at Jerusalem, where the Jews assemble to weep over the foundation
stones of the old temple, is a proof that their habit of weeping over
crushed hopes is not yet extinct.

32.—[*Then when Mary, etc.*] We see in this verse that as soon as
Mary met our Lord, the first thing she said was almost exactly

what Martha had said in the twenty-first verse, and the remarks made there need not be repeated. The similarity shows, at any rate, that throughout the illness of Lazarus, the thoughts of the two sisters had been running in one and the same direction. Both had built all their hopes on Jesus coming. Both had felt confidence that His coming would have saved their brother's life. Both were bitterly disappointed that He did not come. Both had probably kept saying the same words repeatedly, "If our Master would only come, Lazarus would not die." There are, however, one or two touches of difference between the two sisters, here as elsewhere. Let us note them.

Mary "fell down" at our Lord's feet, and Martha did not. She was made of softer, feebler character than Martha, and was more completely crushed and overcome than her sister.

Mary fell down at our Lord's feet when she "saw" Him. Up to that moment probably she had borne up, and had run to the place where Martha told her Jesus was waiting. But when she actually saw her Master, and remembered how she had longed for a sight of Him for some days, her feelings overcame her, and she broke down. The eyes have a great effect on the feelings of the heart. People often bear up pretty well, till they *see* something that calls up thoughts.

I do not perceive any ground for thinking, as Calvin does, that this "falling at our Lord's feet" was an act of worship, a recognition of our Lord's divinity. It is much more natural and reasonable to regard it as the mere expression of Mary's state of feeling.

Trapp remarks that the words of Mary in this verse and of Martha in the former one, show that we are all naturally disposed to make too much of Christ's bodily presence.

33.—[*When Jesus therefore, saw her, etc.*] This is one of those verses which bring out very strongly the real humanity of our Lord, and His power to sympathize with His people. As a real man, He was specially moved when He saw Mary and the Jews weeping. As God, He had no need to hear their plaintive language, and to see their tears in order to learn that they were afflicted. He knew perfectly all their feelings. Yet as man He was like ourselves, peculiarly stirred by the *sight* of sorrow : for human nature is so constituted, that grief is eminently contagious. If one in a company is deeply touched, and begins to weep, it is extremely likely that others will weep also. This power of sympathy our Lord evidently had in full possession. He *saw* weeping, and He wept.

Let us carefully remark that our Lord never changes. He did not leave behind Him His human nature when He ascended up into heaven. At this moment, at God's right hand, He can be touched with the feeling of our infirmities, and can understand tears as well as ever. Our great High Priest is the very Friend that our souls need, able to save as God, able to feel as man. To talk of the Virgin Mary feeling for sinners more than Jesus, is to say that which is ignorant and blasphemous. To teach that we can need any other priest, when Jesus is such a feeling Saviour, is to teach what is senseless and absurd.

[*He groaned in spirit.*] There is considerable difficulty about this expression. The word rendered "groaned," is only used five times in the New Testament. In Matt. ix. 30, and Mark i. 43, it is "straitly charged." In Mark xiv. 5, it is "murmured." Here, and at the thirty-eighth verse above, it is "groaned." Now what is precisely meant by the phrase?

(*a*) Some, as Ecolampadius, Brentius, Chemnitius, Flacius, and Ferus, maintain firmly that the notion of anger, indignation, and stern rebuke, is inseparable from the word "groaned." They think that the latent idea is the deep and holy indignation with which our Lord was moved at the sight of the ravages which death had made, and the misery sin and the devil had brought into the world. They say it implies the stern and righteous wrath with which the deliverer of a country tyrannized over and trampled down by a rebel, regards the desolation and destruction which the rebel has caused.

(*b*) Some add to this view the idea that "in spirit" means that our Lord groaned through the Holy Ghost, or by the Divine Spirit which dwelt in Him without measure, or by the power of His Godhead.

(*c*) Some, as Chrysostom, Theophylact, and Euthymius, think "groaned in spirit" means that Christ rebuked His own natural feelings by His Divine nature, or restrained His trouble, and in so doing was greatly disturbed.

(*d*) Some, as Gomarus and Lampe, consider that our Lord was moved to holy sorrow and indignation at the sight of the unbelief even of Martha and Mary (expressed by their immoderate grief, as if the case of Lazarus was hopeless), as well as at the sight of the unbelief of the Jews.

(*e*) Some, as Bullinger, Gualter, Diodati, Grotius, Maldonatus, Jansenius, Rollock, and Hutcheson, consider that the phrase simply expresses the highest and deepest kind of inward agitation of mind, an agitation in which grief, compassion, and holy detestation of sin's work in the world, were all mingled and combined. This agitation, however, was entirely inward at present. it was not bodily, but spiritual; not in the flesh, but in the spirit. As Burgon says, the "spirit" here means Christ's *inward* soul. I prefer this opinon to the former one, though I fully admit it has difficulties. But it is allowed by Schleusner and Parkhurst, and seems the view of Tyndall, Cranmer, and the Geneva version, as well as of our own.

[*And was troubled.*] This expression is to my mind even more difficult than the one which immediately precedes it. It would be literally translated, as our marginal reading has it, "He troubled Himself." In fact, Wycliffe translates it so. Now what can this mean?

Some maintain that in our Lord's mysterious Person the human nature was so entirely subordinated to the Divine, that the human passions and affections never moved unless influenced and actuated by the Divine nature, and that here to show His sympathy, He "troubled Himself." Thus Rupertus remarks that "if He had not troubled Himself, no one else could have troubled Him." I confess that I regard this view with a little suspicion. It seems to me to imply that our Lord's human nature was not like ours, and that His humanity was like an instrument played upon by His divinity, but in itself dead and passive until its music was called out. To my mind there is something dangerous in this.

I prefer to think that our Lord as man had all the feelings, passions, and affections of a man, but all under such perfect control that they never exceeded as ours do, and were never even very demonstrative, excepting on great occasions. As Beza says, there was no "disorder" in His emotions. Here I think He saw an occasion for exhibiting a very deep degree of sorrow and sympathy, partly from the sorrowful sight He beheld, and partly from His love to Mary, Martha, and Lazarus. Therefore He greatly disturbed and "troubled Himself."

It still admits of a question whether the phrase may not be simply a Hebraism for "He was troubled." (Compare 1 Sam. xxx. 6, and 2 Sam. xii. 18.) Hammond says it is a Hebrew idiom.

When all has been said, we must not forget that the phrase touches a very delicate and mysterious subject: that subject is the precise nature of the union of two natures in our Lord's

Person. That He was at the same time perfect God and perfect Man, is an article of the Christian faith ; but how far the Divine nature acted on the human, and to what extent it checked and influenced the action of human passions and feelings, are very deep points, which we have no line completely to fathom. After all, not the least part of our difficulty is that we can form no clear and adequate conception of a human nature entirely without sin.

One thing, at any rate, is abundantly clear from this passage : there is nothing wrong or wicked in being greatly moved by the sight of sorrow, so long as we keep our feelings under control. To be always cold, unfeeling, and unsympathizing, may appear to some very dignified and philosophical. But though it may suit a Stoic, it is not consistent with the character of a Christian. Sympathy is not sinful, but Christ-like.

Theophylact observes that Christ "teaches us by His own example the due measure of joy and grief. The absence altogether of sympathy and sorrow is brutal : the excess of them is womanly."

Melancthon observes that none of Christ's miracles seem to have been done without some great mental emotion. (Luke viii. 46.) He supposes that here at this verse, there was a great conflict with Satan in our Lord's mind, and that He wrestled in prayer for the raising of Lazarus, and then thanked God afterwards that the prayer was heard. Calvin takes much the same view.

Ecolampadius observes that we must not think Christ had a human body only, and not a human soul. He had a soul like our own in all things, sin only excepted, and capable of all our feelings and emotions.

Piscator and Trapp compare the trouble of spirit which our Lord went through, to the disturbance and agitation of perfectly clear water in a perfectly clear glass vessel. However great the agitation, the water remains clear.

Musculus reverently remarks that after all there is something about this "groaning in spirit and troubling Himself," which cannot be fully explained.

34.—[*And said, Where have ye laid him ?*] We cannot suppose that our Lord, who knew all things, even to the moment of Lazarus' death, could really need to be informed where Lazarus was buried. He asks what He does here partly as a kind friend to show His deep sympathy and interest in the grave of His friend, and partly to give further proof that there was no collusion in the matter of

Lazarus' burial, and that He had nothing to do with the choice of his tomb, in order to concert an imposture about raising him. In short, those who heard Him publicly ask this question, would see that this was no pre-arranged and pre-contrived miracle.

Quesnel remarks, "Christ does not ask out of ignorance, any more than God did when He said, "Adam, where art thou?"

[*They said...Lord, come and see.*] Who they were that said this, we do not exactly know. It was probably the common saying of all the party of mourners who stood around while Jesus talked with Mary. They did not know why our Lord wished to see the grave. They may possibly have supposed that He wished to accompany Mary and Martha, and to weep at the grave. At any rate the question and answer secured a large attendance of companions, as the disciples and our Lord went to the place where Lazarus was buried.

35.—[*Jesus wept.*] This wonderful little verse has given rise to an enormous amount of comment. The difficulty is to select thoughts, and not to overload the subject.

The Greek word rendered "wept" is not the same as that used for "weeping" in the thirty-third verse, but totally different. There the weeping is a weeping accompanied by demonstrative lamentation. Here the word would be more literally and accurately rendered "shed tears." In fact it is the only place in the New Testament where this word for "weep" is used.

There are three occasions where our Lord is recorded to have wept, in the Gospels: once when He beheld the city (Luke xix. 41), once in the garden of Gethsemane (Matt. xxvi. 39, and Heb. vi. 7), and here. We never read of His laughing, and only once of His rejoicing. (Luke x. 21.)

The reasons assigned by commentators why our Lord wept here, before He raised Lazarus, are various and curious.

(*a*) Some think that He wept to see the ravages made by death and sin.

(*b*) Some, as Hilary, think that He wept to think of the unbelief of the Jews.

(*c*) Some think that He wept to see how weak and feeble was the faith of Mary and Martha.

(*d*) Some, as Jerome and Ferus, think that He wept at the thought of the sorrow Lazarus would go through by returning to a sinful world.

(e) Some think that He wept out of sympathy with the affliction of His friends at Bethany, in order to give an eternal proof to
His Church that He can feel with us and for us.

I believe this last opinion is the true one.

We learn the great practical lesson from this verse, that there
is nothing unworthy of a Christian in tears. There is nothing
unmanly, dishonourable, unwise, or feeble, in being full of sympathy with the afflicted, and ready to weep with them that weep.
Indeed, it is curious to gather up the many instances we have in
Scripture of great men weeping.

We may draw great comfort from the thought that the Saviour
in whom we are bid to trust is one who can weep, and is as able
to feel as He is able to save.

We may learn the reality of our Lord's humanity very strongly
from this little verse. He was one who could hunger, thirst, sleep,
eat, drink, speak, walk, groan, be wearied, wonder, feel indignant,
rejoice, like any of ourselves, and yet without sin ; and above all,
He could weep. I read that there is "joy in the presence of the
angels of God" (Luke xv.), but I never read of angels weeping.
Tears are peculiar to flesh and blood.

Chrysostom remarks that "John, who enters into higher statements about our Lord's nature than any of the evangelists, also
descends lower than any in describing His bodily affections."

36.—[*Then said...Jews...Behold...loved him.*] This sentence is the
expression partly of surprise, which comes out in the word "behold ;" and partly of admiration,—what a loving and tender-hearted
Teacher this is ! It gives the idea that those who said this were
the few unprejudiced Jews who had come to Bethany to comfort
Mary and Martha, and afterward believed when they saw Lazarus
raised.

Let us observe that of all graces, love is the one which most
arrests the attention and influences the opinion of the world.

37.—[*And some of them said, etc.*] This sentence sounds to me like
the language of enemies determined to believe nothing good of our
Lord, and prepared to pick a hole or find a fault if possible, in anything that He did. Does not a sarcastic sneer ring throughout it ?
"Could not this Man, if He really did open the eyes of that blind
person at Jerusalem last autumn, have prevented this friend of
His from dying ? If He really is the Messiah and the Christ, and
really does work such wonderful works, why has He not prevented

all this sorrow? If he really loved Lazarus and his sisters, why did He not prove His love by keeping him back from the grave? Is it not plain that He is not Almighty? He cannot do everything. He could open the eyes of a blind man, but He could not prevent death carrying off His friend. If He was able to prevent Lazarus dying, why did He not do it? If He was not able, it is clear there are some things He cannot do."

We should note that "the blind" is a word in the singular number. It is evidently the blind man at Jerusalem whose case is referred to.

Let us note that nothing will convince, or satisfy, or silence some wicked men. Even when Christ is before them, they are cavilling, and doubting, and finding fault. What right have Christ's ministers to be surprised if they meet with the same treatment.

Musculus remarks on the Satanic malice which this sentence displays. It is the old sceptical spirit of cavilling and questioning. Unbelief is always saying Why? and why? and why? "If this Man was such a friend of Lazarus, and loved him so much, why did He let him die?"

JOHN XI. 38—46.

38 Jesus therefore again groaning in himself cometh to the grave. It was a cave, and a stone lay upon it.

39 Jesus said, Take ye away the stone. Martha, the sister of him that was dead, saith unto him, Lord, by this time he stinketh: for he hath been *dead* four days.

40 Jesus saith unto her, Said I not unto thee, that if thou wouldest believe, thou shouldest see the glory of God?

41 Then they took away the stone *from the place* where the dead was laid. And Jesus lifted up *his* eyes, and said, Father, I thank thee that thou hast heard me.

42 And I knew that thou hearest me always: but because of the people which stand by I said *it*, that they may believe that thou hast sent me.

43 And when he had thus spoken, he cried with a loud voice, Lazarus, come forth.

44 And he that was dead came forth, bound hand and foot with grave-clothes: and his face was bound about with a napkin. Jesus saith unto them, Loose him, and let him go.

45 Then many of the Jews which came to Mary, and had seen the things which Jesus did, believed on him.

46 But some of them went their ways to the Pharisees, and told them what things Jesus had done.

THESE verses record one of the greatest miracles the Lord Jesus Christ ever worked, and supply an unanswerable proof of His divinity. He whose voice could bring back from the grave one that had been four days dead,

must indeed have been very God! The miracle itself
is described in such simple language that no human
comment can throw light upon it. But the sayings of
our Lord on this occasion are peculiarly interesting, and
demand special notice.

We should mark, first, *our Lord's words about the
stone which lay upon the grave of Lazarus.* We read
that He said to those around Him, when He came to
the place of burial, "Take ye away the stone."

Now why did our Lord say this? It was doubtless
as easy for Him to command the stone to roll away
untouched, as to call a dead body from the tomb. But
such was not His mode of proceeding. Here, as in
other cases, He chose to give man something to do.
Here, as elsewhere, He taught the great lesson that
His almighty power was not meant to destroy man's
responsibility. Even when He was ready and willing
to raise the dead, He would not have man stand by
altogether idle.

Let us treasure up this in our memories. It involves
a point of great importance. In doing spiritual good
to others,—in training up our children for heaven,—
in following after holiness in our own daily walk,—
in all these things it is undoubtedly true that we are
weak and helpless. "Without Christ we can do nothing."
(John xv. 5.) But still we must remember that Christ
expects us to do what we can. "Take ye away the
stone," is the daily command which He gives us. Let us
beware that we do not stand still in idleness, under the
pretence of humility. Let us daily try to do what we

can, and in the trying, Christ will meet us and grant His blessing.

We should mark, secondly, the *words which our Lord addressed to Martha, when she objected to the stone being removed from the grave.* The faith of this holy woman completely broke down, when the cave where her beloved brother lay was about to be thrown open. She could not believe that it was of any use. "Lord," she cries, "by this time he stinketh." And then comes in the solemn reproof of our Lord : "Said I not unto thee, that if thou wouldst believe, thou shouldest see the glory of God?"

That sentence is rich in meaning. It is far from unlikely that it contains a reference to the message which had been sent to Martha and Mary, when their brother first fell sick. It may be meant to remind Martha that her Master had sent her word, "This sickness is not unto death, but for the glory of God." But it is perhaps more likely that our Lord desired to re-call to Martha's mind the old lesson He had taught her all through His Ministry, the duty of always believing. It is as though He said, "Martha, Martha, thou art forgetting the great doctrine of faith, which I have ever taught thee. Believe, and all will be well. Fear not: only believe."

The lesson is one which we can never know too well. How apt our faith is to break down in time of trial! How easy it is to talk of faith in the days of health and prosperity, and how hard to practice it in the days of darkness, when neither sun, moon, nor stars appear!

Let us lay to heart what our Lord says in this place. Let us pray for such stores of inward faith, that when our turn comes to suffer, we may suffer patiently and believe all is well. The Christian who has ceased to say, "I must see, and then I will believe," and has learned to say, "I believe, and by and by I shall see," has reached a high degree in the School of Christ.

We should mark thirdly, *the words which our Lord addressed to God the Father, when the stone was taken from the grave.* We read that he said, "Father, I thank Thee that Thou hast heard Me. And I knew that Thou hearest me always: but because of the people which stand by I said it, that they may believe that Thou hast sent Me."

This wonderful language is totally unlike anything said by Prophets or Apostles, when they worked miracles. In fact, it is not prayer, but praise. It evidently implies a constant mysterious communion going on between Jesus and His Father in heaven, which it is past the power of man either to explain or conceive. We need not doubt that here, as elsewhere in St. John, our Lord meant to teach the Jews the entire and complete unity there was between Him and His Father, in all that He did, as well as in all that He taught. Once more He would remind them that He did not come among them as a mere Prophet, but as the Messiah, who was sent by the Father, and who was one with the Father. Once more He would have them know that as the words which He spake were the very words which the Father gave Him to speak, so the works which He wrought were the very works which the Father gave Him to do. In short, He was the promised Messiah, whom the Father always hears, because He and the Father are One.

Deep and high as this truth is, it is for the peace of our souls to believe it thoroughly, and to grasp it tightly. Let it be a settled principle of our religion, that the Saviour in whom we trust is nothing less than eternal God, One whom the Father hears always, One who in very deed is God's Fellow. A clear view of the dignity of our Mediator's Person, is one secret of inward comfort. Happy is he who can say, "I know whom I have believed, and that He is able to keep that which I have committed to Him." (2 Tim. i. 12.)

We should mark, lastly, *the words which our Lord addressed to Lazarus when he raised him from the grave.* We read that "He cried with a loud voice, Lazarus come forth." At the sound of that voice, the king of terrors at once yielded up his lawful captive, and the insatiable grave gave up its prey. At once, "He that was dead came forth, bound hand and foot with grave-clothes."

The greatness of this miracle cannot possibly be exaggerated. The mind of man can scarcely take in the vastness of the work that was done. Here, in open day, and before many hostile witnesses, a man, four days' dead, was restored to life in a moment. Here was public proof that our Lord had absolute power over the material world! A corpse already corrupt, was made alive!—Here was public proof that our

Lord had absolute power over the world of spirits!
A soul that had left its earthly tenement was called
back from Paradise, and joined once more to its owner's
body. Well may the Church of Christ maintain that
He who could work such works was "over all, God
blessed for ever." (Rom. ix. 5.)

Let us turn from the whole passage with thoughts
of comfort and consolation. Comfortable is the thought
that the loving Saviour of sinners, on whose mercy
our souls entirely depend, is one who has all power in
heaven and earth, and is mighty to save.—Comfortable
is the thought that there is no sinner too far gone in
sin for Christ to raise and convert. He that stood by
the grave of Lazarus can say to the vilest of men,
"Come forth: loose him, and let him go."—Comfortable,
not least, is the thought that when we ourselves lie
down in the grave, we may lie down in the full assu-
rance that we shall rise again. The voice that called
Lazarus forth will one day pierce our tombs, and bid
soul and body come together. "The trumpet shall
sound, and the dead shall be raised incorruptible, and
we shall be changed." (1 Cor. xv. 52.)

NOTES. JOHN XI. 38—46.

38.—[*Jesus...groaning...cometh...grave.*] The word here rendered
"groaning" is the same that was used at 32nd verse, and the
same remarks apply to it. The only difference is that here it is
"groaning in Himself," and there "groaning in the spirit." This,
however, confirms my impression that in the former verse "in
the spirit" simply means "inwardly and spiritually," and that
the general idea is "under the influence of very strong inward
emotion."

The situation of the grave, we need not doubt, was outside the village of Bethany.   There was no such thing as interment within a town allowed among the Jews, or indeed among ancient nations generally.   The practice of burying the dead among the living is a barbarous modern innovation, reflecting little credit on Christians.

Calvin remarks, "Christ approaches the sepulchre as a champion preparing for a contest; and we need not wonder that He groans, as the violent tyranny of death, which He had to conquer, is placed before His eyes."

Ecolampadius and Musculus think that the unbelieving, sneering remark of the Jews in the preceding verse, is the reason why our Lord "again groaned."   Bullinger thinks that the renewed emotion of our Lord was simply occasioned by the sight of the grave.

[*It was a cave, and a stone lay upon it.*]   Graves among the Jews seem to have been of three kinds.   (1) Sometimes, but rarely, they were holes dug down into the ground, like our own.   (See Luke xi. 44.) (2) Most frequently they were caves hewn horizontally into the side of a rock, with a stone placed against the mouth. This was most probably the kind of new tomb in which our Lord was laid.   (3) Sometimes they were caves in which there was a sloping, downward descent.   This appears to have been the description of grave in which Lazarus was buried.   It says distinctly that "a stone lay *upon* it."

No doubt these particulars are specified to supply incidental proof of the reality of Lazarus's death and burial.

39.—[*Jesus said, Take ye away the stone.*]   The expression here conveys the idea of "lifting up" to take away.   It is the same word that is rendered "lifted up" in 41st verse.

The use of this word greatly strengthens the idea that the grave was a descending cave, and not a horizontal one.   When our Lord rose again, the stone was "rolled away from the door," and not lifted up.   (Matt. xxviii. 2.)

By calling on the crowd of attendants to take away the stone, our Lord effected two things.   Firstly, He impressed on the minds of all engaged the reality and truth of the miracle He was about to perform.   Every one who lent a hand to lift the huge stone and remove it, would remember it, and become a witness.   He would be able to say, "I myself helped to lift up the stone.   I myself am sure there was no imposture.   There was a dead body inside the grave." In fact, we cannot doubt that the smell rising from the bottom of the cave would tell any one who helped to lift the stone what there was there.—Secondly, our Lord teaches us the simple lesson that He would have man do what he can. Man cannot raise the soul, and give life, but he can often remove the stone.

Flacius points out the likeness between this command and the command at Cana to fill the water pots with water. (John ii. 7.)

That the stones placed at the mouth of graves in Palestine were very large, and not easily moved, we may see from Mark xvi. 3.

[*Martha, the sister of him, etc., etc.*] This is a remarkable sentence, and teaches several important things.

(*a*) It certifies, for the last time, the reality of Lazarus's death. He was not in a swoon or a trance. His own sister, who had doubtless seen him die, and closed his eyes, declares before the crowd of lookers on, that Lazarus had been dead four days, and was fast going to corruption. This we may well believe in such a climate as that of Palestine.

(*b*) It proves, beyond a reasonable doubt, that there was no imposture, no collusion, no concerted deception, arranged between the family of Bethany and our Lord. Here is the sister of Lazarus actually questioning the propriety of our Lord's order, and publicly saying in effect that it is no use to move the stone, that nothing can now be done to deliver her brother from the power of death. Like the eleven Apostles, after Jesus Himself rose, Martha was not a willing and prepared witness, but a resisting and unwilling one.

(*c*) It teaches, not least, how much unbelief there is in a believer's heart at the bottom. Here is holy Martha, with all her faith in our Lord's Messiahship, shrinking and breaking down at this most critical point. She cannot believe that there is any use in removing the stone. She suggests, impulsively and anxiously, her doubt whether our Lord remembers how long her brother has been dead.

It is not for nothing that we are specially told it was "Martha, the sister of him that was dead," who said this. If even she could say this, and raise objections, the idea of imposture and deception becomes absurd.

Some writers object to putting the full literal meaning on the Greek word rendered "stinketh:" but I can see nothing in the objection. We need not suppose that the body of Lazarus was different to other bodies. Moreover, it was just as easy to our Lord to raise a corpse four days' dead, as one only four hours' dead. In either case, the grand difficulty to be overcome would be the same : viz., to change death into life. Indeed it is worth considering whether this fact about Lazarus is not specially mentioned in order to show our Lord's power to restore man's corrupt and decayed body at the last day, and to make it a glorious body.

Let us note here what a humbling lesson death teaches. So terrible and painful is the corruption of a body, when the breath leaves it, that even those who love us most are glad to bury us out of sight. (Gen. xxiii. 4.)

Musculus suggests that Martha had so little idea what our Lord was going to do, that she supposed He only wanted to see Lazarus's face once more. This is perhaps going too far.

The Greek for "dead four days," is a singular expression, and one that cannot be literally rendered in English. It would be "He is a person of four days ;" and it may possibly mean, "He has been buried four days." Raphelius gives examples from Herodotus und Xenophon, which make it possible that it means either dead or buried.

Lightfoot mentions a very curious tradition of the Jews : "They say after death the spirit hovers about the sepulchre, waiting to see if it may return to the body. But when it sees the look of the face of the corpse changed, then it hovers no more, but leaves the body to itself." He also adds, "They do not certify of the dead, except within three days after decease ; for after three days the countenance changes."

40.—[*Jesus saith, Said I not, etc.*] This gentle but firm reproof is remarkable. It is not clear to what our Lord refers in the words, "Said I not."

(*a*) Some think, as Rupertus, that He refers to the message He sent at the beginning : "This sickness is not unto death, but for the glory of God."

(*b*) Some think that He refers to the conversation He had with Martha when she first met Him outside Bethany.

(*c*) Some think that He refers to words He had often used in discoursing with Martha and Mary, on former occasions.

The point is one which must be left open, as we have no means of settling it. My own impression is that there is probably a

reference to the message which our Lord sent back to the sisters
at first, when Lazarus was sick. I fancy there must have been
something more said at that time which is not recorded, and that
our Lord reminded Martha of this. At the same time I cannot
doubt that our Lord constantly taught the family of Bethany, and
all His disciples, that believing is the grand secret of seeing God's
glorious works.—"If thou canst believe, all things are possible to
him that believeth." "He did not many mighty works because of
their unbelief." (Mark ix. 23 ; Matt. xiii. 58.) Unbelief, in a
certain sense, seems to tie the hands and limit the power of omni-
potence.

Let us note that if we would see much we must first believe.
Man's natural idea is just the reverse : he would first see, and
then believe.

Let us note that even the best believers need reminding of Christ's
sayings, and are apt to forget them. "Said I not unto thee." It
is a little sentence we should often call to mind.

41.—[*Then they took away...stone...laid.*] Martha's interruption seems
to me to have caused a little pause in the proceedings. She being
the nearest relative of Lazarus, and having probably arranged
everything concerning his burial, and provided his tomb, we may
well believe that her speech made the bystanders hesitate to move
the stone. When, however, they heard our Lord's solemn reply,
and observed that she was silenced, and made no further objection,
"then" they proceeded to do what our Lord desired.

Hall remarks, "They that laid their hands to the stone doubtless held still awhile, when Martha spoke, and looked one while
on Christ, another while on Martha, to hear what issue of reso-
lution would follow so important an objection."

[*And Jesus lifted up His eyes, and said.*] We now reach a point
of thrilling and breathless interest. The stone had been removed
from the mouth of the cave. Our Lord stands before the open
grave, and the crowd stands around, awaiting anxiously to
see what would happen next. Nothing appears from the tomb.
There is no sign of life at present : but while all are eagerly
looking and listening, our Lord addressed His Father in heaven
in a most solemn manner, lifting up His eyes, and speaking audibly
to Him in the hearing of all the crowd. The reason He explains
in the next verse. Now, for the last time, about to work His
mightiest miracle, He once more makes a public declaration that
He did nothing separate from His Father in heaven. and that in

this and all His works there is a mysterious and intimate union between Himself and the Father.

We should note how He suits the action to the word. "He lifted up His eyes." (Compare John xvii. 1.) He showed that He was addressing an unseen Father in heaven.

[*Father, I thank thee that Thou hast heard Me.*] This is a remarkable expression. Our Lord begins with "thanks," when man would have expected Him to offer prayer. How shall we explain it?

(*a*) Some think that our Lord refers to prayer He had put up to the Father concerning the death of Lazarus, from the moment that He heard of his illness, and to His present firm conviction that those prayers had been heard, and were going to receive a public answer.

(*b*) Others think that there is no reason to suppose that our Lord refers to any former or remote prayer; that there was a constant, hourly, minutely communication between Himself and His heavenly Father; and that to pray, and return thanks for the answer to prayer, were actions which in His experience were very closely connected.

The subject is a deep and mysterious one, and I shrink from giving a very positive opinion about it. That our Lord constantly prayed on all occasions, we know from the Gospels. That He prayed sometimes with great agony of mind and with tears, we also know. (Heb. v. 7.) But how far He could know anything of that peculiar struggle which we poor sinners have to carry on with doubt, fear, and anxiety, in our prayers, is another question altogether, and very hard to answer. One might suppose that One who was as man, entirely holy, humble, and without sin, might be able to thank for prayer heard, almost as soon as prayer was offered. Upon this theory the sentence before us would be plain : "I pray that Lazarus may be raised; and I thank Thee at the same time for hearing my prayer, as I know Thou dost."

And yet we must not forget two of our Lord's prayers not granted, apparently: "Father, save Me from this hour;"—"Father, let this cup pass from Me." (John xii. 47, and Mark xxvi. 29.) It is however only fair to say that the first of these prayers is greatly qualified by the context, and the second by the words, "If it be possible."

We may note here as elsewhere, what an example of thankfulness, as well as prayerfulness, our Lord always supplies. Well if it was followed! His people are always more ready to ask than to thank. The more grace in a heart the more humility, and the more humility the more praise.

Chrysostom remarks, "Who now ever prayed in this manner? Before uttering any prayer, He saith, 'I thank Thee;' showing that He needed not prayer." He also says that the real cause of our Lord saying this was to show the Jews He was no enemy of God, but did all His works according to His will.

Origen observes, "If to those who pray worthily is given the promise in Isaiah, 'Thou shalt cry, and He shall say, Here I am,' what answer think we could our Lord receive? He was about to pray for the resurrection of Lazarus. He was heard by the Father before He prayed; His request was granted before it was made; and, therefore, He begins with thanks."

Musculus, Flacius, and Glassius, think that our Lord refers to prayer He had been putting up secretly when He was "groaning in spirit and troubled," and that He was then wrestling and agonizing in prayer, though those around Him knew it not. We may remember that at the Red Sea we are not told of any audible prayer Moses offered, and yet the Lord says, "Wherefore criest thou unto Me?" (Exodus xiv. 15.)

Quesnel observes, "Christ being about to conclude His public life and preaching by the last and most illustrious of His miracles, returns solemn thanks to His Father for the power given to His human nature to prove the authority of His mission by miracles."

Hall observes, "Words express our hearts to men, thoughts to God. Well didst Thou know, Lord, out of the self-sameness of Thy will with the Father's, that if Thou didst but think in Thy heart that Lazarus should rise, he was now raised. It was not for Thee to pray vocally and audibly, lest those captious hearers should say, Thou didst all by entreaty, and nothing by power."

12.—[*And I knew that Thou hearest, etc.*] This verse is so elliptical that the meaning can hardly be seen without a paraphrase. "I do not give Thee these thanks as if I had ever doubted Thy willingness to hear Me; on the contrary, I know well that Thou always hearest Me.—Thou dost not only hear all my prayers as Man, both for myself and my people; Thou dost also ever hear Me, even as I hear Thee, from the mystical union there is between the Father and the Son.—But I have now said this publicly, for the benefit of this crowd of people standing by the grave, in order that they may see and believe for the last time that I do no miracle without Thee, and that I am the Messiah whom Thou hast sent into the world. I would have them publicly hear Me declare that I work this last great work as Thy Sent One, and as a last evidence that I am the Christ."

I cannot but think that there is a deep meaning about the expression, "Thou hearest Me alway." (Compare John v. 30.) But I admit the difficulty of the phrase, and would speak with diffidence.

It is impossible to imagine a more thorough open challenge to the attention of the Jews, than the language which preceded the raising of Lazarus. Before doing this stupendous work, our Lord proclaims that He is doing and speaking as He does, to supply a proof that the Father sent and commissioned Him as the Christ. Was He the "Sent One" or not? This, we must always remember, was the great question, of which He undertook to give proof. The Jews, moreover, said that He did His miracles by Beelzebub : let them hear that He did all by the power of God.

Bullinger remarks that our Lord seems to say, "The Jews do not all understand that union and communion between Me and Thee, by which we are of the same will, power, and substance. Some of them even think that I work by the power of the devil. Therefore that all may believe that I come from Thee, am sent by Thee, am Thy Son, equal to Thee, light of light, very God of very God, I use expressions of this sort."

Poole remarks, "There is a great difference between God's hearing of Christ and hearing us. Christ and His Father have one essence, one nature, and one will."

The following miracles were wrought by Christ without audible prayer, and with only an authoritative word, Matt. viii. 3 ; ix. 6 ; Mark v. 41 ; ix. 25 ; Luke vii. 14.

Wordsworth observes, "Christ prayed to show that He was not against God, nor God against Him, and that what He did was done with God's approval."

43.—[*And when...cried ..come forth.*] In this verse we have the last and crowning stage of the miracle. Attention was concentrated on the grave and our Lord. The crowd looked on with breathless expectation ; and then, while they looked, having secured their attention, our Lord bids Lazarus come forth out of the grave. The Greek word for "He cried," is only in this place applied to any voice or utterance of our Lord. In Matt. xii. 19, it is used, where it is said of our Lord, "He shall *not cry*." Here it is evident that He purposely used a very loud and piercing cry, that all around might hear and take notice.

Theophylact thinks that Jesus "cried aloud to contradict the Gentile fable that the soul remained in the tomb with the body. Therefore the soul of Lazarus is called to as if it were absent, and a loud voice were necessary to summon it back." Euthymius suggests the same reason. This however seems an odd idea.

On the other hand, Brentius, Grotius, and Lampe, suggest that Jesus "cried with a loud voice," to prevent the Jews from saying that He muttered or whispered some magical form, or words of enchantment, as witches did.

Ferus observes that our Lord did not say, "In the name of my Father, come forth," or "Raise Him, O my Father," but acts by His own authority.

44.—[*And he that was dead came forth.*] The effect of our Lor''s words was seen at once. As soon as He "cried," Lazarus was seen coming up out of the cave, before the eyes of the crowd. A more plain, distinct, and unmistakable miracle it would be impossible for man to imagine. That a dead man should hear a voice, obey it, rise up, and move forth from his grave alive, is utterly contrary to nature. God alone could cause such a thing. What first began life in him, how lungs and heart began to act again, suddenly and instantaneously, it would be waste of time to speculate. It was a miracle, and there we must leave it.

The idea of some, that Lazarus moved out of the grave without the use of his legs, passing through air like a spirit or ghost, seems to me needless and unreasonable. I agree with Hutcheson, Hall, and Pearce, that though "bound hand and foot," there is no certain proof that his legs were tied together so tightly that he could not move out of the grave, though slowly and with difficulty, like one encumbered, on his own feet. The tardy shuffling action of such a figure would strike all. Pearce remarks, "He must have come forth crawling on his knees." We are surely not required to multiply miracles.—Yet the idea that Lazarus came out with a supernatural motion seems to be held by Augustine, Zwingle, Ecolampadius, Bucer, Gualter, Toletus, Jansenius, Lampe, Lightfoot, and Alford, who think it part of the miracle. I would not press my opinion positively on others, though I firmly maintain it. My own private feeling is that the slow, gradual, tottering movements of a figure encumbered by grave-clothes would impress a crowd far more than the rapid ghost-like gliding out in air of a body, of which the feet did not move.

[*His face bound about...napkin.*] This is mentioned to show that he had been really dead, and his corpse treated like all other corpses.   If not dead, he would have been unable to breathe through the napkin for four days.

[*Jesus saith.. Loose him...let him go.*] This command was given for two reasons : partly that many around might touch Lazarus, and see for themselves that it was not a ghost, but a real body that was raised ; partly that he might be able to walk to his own house before the eyes of the multitude, as a living man.   This, until he was freed from grave-clothes and his eyes were unbandaged, would have been impossible.

Very striking is it to remark how in the least minute particulars the objections of infidels and sceptics are quietly forestalled and met in Gospel narrative !   Thus Chrysostom remarks that the command to "loose him" would enable the friends who bore Lazarus to the grave, to know from the grave-clothes that it was the very person they had buried four days before.   They would recognise the clothes : they could not say, as some had said in the case of the blind man, "This is not he."   He also remarks that both hands, eyes, ears, and nostrils would all convince the witnesses of the truth of the miracle.

45.—[*Then many of the Jews...believed on Him.*] This verse describes the good effect which the raising of Lazarus had on many of the Jews who had come from Jerusalem to comfort Mary and Martha. Their remaining prejudices gave way.   They were unable to resist the extraordinary evidence of the miracle they had just seen. From that day they no longer denied that Jesus was the Christ. Whether their belief was faith unto salvation may well be doubted : but at any rate they ceased to oppose and blaspheme.   And it is more than probable that on the day of Pentecost many of those very Jews whose hearts had been prepared by the miracle of Bethany, came boldly forward and were baptized.

We should observe in this verse what a signal blessing God was pleased to bestow on sympathy and kindness.   If the Jews had not come to comfort Mary under her affliction, they would not have seen the mighty miracle of raising Lazarus, and perhaps would not have been saved.

Lampe remarks on these Jews, "They had come as the merciful, and they obtained mercy."

Bessner observes the beautiful delicacy with which St. John draws a veil over the effect on Martha and Mary of this miracle, while he dwells on the effect it had on strangers.

46.—[*But some of them went...Pharisees, etc.*] We see in this verse the bad effect which the raising of Lazarus had on some who saw it. Instead of being softened and convinced, they were hardened and enraged. They were vexed to see even more unanswerable proofs that Jesus was the Christ, and irritated to feel that their own unbelief was more than ever inexcusable. They therefore hurried off to the Pharisees to report what they had seen, and to point out the progress that our Lord was making in the immediate neighbourhood of Jerusalem.

The amazing wickedness of human nature is strikingly illustrated in this verse. There is no greater mistake than to suppose that seeing miracles will necessarily convert souls. Here is a plain proof that it does not. Never was there a more remarkable confirmation of our Lord's words in the parable of the Rich Man and Lazarus : "If they believe not Moses and the Prophets, neither will they be persuaded though one rose from the dead."

Musculus observes what a wonderful example we have here of the sovereign grace of God, choosing some, and leading them to repentance and faith, and not choosing others. Here is the same miracle, seen under the same circumstances, and with the same evidence, by a large crowd of persons : yet while some believe, others believe not ! It is like the case of the two thieves on the cross, both seeing the same sight, one repenting and the other impenitent. The same fire which melts wax hardens clay.

In leaving this wonderful miracle, there are three things which demand special notice.

(a) We should observe that we are not told of anything that Lazarus said about his state while in the grave, and nothing of his after-history. Tradition says that he lived for thirty years after, and was never known to smile : but this is probably a mere apocryphal invention. As to his silence, we can easily see there is a Divine wisdom about it. If St. Paul "could not utter" the things that he saw in the third heaven, and called them "unspeakable things," it is not strange that Lazarus should say nothing of what he saw in Paradise. (2 Cor. xii. 4.) But there may be always seen in Scripture a striking silence about the feelings of men and women who have been the subjects of remarkable Divine interposition. God's ways are not man's ways. Man loves sensation and excitement, and likes to make God's work on his fellow-creatures a gazing-stock and a show, to their great damage. God almost always seems to withdraw them from the public, both for their own good and His glory.

(b) We should observe that we are told nothing of the feelings of Martha and Mary, after they saw their brother raised to life. The veil is drawn over their joy, though it was not over their sorrow. Affliction is a more profitable study than rejoicing.

(c) We should observe, lastly, that the raising of Lazarus is one of the most signal instances in the Gospels of Christ's Divine power. To Him who could work such a miracle nothing is impossible. He can raise from the death of sin any dead soul, however far gone and corrupt. He will raise us from the grave at His own second appearing. The voice which called Lazarus from the tomb is almighty. "The dead shall hear the voice of the Son of Man, and they that hear shall live." (John v. 25.)

JOHN XI. 47—57.

47 Then gathered the chief priests and the Pharisees a council, and said, What do we? for this man doeth many miracles.

48 If we let him thus alone, all *men* will believe on him: and the Romans shall come and take away both our place and nation.

49 And one of them, *named* Caiaphas, being the high priest that same year, said unto them, Ye know nothing at all,

50 Nor consider that it is expedient for us, that one man should die for the people, and that the whole nation perish not.

51 And this spake he not of himself: but being high priest that year, he prophesied that Jesus should die for that nation:

52 And not for that nation only, but that also he should gather together in one the children of God that were scattered abroad.

53 Then from that day forth they took counsel together for to put him to death.

54 Jesus therefore walked no more openly among the Jews; but went thence unto a country near to the wilderness, into a city called Ephraim, and there continued with his disciples.

55 And the Jews' passover was nigh at hand: and many went out of the country up to Jerusalem before the passover, to purify themselves.

56 Then sought they for Jesus, and spake among themselves, as they stood in the temple, What think ye, that he will not come to the feast?

57 Now both the chief priests and the Pharisees had given a commandment, that, if any man knew where he were, he should shew *it*, that they might take him.

THESE concluding verses of the eleventh chapter of St. John, contain a melancholy picture of human nature. As we turn away from Jesus Christ and the grave at

Bethany, and look at Jerusalem and the rulers of the Jews, we may well say, "Lord, what is man?"

We should observe, for one thing, in these verses, *the desperate wickedness of man's natural heart.* A mighty miracle was wrought within an easy walk of Jerusalem. A man four days dead was raised to life, in the sight of many witnesses. The fact was unmistakable, and could not be denied; and yet the chief priests and Pharisees would not believe that He who did this miracle, ought to be received as the Messiah. In the face of overwhelming evidence they shut their eyes, and refused to be convinced. "This man," they admitted, "does many miracles." But so far from yielding to this testimony, they only plunged into further wickedness, and "took counsel to put Him to death." Great, indeed, is the power of unbelief!

Let us beware of supposing that miracles alone have any power to convert men's souls, and to make them Christians. The idea is a complete delusion. To fancy, as some do, that if they saw something wonderful done before their eyes in confirmation of the Gospel, they would at once cast off all indecision and serve Christ, is a mere idle dream. It is the grace of the Spirit in our hearts, and not miracles, that our souls require. The Jews of our Lord's day are a standing proof to mankind that men may see signs and wonders, and yet remain hard as stone. It is a deep and true saying, "If men believe not Moses and the Prophets, neither would they be persuaded though one rose from the dead." (Luke xvi. 31.)

We must never wonder if we see abounding unbelief in our own times, and around our own homes. It may seem at first inexplicable to us, how men cannot see the truth which seems so clear to ourselves, and do not receive the Gospel which appears so worthy of acceptation. But the plain truth is, that man's unbelief is a far more deeply-seated disease than it is generally reckoned. It is proof against the logic of facts, against reasoning, against argument, against moral suasion. Nothing can melt it down but the grace of God. If we ourselves believe, we can never be too thankful. But we must never count it a strange thing, if we see many of our fellow-Christians just as hardened and unbelieving as the Jews.

We should observe, for another thing, *the blind ignorance with which God's enemies often act and reason.* These rulers of the Jews said to one another, " If we let this Christ alone, we shall be ruined. If we do not stop His course, and make an end of His miracles, the Romans will interfere, and make an end of our nation." Never, the event afterward proved, was there a more short-sighted and erring judgment than this. They rushed madly on the path they had chosen, and the very thing they feared came to pass. They did not leave our Lord alone, but crucified and slew Him. And what happened then? After a few years, the very calamity they had dreaded took place : the Roman armies did come, destroyed Jerusalem, burned the temple, and carried away the whole nation into captivity.

The well-read Christian need hardly be reminded of

many such like things in the history of Christ's Church.
The Roman Emperors persecuted the Christians in the
first three centuries, and thought it a positive duty not
to let them alone.   But the more they persecuted them,
the more they increased.   The blood of the martyrs
became the seed of the Church.—The English Papists,
in the days of Queen Mary, persecuted the Protestants,
and thought that truth was in danger if they were let
alone.   But the more they burned our forefathers, the
more they confirmed men's minds in steadfast attachment
to the doctrines of the Reformation.—In short, the words
of the second Psalm are continually verified in this
world: " The kings of the earth set themselves, and the
rulers take counsel together, against the Lord;" but
" He that sitteth in the heavens shall laugh: the Lord
shall have them in derision."   (Psalm ii. 4.)   God can
make the designs of His enemies work together for
the good of His people, and cause the wrath of man
to praise Him.   In days of trouble, and rebuke, and
blasphemy, believers may rest patiently in the Lord.
The very things that at one time seem likely to hurt
them, shall prove in the end to be for their gain.

   We should observe, lastly, *what importance bad men
sometimes attach to outward ceremonial, while their hearts
are full of sin.*   We are told that many Jews " went up
out of the country to Jerusalem, before the Passover, to
purify themselves."   The most of them, it may be feared,
neither knew nor cared anything about inward purity
of heart.   They made much ado about the washings,
and fasting, and ascetic observances, which formed the

essence of popular Jewish religion in our Lord's time; and yet they were willing in a very few days to shed innocent blood. Strange as it may appear, these very sticklers for outward sanctification were found ready to do the will of the Pharisees, and to put their own Messiah to a violent death.

Extremes like this meeting together in the same person, are unhappily far from uncommon. Experience shows that a bad conscience will often try to satisfy itself by a show of zeal for the cause of religion, while the "weightier matters" of the faith are entirely neglected. The very same man who is ready to compass sea and land to attain ceremonial purity, is often the very man, who, if he had fit opportunity, would not shrink from helping to crucify Christ. Startling as these assertions may seem, they are abundantly borne out by plain facts. The cities where Lent is kept at this day with the most extravagant strictness, are the very cities where the carnival before Lent is a season of glaring excess and immorality. The people in some parts of Christendom, who make much ado one week about fasting and priestly absolution, are the very people who another week will think nothing of murder! These things are simple realities. The hideous inconsistency of the Jewish formalists in our Lord's time has never been without a long succession of followers.

Let us settle it firmly in our minds that a religion which expends itself in zeal for outward formalities, is utterly worthless in God's sight. The purity that God desires to see is not the purity of bodily washing and fasting, of holy water and self-imposed asceticism, but purity of heart. Will-worship and ceremonialism may "satisfy the flesh," but they do not tend to promote real godliness. The standard of Christ's kingdom must be sought in the sermon on the mount: "Blessed are the pure in heart, for they shall see God." (Matt. v. 8; Col. ii. 23.)

NOTES. JOHN XI. 47--57.

47.—[*Then gathered...priests...Pharisees...council.*] This council was probably the great Sanhedrim, or consultative assembly of the Jewish Church. It was for purely ecclesiastical, and not for civil or political purposes. It is the same assembly before which, it is conjectured with much show of reason, our Lord made His defence, in the fifth chapter of this gospel. On receiving the tidings of the astounding miracle which had been wrought at Bethany, our Lord's bitterest enemies, the chief priests and Pharisees, seem to have been alarmed and enraged, and to have felt the absolute necessity of taking decided measures to check our Lord's progress. Ecclesiastical rulers, unhappily, are often the foremost enemies of the Gospel.

[*And said, What do we?*] This question indicates perplexity and irritation. "What are we about? Are we going to sit still, and let this new Teacher carry all before Him? What is the use of trifling with this new heresy? We are doing nothing effectual to check it. It grows: and we let it alone."

[*For this man doeth many miracles.*] This is a marvellous admission. Even our Lord's worst enemies confess that our Lord did miracles, and many miracles. Can we doubt that they would have denied the truth of His miracles, if they could? But they do not seem to have attempted it. They were too many, too public, and too thoroughly witnessed, for them to dare to deny them. How, in the face of this fact, modern infidels and sceptics can talk of our Lord's miracles as being impostures and delusions, they would do well to explain! If the Pharisees who lived in our Lord's time, and who moved heaven and earth to oppose His progress, never dared to dispute the fact that He worked miracles, it is useless to begin denying His miracles now, after eighteen centuries have passed away.

Let us note the desperate hardness and wickedness of man's heart. Even the sight of miracles will not convert any one without the renewing grace of the Holy Ghost.

Brentius remarks that the simple answer to the question of this verse ought to have been, " Our duty is to believe at once that this worker of many miracles is the Christ of God."

48.—[*If we let Him thus alone.*] This means, "If we continue to treat Him as we do now, and take no more active measures to put Him down ; if we only dispute, and reason, and argue, and cavil, and denounce Him, but let Him have His liberty, let Him go where He pleases, let Him do what He pleases, and preach what He pleases."

"Thus " can only mean "as at present, and hitherto."

[*All men will believe on Him.*] This means the bulk of the population will believe that He is what He *professes* to be,—the promised Messiah. The number of His adherents will increase, and faith in His Messiahship will become contagious, and spread all over Palestine."

The word "all," in this sentence, must evidently not be taken literally. It only means "the great mass of the people." It is like "all men come unto Him," said by the angry disciples of John the Baptist about Christ. (John iii. 36.) When men lose their tempers, and talk in passion, they are very apt to use exaggerated expressions.

[*The Romans come...take away...place nation.*] The process of reasoning by which the Pharisees arrived at this conclusion, was probably something of this kind. " This man, if let alone, will gather round Him a crowd of adherents, who will proclaim Him a Leader and King. This our governors, the Romans, will hear, and consider it a rebellion against their authority. Then they will send an army, deal with us as rebels, destroy Jerusalem and the temple, and carry away the whole Jewish nation, as the Babylonians did, into captivity."

In this wretched argument it is difficult to say which appears most prominent, ignorance or unbelief.

It was an *ignorant* argument. The Pharisees ought to have known well that nothing was further from our Lord's teaching than the idea of an earthly kingdom, supported by an armed force. He always proclaimed that His kingdom was not of this world, and not temporal, like Solomon's or David's. He had never hinted at any deliverance from Roman authority. He distinctly taught men to render to Cæsar the things that were Cæsar's, and had distinctly refused, when appealed to, to be "a Judge or divider" among the Jews. Such a person, therefore, was not the least likely to excite the jealousy of the Romans.

It was an *unbelieving* argument. The Pharisees ought to have believed that the Romans could never have conquered and put down our Lord and His adherents, if He really was the Messiah, and could work miracles at His will. The Philistines could not overcome David, and the Romans could not have overcome David's greater Son. By their own showing, the Jewish nation would have had protection enough in the miracle-working power of our Lord.

That there was an expectation throughout the East, at the time of our Lord's ministry, that some remarkable person was about to arise, and become a great leader, is mentioned by Roman historians. But there is no evidence that the Roman Government ever showed jealousy of any one who was merely a religious teacher, like our Lord, and did not interfere with the civil power.

The plain truth is, that this saying of the Pharisees looks like an excuse, caught up as a weapon against our Lord, and a pretext for stirring up enmity against Him. What they really hated was our Lord's doctrine, which exposed their own system, and weakened their authority. They felt that "their craft was in danger." But not daring to say this publicly, they pretended a fear that He would excite the jealousy of the Romans, and endanger the whole nation. They did just the same when they finally accused Him to Pilate, as One that stirred up sedition, and made Himself a King. It is no uncommon thing for wicked people to assign very untrue reasons for their conduct, and to keep back and conceal their true motives. Demetrius, and his friends at Ephesus, said that the temple of the great goddess Diana was in danger, when in reality it was their own "craft" and their own "wealth." The Jews at Thessalonica who persecuted Paul, pretended great zeal for "the decrees of Cæsar," when their real motive was hatred of Christ's Gospel. The Pharisees here pretended fear of the Romans, when in reality they found the growing influence of Jesus pulling down their own power over the people.

Calvin observes, "They double their wickedness by a plausible disguise,—their zeal for the public good. The fear that chiefly distressed them was, that their own tyranny should be destroyed:

but they pretend to be anxious about the temple and worship of God."

Bucer compares the Pharisees' pretended fear of the Romans to the absurd fears of the consequence of printing and literature, which the Papists used to express at the period of the Reformation.

Flacius remarks, that "through fear of Cæsar, God is despised and His Son crucified, and this under pretext of preserving religion, the temple, and the nation. Human wisdom preserves itself by appeasing man and offending God !"

Ferus remarks that the Council entirely forgot that "Rulers, whether the Romans or any others, are not a terror to good works, but to evil. If the Jews had believed and obeyed God, they had nothing to fear."

That the leading Jews at Jerusalem had a strong suspicion that Jesus really was the Messiah, in spite of all their outrageous enmity and unbelief, is evident not only from comparison of other places, but from their nervous anxiety to get rid of Him. They knew that Daniel's seventy weeks were run out. They could not deny the miracles that Jesus did. But they dared not follow out their convictions, and draw the conclusion they ought to have drawn. They willingly shut their eyes against light.

How miserably mistaken the policy of the Pharisees proved to be, it is needless to say. If they had let Jesus alone, and allowed His Gospel to be received and believed, Jerusalem, humanly speaking, might have stood to this day, and the Jews might have been more mighty and prosperous than in the days of Solomon. By not letting Jesus alone, and by killing Him, they filled up the measure of their nation's sin, and brought destruction on the temple, and scattering on the whole people.

"Take away," applied to place here, must mean "destroy." Thus Matt. xxiv. 39 : "The flood took them all away."

Some, as Heinsius and Bloomfield, think that "our place" means the city, Jerusalem.

Some, as Olshausen and Alford, think that "our place" means "our country."

Others, as Maldonatus, Hutcheson, Poole, and Hammond, with whom I entirely agree, think "our place" means the temple. (Compare Acts vi. 13, 14.) Lampe thinks this view is proved by Micah i. 3.

Calvin observes how many people in his day were always hang-
ing back from helping the Protestant Reformation, from the very
same motives as these Jews,—the fear of consequences. "We
must consult public tranquility. There are dangers in the way."

49.—[*And one of them, named Caiaphas.*] This man, by comparing
Acts v. 17, would seem to have been of the sect of the Sadducees.
We also know that he was son-in-law to Annas, of whom Josephus
specially mentions that he was a Sadducee. If this view be correct (and Guyse, Gill, Scott, and Lampe agree with me in it), it
rather accounts for the contemptuous way in which he seems to
speak in replying here to the saying of the Pharisees. It is remarkable, however, to observe how Pharisees and Sadducees, who
disagreed on so many points, were agreed in hating and opposing
Christ. Formalists and sceptics, in all ages, make common cause
against the Gospel.

[*Being...high priest...same year.*] This expression shows the
disorder and irregularity which prevailed in the Jewish Church
in our Lord's time. According to the law of Moses, the office of
high priest was tenable for life. In the last days of the Jews,
the office seems to have been obtainable by election, and to have
been held with great variety of term. Caiaphas was high priest
when John the Baptist began his ministry, and Annas with him.
(Luke iii. 2.) He was also high priest after the Day of Pentecost,
and before the persecution of Stephen. No wonder St. Paul says,
on a subsequent occasion, of Ananias, "I wist not that he was
the high priest." (Acts xxiii. 2.)

Poole remarks, "After Herod's time there was no regard to the
family of Aaron, but the Romans made what high priests they
pleased. Josephus tells us that the Jews had thirteen high priests
from Aaron to Solomon, which was 612 years; eighteen from
Solomon to the Babylonian captivity, which was 460 years; fifteen
from the captivity to Antiochus, which was 414 years: but they
had no less than twenty-eight between the time that Herod began
to reign and Jerusalem was destroyed, which was less than a
century."

[*Said...Ye know nothing at all.*] The word rendered "ye" is
here emphatic in the Greek. It seems not unlikely that it expresses
Caiaphas' contempt for the ignorance and helplessness of the
Pharisees' question. "You and all your party do not understand
what the situation of things requires. You are wasting time in
complaints and expressions of vexation, when a sterner, severer
policy is imperatively demanded."

Chrysostom remarks, "What others made matter of doubt, and put forth in the way of deliberation, this man cried aloud shamelessly, openly, and audaciously. *One must die.*"

Pearce thinks that some of the Jews in council must have talked of only putting a stop to Christ's preaching, as they afterwards tried to stop the Apostles (Acts iv. 18), but that Caiaphas ridiculed such weak counsel, and advised more violent measures. May we not suppose that Nicodemus and others spoke in favour of our Lord?

50.—[*Nor consider.*] The word thus rendered is almost always trans-lated "reason," and is nowhere "consider," except here. It seems to imply that Caiaphas wished the Pharisees to know that they had not reasoned out and properly weighed the right thing to be done. Hence this perplexity. He would now show them the conclusion they ought to have come to.

[*It is expedient...one...die...whole...perish not.*] Caiaphas' con-clusion is short and decisive. He gives it elliptically. "This Man must die. It is far better that one should die, whether inno-cent or not, for the benefit of the whole nation, than that the whole nation should be brought into trouble and perish. You are thinking that if we do not let this Man alone, and interfere, we are injuring an innocent person. Away with such childish scruples. Let Him be put out of the way. It is expedient to kill Him. Better He should die to save the nation from further trouble, than live, and the nation be brought into trouble by Him."

I cannot suppose that Caiaphas meant anything more than this. He simply argues that Christ's death would be a public benefit, and that to spare Him might bring destruction on the nation. Of the full meaning that His words were capable of bearing, I do not believe he had the least idea.

Let us carefully note here what crimes and sins may be committed on the ground of *expediency*. None are so likely to be tempted to commit such sins as rulers and governors. None are so likely to do things unjust, dishonest, and oppressive, as a Government under the pressure of the spurious argument that it is "expedient" that the few should suffer, rather than the many should take harm. For political expediency Christ was crucified. What a fact that is! Ought we not rather to ask always what is just, what is right, what is honourable in the sight of God? That which is morally wrong can never be politically right. To govern only for the sake of pleasing and benefiting the majority, without any reference to the eternal principles of justice, right, and mercy, may be *expedient*, and please man ; but it does not please God.

Calvin observes, "Let us learn never to separate what is useful and expedient from what is lawful, since we ought not to expect any prosperity and success but from the blessing of God."

Ecolampadius remarks that we must never do evil that good may come. "If you could, by the slaying of one good man, work the saving of many, it would be unlawful."

Poole observes, "Never was anything spoken more diabolically. Like a wretched politician, concerned for nothing but the people's safety, Caiaphas saith not 'it is lawful,' but 'it is expedient' for us that one Man, be He never so good, never so innocent and just, should die."

Doddridge remarks, "When will the politicians of this world learn to trust God in His own ways, rather than to trust themselves and their own wisdom, in violation of all rules of truth, honour, and conscience ?"

51, 52.—[*And this spake he not of himself, etc.*] These two verses contain a parenthetical comment by St. John, on the address of Caiaphas to the Pharisees. It is a peculiar passage, and not without difficulty. That a man like Caiaphas should be said to prophesy, and that his prophecy should be of so wide and extensive a character, is undoubtedly strange. I offer a few remarks that may help to throw light on the passage.

That God can employ a wicked man to declare prophetical truth, is clearly proved by the case of Balaam. But the positions of Balaam and Caiaphas were very different.

That the Jewish high priest at any time possessed, by virtue of his office, the power of predicting things to come, I can nowhere find. David certainly speaks of Zadok as "a seer." (2 Sam. xv. 27.) The high priest's ephod conveyed a certain mysterious power to the wearer, of foreseeing things immediately near. (1 Sam. xxiii. 9.) The "urim and thummim," whatever they were, which dwelt in the breast-plate of the high priest, appear to have given the wearer peculiar powers of discernment. But even they were withdrawn at the destruction of the first temple. In short, there is an utter absence of proof that a Jewish high priest, in the time of our Lord, had any power of prophesying.

I believe that the verses before us are very elliptical, and require much to be supplied in order to convey the meaning of St. John.

The only satisfactory sense I can put upon the passage will be found in the following free paraphrase.

[*This spake he not of himself.*] He spoke these words, though he was not aware of it, under the influence of an overruling power, making him say things of far deeper meaning than he was conscious of himself. As Ecolampadius says, "God used him as an instrument." (See Isa. x. 15.)

[*But being high priest that year, he prophesied.*] He spoke words which as the event showed afterwards, were eminently prophetical ; and the fact that they fell from his lips when he was high priest, made them more remarkable, when afterwards remembered and noted.

[*That Jesus should die for that nation.*] He actually foretold, though the fulfilment was in a manner very different from his intentions, that Jesus would die for the benefit of the Jewish nation.

[*And not for that nation only, etc.*] And He also foretold what was practically fulfilled afterwards, though in a way marvellously unlike what he thought,—that Jesus would not only die for the Jewish nation, but for the benefit of all God's children at present scattered all over the world.

The utmost, in fact, that I can make of John's explanatory comment, is that he remarks on the extraordinary manner in which Caiaphas' words proved true, though in a way that he never intended, wished, or expected. He lets fall a saying on a great public occasion, which comes from his lips with great authority, on account of his office as high priest. That saying was afterwards fulfilled in the most marvellous manner by the overruling providence of God, but in a way that the speaker never dreamed of. The thing was afterwards remembered and remarked on ; and it seemed, says St. John, as if being high priest that year, he was miraculously compelled by the Holy Ghost to prophesy the redemption of mankind, at the very time that he thought he was only speaking of putting Christ to death. Caiaphas in short meant nothing but to advise the murder of Christ. But the Holy Ghost obliged him unconsciously to use words which were a most remarkable prediction of Christ's death bringing life to a lost world.

The Greek word rendered "should die," would be more literally, "was about to die." It simply expresses a future coming event.

The "children of God scattered abroad," I believe, mean the elect of God among the Gentiles. They are put in contrast with "that nation," or "the nation," as it would be more literally rendered.

The "gathering together in one," I believe to be that final gathering of all Christ's members which is yet to come at His second advent. (See Eph. i. 10 ; John xii. 32 ; Gen. xlix. 10.)

Lightfoot says, the Jews thought the greatest work of Messiah was to be the "reduction, or gathering together of the captivities."

I leave the passage with a very deep sense of its difficulty, and desire not to press my views on others dogmatically, if they are not satisfied with them.

Chrysostom remarks, "Caiaphas prophesied, not knowing what he said ; and the grace of God merely made use of his mouth, but touched not his accursed heart."

Musculus and Ferus remark how striking the resemblance is between Caiaphas unintentionally using language fulfilled in a sense totally unlike what he meant, and the Jews saying of Christ to Pilate, "His blood be on us and on our children." They little knew the awful and tremendous extent of the saying.

The absurdity of the Roman Catholic claim, that the Pope's words and decrees are to be received as partially inspired because of his office, on the ground of this passage, is noted and exposed by all the Protestant commentators of the seventeenth century.

Lightfoot thinks we should lay great emphasis on the expression, "that same year," and justly so.—He observes that it was the very year when the high priest's office ended, and the veil was rent, and the Jewish dispensation wound up, and the Mosaic priesthood abrogated by Christ's becoming manifestly our priest.—He thinks St. Paul, in Acts xxiii. 5, "I wist not that he was the high priest," may have meant "that he did not know there was any high priest at all."—He also observes that this very year at Pentecost, the Holy Ghost was poured out as the spirit of prophecy and revelation in an extraordinary measure. What wonder if "that year" the last high priest, like Balaam, should prophesy.

53.—[*Then from that day...counsel...death.*] We see here the result of Caiaphas' counsel. His stern, bold, outspoken proposal carried all the Council with him, and even if Gamaliel, Nicodemus, and Joseph were there, their voices were silenced. From that very day it became a settled thing with the Jewish leaders at Jerusalem, that Jesus was to be put to death. The only difficulty was to find

the way, the time, and the means of doing it, without creating a
tumult. The great miracle just wrought at Bethany would doubtless increase the number of our Lord's adherents, and make it
necessary to use caution in carrying out the murderous plan.

The conclusions of great Ecclesiastical Councils are seldom wise
and good, and sometimes are wicked and cruel. Bold, forward,
unscrupulous men, like Caiaphas, generally silence the quieter
members, and carry all before them.

54.--[*Jesus therefore walked...Jews.*] From this time our Lord found
it necessary to give up appearing openly at Jerusalem, and came
there no more till the week of His crucifixion. He knew the result
of the Council just held, either from His own Divine knowledge,
or from the information of friends like Nicodemus ; and as His
time was not fully come, he retired from Judæa for a season.

The expression "no more," is literally "not yet." It must mean
"no more at present."

May we not learn from our Lord's conduct, that it may be a
duty sometimes not to court danger or death ? There are seasons
when it is a duty to retire, as well as seasons for going forward.
There are times to be silent, as well as times to speak.

Hutcheson remarks, "It is lawful for Christ's servants to flee
when their death is decreed by enemies, and the persecution is
personal."

[*Went thence...wilderness...Ephraim...disciples.*] Nothing whatever is known for certain of the distinct locality to which our
Lord retired, or of the city here named. It seems, purposely,
to have been a quiet, isolated, and little frequented place. The
probability is that it was beyond Jordan, in Perea, because when our
Lord came to Jerusalem the last time He passed through Jericho.

Ellicott suggests that Ephraim was a town called also Ophrah,
about twenty miles north of Jerusalem, on the borders of Samaria.
He also thinks that on leaving Ephraim those words of St. Luke
(chapter xvii. 11) come in, which say, that our Lord "passed
through the midst of Samaria and Galilæ." After that he thinks
He went through Perea, to Jericho. But I am not satisfied that
he proves these points.

It is worth noticing that our Lord chose a scene of entire quiet
and seclusion as His last abode, before going up to His last great
season of suffering at the crucifixion. It is well to get alone and
be still, before we take in hand any great work for God. Our

Saviour was not above this. How much more should His disciples remember it ! In saying this, I would not be thought to commend the ostentatious "retreats" of the Romish Church and its followers. It is of the very essence of Christian retirement, if it is to be profitable, that it should be without parade, and should not attract the notice of men. The life of the Eremite has no warrant in Scripture.

When it says that our Lord continued or tarried at Ephraim "with His disciples," it is worth noticing that we do not hear a word of any public works that He did there. It looks as if He devoted the last few quiet days that remained before His crucifixion, to uninterrupted communion with the Father, and private instruction of His disciples.

55.—[*And...Jews' passover...nigh at hand.*] This expression, like many others in John's Gospel, shows that he wrote for the Church generally, and for many readers who were not familiar with Jewish feasts and customs.

[*And many went...country...before...passover.*] This seems mentioned as a simple matter of custom among the Jews, and not as a thing done this year more than any other. They always did so ; and thus drew together, for seven days before the passover, a larger collection of people at Jerusalem than at any other time of the year. Hence the crowds and expectation when our Lord appeared. He had been talked of by people from all parts of Palestine.

[*To purify themselves.*] This refers to the ceremonial washings, purifications, and atonements for ceremonial uncleanness, which all strict Jews were careful to go through before eating the passover. (See 2 Chron. xxx. 18, 19.) It is impossible to read the book of Leviticus carefully, and not to be struck with the almost endless number of ways in which an Israelite could become ceremonially unclean, and need going to the priest to have an atonement made. (See Numbers ix. 6—11.) That the Pharisees, in such matters, added to legal strictness by their absurd scrupulosity, such as "straining out a gnat," as if the dead body of such an insect could defile them, we cannot doubt : but the simple law as it stood was a yoke that was very hard to bear. No wonder that thousands of devout Jews came anxiously before the passover to Jerusalem, to be made ceremonially clean and fit for the feast.

It is worth noting how singularly particular men are sometimes about forms and ceremonies and outward correctness, while they coolly plan and execute enormous crimes. The Jews, zealous about "purifying" themselves while they were planning the murder of Christ, have had imitators and followers in every age of the Church. Strictness about forms and ceremonies, and utter recklessness about gross sin, are found quite compatible in many hearts.

56.—[*Then sought they...Jesus, and spake, etc., etc.*] The persons here mentioned seem to me to have been the Jews from all parts of Palestine, mentioned in the last verse, who had come up to prepare for the passover. The fame and history of our Lord were probably so great throughout Palestine, that one of the first inquiries the comers would make of one another would be about Him. And as they stood in the temple court, waiting for their turn to go through ceremonial purification, or talking with old friends and acquaintances who had come up, like themselves, from the country, Jesus would probably be a principal topic of conversation.

[*What think ye...that.. not come..feast.*] This is mentioned as one of the principal inquiries made by the Jews of one another. Our Lord, on a former occasion, had not come up to the passover. (See John vi.) They might, therefore, naturally feel doubtful whether He would come now.

It is noteworthy that the question admits of being taken as one, or divided into two distinct ones.

Some think that it means, "What think ye of the question, whether He will come to the feast or not?"

Others hold that it means, "What think ye of Christ, and especially of His position at this time? Do you think that He will not come to the feast?" I myself prefer this view.

It is noteworthy that the very question with which our Lord confounded the Pharisees a few days after, as recorded in St. Matthew xxii. 42, begins with precisely the same Greek words as those here used, "What think ye of Christ?"

57.—[*Now both ..priests...Pharisees, etc., etc.*] This verse shows the first steps which had been taken after the session of the Council which adopted the advice of Caiaphas to kill Jesus. A general order had been given that if any man knew where Jesus lodged in Jerusalem, he was to give information, in order that He might be apprehended.

I cannot help thinking myself that this order must only have referred to Jerusalem, and the house where our Lord might lodge when He came to the passover, if He did come. I cannot suppose that our Lord's enemies could be ignorant where He was between the miracle of Bethany and the passover. But I fancy they dared not run the risk of a tumult or rebellion, which might be caused if they sent into the rural districts to apprehend Him. Indeed, it is doubtful whether the jurisdiction of the priests and Pharisees extended beyond the walls of Jerusalem, and whether they could lay hands upon our Lord anywhere outside the city. This may have been the reason why He often lodged at Bethany.

Musculus here discusses the question, whether obedience to the powers that be, obliges us to give up a man to those who are seeking to apprehend him. He answers, " Decidedly not ; if we believe him to be an innocent man."

JOHN XII. 1—11.

1 Then Jesus six days before the passover came to Bethany, where Lazarus was which had been dead, whom he raised from the dead.

2 There they made him a supper; and Martha served : but Lazarus was one of them that sat at the table with him.

3 Then took Mary a pound of ointment of spikenard, very costly, and anointed the feet of Jesus, and wiped his feet with her hair : and the house was filled with the odour of the ointment.

4 Then saith one of his disciples, Judas Iscariot, Simon's *son*, which should betray him,

5 Why was not this ointment sold for three hundred pence, and given to the poor ?

6 This he said, not that he cared for the poor ; but because he was a thief, and had the bag, and bare what was put therein.

7 Then said Jesus, Let her alone : against the day of my burying hath she kept this.

8 For the poor always ye have with me : but me ye have not always.

9 Much people of the Jews therefore knew that he was there : and they came not for Jesus' sake only, but that they might see Lazarus also, whom he had raised from the dead.

10 But the chief priests consulted that they might put Lazarus also to death ;

11 Because that by reason of him many of the Jews went away, and believed on Jesus.

THE chapter we have now begun, finishes a most important division of St. John's Gospel. Our Lord's public addresses to the unbelieving Jews of Jerusalem are here brought to an end. After this chapter, St. John records nothing but what was said in private to the disciples.

We see, for one thing, in this passage, *what abounding proofs exist of the truth of our Lord's greatest miracles.*

We read of a supper at Bethany, where Lazarus "sat at the table" among the guests,—Lazarus, who had been publicly raised from the dead, after lying four days in the grave. No one could pretend to say that his resurrection was a mere optical delusion, and that the eyes of the bystanders must have been deceived by a ghost or vision. Here was the very same Lazarus, after several weeks, sitting among his fellow-men with a real material body, and eating and drinking real material food. It is hard to understand what stronger evidence of a fact could be supplied. He that is not convinced by such evidence as this may as well say that he is determined to believe nothing at all.

It is a comfortable thought, that the very same proofs which exist about the resurrection of Lazarus, are the proofs which surround that still mightier fact, the resurrection of Christ from the dead. Was Lazarus, seen for several weeks by the people of Bethany, going in and coming out among them? So was the Lord Jesus seen by His disciples.—Did Lazarus take material food before the eyes of his friends? So did the Lord Jesus eat and drink before His ascension.—No one in his sober senses, who saw Jesus take "broiled fish and a honeycomb," and eat it before several witnesses, would doubt that He had a real body. (Luke xxiv. 42.)

We shall do well to remember this. In an age of abounding unbelief and scepticism, we shall find that the resurrection of Christ will bear any weight that we can lay upon it. Just as He placed beyond reasonable doubt the rising again of a beloved disciple within two miles of Jerusalem, so in a very few weeks He placed beyond doubt His own victory over the grave. If we believe that Lazarus rose again, we need not doubt that Jesus rose again also. If we believe that Jesus rose again, we need not doubt the truth of His Messiahship, the reality of His acceptance as our Mediator, and the certainty of our own resurrection. Christ has risen indeed, and wicked men may well tremble. Christ has risen from the dead, and believers may well rejoice.

We see, for another thing, in this passage, *what unkindness and discouragement Christ's friends sometimes meet with from man.*

We read that at the supper in Bethany, Mary, the sister of Lazarus, anointed the feet of Jesus with precious ointment, and wiped them with the hair of her head. Nor was this ointment poured on with a niggardly hand. She did it so liberally and profusely that "the house was filled with the odour of the ointment." She did it under the influence of a heart full of love and gratitude. She thought nothing too great and good to bestow on such a Saviour. Sitting at His feet in days gone by, and hearing His words, she had found peace for her conscience, and pardon for her sins. At this very moment she saw Lazarus alive and well, sitting by her Master's side,—her own brother Lazarus, whom He had brought back to her from the grave. Greatly loved, she thought she could not show too much love in return. Having freely received, she freely gave.

But there were some present who found fault with Mary's conduct, and blamed her as guilty of wasteful extravagance. One especially, an apostle, a man of whom better things might have been expected, declared openly that the ointment would have been better employed if it had been sold, and the price "given to the poor." The heart which could conceive such thoughts must have had low views of the dignity of Christ's person, and still lower views of our obligations to Him. A cold heart and a stingy hand will generally go together.

There are only too many professing Christians of a like spirit, in the present day. Myriads of baptized people cannot understand zeal of any sort for the honour of Christ. Tell them of any vast outlay of money to push trade or to advance the cause of science, and they approve of it as right and wise. Tell them of any expense incurred for the preaching of the Gospel at home or abroad, for spreading God's Word, for extending the knowledge of Christ on earth, and they tell you plainly that they think it "waste." They never give a farthing to such objects as these, and count those people fools who do. Worst of all, they often cover over their own backwardness to help purely Christian objects, by a pretended concern for the poor at home. Yet they find it convenient to forget the notorious fact that those who do most for the cause of Christ, are precisely those who do most for the poor.

We must never allow ourselves to be moved from "patient continuance in well doing," by the unkind remarks of such persons. It is vain to expect a man to do much for Christ, when he has no sense of debt to Christ.

We must pity the blindness of our unkind critics, and work on. He who pleaded the cause of loving Mary, and said, "Let her alone," is sitting at the right hand of God, and keeps a book of remembrance. A day is soon coming when a wondering world will see that every cup of cold water given for Christ's sake, as well as every box of precious ointment, was recorded in heaven, and has its reward. In that great day those who thought that any one could give too much to Christ, will find they had better never have been born.

We see, lastly, in this passage, *what desperate hardness and unbelief there is in the heart of man.*

Unbelief appears in the chief priests, who "consulted that they might put Lazarus to death." They could not deny the fact of his having been raised again. Living, and moving, and eating, and drinking within two miles of Jerusalem, after lying four days in the grave, Lazarus was a witness to the truth of Christ's Messiahship, whom they could not possibly answer or put to silence. Yet these proud men would not give way. They would rather commit a murder than throw down the arms of rebellion, and confess themselves in the wrong. No wonder that the Lord Jesus in a certain place "marvelled" at unbelief. Well might He say, in a well known parable, "If they believe not Moses and the Prophets, neither will they be persuaded though one rose from the dead." (Mark vi. 6 ; Luke xvi. 31.)

Hardness especially appears in Judas Iscariot, who, after being a chosen Apostle and a preacher of the kingdom of heaven, turns out at last a thief and a traitor. So long as the world stands, this unhappy man will be a lasting proof of the depth of human corruption.   That any one could follow Christ as a disciple for three years, see all His miracles, hear all His teaching, receive at His hand repeated kindnesses, be counted an Apostle, and yet prove rotten at heart in the end, all this at first sight appears incredible and impossible! Yet the case of Judas shows plainly that the thing can be. Few things, perhaps, are so little realized as the extent of the fall of man.

Let us thank God if we know anything o: faith, and can say, with all our sense of weakness and infirmity, " I believe." Let us pray that our faith may be real, true, genuine, and sincere, and not a mere temporary impression, like the morning cloud and the early dew. Not least, let us watch and pray against the love of the world. It ruined one who basked in the full sunshine of privileges, and heard Christ Himself teaching every day.   Then "let him that thinketh he standeth take heed lest he fall." (1 Cor. x. 12.)

NOTES. JOHN XII. 1—11.

1.—[*Then Jesus six days...passover...Bethany.*] Every intelligent reader of the Gospel will see that John purposely omits at this point certain events which are recorded by Matthew, Mark, and Luke. He passes at once from our Lord's retirement to the city called Ephraim to His return to Bethany for the last time. In this interval will be found the things related in Matthew xx. 17—34 ; Mark x. 32—52 ; Luke xviii. 31, to xix. 1—28. In whatever part of Palestine this city Ephraim was, it is almost certain that between it and Bethany Jesus passed through Jericho, healed two blind men there, converted the publican Zacchæus, and spoke the parable of the nobleman who went into a far country, after giving to his ten servants ten pounds.

Why St. John did not record these facts we do not know, and it is mere waste of time to inquire. A reverent mind will be content to remember that John wrote by inspiration of God, and was guided by infallible direction, both as to what he recorded and what he did not record. Reason and common sense, moreover, tell us that if the four Evangelists had all narrated exactly the same things, their value as independent witnesses would have been greatly damaged. Their variations and diversities are a strong indirect proof of their credibility. Too close an agreement would raise a suspicion of collusion, and look like an attempt to deceive.

The expression, "six days before the passover," is remarkable, because at first sight it seems to contradict Mark's narrative of the anointing, which Mark expressly says was "two days before the passover." (Mark xiv. 1.) Hence some maintain that the Greek words should be translated, "Before the six days of the passover feast," leaving the precise day indefinite and uncertain. To this, however, it is reasonably objected that the passover feast was more than six days, and that the proposed translation is not a probable rendering of the Greek words.—To this I must add, that in my opinion there seems no necessity for departing from the English version. It is not only possible, but probable, as Lightfoot maintains, that there were two distinct anointings of our Lord, one six days before the passover, and the other two days before. [The reader is requested to refer back to the notes on John ii. 2, where he will find this point fully discussed.]

The passover was slain on the Thursday evening. At this rate our Lord must have arrived at Bethany on Friday, the afternoon or evening before the Sabbath. Thus He must have spent His last earthly Sabbath with Mary, Martha, and Lazarus, at Bethany.

That the disciples must have journeyed to Bethany with a full impression that a great crisis was at hand, and the end of their Master's ministry approaching, one can hardly doubt, after reading the plain warnings recorded in Matthew, Mark, and Luke. But whether they really thought their Master would be put to death, or whether they did not secretly expect He would soon manifest His Divine power, take His kingdom and reign, is more than questionable.

A more deliberate, voluntary, calm walking up to death than our Lord's last journey into Judæa, it is impossible to conceive.

[*Where Lazarus...been dead...raised from the dead.*] These words seem to show that Lazarus lived at Bethany, and was not merely a visitor or lodger there. They also show the immense importance of the miracle wrought on him. Within two miles of Jerusalem and the temple, there lived for weeks, if not months, a man well known to many Jews, who had been actually raised from his grave after being four days buried. He had not been raised only, and then had disappeared from public notice, but he lived where he was raised.

Lightfoot draws out the following interesting scheme of our Lord's disposal of time during the last six days before His crucifixion:—(1) On Saturday He supped with Lazarus. (2) On Sunday He rode into Jerusalem publicly on an ass. This was the day when the Jews used to take out a lamb from the flock, for each family, and to keep it separate for the passover. On this day the Lamb of God publicly presented Himself in Zion. (3) On Monday He went to Jerusalem again, and cursed the barren fig-tree on the way. (4) On Tuesday He went again to Jerusalem, and spoke for the last time to the people. Returning, He sat on the Mount of Olives and delivered the famous prophecy of Matthew xxiv. and xxv., and supped that night with Simon the leper. (5) On Wednesday He tarried in Bethany. (6) On Thursday He went to Jerusalem, ate the passover, appointed the Lord's Supper, and the same night was taken before the priests as a prisoner. (7) On Friday He was crucified.

2. —[*There they made Him a supper.*] These words show the joyful hospitality with which the Master was received by the disciples. The expression, "they," may perhaps be used indefinitely, according to a common Hebraism. (Compare Matthew v. 15, x. 10, xiii. 48, and John xv. 6.) It then simply means, "a supper was made." If not so used, it evidently can apply to none but Mary, Martha, and Lazarus.—Whether the supper was on Friday evening, when our Lord arrived, after the Sabbath began, or on the Saturday, or the Sabbath Day, is immaterial. It is evident that hospitality was thought no breach of the Sabbath among the Jews.

Lightfoot says the feast of the Jews, on this particular day, six days before the passover, was always peculiarly liberal and sumptuous.

Hutcheson observes, "It is not unlawful at some times to enjoy the liberal use of the creatures in a sober manner. Christ doth not decline this supper; sometimes He went to the feasts of Pharisees, and sometimes of Publicans." (Luke vii. 36; Matt. ix. 11.)

[*And Martha served.*] The natural temperament of this good woman comes out here as elsewhere. She could not sit still and do nothing while her Lord was in her house. She must be actively stirring and trying to do something. Grace does not take away our peculiar characteristics.

[*But Lazarus...sat at the table with Him.*] This appears to most commentators, from Chrysostom downwards, to be purposely mentioned, in order to show the reality of Lazarus's resurrection. He was not a ghost or a spirit. He had really been raised to life with a real body, and flesh and bones, and all the wants and conditions of a body. Thus we are practically taught that though a man's body dies, it may yet live again.

Is not this feast a faint type of the Marriage Supper of the Lamb? Jesus Christ will be there ; those believers who died and are raised again at His second advent will be there ; and those who never died, but are found alive and believing when He comes, will be there. Then the number of guests will be complete.

3.—[*Then took Mary...ointment...anointed..feet...Jesus, etc., etc.*] This remarkable action of Mary, which according to our Lord's saying in Matthew and Mark, is related all over the world, deserves our special consideration.

The action itself was not an uncommon one in Eastern countries, where the heat is very great, and the feet exposed to it by wearing sandals are liable to suffer much from dryness and scorching. There was nothing, moreover, out of the common way in a woman doing this service. To "wash the saints' feet," St. Paul names among the good works of a Christian widow. (1 Tim. v. 10.)

The motive of Mary, in doing what she did, was evidently strong and grateful love to her Lord and Saviour. Not only from what she had learned from Him for her own spiritual benefit, but also for what He had done for her brother Lazarus, she felt there was nothing too great or too good to do for Him. Her feelings made her anxious to do her Master the highest honour, regardless of expense, and indifferent to any remark that witnesses might make.

The extent of her gratitude is shown by the lavish profuseness with which she used the ointment on this occasion, although it was very costly. This seems indicated by her "wiping our Lord's feet with her hair," having poured on them so much ointment that they needed wiping ; and also by the "house being filled with the odour of the ointment." She poured out so much ointment that the scent of it filled the whole apartment and the whole house where the guests were. Any one who knows the powerful odour of otto of roses, in the present day, will easily understand this.

What this "ointment of spikenard" was has puzzled the commentators in every age, as the Greek word throws no certain light on the question. Some think that it means "potable" ointment, that might be drunk ; some that it means perfectly "pure" ointment, that might be trusted as genuine and unadulterated. Augustine thinks that the expression denotes the place from which the ointment came. The question is of no importance, and must be left unexplained for want of materials to explain it. Enough for us to know that it was something very valuable and costly. How costly an ointment might be, any one can guess who knows the value of pure otto of roses.

I can only repeat the opinion already expressed, that this anointing was certainly not the anointing which is described in Luke vii. ; and most probably was not the anointing of Mark xiv. The anointing in Mark was two days before the passover, while this was six. In Mark the ointment was poured on the head, and here it was poured on the feet. In Matthew and Mark several "disciples" murmured, but here only Judas is named. These discrepancies, in my judgment, are insuperable, and make it necessary to believe that there were two distinct anointings at Bethany during the last six days preceding the crucifixion. I grant that it is a choice between difficulties, and that there are difficulties in the view I maintain. But I do not think them so weighty as those of the other view. At any rate, I am supported by the great authority of Chrysostom, Chemnitius, Lightfoot, Whitby, and Henry.

What the significance of Mary's wiping our Lord's feet with the hairs of her head may be, is a difficult question. Perhaps, from our ignorance of Eastern customs in the days of our Lord's earthly ministry, we are hardly qualified to give an opinion about it now. On points like these, where we are ignorant, it is wisest not to conjecture.

Calvin says, "The usual practice was to anoint the head, and on this account Pliny reckons it an instance of excessive luxury that some anointed the ancles. What John says about the feet amounts to this,—that the whole body of Christ, down to the feet, was anointed."

Rollock observes that at this time Mary seems to have had a deeper and more intimate perception of what there was in Christ, and of the real dignity of His person, than any of His disciples.

1.—[*Then saith…Judas Iscariot, Simon's son.*] We know nothing of this Simon, who he was, or why he is specially mentioned here.

It is worth notice, that hardly any name occurs so frequently in the New Testament as this. We have the following :—

1. The Apostle Simon, called also Peter.
2. The Apostle Simon, called also Zelotes, and the Canaanite.
3. Simon the brother of our Lord, mentioned with James and Joses. (Matt. xiii. 55.)
4. Simon the leper, in whose house the anointing took place. (Matt. xxvi. 6.)
5. Simon the Cyrenian, who carried the cross. (Matt. xxvii. 32.)
6. Simon the Pharisee. (Luke vii. 40.)
7. Simon the sorcerer at Samaria. (Acts viii. 9.)
8. Simon the tanner. (Acts ix. 43.)

It would of course be interesting to know if Judas Iscariot was son of any of these. But we have no clue to guide us.

Wordsworth sees in the mention of Judas by name a strong internal evidence of the late date of St. John's Gospel. Compare with this the fact that John alone mentions Peter and Malchus by name. (John xviii. 10.)

[*Which should betray him.*] These words would be more literally rendered, "the one who was about to betray Him."

On the occasion of the anointing related in Matt. xxvi. and Mark xiv. it is worth noticing, that "some of the disciples," and not Judas only, found fault with the action. It rather adds probability to the theory that there were two anointings at Bethany.

Chrysostom remarks that Jesus knew from the beginning that Judas was a traitor, and rebuked him with such words as, "One of you is a devil." (John vi. 64.) Augustine also remarks that we must not suppose Judas never fell till he received money from the Jews. He was false from the beginning. He also says that he was present at the institution of the Lord's Supper, and was a communicant.

5.—[*Why was not this ointment sold for three hundred pence.. poor ?*] This carping question is a specimen of the way in which wicked men often try to depreciate a good action, and specially in the matter of giving money. When the deed is done they do not say downright that it ought not to have been done, but suggest that something better might have been done! Those who do good must be prepared to find their actions carped at and their motives depreciated, and themselves charged with neglecting one class of duties in over-zeal for doing others. If we do nothing until everybody commends and praises us, we shall never do any good in the world.

We may learn from this verse the costly nature of Mary's oint-ment. If workmen's wages were "a penny a day" (Matt. xx. 2), about 7½d. of our money, this holy woman must have poured on our Lord's feet what was worth between £9 and £10 of our money, according to the estimate of Judas. But allowances must perhaps be made for an exaggerated statement being made by an envious and wicked man.

We may note here that giving to the poor was evidently assumed to be a part of every Christian's duty. Compare this with Gal. ii. 10. In a country like England, where there is a poor law, Christians are sadly apt to forget this. The duty of "giving to the poor," and not merely paying rates in obedience to law, is just as obligatory now as it was 1800 years ago.

Ecolampadius remarks that the more wicked and graceless people are, the more ready they are to find fault with and blame others, and to see no beauty in what they do.

Quesnel remarks, that Judas made a great ado about 300 pence (viz., £10) and a little ointment, when he was about to sell the Son of God for 30 pieces of silver : viz., £3 15s.

Henry observes, "Coldness of love to Christ, and a secret con-tempt of serious piety, when they appear in professors of religion, are sad presages of final apostasy."

Stier remarks, "We have in the words of Judas an example of those judgments which have their foundation in the favourite principles of utilitarianism, and which may too often be applied falsely, to the wounding of pious hearts."—"This lays bare the root of that suspicion with which Missionary offerings for the extension of Christ's kingdom are looked at, because of the poor whom we have at home."—"We have here, furthermore, an ex-ample of all cold judgments passed on the virtuous emotions of warm hearts, of all more or less conscious or unconscious censures of the artless outgoings and acts of honest feelings, and of all narrow-hearted criticism of others according to our own mind and temper."

6.—[*This he said, not...cared for the poor.*] This is one of those parenthetical explanations or glosses, which are so frequent in St John's Gospel. The Evangelist tells us the true character of Judas, and the reason why he said what he did. He did not really care about the poor, but put their interest forward as a special and plausible argument for depreciating Mary's action, and discouraging such actions in others.

There is something very instructive in this. The argument of Judas is frequently reproduced in the present day. Hundreds of people excuse themselves from one class of duties by pretended zeal for others, and compensate for neglecting Christ's cause by affecting great concern for the poor. Yet in reality they care nothing for the poor, and only want to save their own money, and to be spared contributing to religious objects.

Some, for instance, will never give money to benefit the souls of their fellow-countrymen, and tell us we must first relieve their poverty and feed their bodies.—Some again will give nothing to help Missions abroad, and tell us we must first mind the poor at home.—Even the shareholders of some great joint-stock companies have been known to express great concern for the poor and working classes, as an excuse for carrying on their business on Sundays.—The language of St. John about Judas Iscariot shows us that this apparent zeal for the poor should always be regarded with suspicion, and submitted to close analysis and cross examination. He talked brave words about the poor, as if he cared more for them than any one! Yet there is not the slightest proof in the Gospels that he cared more for them than others. Above all the conclusion of the verse lets out the truth, and the unerring pen of inspiration reveals the man's true motives. These things are written for our learning. There are few greater impostors in the world than some of those who are pretending perpetually to care about the poor. The truest and best friends of the working classes and the poor, the people who give most and do most for them, will always be found among those who do most for Christ. It is the successors of Mary of Bethany, and not of Judas Iscariot, who really "care for the poor." But they do not talk about it. While others talk and profess, they act.

[*But because he was a thief.*] This is strong language, and a very heavy accusation. It seems to indicate that this was the habitual character of Judas. He always had been, and always was a dishonest man. So says an inspired Apostle. In the face of this expression, it appears to me impossible to prove that Judas ever had the grace of God at any time, and that he only fell away at last. He was inwardly wrong at heart all the way through. Again, I find it impossible to believe that Judas was a high-souled and noble-minded, though greatly erring, man, and that his motive in betraying his Lord was to hasten His kingdom, and to cut short the period of His humiliation. I cannot reconcile this with the word "thief."

Let us note here how far a man may go in Christian profession without any inward grace. There is no evidence that Judas up to this time was unlike other Apostles. Like them he had seen all Christ's miracles, heard Christ's teaching, lived in Christ's company, and had himself preached the kingdom of God. Yet he was at bottom a graceless man. Privileges alone convert nobody.

Ferus remarks, "Let us never put confidence in man, or in any sanctity of position, office, or dress. If apostleship did not make Judas a saint, neither will position, office, nor dress make thee a saint. In fact, unless you first have inward holiness, and have sought it from God, it may be that your office may render you more wicked."

Let us note the amazing power of the love of money. No besetting sin seems so thoroughly to wither up and blight and harden the heart. No wonder it is called "the root of all evil." (1 Tim. v. 10.) However many the faults and infirmities recorded of saints in the Bible, we have not a single example of one that was covetous.

Chrysostom observes, "A dreadful thing is the love of money! It disables both eyes and ears, and makes men worse to deal with than a wild beast, allowing a man to consider neither conscience, nor friendship, nor fellowship, nor salvation."

Quesnel observes that "Christ allows His money to be taken from Him, but never His sheep."

[*And had the bag.*] The Greek word rendered "bag" is a curious one. The original idea is that of a bag in which musicians kept the mouthpieces or reeds of their instruments. From that, the idea evidently was attached to it of a bag carried about by any member of a company, such as that of the disciples, on behalf of his companions. Whether the common stock of provisions as well as of money was not kept in this bag, perhaps admits of a question.

Theophylact says, that some think that Judas was trusted with the care of the money as one of the meanest and most inferior of Christian duties. Thus in Acts, the Apostles would not "serve tables." (Acts vi. 2.)

[*And bare what was put therein.*] The last words would be more literally rendered, "the things put therein." Some, as Origen, Theophylact, Pearce, Lampe, Tittman, Bloomfield, and Clarke, have thought that the word "bare" means "took away, carried off, stole, secreted, or set apart for himself."—I doubt this. I prefer the simple idea of "carrying about." It was the office of Judas to be the purse-keeper of the little company of disciples. The contributions in money and provisions of those friends who ministered to our Lord, such as "Joanna, Susanna, and many others" (Luke viii. 3), were probably meant by the things here mentioned. It is clear that our Lord had no earthly wealth, nor His disciples. It is equally clear that His friends, scattered all over Palestine, must have thought it a privilege, whenever He came among them, to contribute to His maintenance and support Of these contributions in all probability Judas was treasurer.

Let professing Christians note that to have money passing through their hands, is a snare and a temptation. It is a snare by which many in every age have been cast down.

7.—[*Then said Jesus, Let her alone.*] This is unquestionably a rebuke to Judas, and a somewhat sharp one. It shows how jealously our Lord regards any attempt to hinder, check, or discourage the zeal of His own people. Even now, when some of His weak disciples undertake work which calls forth enmity and opposition, He can make all difficulties vanish, and say, "Let them alone."

[*Against the day...burying...kept this.*] The first word here would be more literally rendered, "for" the day. I believe we must not interpret this sentence as if our Lord meant that Mary really knew that our Lord's burial was at hand. I think it rather signifies, "The ointment which Mary has poured on my feet, though she meant it only as a mark of honour, happens to be a most suitable thing, as my death and burial are approaching. She little knew, in doing what she did, the nearness of my death; but as it happens, her action is most seasonable."

Some, as Chrysostom, think that our Lord intended to prick the conscience and soften the feelings of Judas by talking of His "burial," and by the language of the next verse, "Me ye have not always." It may possibly be so. But I rather think that in both instances He intended to direct the minds of all around Him, as He had evidently been doing for some weeks, to His approaching death and the conclusion of His ministry. He brings that conclusion in at every turn now.

Some think that the word "kept" refers to the ointment having been originally got by Mary for her brother Lazarus, and that there had been a long hoarding up of it from the day when Lazarus died, and that Judas blamed Mary for having "kept" it so long, and not having sold it. But this is purely conjectural.

May we not learn from our Lord's words here, that Christians do not always know the full meaning of what they do? God uses them as His instruments, without their being aware of it at the time. (Compare John xii. 16.)

Calvin says, "Those are absurd interpreters who infer from Christ's reply, that costly and magnificent worship is pleasing to God He rather excuses Mary, on the ground of her having rendered an extraordinary service, which ought not to be regarded as a perpetual rule for the worship of God."

8.—[*For the poor always...with you.*] It is clear from these words that poverty will always exist; and we need not wonder. So long as human nature is what it is, some will always be rich and some poor, because some are diligent and some idle, some are strong and some weak, some are wise and some foolish. We need never dream that by any arrangement, either civil or ecclesiastical, poverty can ever be entirely prevented. The existence of pauperism is no proof whatever that States are ill governed, or that Churches are not doing their duty.

Ecolampadius thinks that our Lord here refers to the poor as being His members, and that there is a latent reference to the language of the twenty-fifth chapter of Matthew, about works of mercy being regarded as works done to Christ's brethren and to Christ Himself. (Matt. xxv. 40.)

It is noteworthy that Jesus in this sentence passes from a singular verb to a plural one, and seems to address not Judas only, but all present.

[*But Me ye have not always.*] These words show, for one thing, that our Lord's bodily presence on earth was a great and miraculous event, and as such deserved to be marked with peculiar honour: and for another thing, that His departure was at hand, so that the opportunities for doing Him honour were becoming very few. Moreover, if words mean anything, the sentence completely overthrows the whole theory of Christ's body being present under the forms of bread and wine, in the Lord's Supper. That favourite Romish doctrine can never be reconciled with "Me ye have not always."

We may surely learn from this verse, that relieving the poor, however good a work, is not so important a work as doing honour to Christ. In times like these it is well to remember this. Not a few seem to think all religion consists in giving temporal help to the poor. Yet there are evidently occasions when the relief of the poor must not be allowed to supersede the direct work of honouring Christ. Doubtless it is well to feed, and clothe, and nurse the poor ; but it is never to be forgotten, that to glorify Christ among them is far better. Moreover, it is much easier to give temporal than spiritual help, for we have our reward in thanks, and gratitude, and the praise of man. To honour Christ is far harder, and gets us no praise at all.

Augustine remarks, "In respect of the presence of His Majesty, we have Christ always ; in respect to the presence of the flesh, it was rightly said, 'Me ye will not have always.' The Church had Him in respect of the flesh for a few days ; now by faith it holds, not with eyes beholds Him."

Zwingle observes that this sentence "excludes Christ's corporal presence from the Lord's Supper. According to His Divine nature, Christ is always present with His people. According to His human nature, He is in one place in heaven, at the right hand of God." Most of the other Reformers make the same comment.

Rollock remarks, that our Lord's defence of Mary in this passage must not be alleged as a warrant for extravagant and profuse expenditure in the public worship of Christians. Jesus Himself points out that the occasion was extraordinary and singular : viz., on the eve almost of His burial,—an occasion which could only happen once. This seems to imply that on ordinary occasions such an expenditure as that of Mary would not have been justifiable.

9.—[*Much people...knew...there.*] We need not doubt that the news of our Lord's arrival at Bethany would soon spread, like lightning, partly because Bethany was so near Jerusalem, partly because of the recent miracle wrought there, partly because of the order of the rulers to give information where Christ was, partly because of the approach of the Passover, and the crowds assembling all around Jerusalem.

[*They came...not...Jesus' sake...see Lazarus...dead.*] This sentence is a genuine exhibition of human nature. Curiosity is one of the most common and powerful motives in man. The love of seeing something sensational and out of the common way, is almost universal. When people could see at once both the subject of the miracle and Him that worked the miracle, we need not wonder that they resorted in crowds to Bethany. Yet within ten days a far greater miracle was to take place, viz., our Lord's own resurrection.

10.—[*But the chief priests consulted.*] It admits of doubt whether the word rendered "consulted" would not be better rendered "purposed" or "determined," as in Acts xv. 37, xxvii. 39 ; 2 Cor. i. 17. This is the view of Schleusner and Parkhurst.

[*That they might put Lazarus...death.*] It is difficult to conceive a greater proof of hardened and incorrigible wickedness of heart than this sentence exhibits. The chief priests could not possibly deny the fact of Lazarus having been raised, or explain it away. He was a witness whose testimony against their unbelief was overwhelming. They must therefore stop his mouth by killing him. And these were the chief ecclesiastical leaders of Israel !—Moreover Lazarus had done them no harm. Though a disciple, there is no proof that he was a leading follower of Christ, much less a preacher of the Gospel. But he was an inconvenient standing evidence, and so he must be removed !

11.—[*Because...many...Jews went away.*] This sentence shows the immense effect that the raising of Lazarus had on the public mind, in spite of all the priests could do to prevent it. In every age people will think for themselves, when God's truth comes into a land. Prisons and threats and penalties cannot prevent men thinking. Mind and thought cannot be chained. When ecclesiastical tyrants burn martyrs, and destroy Bibles, and silence preachers, they forget there is one thing they cannot do. They cannot stop the inward machinery of people's thoughts.

The expression "went away" will hardly bear the sense put on it by Pearce, of "withdrawing themselves from the service of the synagogue." It probably only means "went to Bethany." Bloomfield says, "it denotes their ceasing to pay that regard to the teaching of the Scribes which they formerly had done."

[*And believed in Jesus.*] I dare not think that this "believing" means more than an intellectual conviction that Jesus must be the Messiah. I see no evidence that it means the faith of the heart. Yet it is probable this was exactly the state of mind in which many hundreds or thousands of Jews were before the crucifixion, the resurrection, and the day of pentecost ; convinced but not converted, persuaded that Jesus was the Christ of God but afraid to confess Him. Hence on the day of Pentecost we cannot doubt that many hundreds of Peter's hearers were prepared to believe. The

stony ground of prejudice and ignorant adhesion to Judaism had
been broken to pieces, and the seed fell into soil prepared for it.

Poole thinks that Lazarus after his marvellous resurrection,
"possibly spake of it, to the honour and glory of God," and that
this excited the special anger of the priests.

JOHN XII. 12—19.

12 On the next day much people that
were come to the feast, when they heard
that Jesus was coming to Jerusalem,

13 Took branches of palm trees, and
went forth to meet him, and cried, Hosanna: Blessed *is* the King of Israel
that cometh in the name of the Lord.

14 And Jesus, when he had found a
young ass, sat thereon; as it is written,

15 Fear not, daughter of Sion: behold,
thy King cometh, sitting on an ass's
colt.

16 These things understood not his
disciples at the first: but when Jesus
was glorified, then remembered they
that these things were written of him,
and *that* they had done these things
unto him.

17 The people therefore that was with
him when he called Lazarus out of his
grave, and raised him from the dead,
bare record.

18 For this cause the people also met
him, for that they heard that he had
done this miracle.

19 The Pharisees therefore said among
themselves, Perceive ye how ye prevail
nothing? behold, the world is gone after
him.

A CAREFUL reader of the Gospels can hardly fail to
observe that our Lord Jesus Christ's conduct, at this
stage of His earthly ministry, is very peculiar. It is
unlike anything else recorded of Him in the New
Testament. Hitherto we have seen Him withdrawing
as much as possible from public notice, retiring into the
wilderness, and checking those who would have brought
Him forward, and made Him a king. As a rule He
did not court popular attention. He did not "cry or
strive, or cause His voice to be heard in the streets."
(Matt. xii. 19.) Here, on the contrary, we see Him
making a public entry into Jerusalem, attended by an
immense crowd of people, and causing even the Pharisees to say, "Behold the world is gone after Him."

The explanation of this apparent inconsistency is not

hard to find out. The time had come at last when
Christ was to die for the sins of the world. The time
had come when the true passover Lamb was to be slain,
when the true blood of atonement was to be shed, when
Messiah was to be "cut off" according to prophecy
(Dan. ix. 26), when the way into the holiest was to
be opened by the true High Priest to all mankind.
Knowing all this, our Lord purposely drew attention
to Himself. Knowing this, He placed Himself prominently under the notice of the whole Jewish nation.
It was only meet and right that this thing should not
be "done in a corner." (Acts xxvi. 26.) If ever there
was a transaction in our Lord's earthly ministry which
was public, it was the sacrifice which He offered up on
the cross of Calvary. He died at the time of year when
all the tribes were assembled at Jerusalem for the passover feast. Nor was this all. He died in a week when
by His remarkable public entry into Jerusalem He had
caused the eyes of all Israel to be specially fixed upon
Himself.

We learn, for one thing, in these verses, *how entirely
voluntary the sufferings of Christ were.*

It is impossible not to see in the history before us
that our Lord had a mysterious influence over the
minds and wills of all around Him, whenever He
thought fit to use it. Nothing else can account for the
effect which His approach to Jerusalem had on the
multitudes which accompanied Him. They seem to
have been carried forward by a secret constraining
power, which they were obliged to obey, in spite of the

disapproval of the leaders of the nation. In short, just as our Lord was able to make winds, and waves, and diseases, and devils obey Him. so was He able, when it pleased Him, to turn the minds of men according to His will.

For the case before us does not stand alone. The men of Nazareth could not hold Him when He chose to "pass through the midst of them and go His way." (Luke iv. 30.) The angry Jews of Jerusalem could not detain Him when they would have laid violent hands on Him in the temple; but, "going through the midst of them, He passed by." (John viii. 59.) Above all, the very soldiers who apprehended Him in the garden, at first "went backward and fell to the ground." (John xviii. 6.) In each of these instances there is but one explanation. A divine influence was put forth. There was about our Lord during His whole earthly ministry a mysterious "hiding of His power." (Hab. iii. 4.) But He had almighty power when He was pleased to use it.

Why then did He not resist His enemies at last? Why did He not scatter the band of soldiers who came to seize Him, like chaff before the wind? There is but one answer. He was a willing Sufferer in order to procure redemption for a lost and ruined soul. He had undertaken to give His own life as a ransom, that we might live for ever, and He laid it down on the cross with all the desire of His heart. He did not bleed, and suffer, and die, because He was vanquished by superior force, and could not help Himself, but because

He loved us, and rejoiced to give Himself for us as our Substitute. He did not die because He could not avoid death, but because He was willing with all His heart to make His soul an offering for sin.

For ever let us rest our hearts on this most comfortable thought. We have a most willing and loving Saviour. It was His delight to do His Father's will, and to make a way for lost and guilty man to draw near to God in peace. He loved the work He had taken in hand, and the poor sinful world which He came to save. Never then let us give way to the unworthy thought that our Saviour does not love to see sinners coming to Him, and does not rejoice to save them. He who was a most willing Sacrifice on the cross, is also a most willing Saviour at the right hand of God. He is just as willing to receive sinners who come to Him now for peace, as He was to die for sinners, when He held back His power, and willingly suffered on Calvary.

We learn, for another thing, in these verses, *how minutely the prophecies concerning Christ's first coming were fulfilled.*

The riding into Jerusalem on an ass, which is here recorded, might seem at first sight a simple action and in no way remarkable. But when we turn to the Old Testament, we find that this very thing had been predicted by the Prophet Zechariah five hundred years before. (Zech. ix. 9.) We find that the coming of a Redeemer some day, was not the only thing which the Holy Ghost had revealed to the Fathers but that even the least particulars of His earthly career were predicted and written down with precise accuracy.

Such fulfilments of prophecy as this deserve the special attention of all who love the Bible and read it with reverence. They show us that every word of Holy Scripture was given by inspiration of God. They teach us to beware of the mischievous practice of spiritualizing and explaining away the language of Scripture. We must settle it in our minds that the plain, literal meaning of the Bible is generally the true and correct meaning. Here is a prediction of Zechariah literally and exactly fulfilled. Our Lord was not merely a very humble person, as some spiritualizing interpreters would have explained Zechariah's words to mean, but He literally rode into Jerusalem on an ass. Above all, such fulfilments teach us what we may expect in looking forward to the second advent of Jesus Christ. They show us that we must look for a literal accomplishment of the prophecies concerning that second coming, and not for a figurative and a spiritual one. For ever let us hold fast this great principle. Happy is that Bible-reader who believes the words of the Bible to mean exactly what they seem to mean. Such a man has got the true key of knowledge in looking forward to things to come. To know that predictions about the second advent of Christ will be fulfilled literally, just as predictions about the first advent of Christ were fulfilled literally, is the first step towards a right understanding of unfulfilled prophecy.

NOTES. JOHN XII. 12—19.

12.—[*On the next day.*] This day must have been the Sunday before Easter, which is commonly known in England as "Palm Sunday," from the circumstance here related.

[*Much people...come to the feast.*] This must include many of the Jews who had come up to the passover from Galilee, and were doubtless well acquainted with our Lord's ministry and the numerous miracles He had wrought in Galilee. Some of them in all human probability had formed part of the multitude whom He fed with a few loaves in the wilderness.

[*When they heard that Jesus was coming to Jerusalem.*] We must suppose that by some means our Lord's intention of coming to Jerusalem must have become known, either by Himself communicating it, or by His disciples learning it and telling others. This information would be carried back to the city by those who came from thence to Bethany on Saturday. Bethany however was on the direct road from Jericho to Jerusalem, and the tidings of our Lord's approach may have travelled before Him for some days.

Rollock thinks this multitude must have been chiefly composed of Jews not residing in Jerusalem. The Jerusalem Jews, he thinks, are an instance of the old proverb, which he quotes, "the nearer the Church the further from God."

13.—[*Took branches of palm trees, and went...meet Him.*] The precise motive of this action we are left to conjecture. Palm branches were carried by processions attending kings or victorious generals on public occasions. The triumphant host in heaven, which John saw in vision, was composed of persons having "palms in their hands." (Rev. vii. 9.) It may be that some of the crowd on this occasion believed that Jesus was the Messiah. Others, we may be sure, did what the rest did, without any special motive at all. At most we can only suppose that the multitude had a vague idea that Jesus was somebody very remarkable,—a prophet, or some one raised up by God,—and as such did Him honour.

Rollock thinks the custom of carrying branches at the feast of tabernacles, as the expression of joy, was the motive of the crowd here.

[*And cried, Hosanna.*] This Hebrew word is taken from Psalm cxviii. 25, and signifies "save now, we beseech Thee."

Calvin thinks this phrase testified that they acknowledged Christ to be the Messiah, and considers that Psalm cxviii. had special reference to Messiah's coming.

[*Blessed...King of Israel that cometh...name...Lord.*] This sentence would be more literally rendered "Blessed is He that cometh in the name of the Lord, the King of Israel." It is partly taken from Psalm cxviii. 26 ; but there the words are simply " Blessed be He that cometh in the name of the Lord," and no mention is made of "the King."—We can only conjecture that some of the multitude had a vague idea that Jesus had come to be a temporal King, and a conquering Messiah, who would set Israel free from all foreign dominion. These few caught up the words of the Psalm, and their cry was taken up by the many around them, perhaps without knowing distinctly what they did or said. Nothing is so soon caught up as a popular cry. From "Hosanna" to "Crucify Him" there was only an interval of a very few days ! Nothing is so worthless as popular applause.

Theophylact holds decidedly that the multitude honoured our Lord as God. But I cannot think it.

14.—[*And Jesus...found...ass, sat thereon.*] That there was no chance or accident in the ass being found, we know from St. Matthew's Gospel, where we read that the disciples were sent to get the ass ready. (Matt. xxi. 7.) Every step of this triumphal progress into Jerusalem was pre-arranged.

To ride upon an ass, we must always remember, was not so low and igominious a mode of travelling as it may seem to us. The Eastern ass is a very different creature to the English ass,—larger, stronger, and far more valuable. Asses are specially named as part of the wealth of Abraham, Jacob, and Job. (Gen. xii. 16 ; xxx. 43. Job xlii. 12.) Solomon had an officer specially over the asses. (1 Chron. xxvii. 30.) Abraham, Balaam, Achsah, Abigail, and the Shunamite rich woman, all rode on asses. To ride on white asses was a mark of great men in the days of the Judges. (Judges v. 10.) The idea therefore of anything degrading in riding on an ass must be entirely dismissed from our minds.

On the other hand, it is undeniable that the ass is not the animal that a king or ruler, in any age, has ever chosen to use on public occasions, in heading a procession. The horse has always been preferred. The use of an ass, we cannot doubt, was meant to show that our Lord's kingdom was utterly unlike the kingdoms of this world. No Roman soldier in the garrison of Jerusalem, who, standing at his post or sitting in his barrack-window, saw our Lord riding on an ass, could report to his centurion that He looked like one who came to wrest the kingdom of Judæa out of the hand of the Romans, drive out Pontius Pilate and his legions from the tower of Antonia, and achieve independence for the Jews with the sword!

The Greek word rendered "young ass" here, is a diminutive, and seems used intentionally to show that it was a very young or small ass.

[*As it is written.*] By riding on an ass our Lord had fulfilled the prophecy of Zechariah, in which 500 years before, the prophet had foretold that the King of Zion would one day appear "riding upon an ass." At the time when he prophesied this, there were no kings in Jerusalem. The kingdom had ceased at the captivity. We cannot doubt that this prophecy was well known among the scribes and Pharisees, and, taken together with the fact that Daniel's 70 weeks were expiring, our Lord's entry into Jerusalem in this fashion must have raised many thoughts in their hearts.

Let it be noted that many like events in our Lord's earthly ministry were foreknown and foretold long before they happened, and with increasing minuteness and particularity as the roll of prophecy drew near to an end.

15.—[*Fear not, daughter of Sion, etc.*] It will be observed, of course, that John does not quote literally and exactly all that Zechariah said. He omits several words. The explanation is simple. He did not quote from memory only, and so forget part; but he purposely only quoted that part of the prediction which was now specially fulfilled: viz., the "riding on the ass." The object of the prophecy, when it was first delivered, was to comfort the Jews in their low and decayed state, after their return from Babylon, by a promise of Messiah. Therefore Zechariah was taught by the Holy Ghost to say things which may be paraphrased as follows: "Fear not; be not cast down or depressed, O daughter of Sion, or inhabitants of Jerusalem. Low and depressed as your condition may be now, there will be a day when you shall have a King again. There shall come One who will ride on a certain public occasion into thy gates,—a King on an ass's colt; not as a warrior, with a sword in hand, but as a peaceful Prince, a just and holy King, better even than David, Solomon, Hezekiah, or Josiah, and bringing with Him salvation for souls. Therefore think not thyself forsaken, because thou art poor now, and hast no King. Look forward to thy coming King."

Let it be noted that Christ's coming, first or second, is always the great topic of comfort in prophetical writings.

16.—[*These things understood not ..disciples...first.*] It is clear from.

this and other kindred passages, that our Lord's own immediate followers had a very imperfect knowledge of our Lord's Person and work, and of the fulfilment of Scripture which was going on around them. Brought up amidst Jewish notions of a glorious temporal Messiah, they failed to see the full meaning of many of our Lord's doings.

Let us never forget that men may be true Christians, and right hearted, and yet be very ignorant on some points. "Faith," says Zwingle, on this verse, "admits of degrees and increase." In estimating others, we must make great allowance for early training and associations.

[*But when Jesus was glorified.*] This must mean, as Theophylact says, our Lord's ascension. After that time, and the day of Pentecost, the minds of the disciples were greatly enlightened. Compare John vii. 39 : "The Holy Ghost was not yet given, because Jesus was not yet glorified."

[*Then remembered...these things...written of Him.*] The power of memory to see things long after they happen, in a new light, and then to recollect them vividly, is very remarkable. In no case does it appear more curiously than in the rising again in our minds of texts and sermons heard long ago, which at the time apparently left no impression on us. Preachers and teachers may take comfort in this. All is not lost that they say, although their hearers and scholars may seem at the time to pay no attention. Their words in many cases shall have a resurrection. One great cause of this is, that it is part of the Holy Ghost's office "to bring things to remembrance." (John xiv. 26.)

[*And...they...done these things...Him.*] The disciples found, long after the triumphant entry into Jerusalem, that they had been unconscious actors in a mighty accomplishment of Scripture. This is a thought for us all. We have not the least idea, during the greater part of our lives, how much of God's great purposes on earth are being carried on through us and by us, without our being conscious of it. The full extent to which they are carried on we shall never know till we wake up in another world. We shall then discern with wonder and amazement the full meaning of many a thing in which we were unconscious agents during our lives.

Calvin remarks, "Then, after the ascension, did it occur to the disciples that Christ did not do these things rashly, and that these men were not employed in idle amusement, but that the whole transaction had been regulated by the providence of God."

Poole observes, that here St. John "confesseth his own ignorance." He was present, and saw all that was done, but did not understand it at the time.

17.—[*The people therefore...Lazarus...bare record.*] I feel no doubt that this verse describes one part of the multitude which met our Lord, and the following verse describes another part. One part, and of course a small one, consisted of those who had seen the raising of Lazarus. The other, and a much larger one, consisted of those who had only heard the report.

That there must have been a very large number of persons present at the miracle of Bethany, is, I think, indirectly proved by the expression here used, "people that were with Him."

The word "bare record," must mean that they testified that a great miracle really had been wrought, and that this same Jesus, now riding on an ass before the eyes of the people, was that very Person who had wrought it. I do not see that we can possibly get more out of the expression, and I cannot suppose that these people testified their belief in Christ's Messiahship.

The double expression, "called out of his grave," and "raised from the dead," deserves notice. It is doubtless meant to keep before our minds the mighty simplicity of the means used by our Lord. He spoke, and it was done. He "called" to Lazarus to come forth, and he was "raised" at once.

18.—[*For this cause...people met Him, etc.*] This verse describes the state of mind of the larger part of the multitude which surrounded our Lord at His entry into Jerusalem. It consisted of those who had heard the report of His raising Lazarus,—a story magnified, no doubt, in the telling. Strong curiosity to see the Person who had done such a miracle, would call forth an immense crowd in any city. But among Jews, familiar with Old Testament miracles, assembled in enormous numbers for the Passover, excited by the rumour of Messiah coming,—among such we may well believe that the report of Jesus coming in from Bethany, would draw together many myriads of spectators to meet Him.

The Greek words, "for this cause," here seem to refer forward to the latter part of the verse, and not backward to the preceding verse. Compare John x. 17, where the same form of language is used.

19.—[*The Pharisees...said...prevail nothing.*] This is the language of men baffled, angry, and at their wits' end from vexation, to see their plans defeated. Instead of finding people willing to lay hands on Jesus as a malefactor, and to deliver Him up into their power, they beheld a large multitude surrounding Him with joyful acclamations, and saluting Him as a King! Of course they could do nothing but sit still and see it. The least attempt to use violence against our Lord would have raised a tumult, and endangered their own lives. So that they were obliged to see their most hated enemy entering Jerusalem in triumph, like Mordecai led by Haman. (Esther vi. 11.)

"Perceive ye." I believe, should be taken as an imperative, and not as an interrogative indicative. It sounds like the language of men looking on from the city walls or the temple courts, as the huge procession wound slowly through the gates of the city. "Behold this sight! Behold how you do nothing effectual to stop this fellow's course! Your order to denounce Him, and have Him apprehended, is utterly useless and unprofitable."

Chrysostom and Theophylact think that those who said this had some faith and felt rightly, but had not courage enough to confess Christ. But I cannot agree with them. Calvin and other Reformers think, on the contrary, that it was the language of Christ's enemies.

Bullinger observes that wicked men show their wickedness especially by their dislike of true religion, and their annoyance when, as in the case before us, it seems to enjoy a temporary popularity. For neglect and contempt of religion they show no concern at all.

[*Behold...world...gone after Him.*] Some allowance must of course be made for the exaggerated language which angry and disappointed men use under the influence of passion. Nevertheless the word "world" may not be really so extravagant as it appears at first, when we consider the immense number of Jews who attended the passover feast. According to a computation made by Josephus there were nearly three millions of people assembled on such occasions at Jerusalem. At this rate we can understand that the crowd drawn together by our Lord's public entry might well be so large as to warrant the saying, "The world is gone after Him." Most of the crowd, it may be remembered, were not dwellers in Jerusalem, but strangers, who were only visitors or sojourners, absent from home, and would materially swell a crowd.

In leaving this passage it is impossible not to feel that there must have been an overruling, constraining influence on the minds of the Jewish people on the occasion of the Lord's triumphant entry into Jerusalem. This no doubt was an influence miraculously exercised by our Lord in order to draw all men's attention to Himself, and to make His approaching Sacrifice on the cross as public an event as possible.

Rollock observes, "A secret power of royal authority stirred up the minds of the multitude to receive Christ as a King." He also observes that it is the same power which Christ will put forth when He comes at the last day to judge the world.

JOHN XII. 20—26.

20 And there were certain Greeks among them that came up to worship at the feast:

21 The same came therefore to Philip, which was of Bethsaida of Galilee, and desired him, saying, Sir, we would see Jesus.

22 Philip cometh and telleth Andrew: and again Andrew and Philip tell Jesus.

23 And Jesus answered them, saying, The hour is come, that the Son of man should be glorified.

24 Verily, verily, I say unto you, Except a corn of wheat fall into the ground and die, it abideth alone: but if it die, it bringeth forth much fruit.

25 He that loveth his life shall lose it; and he that hateth his life in this world shall keep it unto life eternal.

26 If any man serve me, let him follow me; and where I am, there shall also my servant be: if any man serve me, him will my Father honour.

THERE is more going on in some people's minds than we are aware of. The case of the Greeks before us is a remarkable proof of this. Who would have thought when Christ was on earth, that foreigners from a distant land would have come forward in Jerusalem, and said, "Sir, we would see Jesus"? Who these Greeks were, what they meant, why they desired to see Jesus, what their inward motives were,—all these are questions we cannot answer. Like Zacchæus, they may have been influenced by curiosity. Like the wise men from the East, they may have surmised that Jesus was the promised King of the Jews, whom all the Eastern world was expecting. Enough for us to know that they showed more interest in Christ than Caiaphas and all his com-

panions.   Enough to know that they drew from our
Lord's lips sayings which are still read in one hundred
and fifty languages, from one end of the world to the
other.

We learn, for one thing, from our Lord's words in
this passage, that *death is the way to spiritual life and
glory.* "Except a corn of wheat fall into the ground,
it abideth alone; but if it die, it bringeth forth much
fruit."

This sentence was primarily meant to teach the
wondering Greeks the true nature of Messiah's kingdom.
If they thought to see a King like the kings of this
world, they were greatly mistaken. Our Lord would
have them know that He came to carry a cross, and not
to wear a crown. He came not to live a life of honour,
ease, and magnificence, but to die a shameful and dishonoured death. The kingdom He came to set up was
to begin with a crucifixion, and not with a coronation.
Its glory was to take its rise not from victories won by
the sword, and from accumulated treasures of gold and
silver, but from the death of its King.

But this sentence was also meant to teach a wider
and broader lesson still. It revealed, under a striking
figure, the mighty foundation-truth, that Christ's death
was to be the source of spiritual life to the world. From
His cross and passion was to spring up a mighty harvest
of benefit to all mankind. His death, like a grain of
seed-corn, was to be the root of blessings and mercies to
countless millions of immortal souls. In short the great
principle of the Gospel was once more exhibited,—that

Christ's vicarious death (not His life, or miracles, or
teaching, but His *death*) was to bring forth fruit to the
praise of God, and to provide redemption for a lost
world.

This deep and mighty sentence was followed by a
practical application, which closely concerns ourselves.
"He that hateth his life shall keep it." He that would
be saved must be ready to give up life itself, if necessary,
in order to obtain salvation. He must bury his love of
the world, with its riches, honours, pleasures, and rewards, with a full belief that in so doing he will reap
a better harvest, both here and hereafter. He who
loves the life that now is so much that he cannot deny
himself anything for the sake of his soul, will find at
length that he has lost everything. He, on the contrary,
who is ready to cast away everything most dear to him
in this life, if it stands in the way of his soul, and to
crucify the flesh with its affections, and lusts, will find
at length that he is no loser. In a word, his losses
will prove nothing in comparison to his gains.

Truths such as these should sink deeply into our
hearts, and stir up self-inquiry. It is as true of Christians as it is of Christ,—there can be no life without
death, there can be no sweet without bitter, there can
be no crown without a cross. Without Christ's death
there would have been no life for the world. Unless
we are willing to die to sin, and crucify all that is
most dear to flesh and blood, we cannot expect any
benefit from Christ's death. Let us remember these
things, and take up our cross daily, like men. Let us

for the joy set before us endure the cross and despise
the shame, and in the end we shall sit down with our
Master at God's right hand. The way of self-crucifixion
and sanctification may seem foolishness and waste to
the world, just as burying good seed-corn seems waste
to the child and the fool. But there never lived the
man who did not find that by sowing to the Spirit, he
reaped life everlasting. (Gal. vi. 8.)

We learn, for another thing, from our Lord's words,
that *if we profess to serve Christ, we must follow Him.*
" If any man serve Me," is the saying, " let him follow
Me."

That expression, "following," is one of wide signification, and brings before our minds many familiar ideas.
As the soldier follows his general, as the servant follows
his master, as the scholar follows his teacher, as the
sheep follows its shepherd, just so ought the professing
Christian to follow Christ. Faith and obedience are the
leading marks of real followers, and will always be seen
in true believing Christians. Their knowledge may be
very small, and their infirmities very great; their grace
very weak, and their hope very dim. But they believe
what Christ says, and strive to do what Christ commands.
And of such Christ declares, "They serve Me: they are
mine."

Christianity like this, receives little praise from man.
It is too thorough, too decided, too strong, too real. To
serve Christ in name and form is easy work, and satisfies
most people; but to follow Him in faith and life demands
more trouble than the generality of men will take about

their souls. Laughter, ridicule, opposition, persecution, are often the only reward which Christ's followers get from the world. Their religion is one, " whose praise is not of men but of God." (Rom. ii. 29.)

Yet to him that followeth, let us never forget, the Lord Jesus holds out abundant encouragement : " Where I am," He declares, "there also shall my servant be: if any man serve Me, him will my Father honour." Let us lay to heart these comfortable promises, and go forward in the narrow way without fear. The world may cast out our name as evil, and turn us out of its society ; but when we dwell with Christ in glory, we shall have a home from which we can never be ejected.—The world may pour contempt on our religion, and laugh us and our Christianity to scorn ; but when the Father honours us at the last day, before the assembly of angels and men, we shall find that His praise makes amends for all.

NOTES. JOHN XII. 20—26.

20.—[*And there were certain Greeks, etc., etc.*] Who these Greeks were has exercised the conjectural ingenuity of commentators. They were not downright heathens, it is clear, from the expression that they were of those "that came to worship" at the feast. No heathen would be admitted to the Passover.—They were not, in my judgment, Jews who had lived among Greeks until they were more Grecian than Jewish in their language. The word we have rendered "Greeks" seems to me to make that impossible.—I believe they were men who were by birth heathens, but had become proselytes to Judaism, and as such were regular attendants on the Jewish feasts. That there were many such proselytes wherever Jews lived, is a simple matter of fact. So in Acts xvii. 4, we read of "devout" or "worshipping" Greeks. The leavening influence of Judaism, in every part of the heathen world where the scattered Jews dwelt, before the coming of Christ, was probably very considerable. It is worth notice that as Gentiles, the wise men from the East, were among the first to honour our Lord when He was born, so Gentiles were among the first to show interest in Him just before His crucifixion.

Whether the circumstance recorded in the passage before us took place the same day that our Lord rode in triumph into Jerusalem, or whether there was not a break or interval of a day or two, admits of question. Judging from the inquiry of the Greeks, "We would see Jesus," it seems unlikely that it happened the same day. It stands to reason that our Lord, at a time when He was riding into Jerusalem on an ass, and was the object of popular enthusiasm, would easily have been distinguished and recognised by the Greeks. Moreover one cannot suppose that the words spoken in the following verse, and the miracle of the voice from heaven, belong to a time of noise, shouting and popular acclamation, such as there must have been during the procession. For these reasons I incline to the opinion that we must suppose an interval of a day or two between this verse and the preceding one.

21.—[*The same came...Philip...Bethsaida...Galilee.*] Why the Greeks came to Philip more than any other disciple we do not know. It is conjectured that Philip, being an inhabitant of a town in North Galilee, was more likely than the other disciples to be acquainted with Greeks, from being near Tyre and Sidon. But this reason applies quite as much to Andrew, Peter, James, and John, who were all Galileans, as it does to Philip.—Is it not worth noticing that Philip's name is a more purely Greek name than that of any of the apostles? Does not this indicate that he probably had Greek relatives and connections?

The mention of Bethsaida accounts for Philip speaking to Andrew, in the next verse. Bethsaida was the native place of Andrew and Peter, and Philip therefore was their fellow-townsman.

[*And desired him, saying, Sir.*] The Greek word rendered "desired" is more frequently translated, "asked," "besought," "prayed." It implies the desire of an inquirer who expresses a wish for a thing, and asks whether it is possible for him to have it.

The word we render "sir" is almost always rendered "lord." When rendered "sir" it is addressed by an inferior to a superior. Thus the servant of the householder says, "Sir, didst thou not sow good seed?" (Matt. xiii. 27.) The Pharisees said to Pilate, "Sir, we remember that deceiver said." (Matt. xxvii. 63.) The Samaritan woman says to Jesus three times, "Sir." (John iv. 11, 13, 19.) Here the use of the word marks the respect of the Greeks for our Lord and His apostles.

[*We would see Jesus.*] The English here fails to express the Greek fully. It is literally, "we wish : we desire to see."

Concerning the motive of the Greeks in asking to see our Lord, we know nothing certain. It may have been nothing but curiosity, like that of Zacchæus, aroused by hearing rumours about Jesus, and sharpened by seeing the procession of the palm-bearing multitude at His entry into the city. This alone was enough to excite the attention of Greeks accustomed to the demonstrations of their own countrymen on public occasions.—It may possibly be that, like the Canaanitish woman, the Centurion of Capernaum, and Cornelius, they had as proselytes, got hold of the great truths which underlaid Judaism, and were actually looking for a Redeemer. But we do not know.

Bengel thinks that at this moment "Jesus was engaged in the inner part of the temple, to which an entrance was not open to the Greeks," and for this reason the Greeks could not get at Him, and have a personal interview.

These Greeks, we should note, sought to see Jesus at the very time when the Jews sought to kill Him.

22.—[*Philip cometh and telleth Andrew.*] This expression seems to favour the idea that this whole transaction was not on the same day that Jesus entered Jerusalem. On such a day there would hardly be an opportunity for one disciple coming quietly and telling a thing to another. Why Philip chose to tell Andrew we have seen. He was his fellow-townsman.

[*And again Andrew and Philip tell Jesus.*] This expression seems to imply that the two Apostles consulted together before they told our Lord. Perhaps, as thorough Jews, they did not feel sure that our Lord would care to give an interview to Gentiles, and at first hesitated about telling Him. They remembered that at one time Jesus had said, "Go not into the way of the Gentiles." (Matt. x. 5.) On reflection they probably remembered our Lord's kindness to the Canaanitish mother, and the Roman centurion, and resolved to tell Him.

Of course it is possible that the Greeks only wanted to look at our Lord and see what He was like, and not to converse with Him. If this was all, the disciples may have doubted whether it was worth mentioning to Jesus.

23.—[*And Jesus answered them, saying.*] It is doubtful whether this was spoken to the two disciples only,—or to them and the

Greeks before mentioned,—or to the twelve alone. I incline to think it must mean to the twelve, and specially to Andrew and Philip.

[*The hour is come...Son of man...glorified.*] The true key-note to this verse, and the two which follow, is probably this. Our Lord saw the state of mind in which His followers were. He saw them excited by His triumphant entry into Jerusalem, and the desire of strangers like the Greeks to see their Master. He saw they were secretly expecting a glorious kingdom to be immediately set up, in which they would have chief places, power, and authority. He proceeds to rectify their conceptions, and to remind them of what He had repeatedly told them, His own death :—

" The hour has certainly arrived for my being glorified. I am about to leave the world, ascend up to my Father, finish the work I came to do, and be highly exalted. My earthly ministry of humiliation is ending, and my time of glory is drawing nigh. But all this is to be brought about in a way very different from that which you are thinking about. I am going to a cross first, and not a throne. I am going first to be condemned, crucified, and slain."

That "glorified" means "to be crucified," I cannot admit, with such texts as John vii. 39 and xii. 16 before me. That the cross led to glory, and that through the crucifixion came the glorification, I believe firmly. But the glory came after the suffering. (Luke xxiv. 26.)

Let us note that "the hour" or season for Christ to finish His ministry was fixed and appointed. Till it came the Jews could do nothing to stop His preaching or harm His person. Just so it is with His people in one sense. Each is immortal till his work is done.

Does it not seem that the inquiry of the Greeks has much to do with our Lord's opening words?—"The Gentiles are beginning to inquire after Me. Thus the hour is manifestly come that my work should be finished, and my kingdom fully set up in the world, by my crucifixion, resurrection, and ascension."

24.—[*Verily, verily I say unto you.*] This is one of those solemn prefaces which are so frequent in John's Gospel, and indicate some very weighty truth coming. I think "to you" must surely include not only Andrew and Philip, but all the company around our Lord.

[*Except a corn of wheat, etc., etc.*] Our Lord here illustrates a great Scriptural truth by a very familiar fact in nature. That fact is, that in plants and seeds life comes by death. The seed must be put into the ground, must rot, decay, and die, if we want it to bear fruit and produce a crop. If we refuse to bury the seed, and will keep it without sowing it, we shall never reap any harvest. We must be content to let it die if we want corn.

The wealth of spiritual truth which this beautiful figure unfolds is very great. The death of Christ was the life of the world. From it, as a most prolific seed, was to spring an enormous harvest of blessing to souls, and of glory to God. His substitution on the cross, His atoning death, were to be the beginning of untold blessings to a lost world. To wish Him not to die, to dislike the idea of His death (as the disciples evidently did), was as foolish as to keep seed-corn locked up in the granary, and to refuse to sow it. "I am the corn of wheat," Jesus seems to say. "Unless I die, whatever you in your private opinion may think, my purpose in coming into the world will not be accomplished. But if I die, multitudes of souls will be saved."

Let us carefully mark here the immense importance which our Lord attaches to His death. Nothing can explain this but the old foundation-doctrine of the Bible, that Christ's sacrificial death on the cross is the only Satisfaction and Atonement for the sin of the world. A passage like this can never be thoroughly explained by those who regard Christ's death as nothing more than a martyrdom or an example of self-denial. It was something far greater and more important than this. It was the dying of a corn of wheat, in order that out of its death should spring up an enormous spiritual harvest. Christ's vicarious death is the world's life.

Let us notice here, as elsewhere, the Divine wisdom with which our Master illustrated spiritual truth by earthly figures. Illustrations fitly chosen, strike men much more than abstract arguments. Ministers and teachers of religion should study to "use similitudes."

Theophylact thinks our Lord meant by this beautiful figure, to encourage His disciples not to be offended and shaken in mind by His coming death. In His case, as in the natural world, they must remember life comes through death.

Zwingle thinks that as with the corn, when sown, so it is with the body of Christ. It does us good by dying for us, and not by our eating it.

Gill remarks, that by "abiding alone," in this simile, Christ meant that if He did not die, He would be "alone" in heaven with the Father and the elect angels, but without any of the sons of men. Scott says the same.

25.—[*He that loveth his life, etc.*] There are few of our Lord's sayings more frequently recorded by the Holy Ghost, than this pair of paradoxes. The repetition shows its great importance. It will be found in Matt. x. 39 ; xvi. 25 ; Mark viii. 35 ; Luke ix. 24 ; xvii. 33 ; as well as here.

The meaning is plain. "He that loves his life, or thinks more of the life that now is than that which is to come, shall lose that which is the best part of his life, his soul. He that hateth his life, or cares little for it compared to the life to come, shall preserve to eternal glory that which is the best part of his life, to wit, his soul."

One object of our Lord in saying these words, was evidently to prevent His disciples looking for good things in this life, if they followed Him. They must give up their Jewish ideas about temporal rewards and honours in Messiah's service. They must understand that His kingdom was entirely spiritual, and that if they were His disciples they must be content to lose much in this life, in order to gain the glory of the life to come. So far from promising them temporal rewards, He would have them distinctly know that they must give up much and sacrifice much, if they wanted to be saved.

The other object our Lord had in view in saying these words, was to teach all Christians in every age, that, like Him, they must make up their minds to sacrifice much, and to die to the world, in the hope of a harvest of glory in a world to come. Through death we must seek life. Eternal life must be the great end a Christian looks to. To attain it he must be willing to give up everything.

The practical condemnation which this verse passes on the life lived by many, should never be overlooked. How few hate their lives here ! How many love them, and care for nothing but how to make them comfortable and happy ! The eternal loss or the eternal gain are often entirely forgotten.

Augustine gives a wise caution : "Take heed lest there steal upon thee a will to make away with thyself, while thou takest in the sense that it is a duty to hate thine own life in this world. Hence certain malignant and perverse men give themselves to the flames, choke themselves in the water, dash themselves in pieces, and so perish. Christ taught not this. Not by himself, but by another, must that man be put to death who would follow in Christ's footsteps."

The word "hate" here must be taken comparatively. It is a Hebraism, like "Jacob have I loved, and Esau have I hated."— "Your appointed feasts my soul hateth." (Rom. ix. 13; Isa. i. 14.)

Scott thinks this verse was meant to teach the Greeks and all the disciples to arm themselves with a mind like their Master's, if they wanted to follow Him.

26.—[*If any man serve Me...follow Me.*] This verse seems spoken for the benefit and information of the Greeks who sought to see Jesus, and of all who desired to become His disciples. If any man desires to serve Christ, and be a Christian, he must be content to follow His Master, walk in His footsteps, share His lot, do as He did, and partake of His Master's inheritance in this world. He must not look for good things here,—for crowns, kingdoms, riches, honours, wealth, and dignity. Like His Master, he must be content with a cross. He must, in a word, "take up his cross and follow Me." (Matt. xvi. 24.) As St. Paul says, "We are heirs of God, and joint-heirs with Christ; if so be that we suffer with Him. that we may be also glorified together." (Rom. viii. 17.)

[*And where I am, there...my servant be.*] This is the first thing that Christ promises to those who follow Him. They shall be with Christ wherever He is, in paradise, and in His glorious kingdom. He and His servant shall not be parted. Whatever the Master has, the servant shall have also.

It is a comfortable thought, that however little we know of the life to come and the state after death, we do know that we shall be "with Christ, which is far better." (Phil. i. 23.)

[*If any man serve me...my Father honour.*] This is the second thing which Jesus promises to His disciples. The father shall give to those who love Christ such honour as eye hath not seen nor ear heard. Honour from the men of this world they may not have. Honour from the Father shall make amends for all.

It is impossible not to see throughout this verse that our Lord's intention is to discourage the carnal and earthly expectation of His Jewish followers, and yet to encourage them by showing what they might confidently look for. They must follow in His steps if they were His true servants, and in so following they would find a cross and not a crown, whatever they might be thinking, at that moment, while the Hosannas of an excited crowd were sounding in their ears. But though they had a cross, they should not miss a reward finally, which would make amends for all. They would be with Christ in glory. They would be honoured by God the Father.

The words, "Him will my Father honour," of course admit of being applied to this life in a certain sense : "Them that honour Me I will honour." (1 Sam. ii. 30.) But it is much more agreeable to the context, I think, to apply them to the honour which shall be given in another world.

The clearest conception we can form of heaven, is that which is here stated. It is being with Christ, and receiving honour from God. Heaven is generally described by negatives. This is, however, an exceptional positive. It is being "with Christ." (Compare John xiv. 3 ; xvii. 24 ; 1 Thess iv. 17.)

Let us note how wisely and mercifully our Lord always damped and checked the unscriptural expectations of His disciples. Never on any occasion do we find Him keeping back the cross, or bribing men to follow Him, as Mahomet did, by promising temporal comfort and happiness.

JOHN XII. 27–33.

27 Now is my soul troubled : and what shall I say ? Father, save me from this hour : but for this cause came I unto this hour.

28 Father, glorify thy name. Then came there a voice from heaven, *saying*, I have both glorified *it*, and will glorify *it* again.

29 The people therefore, that stood by, and heard *it*, said that it thundered : others said, An angel spake to him.

30 Jesus answered and said, This voice came not because of me, but for your sakes.

31 Now is the judgment of this world : now shall the prince of this world be cast out.

32 And I, if I be lifted up from the earth, will draw all *men* unto me.

33 This he said, signifying what death he should die.

THESE verses show us what St. Peter meant when he said, "There are some things hard to be understood" in Scripture. (2 Peter. iii. 16.) There are depths here which we have no line to fathom thoroughly. This need not surprise us, or shake our faith. The Bible would not be a book "given by inspiration of God," if it did not contain many things which pass man's finite understanding. With all its difficulties it contains thousands of passages which the most unlearned may easily comprehend. Even here, if we look steadily at these verses, we may gather from them lessons of no mean importance.

We have, first, in these verses, *a great doctrine indirectly proved.* That doctrine is the imputation of man's sin to Christ.

We see the Saviour of the world, the eternal Son of God troubled and disturbed in mind: "Now is my soul troubled." We see Him who could heal diseases with a touch, cast out devils with a word, and command the waves and winds to obey Him, in great agony and conflict of spirit. Now how can this be explained?

To say, as some do, that the only cause of our Lord's trouble was the prospect of His own painful death on the cross, is a very unsatisfactory explanation. At this rate it might justly be said that many a martyr has shown more calmness and courage than the Son of God. Such a conclusion is, to say the least, most revolting. Yet this is the conclusion to which men are driven if they adopt the modern notion, that Christ's death was only a great example of self-sacrifice.

Nothing can ever explain our Lord's trouble of soul, both here and in Gethsemane, except the old doctrine, that He felt the burden of man's sin pressing Him down. It was the mighty weight of a world's guilt imputed to Him and meeting on his head, which made Him groan and agonise, and cry, "Now is my soul troubled." For ever let us cling to that doctrine, not only as untying the knot of the passage before us, but as the only ground of solid comfort for the heart of a Christian. That our sins have been really laid on our divine Substitute, and borne by Him, and that His righteousness is really imputed to us and accounted ours,—this is the real warrant for Christian peace. And if any man asks how we know that our sins were laid on Christ, we bid him read such passages as that which is before us, and explain them on any other principle if he can. Christ has borne our sins, carried our sins, groaned under the burden of our sins, been "troubled" in soul by the weight of our sins, and really taken away our sins. This, we may rest assured, is sound doctrine : this is Scriptural theology.

We have, secondly, in these verses, *a great mystery unfolded*. That mystery is the possibility of much inward conflict of soul without sin.

We cannot fail to see in the passage before us, a mighty mental struggle in our blessed Saviour. Of its depth and intensity we can probably form very little conception. But the agonizing cry, "My soul is troubled,"— the solemn question, "What shall I say ?"—the prayer of suffering flesh and blood, "Father, save Me from this hour,"—the meek confession, "For this cause came I unto this hour,"—the petition of a perfectly submissive will, "Father, glorify Thy name,"—what does all this mean ? Surely there can be only one answer. These sentences tell of a struggle within our Saviour's breast, a struggle arising from the natural feelings of one who was perfect man, and as man could suffer all that man is capable of suffering. Yet He in whom this struggle took place was the Holy Son of God, "In Him is no sin." (1 John iii. 5.)

There is a fountain of comfort here for all true servants of Christ, which ought never to be overlooked. Let them learn from their Lord's example that inward conflict of soul is not necessarily in itself a sinful thing. Too many, we believe, from not understanding this point, go heavily all their days on their way to heaven. They fancy they have no grace, because they find a fight in their own hearts. They refuse to take comfort in the Gospel, because they feel a battle between the flesh and the Spirit. Let them mark the experience of their Lord and Master, and lay aside their desponding fears. Let them study the experience of His saints in every age, from St. Paul downwards, and understand that as Christ had inward conflicts so must Christians expect to have them also. To give way to doubts and unbelief, is certainly wrong, and robs us of our peace. There is a faithless despondency, unquestionably, which is blame-worthy, and must be resisted, repented of, and brought to the fountain for all sin, that it may be pardoned. But the mere presence of fight and strife and conflict in our hearts, is in itself no sin. The believer may be known by his inward warfare as well as by his inward peace.

We have, thirdly, in these verses, *a great miracle exhibited*. That miracle is the heavenly Voice described in this passage—a voice which was heard so plainly that people said "it thundered,"—proclaiming, "I have glorified my name, and will glorify it again."

This wondrous Voice was heard three times during our Lord's earthly ministry. Once it was heard at His baptism, when the heavens were opened and the Holy Ghost descended on Him.—Once it was heard at His transfiguration, when Moses and Elias appeared for a season with Him, before Peter, James, and John.—Once it was heard here at Jerusalem, in the midst of a mixed crowd of disciples and unbelieving Jews. On each occasion we know that it was the Voice of God the Father. But why and wherefore this Voice was only heard on these occasions, we are left to conjecture. The thing was a deep mystery, and we cannot now speak particularly of it.

Let it suffice us to believe that this miracle was meant to show the intimate relations and unbroken union of God the Father and God the Son, throughout the period of the Son's earthly ministry. At no period during His incarnation was there a time when the eternal Father was not close to Him, though unseen by man.—Let us also believe that this miracle was meant to signify to bystanders the entire approval of the Son by the Father, as the Messiah, the Redeemer, and the Saviour of man. That approval the Father was pleased to signify by voice three times, as well as to declare by signs and mighty deeds, performed by the Son in His name. These things we may well believe. But when we have said all, we must confess that the Voice was a mystery. We may read of it with wonder and awe, but we cannot explain it.

We have, lastly, in these verses, *a great prophecy delivered.* The Lord Jesus declared, "I, if I be lifted up from the earth, will draw all men unto Me."

Concerning the true meaning of these words there can be but one opinion in any candid mind. They do not mean, as is often supposed, that if the doctrine of Christ crucified is lifted up and exalted by ministers and teachers, it will have a drawing effect on hearers. This is undeniably a truth, but it is not the truth of the text. They simply mean that the death of Christ on the cross would have a drawing effect on all mankind. His death as our Substitute, and the Sacrifice for our sins, would draw multitudes out of every nation to believe on Him and receive Him as their Saviour. By being crucified for us, and not by ascending a temporal throne, He would set up a kingdom in the world, and gather subjects to Himself.

How thoroughly this prophecy has been fulfilled for eighteen centuries, the history of the Church is an abundant proof. Whenever Christ crucified has been preached, and the story of the cross fully told, souls have been converted and drawn to Christ, just as iron-filings are drawn to a magnet, in every part of the world. No truth so exactly suits the wants of all children of Adam, of every colour, climate, and language, as the truth about Christ crucified.

And the prophecy is not yet exhausted. It shall yet receive a more complete accomplishment. A day shall come when every knee shall bow before the Lamb that was slain, and every tongue confess that He is Lord, to the glory of God the Father. (Phil. ii. 10, 11.) He that was "lifted up" on the cross shall yet sit on the throne of glory, and before Him shall be gathered all

nations.   Friends and foes, each in their own order,
shall be " drawn " from their graves, and appear before
the judgment-seat of Christ.   Let us take heed in that
day that we are found on His right hand !

NOTES.   JOHN XII. 27—33.

27.—[*Now is my soul troubled, etc., etc.*]   This remarkable verse
comes in somewhat abruptly.   Yet the connection is not hard to
trace.   Our Lord had just been speaking of His own atoning death.
The thought and prospect of that death appears to draw from Him
the expressions of this verse, which I will now examine in order.

[*Now is my soul troubled.*]   This sentence implies a sudden,
strong mental agony, which came over our Lord, troubling, distressing, and harassing Him.—What was it from ?   Not from the
mere foresight of a painful death on the cross, and the bodily
suffering attending it.   No doubt human nature, even when sinless,
naturally revolts from pain and suffering.   Yet mere bodily pain
has been endured for weeks by many a martyr, and even by heathen fanatics in India, without a groan or a murmur.—No : it was
the weight of the world's imputed sin laid upon our Lord's head,
which pressed Him downward, and made Him cry, "Now is my
soul troubled."   It was the sense of the whole burden of man's
transgression imputed to Him, which, as He drew near to the
cross, weighed Him down so tremendously.   It was not His bodily
sufferings, either anticipated or felt, but our sins, which here, at
Gethsemane, and at Calvary, agonized and racked His soul.

Let us notice here the reality of Christ's substitution for us.
He was made "a curse " for us, and "sin"for us, and He felt it for a
time most deeply.   (Gal. iii. 13 ; 2 Cor. v. 21.)   Those who deny
the doctrine of substitution, imputation, and atonement, can never
explain the expressions before us satisfactorily.

Poole remarks, "There is a vast difference between this trouble
of spirit in Christ, and that which is in us.   Our troubles are upon
reflection for our own sins, and the wrath of God due to us therefore ; His troubles were for the wrath of God due to us for our
sins.—Our troubles are because we have personally grieved God ;
His were because those given to Him had offended God.—We are
afraid of our eternal condemnation ; He was only afraid by a
natural fear of death, which naturally riseth higher according to

the kind of death we die.—Our troubles have mixture of despair, distrust, sinful horror: there was no such thing in His trouble.—Our troubles, in their natural tendency, are killing and destroying: only by accident and the wise ordering of Divine providence do they prove advantageous, and lead us to Him. His trouble, in the very nature of it, was pure, and clean, and sanative, and healing.—But that He was truly troubled, and that such a trouble did truly agree to His office as Mediator, and is a great foundation of peace, quiet, and satisfaction to us, is out of question. By some of these stripes we are healed."

We should remember and admire the prayer in the Litany of the Greek Church: "By Thine unknown sufferings, good Lord deliver us."

Rollock observes here, "If you ask me what the Divine nature in Christ was doing when He said, 'My soul is troubled,' and whether it was divided asunder from His human nature? I reply that it was not divided, but contained itself, or held itself passive, while the human nature was suffering. If it had exercised itself in its full power and glory, our Lord could not possibly have suffered."

(The whole of Rollock's remarks on this difficult verse are singularly good, and deserve close study.)

Hutcheson observes, "The rise and cause of this trouble was thus: the Godhead hiding itself from the humanity's sense, and the Father letting out not only an apprehension of sufferings to come, but a present taste of the horror of His wrath due to man for sin. Christ was amazed, perplexed, and overwhelmed with it in His humanity. And no wonder, since He had the sins of all the elect laid upon Him, by imputation, to suffer for."

Hengstenberg remarks, "The only solution of this extreme trouble is the vicarious significance of the sufferings and death of Christ. If our chastisement was upon Him, in order that we might have peace, then in Him must have been concentrated all the horror of death. He bore the sin of the world, and the wages of that sin was death. Death therefore must to Him assume its most frightful form. The physical suffering was nothing compared to the immeasurable suffering of soul which impended over the Redeemer, and the full greatness and depth of which He clearly perceives. Therefore, in Heb. v. 7, "a fear" is described as that which pressed with such awful weight upon our Lord. When God freed Him from that He saved Him from death. Thus, when the suffering of Christ is apprehended as vicarious and voluntary, all the accompanying circumstances can be easily understood."

Let us note the exceeding guilt and sinfulness of sin. The thing
which made even God's own Son, who had power to work works
that none else did beside Him, groan, and cry, "My soul is
troubled," can be no light thing. He that would know the full
measure of sin and guilt should mark attentively this verse, and
the expressions used by our Lord at Gethsemane and Calvary.

It is worth noticing that this verse, Matt. xxvi. 38, and Mark
xiv. 34, are the only three places in the Gospels where our Lord
speaks of "My soul."

The word "now," I suspect, is emphatic: "Now, at this
special time, my soul has begun to be specially troubled."

[*And what shall I say?*] These words are thought by some, as
Theophylact, Grotius, Bloomfield, and Barnes, to be wrongly translated in our English version. They would render them, "And
what? What is my duty? What does the hour require of Me?
Shall I say, Save Me," etc., etc.—I much prefer our English version
as it is. I believe the question is strongly significant of the agony
and conflict through which our Lord's soul was passing.—"What
shall I say under this sense of pressing, overwhelming trouble? My
human nature bids me say one thing,—acting alone and urging me
alone. My knowledge of the purpose for which I came into the
world bids me say another thing. What then shall I say?"
Such a question as this is a strong proof of our Lord's real, true
humanity.

Rollock observes, "'What shall I say?' is the language of the
highest perplexity and anxiety of mind. In the height of anguish
is the height of perplexity, so that a man knows not what to say
or do. The Lord found deliverance in prayer. But the perpetual
cry of the lost will be, 'What shall I say? What shall I do?'
From that perplexity and anguish they will never be delivered."

Bengel remarks, "Jesus says, 'What shall I say?' not, What
shall I choose? Compare with this the different expression of St.
Paul, 'What I shall choose I wist not, for I am in a strait betwixt
two, having a desire to depart.'" (Phil. i. 22.)

Ecolampadius thinks the question means, "In what words shall
I unfold my pain, or the bitterness and ingratitude of the Jews?"
I prefer taking it as the language of perplexity and distress.

The presence of two natures in our Lord Jesus Christ's person
seems clearly taught when we compare the language used by our
Lord in this verse, with the language of the fifth and seventeenth
chapters of this Gospel. *Here* we see unmistakably our Lord's

true humanity. *There*, on the other hand, we see no less plainly His divinity. Here He speaks as man : there as God.

[*Father, save Me from this hour.*] This is undoubtedly a prayer to be saved from, or delivered from the agony and suffering of this hour. It is the language of a human nature which, though sinless, could suffer, and instinctively shrank from suffering. It would not have been real human nature if it had not so shrunk and recoiled.

The idea of the prayer is just the same as that of the prayer in Gethsemane : "Let this cup pass from Me." (Matt. xxvi. 39.)

Let us learn from our Lord's example that there is nothing sinful in praying to be delivered from suffering, so long as we do it in submission to the will of God. There is nothing wrong in a sick person saying, "Father, make me well," so long as the prayer is offered with proper qualification.

Rollock observes, "In agony there is a certain forgetfulness of all things except present pain. This seems the case of our Lord here. Yet even here He turns to His Father, showing that He never loses the sense of the Father's love. The lost in hell will never turn to the Father."

It is worth noticing that our Lord speaks of "the Father" and "My Father" at least 110 times in John's Gospel.

[*But for this cause came I unto this hour.*] This sentence is an elliptical way of declaring our Lord's entire submission to His Father's will, in the matter of the prayer He had just prayed. "But I know that for this cause I came into the world and have reached this hour, to suffer, as I am now suffering, and to agonize as I am now agonizing. I do not refuse the cup. If it be Thy will, I am willing to drink it. Only I tell Thee my feelings, with entire submission to Thy will."

We may surely learn from the whole verse that Christians have no cause to despair because they feel trouble of soul,—because they feel perplexed, and know not what to say in the agony of inward conflict,—because their nature shrinks from pain, and cries to God to take it away. In all this there is nothing wicked or sinful. It was the expression of the human nature of our Lord Jesus Christ Himself. And in Him was no sin.

Rollock says, "This is the language of one recollecting himself, and collecting his thoughts to remember something besides his agony and pain."

[*Father, glorify Thy name.*] This passage seems the conclusion

of the strife and agony of soul which came over our Lord at this
particular period. It is as though He said, "I leave the matter in
Thy hand, O my Father: do what Thou seest best. Glorify Thy
name and Thy attributes in Me: do what is meet for setting forth
Thy glory in the world. If it be for Thy glory that I should
suffer, I am willing to suffer even unto the bearing of the world's
sins."

I see in the whole event here described, a short summary of
what took place afterwards more fully at Gethsemane. There is a
remarkable parallelism at every step.

(*a*) Does our Lord say here, "My soul is troubled"? Just so
He said in Gethsemane: "My soul is exceeding sorrowful, even
unto death." (Matt. xxvi. 38.)

(*b*) Does our Lord say here, "Father, save Me from this hour"?
Just so He says in Gethsemane: "O My Father, if it be possible,
let this cup pass from Me." (Matt. xxvi. 39.)

(*c*) Does our Lord say here, "For this cause came I unto this
hour"? Just so He says in Gethsemane: "If this cup may not
pass away from Me except I drink it, Thy will be done."

(*d*) Does our Lord say, finally, "Father, glorify thy name"?
Just so our Lord says, lastly, "The cup which my Father hath
given Me, shall I not drink it?" (John xviii. 11.)

The brief prayer which our Lord here offers, we should remember,
is the highest, greatest thing that we can ask God to do. The
utmost reach of the renewed will of a believer, is to be able to
say always, "Father, glorify Thy name in Me. Do with Me what
Thou wilt, only glorify Thy name." The glory of God after all
is the end for which all things were created. Paul's joyful hope,
he told the Philippians, when a prisoner at Rome, was "that in
all things, by life or by death, Christ might be magnified in his
body." (Philip i. 20.)

Rollock says, "This is the language of one who now forgets the
agony and pain, remembers only His Father's glory, and desires it
even together with His own passion and death."—He also remarks
that the experience of God's saints in great trouble, is in a sense
much the same. For a time they forget everything but present
pain. By and by they rise above their sufferings, and remember
only God's glory.

[*Then came there a voice from heaven.*] This voice was undoubtedly a great miracle. God the Father was heard speaking audibly with man's voice to the Son. Three times in our Lord's ministry this miracle took place: first, at His baptism; secondly, at His transfiguration; thirdly, just before His crucifixion. Rarely has the voice of God been heard by large crowds of unconverted men. Here, at mount Sinai, and perhaps at our Lord's baptism, are the only three occasions on record.

Of course we can no more explain this wonderful miracle, than any other miracle in God's Word. We can only reverently believe and admire it. The intimate nearness of the Father to the Son, all through His ministry, is one of the many thoughts which may occur to our minds as we consider the miracle. Our Lord was never left alone. His Father was alway with Him, though men knew it not. How could it indeed be otherwise? So far as concerned His Divine nature, He and the Father were "one."

How any one in the face of this passage can deny that the Father and the Son are two distinct Persons, it is very hard to understand. When one person is heard speaking to another, common sense seems to point out that there are two persons, and not one.

Hammond maintains that there really was a loud clap of thunder, as well as a voice from heaven. Burkitt also seems to think the same, and compares it to the thunder which accompanied the giving of the law at Sinai.

[*I have both glorified it and will glorify it again.*] This solemn sentence,—far more solemn in the pithy and expressive Greek language than it can possibly be made in our translation,—admits, as Augustine says, of being interpreted two ways.

(*a*) It may be applied solely and entirely to the Lord Jesus Christ Himself. It would then be a special declaration of the Father to the Son. "I have glorified my name in Thy incarnation, Thy miracles, Thy words, Thy works; I will yet glorify it again in Thy voluntary suffering for mankind, Thy death, Thy resurrection, and Thy ascension."

Lightfoot thinks there is a special reference to our Lord's conflict with the devil. "I have glorified my name in the victory Thou formerly didst obtain over Satan's temptation in the wilderness. I will glorify my name again, in the victory Thou shalt have in this conflict also."

(*b*) It may be applied to the whole course of God's dealings with creation from the beginning. It would then be a declaration of the Father: "I have continually glorified my name in all the dispensations which have been,—before the flood, in the days of the Patriarchs, in the time of Moses, under the Law, under the Judges, under the Kings. I will yet glorify it once more at the end of this dispensation, by finishing up the types and figures, and accomplishing the work of man's redemption."

Which of these views is the true one, I cannot pretend to decide. Either makes excellent divinity, and is reasonable and consistent. But we have no means of ascertaining which is correct. If I have any opinion on the point I lean to the second view.

29.—[*The people therefore, etc.*] This verse apparently is meant to describe the various opinions of the crowd which stood around our Lord, about the voice which spoke to Him.—Some who were standing at some little distance, and were not listening very attentively, said it thundered. Others, who were standing close by, and paying great attention, declared that an invisible being, an angel, must have spoken.—Both parties entirely agreed on one point: something uncommon had happened. An extraordinary noise had been heard, which to some sounded like thunder, and to others like words. But nobody said they heard nothing at all.

That the voice must have been very loud, seems proved by the supposition that it was "thunder." That the reality and existence of angels formed part of the popular creed of the Jews, seems proved by the readiness of some to take up the idea that an angel had spoken.

Some think that the Greeks before mentioned, not knowing the Hebrew language, in which probably the voice spoke, fancied the voice was thunder, and the Jews of the crowd thought it an angel's voice.

30.—[*Jesus answered...This voice...not...Me...your sakes.*] In this verse our Lord tells the Jews the purpose of this miraculous voice. It was not for His sake,—to comfort Him and help Him; but for their sakes,—to be a sign and a witness to them. The voice could tell Him nothing that He did not know. It was meant to show them what they did not know or doubted.—The sentence would be more literally rendered, "Not on account of Me was this voice, but on account of you." It was just one more public miraculous evidence of His Divine mission, and apparently the last that was given. The first evidence was a voice at His baptism, and the last a voice just before His crucifixion.

Augustine remarks, "Here Christ shows that this voice was not to make known to Him what He already knew, but to them to whom it was meet to be made known."

31.—[*Now is the judgment of this world.*] This is undeniably a difficult saying. The difficulty lies principally in the meaning of the word "judgment."

(*a*) Some, as Barnes, think that it means, "This is the crisis, or most important time in the world's history." I cannot receive this. I doubt whether the Greek word used here will ever bear the signification of our word "crisis." That our Lord's atoning death was a crisis in the world's history, is undoubtedly true. But that is not the question. The question is, What do the Greek words mean?

(*b*) Some, as Theophylact, and Euthymius, think it means "Now is the vengeance of this world."—"I will cast out him by whom the world has been enslaved."—I doubt this also.

(*c*) Some, as Zwingle, think that "judgment" means the discrimination or separation between the believing and the unbelieving in the world. (Compare John ix. 39.)

(*d*) Some, as Calvin, Brentius, Beza, Bucer, Hutcheson, Flacius, and Gualter, think that "judgment" means the reformation, or setting in right order of the world.

(*e*) Some, as Grotius, Gerhard, Poole, Toletus, and à Lapide, think "judgment" means the deliverance, and setting free from bondage, of this world.

(*f*) Some, as Pearce, think it means, "Now is the Jewish world or nation about to be judged or condemned for rejecting Me."

(*g*) Some, as Bengel, think it means, "Now is the judgment concerning this world, as to who is hereafter to be the rightful possessor of it."

I take it that the word we render "judgment," can only mean condemnation, and that the meaning of the sentence is this: "Now has arrived the season when a sentence of condemnation shall be passed by my death on the whole order of things which has prevailed in the world since the creation. The world shall no longer be let alone, and left to the devil and the powers of darkness. I am about to spoil them of their dominion by my redeeming work, and to condemn and set aside the dark, godless order of things which has so long prevailed upon earth. It has long been winked at and tolerated by my Father. The time has come when it will be tolerated no longer. This very week, by my crucifixion, the religious systems of the world shall receive a sentence of condemnation." This seems the view of Bullinger and Rollock, and I agree with it.

In order to realize the full meaning of this sentence, we must call to mind the extraordinary condition of all the world with the exception of Palestine, before Christ's death. To an extent of which now we can form no conception, it was a world without God, plunged in idolatry, worshipping devils,—in open rebellion against God. (Compare 1 Cor. x. 20. When Christ died, this order of things received its sentence of condemnation.

Rollock says, "I understand by this judgment, the condemnation of that sin of which the world was so full when Christ came, and which had reigned from Adam to Moses." Of this undisturbed reign of idolatry Christ's advent made an end.

Augustine, on this verse, says, "The devil kept possession of mankind, holding men as crimnals bound over to punishment by the handwriting of their sins, having dominion in the hearts of the unbelieving, dragging them, deceived and captive, to the worship of the creature, for which they had deserted the Creator. But by the faith of Christ, confirmed by His death and resurrection, through His blood shed for the remission of sins, thousands of believing persons obtain deliverance from the dominion of the devil, are joined to the body of Christ, and quickened by His Spirit, as faithful members under so great a Head. This it was that He called *judgment.*"

[*Now shall...prince of this world...cast out.*] In this remarkable sentence, there can be no doubt that Satan is meant by the "prince of this world." Up to the time of our Lord's redeeming work, the entire world was in a certain sense completely under his domi-nion. When Christ came and died for sinners, Satan's usurped power was broken, and received a deadly blow. Heathenism and idolatry and devil worship no longer governed all the earth, except Palestine, as they had done for four thousand years, because un-disturbed. In a wonderful and mysterious manner Christ on the cross "spoiled principalities and powers, and made a show of them openly, triumphing over them." (Coloss. ii. 15.) To this victory our Lord clearly refers. "Now in this week, by my vicarious death as man's Redeemer on the cross, Satan, the prince of this world, shall receive a deadly blow, and be dethroned from his supremacy over man, and cast out. The head of the serpent shall be bruised."

Of course our Lord did not mean that Satan would be "cast out" of this world entirely, and tempt it no more. That will be done at the second advent, we know from Rev. xx. ; but it was not done at the first. It only means that he should be cast out of a large portion of the dominion, and power, and undisturbed authority he had hitherto exercised over men's souls.—The result of the change which took place in this respect, when Christ died, is perhaps not enough considered by Christians. We probably have a very inadequate idea of the awful extent to which Satan carried his dominion over men's souls, before the "kingdom of heaven" was set up. Bodily possession, familiar spirits, wizards, heathen oracles, heathen mysteries,—all these are things which before the crucifixion of Christ were much more real and powerful than we suppose. And why? Because the "prince of this world" had not yet been cast out. He had a power over men's bodies and minds far greater than he has now. When Christ came to the cross He did battle with Satan, won a victory over him, stripped him of a large portion of his authority, and cast him out of a large portion of his dominion. Does not the whole of the vision in Rev. xii. 7—17, point to this? This view is supported by Lightfoot.

This sentence shows clearly the reality and power of the devil. How any one can say there is no devil, in the face of such expressions as "the prince of this world," is strange. How any one can scoff and think lightly of a being of such mighty power, is stranger still. The true Christian, however, may always take comfort in the thought that Satan is a vanquished enemy. He was stripped of a large part of his dominion at Christ's first advent. He is still "going to and fro," seeking whom he may devour ; but he shall be completely bound at the second advent. (1 Pet. v. 8 ; Rom. xvi. 20 ; Rev. xx. 2.)

The whole verse appears to me inexplicable, unless we receive and hold the doctrine of Christ's death being an atonement and satisfaction for man's sin, and a payment of man's debt to God. That thought underlies the deep statement here made of the mighty work about to be done by our Lord, in the week of His crucifixion, against the prince of this world. Once adopt the modern notion that Christ's death was only a beautiful example of self-sacrifice and martyrdom for truth, like that of Socrates, and you can make nothing of this verse. Hold, on the other hand, the old doctrine that Christ's death was the payment of man's debt, and the redemption of man's soul from the power of sin and the devil, and the whole verse is lighted up and made comparatively clear.

Augustine observes, "the Lord in this verse was foretelling that which He knew,—that after His passion and glorifying, throughout the whole world many a people would believe, within whose hearts the devil once was, whom when by faith they renounce, then is he cast out." He also says that what formerly took place in a few hearts, like those of the patriarchs and prophets, or very few individuals, is now foretold as about to take place in many a great people.

Euthymius remarks, that as the first Adam by eating of the tree was cast out of Paradise, so the Second Adam by dying on the tree cast the devil out of his usurped dominion in the world.

Bucer thinks there is a latent reference to our Lord's former words about the "strong man armed keeping his house," till a stronger comes upon him and spoils him. (Luke xi. 21, 22.)

32.—[*And I...lifted up...draw all men unto Me.*] In this remarkable verse our Lord plainly points to His own crucifixion, or being lifted up on the cross. It is the same expression that He used to Nicodemus: "As Moses lifted up the serpent in the wilderness, even so must the Son of Man be lifted up." (John iii. 15.)

The promise, "I will draw all men unto Me," must, I think, mean that our Lord after His crucifixion would draw men of all nations and kindreds and tongues to Himself, to believe on Him and be His disciples. Once crucified, He would become a great centre of attraction, and draw to Himself, and release from the devil's usurped power, vast multitudes of all peoples and countries, to be his servants and followers. Up to this time all the world had blindly hastened after Satan and followed him. After Christ's crucifixion great numbers would turn away from the power of Satan and become Christians.

The promise doubtless looks even further than this. It points to a time when every knee shall bow to the crucified Son of God, and every tongue confess that Jesus is the Lord. The whole world shall finally become the kingdom of our God and of His Christ.

Of course the words must not be pressed too far. We must not think that they support the deadly heresy of universal salvation. We must not suppose them to mean that all men shall be actually saved by Christ's crucifixion, any more than we must suppose that Christ actually "lights" every one in the world. (See John i. 9.) The analogy of other texts shows plainly that the only reasonable sense is, that Christ's crucifixion would have a "drawing" influence on men of all nations, Gentiles as well as Jews. Scripture and facts under our eyes, both show us that all persons are not actually drawn to Christ. Many live and die and are lost in unbelief.

The word "draw" is precisely the same that is used in John vi. 44: "No man can come to Me except the Father draw him." Yet I doubt whether the meaning is precisely the same. In the one case it is the drawing of election, when the Father chooses and draws souls. In the other case, it is the drawing influence which Christ exercises on labouring and heavy-laden sinners, when He draws them by His Spirit to come to Him and believe. The subjects of either "drawing" are the same men and women, and the drawing in either case is irresistible. All who are drawn to believe are drawn both by the Father and the Son. Without this drawing no one would ever come to Christ.

The idea of some, that the verse may be applied to the "lifting up" or exalting of Christ by ministers in their *preaching*, is utterly baseless, and a mere play upon words. That the preaching of Christ will always do good, more or less, and draw souls to Christ by God's blessing, is no doubt true. But it is not the doctrine of this text, and ought to be dismissed as an unfair accommodation of Scriptural language.

Euthymius observes that the mission of Christ began to draw souls at once, as in the case of the penitent thief and the centurion.

33.—[*This He said...what death...die.*] This explanatory comment of St. John on our Lord's words is evidently intended to make His meaning plain. He spoke of "being lifted up" with a special reference to His being lifted up on the cross.—Of course it is just possible that the reference is to the drawing all men, and that it means, "He spoke of drawing all men, with a reference to His death being a sacrificial and atoning death, which would affect the position of all men." But I doubt this being so correct a view as the other.

"He should die," is literally, He was "about to die."

It is curious that, in the face of this verse, some, as Bucer and Diodati, maintain that our Lord by "being lifted up," refers to His exaltation into heaven after His resurrection. They think that then, and not till then, could He be said to "draw" men. I cannot see anything in this. Our Lord appears to me to teach plainly, that after His crucifixion, and through the virtue of His crucifixion, He would draw men. That "lifting up" means cruci-fixion, is, in my judgment, plainly taught by John iii. 15

JOHN XII. 34—43.

34 The people answered him, We have heard out of the law that Christ abideth for ever: and how sayest thou, The Son of man must be lifted up? who is this Son of man?

35 Then Jesus said unto them, Yet a little while is the light with you. Walk while ye have the light, lest darkness come upon you; for he that walketh in darkness knoweth not whither he goeth.

36 While ye have light, believe in the light, that ye may be the children of light. These things spake Jesus, and departed, and did hide himself from them.

37 But though he had done so many miracles before them, yet they believed not on him:

38 That the saying of Esaias the prophet might be fulfilled, which he spake,

Lord, who hath believed our report! and to whom hath the arm of the Lord been revealed?

39 Therefore they could not believe, because that Esaias said again,

40 He hath blinded their eyes, and hardened their heart; that they should not see with *their* eyes, nor understand with *their* heart, and be converted, and I should heal them.

41 These things said Esaias, when he saw his glory, and spake of him.

42 Nevertheless among the chief rulers also many believed on him: but because of the Pharisees they did not confess *him*, lest they should be put out of the synagogue:

43 For they loved the praise of men more than the praise of God.

WE may learn, from these verses, the *duty of using present opportunities*. The Lord Jesus says to us all, "Yet a little while is the light with you. Walk while ye have the light, lest darkness come upon you.—While ye have light believe in the light." Let us not think that these things were only spoken for the sake of the Jews. They were written for us also, upon whom the ends of the world are come.

The lesson of the words is generally applicable to the whole professing Church of Christ. Its time for doing good in the world is short and limited. The throne of grace will not always be standing: it will be removed one day, and the throne of judgment will be set up in its place. The door of salvation by faith in Christ will not always be open: it will be shut one day for ever, and the number of God's elect will be completed. The fountain for all sin and uncleanness will not always be accessible: the way to it will one day be barred, and there will remain nothing but the lake that burns with fire and brimstone.

These are solemn thoughts : but they are true. They cry aloud to sleeping Churchmen and drowsy congregations, and ought to arouse great searchings of heart. "Can nothing more be done to spread the Gospel at home and abroad ? Has every means been tried for extending the knowledge of Christ crucified ? Can we lay our hands on our hearts, and say that the Churches have left nothing undone in the matter of missions ? Can we look forward to the Second Advent with no feelings of humiliation, and say that the talents of wealth and influence and opportunities have not been buried in the ground ?"—Such questions may well humble us, when we look, on one side, at the state of professing Christendom, and, on the other, at the state of the heathen world. We must confess with shame that the Church is not walking worthy of its light.

But the lesson of the words is specially applicable to ourselves as individuals.   Our own time for getting good is short and limited ; let us take heed that we make a good use of it. Let us "walk while we have the light." Have we Bibles ? Let us not neglect to read them.—Have we the preached Gospel ? Let us not linger halting between two opinions, but believe to the saving of our souls.—Have we Sabbaths ? Let us not waste them in idleness, carelessness, and indifference, but throw our whole hearts into their sacred employments, and turn them to good account.—Light is about us and around us and near us on every side. Let us each resolve to walk in the light while we have it, lest we find ourselves at length cast out into outer darkness for ever. It is a true saying of an old divine, that the recollection of lost and mis-spent opportunities will be the very essence of hell.

We may learn, secondly, from these verses, *the desperate hardness of the human heart.* It is written of our Lord's hearers at Jerusalem, that "though He had done so many miracles before them, yet they believed not on Him."

We err greatly if we suppose that seeing wonderful things will ever convert souls. Thousands live and die in this delusion. They fancy if they saw some miraculous sight, or witnessed some supernatural exercise of Divine grace, they would lay aside their doubts, and at once become decided Christians. It is a total mistake. Nothing short of a new heart and a new nature implanted in us by the Holy Ghost, will ever make us real disciples of Christ. Without this, a miracle might raise within us a little temporary excitement; but, the novelty once gone, we should find ourselves just as cold and unbelieving as the Jews.

The prevalence of unbelief and indifference in the present day ought not to surprise us. It is just one of the evidences of that mighty foundation doctrine, the total corruption and fall of man. How feebly we grasp and realize that doctrine is proved by our surprise at human incredulity. We only half believe the heart's deceitfulness. Let us read our Bibles more attentively, and search their contents more carefully. Even when Christ wrought miracles and preached sermons, there were numbers of His hearers who remained utterly unmoved. What right have we to wonder if the hearers of modern sermons in countless instances remain un-believing ? " The disciple is not greater than his Master." If even the hearers of Christ did not believe, how much more should we expect to find unbelief among the hearers of His ministers. Let the truth be spoken and confessed. Man's obstinate unbelief is one among many indirect proofs that the Bible is true. The clearest prophecy in Isaiah begins with the solemn question, " Who hath believed ? " (Isai. liii. 1.)

We may learn, thirdly, from these verses, *the amazing power which the love of the world has over men.* We read that "among the chief rulers many believed on Christ : but because of the Pharisees they did not confess Him, least they should be put out of the synagogue. For they loved the praise of men more than the praise of God."

These unhappy men were evidently convinced that Jesus was the true Messiah. Reason, and intellect, and mind, and conscience, obliged them secretly to admit that no one could do the miracles which He did, unless God was with Him, and that the preacher of Nazareth really was the Christ of God. But they had not courage to confess it. They dared not face the storm of ridicule, if not of persecution, which confession would have entailed. And so, like cowards, they held their peace, and kept their convictions to themselves.

Their case, it may be feared, is a sadly common one. There are thousands of people who know far more in religion than they act up to. They know they ought

to come forward as decided Christians.   They know
that they are not living up to their light.   But the fear
of man keeps them back.   They are afraid of being
laughed at, jeered at, and despised by the world.   They
dread losing the good opinion of society, and the favourable judgment of men and women like themselves.   And
so they go on from year to year, secretly ill at ease and
dissatisfied with themselves,—knowing too much of
religion to be happy in the world, and clinging too
much to the world to enjoy any religion.

Faith is the only cure for soul ailments like this.
A believing view of an unseen God, an unseen Christ,
an unseen heaven, and an unseen judgment day,—this
is the grand secret of overcoming the fear of man.   The
expulsive power of a new principle is required to heal
the disease.   "This is the victory that overcometh the
world, even our faith."   (1 John v. 4.)   Let us pray for
faith, if we would conquer those deadly enemies of souls,
the fear of man and the love of man's praise.   And if
we have any faith, let us pray for more.   Let our daily
cry be, "Lord, increase our faith."   We may easily have
too much money, or too much worldly prosperity.   But
we can never have too much faith.

NOTES.   JOHN XII. 34—43.

34.—[*The people answered, etc.*]   This verse supplies a remarkable
   instance of the perverse and hardened blindness of the Jews in our
   Lord's time.   They pretended to be unable to reconcile the Lord's
   language about being "lifted up," with the Old Testament prophecies about the eternity and never dying of Christ.—That "lifted
   up" meant being put to death on the cross, they seem to have
   understood.   That our Lord, or the Son of man, as He called

Himself, claimed to be the Christ, they quite understood. What they stumbled at was the idea of the eternal Christ being put to death. They had got hold of the idea of a glorious, eternal Messiah. They had not got hold of the idea of a suffering, dying Messiah.

Of course they were right in holding that "Christ abideth for ever." It is the universal doctrine of the Old Testament. (Compare Isa. ix. 7; Psalm cx. 4; Ezek. xxxvii. 25; Daniel vii. 14; Micah iv. 7.) Our Lord had never for a moment denied this. He was the promised Saviour, who as Gabriel said to Mary, was to "reign over the house of Jacob for ever." (Luke i. 33.)

On the other hand, they were entirely wrong in not understanding that Christ had to suffer before He reigned, and to go to the cross before He wore the crown. They were wrong in not seeing that His sacrifice as our Substitute and our Passover, was the very corner-stone of revealed religion, and that the very "law" of which they made so much, pointed to His sacrifice as clearly as to His eternal glory. They forgot that Isaiah says that Messiah is to be "brought as a lamb to the slaughter," and that Daniel speaks of His being "cut off." (Isai. liii. 7; Dan. ix. 26.)

The words "we" and "thou," in this verse, in the Greek are emphatic. "WE Jews have always been taught to believe the eternity of Messiah. THOU, on the other hand, sayest that Messiah must be put to death, and lifted up on the cross. How is this? How are we to understand it?"

"The law," in this verse, must evidently be taken for the whole of the Old Testament Scriptures.

It is worthy of remark that the Jews charge our Lord with saying "the Son of man must be lifted up." Yet our Lord in the last verse but one had not mentioned the Son of man, but had only said, "I, if I be lifted up."—It is also singular that our Lord nowhere uses the expression "lifted up" except in His conversation with Nicodemus, in John iii. 14. We must therefore either suppose that the Jews referred to the saying of Christ when He spoke to Nicodemus (which is very unlikely); or else that the expression, "The Son of man must be lifted up," was so frequently on our Lord's lips, that the Jews caught it up and pressed it on Him here; or else that our Lord so frequently spoke of Himself as the Son of man, that when He said, "If I be lifted up," the Jews thought it equivalent to saying, "If the Son of man be lifted up."

The question, "Who is this Son of man?" can hardly imply that the Jews did not know that Christ was speaking of Himself. Does it not rather mean, "Who, and what kind of a Person dost Thou claim to be, calling Thyself the Son of man, and yet talking of being lifted up on the cross? Dost Thou really mean that one and the same person can be a dying person, and yet also the eternal Christ? Dost thou claim to be the eternal Christ, and yet talk of being lifted up on a cross? Explain this apparent contradiction, for we cannot understand it."—It is just the old story over again. The Jews could not and would not understand that Messiah was to suffer as well as to reign, to die as a Sacrifice as well as to appear in glory. They could not and would not see that the two things could be reconciled, and could meet in one person. Hence their perplexity exhibited in the question of the text.

The title, "Son of man," is first found applied to Messiah in Daniel vii. 13. We cannot doubt that the Jews understood and remembered that passage.

Let us note that a half knowledge of Scripture, a suppression of some texts, and a misapplication of other texts, will account for a large portion of mistakes in religion. In this way people get a heresy or a crotchet into their heads on some doctrinal point, and seem blind to the truth. No heresies are so obstinately defended, and so difficult to meet, as those which are based on a perverted view of some portion of Scripture. In reading our Bibles we must be careful to give every part and portion its due weight.

Let us remember, before we judge the blindness of the Jews too severely in this place, that many Christians are just as slow to see the whole truth about the second advent of Christ and His coming glory, as the Jews were to see the whole truth about the first advent and the cross. Multitudes apply texts to the first advent which only belong to the second advent, and are just as much prejudiced against the second personal coming of Christ to reign, as the Jews were against the first personal advent to suffer. Not a few Christians, I fear, are ready to say, "We have heard out of the Scriptures that Christ was to come in humiliation to be crucified; and how say ye, then, that Christ must come in power to reign?"

The expression, "this," is rather emphatic, and has something contemptuous about it. "We have heard of a Son of man who is eternal. Who is THIS Son of man about to be lifted up on the cross, of whom you speak?"

35.—[*Then Jesus said unto them...light with you.*] It is noteworthy, that our Lord makes no direct answer to the question of the Jews. He only warns them in a very solemn manner, of the danger they were in of letting their day of grace slip away unimproved. He draws a figure from the light of day, and the acknowledged importance of walking and journeying while we have the light. By "the light" He evidently means Himself. "I, the Light of the world, am only going to be with you a very little longer. My day is drawing to a close. The sun will soon set." (Compare Jer. xiii. 15.)

Here, as elsewhere, we see how clearly and distinctly our Lord saw His own approaching death and withdrawal from the world.

Ecolampadius thinks that there is a latent connection between this verse and the question of the Jews. "You ask who is this Son of man? I reply that He is the Light of the world, as I have often told you. Like the sun, He is about to be eclipsed, or withdrawn from your eyes very shortly. Make haste, and delay not to believe on Him."

Gerhard justly remarks on this sentence, how far from infallibility the best of the Fathers were. Even Augustine, from his slight acquaintance with Greek, renders the sense, "There is yet a *little light* in your *hearts!*"

A German commentator remarks, that Christ seems here to rebuke this quibbling and questioning about phrases. "There was no time now for sophistry and circumlocution. It was a solemn matter. How differently ought they to demean themselves in their little residue of time, and not to fritter it away with affected contradictions! How earnestly they ought to seek at once for refuge to the light, and shield themselves against coming darkness?"

[*Walk while ye have the light.*] This solemn exhortation was meant to urge the Jews to do for their soul's safety what a wise traveller would do to get safely to his journey's end. "Enter in at the strait gate: walk in the narrow way: flee from the city of destruction: set out on your journey towards eternal life: rise, and be moving, while I and my Gospel are close to you, shining on you, and within your reach."

Hengstenberg remarks, that "walking here denotes activity, and stands opposed to an idle and indifferent rest."

[*Lest darkness come upon you.*] Our Lord here warns the Jews of the things to be feared, if they neglected his advice. Darkness would overtake, catch, and come upon them. He would leave the world, and return to His Father. They would be left in a state of judicial darkness and blindness as a nation, and with the exception of an election, would be given over to untold calamities, scattering, and misery. How true these words were we know from the history of the Jews written by Josephus, after our Lord left the world. His account of the extraordinary state of the inhabitants of Jerusalem, during the siege of the city by Titus, is the best commentary on the text before us. The state of the Jews, as a nation, during the last days of Jerusalem, can only be described as "darkness that might be felt."

[*For he...darkness...knoweth not...goeth.*] This is an argument drawn from the acknowledged helplessness of one who attempts a difficult journey in a dark night. He cannot see his way. He only gets into trouble, and perhaps loses his life. This was exactly the case of the Jewish nation, after our Lord left the world. Up to the time of the destruction of the temple, they seemed like a nation of madmen, and a people judicially blinded,—conscious that they were in a wrong position, struggling furiously to get out of it, and yet only plunging deeper into the mire of hopeless misery, till Titus took the city, and carried the whole race into captivity. They had put out their own eyes by rejecting Christ, and were like a strong man blinded, maddened by a sense of his own misery, and yet impotent to get out of it.

36.—[*While light...believe...children of light.*] This sentence would have been more accurately rendered, "While ye have THE Light ;" that is, "while ye have ME, the Light of the world, with you." It is a final, affectionate entreaty to the Jews, repeating in more plain words the exhortation of the last verse, "To walk in the light." It is as though our Lord said, "Once more I beseech you to believe in Me as the Light of the world, while I am with you." The end and object for which they are to believe is also added, "That ye may become my children, have light in your hearts, light in your consciences, light in your lives, light on your present path, light in your future prospects." There can be no doubt that the expression "children of light" is a Hebraism, signifying, "to be brought in close connection with or under the full influence of light."

Let us note that here, as elsewhere, believing is the first step, —the one thing needful. The exhortation is still to be offered to every sinner, directly and personally : "Believe, that thou mayest be a child of light."

[*These things...spake...departed.. hide...them.*] We know not exactly on what day in the last week of our Lord's life the words just recorded had been spoken. The sentence before us certainly seems to mark a break and interval, and we can hardly suppose that the short address from the forty-fourth verse to the end of the chapter was spoken the same day, or was continuously connected with the discourse ending in this verse.

To me it seems probable that our Lord "departed" to Bethany after the miracle of the Voice from the heavens, and the commotion that followed it.—The words of our English version "Did hide Himself," seem to me rather stronger than the Greek warrants. It would be more literally, "Was concealed from them." Whether this was by miracle, as on other occasions, is not clear.

Calvin seems to think that our Lord only departed from the hearers immediately round Him, and went to the temple, where He met with another audience of a more believing kind. Flacius, too, thinks it was only a short and temporary withdrawal. Poole on the contrary takes the view that I adopt, and says that our Lord withdrew to Bethany.

37.—[*But though...so many miracles...them.*] This verse begins a long parenthetical comment which John was inspired to make at this point, on the peculiar unbelief of the Jerusalem Jews. He remarks on the singular hardness of this section of the nation, in the face of the singularly strong evidence which they enjoyed of Christ's Messiahship.

The expression, "So many miracles," seem to point out that the miracles recorded by St. John are by no means all the miracles that our Lord performed in and near Jerusalem. Beside the purifying of the temple, John only records three,—the healing of the impotent man, the healing of the blind, and the raising of Lazarus. (John v., ix., xi.) Yet John expressly speaks of *miracles* (both here, and in John ii. 23); and the Pharisees say, "This Man doeth many miracles." (John xi. 47.)

The Greek word rendered "before," is very strong. It is the same that is "In the sight of," in 1 Thess. i. 3; and "In the presence of," in 1 Thess. ii. 19.

[*Yet they believed not on Him.*] In estimating the peculiar hardness and unbelief of the Jews at Jerusalem, it is worth remembering that all experience proves that where there is the greatest quantity of the form of religion, there is often the greatest proportion of formality and unbelief. The places where men become most familiar with the outside and ceremonial of Chistianity are precisely the places where the heart seems to become most hard. Witness the state of Rome at this day. Witness too often the state of cathedral cities in our own land. We need not wonder that the city in which was the temple, the daily sacrifice, and the priesthood, was the most unbelieving place in Palestine.

38.—[*That.. saying...Esaias...fulfilled...spake.*] We must not suppose this means that the Jews did not believe, *in order that* the prophecy of Isaiah might be fulfilled. This would be teaching sheer fatalism. and would destroy man's responsibility. The true meaning is, " So that by this unbelief the saying of Isaiah was fulfilled." (See John **v.** 20 ; Rom. v. 20 ; 2 Cor. i. 17.)

Chrysostom observes, "It was not because Isaiah spake that they believed not, but because they were not about to believe, that he spake."

Augustine says, "The Lord, by the Prophet, did predict the unbelief of the Jews,—predict, however, not cause. It does not follow that the Lord compels any man to sin, because He knows men's future sins."

Theophylact and Euthymius say much the same.

[*Lord, who...believed our report.*] This question begins the well known fifty-third chapter of Isaiah, which describes with such extraordinary accuracy our Lord's sufferings. It is certainly a most singular fact, that the very chapter which the Jews in every age have been most obstinately unwilling to believe, should begin with this question. It is a Hebraism tanamount to saying, "Nobody believes our report." The unbelief of the Jews was a thing as clearly foretold in Scripture as the sufferings of Christ. If they had not been unbelieving the Scriptures would have been untrue.

[*To whom...arm of...Lord revealed.*] The expression, "Arm of the Lord," is thought by Augustine to mean Christ Himself. It may be so. If not, it must mean, "To whom is the Lord's power in raising up a Redeemer and an atoning sacrifice revealed?" That is, the Lord's power is revealed to and received by none. The question here again is a Hebraism, equivalent to an assertion.

Bullinger observes, that "some might perhaps wonder that the

Jews did not believe Jesus to be the Messiah. To this John replies, that Isaiah long ago foretold that they would prove an unreasonable and unbelieving nation."

The quotation of Isaiah in this place is strong evidence that the fifty-third chapter of his prophecy applies to Christ, and none else.

39.—[*Therefore they could not believe, because, etc.*] This is undeniably a difficult verse. It cannot of course mean that the Jews were unable to believe, although really desirous to do so, and were prevented by the prophecy of Isaiah. What then can it mean? The following paraphrase is offered. "This was the cause why they could not believe : they were in that state of judicial blindness and hardness which Isaiah had described ; they were justly given over to this state because of their many sins : and for this cause they had no power to believe."

"Therefore," is literally, "on account of this." It cannot, I think, look backward, but forward. (Compare 10, 17, and 12, 18.)

"They could not," is literally, "they were not able." It precisely describes the moral inability of a thoroughly hardened and wicked man to believe. He is thoroughly under the mastery of a hardened and seared conscience, and has, as it were, lost the power of believing.—They had no will to believe, and so they had no power. They could have believed if they would, but they would not, and so they could not.—The expression is parallel to the well known words, "No man can come to Me, except the Father which hath sent Me draw him." There the meaning is, "No man has any will to come unless he is drawn, and so no man can come."

Even in our own English language the expression, "could not," is sometimes used in the sense of "would not." Thus the brethren of Joseph "hated him, and could not speak peaceably unto him." (Gen. xxxvii. 4.)

The word "because" is a needlessly strong rendering of the Greek. It would be just as correctly translated, "for."

Chrysostom observes, "In many places Christ is wont to term choice, power. So, "The world *cannot* hate you, but Me it hateth." So in common conversation a man says, "I cannot love this or that person," calling the force of his will power.

Augustine says, "If I be asked why they could not believe, I answer in a word, Because they would not."—He also says, "It is said of the Omnipotent, He *cannot* deny Himself : and this is the power of the Divine will. So 'they could not believe' is the fault of the human will."

Zwingle also says that "could not" means "would not."

Ecolampadius observes, "They would not, and therefore they could not believe. God is wont to punish those who commit some sin by giving them up to other sins." This, he remarks is the heaviest judgment to which we can be given up,—to have sins punished by sins; that is, by being let alone to commit them.

Bishop Hall says, "They could not believe because, as Isaiah says, in a just punishment for their maliciousness and contempt, God had stricken them with a reprobate sense, so that their eyes were blinded."

Quesnel says here, "Let us bewail this inability of will, with which by means of Adam's sin we are all born, and which by our own sins we daily increase. Let us continually have recourse to Him who said, 'Without Me ye can do nothing,' and, 'No man can come to Me, unless the Father draw him.'"

10.—[*He hath blinded their eyes, etc.*] This quotation is a free paraphrase of the general view of a verse in Isaiah vi. 9, 10. I think it can only have one meaning. That meaning is, that "God had given over the Jews to judicial blindness, as a punishment for their long continued and obstinate rejection of His warnings." That God does in some cases give people over, as a punishment for obstinate unbelief, and that He may be justly termed the cause of such unbelief, is I think quite plain in Scripture. Pharaoh is a case in point. He obstinately refused God's warnings, and so at last He was given over, and God is said to have "hardened his heart." Compare Joshua xi. 20: "It was of the Lord to harden their hearts, that they should come against Israel in battle, that He might destroy them." (So Deut. ii. 30; 1 Sam. ii. 25; Rom. ix. 18.)

This is no doubt a very solemn and awful subject. It seems at first sight to make God the author of man's destruction. But surely a moment's reflection will show us that God is a Sovereign in punishing, and may punish in any way He pleases. Some He cuts off suddenly the moment they sin. Others He gives over to judicial blindness, and ceases to strive with their consciences. "The Judge of all the earth will certainly do right." Those whom He is said to "harden and blind" will always be found to be persons whom He had previously warned, exhorted, and constantly summoned to repent. And never is He said to harden and blind, and give men up to judicial hardness and blindness, till after a long course of warnings. This was certainly the case with Pharaoh and with the Jews.

The consequence of God blinding and hardening a person, is that he does not "see" his danger with his eyes, or "understand" his position with his heart. The result is that he holds on his way unconverted, and dies without his soul's disease being healed. "Seeing" and "understanding" are essential parts of conversion. No simpler reason can be given why myriads of church-goers continue careless, unaffected, unmoved, and unconverted: they neither "see" nor "understand." God alone can give them seeing eyes and understanding hearts, and ministers cannot. And one solemn reason why many live and die in this state is, that they have resisted God's warnings, and are justly punished already with a judicial blindness and hardness, by Him whom they have resisted.

The key to the whole difficulty, after all, lies in the answer we are prepared to give to the question, "Is God just in punishing the sinner?"—The true Christian and honest Bible reader will find no difficulty in answering that question in the affirmative. Once grant that God is just in punishing the ungodly, and there is an end of the problem. God may punish by giving over the obstinate sinner to a reprobate mind, as really as by sentencing him to everlasting fire at the last day.

One thing only must never be forgotten. God "willeth not the death of any sinner." He is willing to soften the hardest heart, and to open the blind eyes of the greatest sinner. In dealing with men about their souls we must never forget this. We may well remind them that by hardened impenitence they may provoke God to give them up. But we must also press on them that God's mercies in Christ are infinite, and that if they are finally lost, they will have none but themselves to blame.

Burgon thinks that the nominative to "blinded" at the beginning of the verse is not God, but "the Jewish people;" and that the meaning is, "This people hath blinded their own eyes." But I cannot see that this idea can be supported by reference to Isaiah, and though it smooths over difficulties, I dare not receive it.

Calvin thinks that the passage applies to the hardness by which God punishes the wickedness of an ungrateful people. They are given over justly to an unbelieving and judicially blinded state of mind.

Poole observes, "We have this text, than which there is none more terrible, no less than six times quoted in the New Testament. In all places it is quoted and given as a reason for the Jews' unbelief in Christ. (Matt. xiii. 14, 15; Mark iv. 12; Luke viii. 10; Acts xxviii. 26, 27; Rom. xi. 8.) It is not quoted alike in all places, but for substance it is the same. In the original, Isaiah is made the instrumental cause. Matthew and Luke, in Acts, mention the people themselves as the cause. All the other texts speak of it as God's act. The thing is easily reconciled."— He then says, "The Jews first shut their own eyes, and hardened their own hearts. Thus behaving themselves, God judicially gave them up to their own lusts, permitted their hearts to harden, and suffered them to close their own eyes, so that they could not repent, believe, or return. God did not infuse any malice into their hearts, but withdrew His grace from them."

Rollock makes the wise and deep remark, that "Darkness does not blind men so much as light, unless God renews their minds by His Spirit."

It is of course noteworthy that this quotation is not given literally and exactly as it stands in the Old Testament. But it is particularly mentioned by Surenhusius, in his book upon the quotations in the New Testament, that it was a common thing with the Hebrew doctors to abbreviate texts in quoting them, and to be content with giving the general sense. The abbreviation, therefore, in the text quoted before us, would not strike John's contemporaries as at all extraordinary.

Let us not fail to remark how "seeing, understanding, being converted, and being healed," are linked together.

41.—[*These things...Esaias.. his glory.. him.*] To see the full force of this verse we should read the sixth chapter of Isaiah in its entirety. We should there see a magnificent description of the Lord's glory, before which even the seraphim veiled their faces. We should observe their cry, "Holy, holy, is the Lord of Hosts!" We should mark how Isaiah says, "My eyes have seen the King, the Lord of Hosts." And then let us remember that John says, "Esaias saw Christ's glory, and spake of Christ!"—How any one, in the face of this evidence, can say that Jesus Christ is not very God. it seems hard to understand.

Lightfoot thinks that Isaiah in this chapter had a view of the glory which our Lord would have when He came to punish the Jewish nation. He thinks this is pointed out by "the posts of the door being shaken;" by "the temple being filled with smoke;" and by "the cities being wasted." (See Isaiah vi.)

42—. [*Nevertheless...rulers.. many believed Him.*] Here St. John mentions a fact which he would have us take together with his account of the hardened unbelief of most of the Jews. There were some who were not so utterly hardened as the rest. They were in a different state of mind : not blind, but convinced ; not hardened against our Lord, but secretly persuaded that He was the Christ. Many even of the chief people at Jerusalem believed, in their own secret minds, that Jesus was the Christ. This faith no doubt was only the faith of the head, and not of the heart. But they did believe.

Let us note that there is often far more going on in people's minds than preachers are aware of. There is much secret conviction.

[*But because...Pharisees...not confess Him.*] They dared not openly confess their faith in our Lord, for fear of the persecution of the Pharisees. They were cowards, and influenced by the fear of man. No wonder that our Lord spoke so strongly in other places about the duty of confessing Him.

[*Lest ..put out of...synagogue.*] The thing that they feared was excommunication. We can have little idea perhaps of the extreme dread with which a Jew regarded exclusion from the visible Jewish Church. Unlike ourselves, he knew no other Church in the whole world. To be shut out of this Church was equivalent to being shut out of heaven. The dread of excommunication in the Irish Catholic Church is perhaps the nearest thing to it in our days.

43.—[*For...loved...praise...man more...God.*] St. John here tells us plainly the prevailing motive in the minds of the cowardly Jews. They loved above everything to be well thought of by their fellow-men. They thought more of having the good opinion of man than the praise of God. They could not bear the idea of being laughed at, ridiculed, reviled, or persecuted by their fellow-men. To keep in with them and have their praise, they sacrificed their own convictions, and acted contrary to their conscience. How much this feeling injures the soul, is shown by our Lord's words in a former place : "How can ye believe which receive honour one from another?" (John v. 44.)

Let us remember that all over the world the same miserable motive is still ruining myriads of souls. "The fear of man

bringeth a snare." (Prov. xxix. 25.) Nothing seems so difficult
to overcome as the desire of pleasing man, keeping in with man,
and retaining man's praise. Nothing will overcome it but thorough
faith. "This is the victory that overcometh the world, even our
faith." (1 John v. 4.) The expulsive power of a new principle,
making us see God, Christ, heaven, hell, judgment, eternity, as
realities, is the grand secret of getting the victory over the fear of
man.

Poole says, "They were not willing to part with their great
places in the magistracy, which brought them respect, honour,
and applause from men. They valued this more than God's praise."

JOHN XII. 44—50.

44 Jesus cried and said, He that believeth on me, believeth not on me, but on him that sent me.

45 And he that seeth me seeth him that sent me.

46 I am come a light into the world, that whosoever believeth on me should not abide in darkness.

47 And if any man hear my words, and believe not, I judge him not: for I came not to judge the world, but to save the world.

48 He that rejecteth me, and receiveth not my words, hath one that judgeth him: the word that I have spoken, the same shall judge him in the last day.

49 For I have not spoken of myself: but the Father which sent me, he gave me a commandment, what I should say, and what I should speak.

50 And I know that his commandment is life everlasting: whatsoever I speak therefore, even as the Father said unto me, so I speak.

THESE verses throw light on two subjects which we can
never understand too well. Our daily peace and our
practice of daily watchfulness over ourselves, are closely
connected with a clear knowledge of these two subjects.

One thing shown in these verses is, *the dignity of our
Lord Jesus Christ*. We find Him saying, "He that
seeth Me, seeth Him that sent Me. I am come a Light
into the world, that whosoever believeth on Me should
not abide in darkness." Christ's oneness with the Father,
and Christ's office, are clearly exhibited in these words.

Concerning the unity of the Father and the Son, we
must be content to believe reverently what we cannot
grasp mentally or explain distinctly. Let it suffice us

to know that our Saviour was not like the prophets and
patriarchs, a man sent by God the Father, a friend of
God, and a witness for God.   He was something far
higher and greater than this.   He was in His Divine
nature essentially one with the Father; and in seeing
Him, men saw the Father that sent Him.   This is a
great mystery, but a truth of vast importance to our
souls.   He that casts His sins on Jesus Christ by faith
is building on a rock.   Believing on Christ, he believes
not merely on Him, but on Him that sent Him.

Concerning the office of Christ, there can be little
doubt that in this place He compares Himself to the
sun.   Like the sun, He has risen on this sin-darkened
world with healing on His wings, and shines for the
common benefit of all mankind.   Like the sun, He is
the great source and centre of all spiritual life, comfort,
and fertility.   Like the sun, He illuminates the whole
earth, and no one need miss the way to heaven, if he
will only use the light offered for his acceptance.

For ever let us make much of Christ in all our religion.   We can never trust Him too much, follow Him
too closely, or commune with Him too unreservedly.
He has all power in heaven and earth.   He is able to
save to the uttermost all who come to God by Him.
None can pluck us cut of the hand of Him who is one
with the Father.   He can make all our way to heaven
bright and plain and cheerful, like the morning sun
cheering the traveller.   Looking unto Him, we shall
find light in our understandings, see light on the path
of life we have to travel, feel light in our hearts, and

find the days of darkness which will come sometimes, stripped of half their gloom. Only let us abide in Him, and look to Him with a single eye. There is a mine of meaning in His words, "If thine eye be single, thy whole body shall be full of light." (Matt. vi. 22.)

Another thing shown in these verses is, *the certainty of a judgment to come.* We find our Lord saying, " He that rejecteth Me, and receiveth not my words, hath One that judgeth Him : the word that I have spoken, the same shall judge him in the last day."

There is a last day ! The world shall not always go on as it does now. Buying and selling, sowing and reaping, planting and building, marrying and giving in marriage,—all this shall come to an end at last. There is a time appointed by the Father when the whole machinery of creation shall stop, and the present dispensation shall be changed for another. It had a beginning, and it shall also have an end. Banks shall at length close their doors for ever. Stock exchanges shall be shut. Parliaments shall be dissolved. The very sun, which since Noah's flood has done his daily work so faithfully, shall rise and set no more. Well would it be if we thought more of this day ? Rent days, birth days, wedding days, are often regarded as days of absorbing interest. But they are nothing compared to the last day.

There is a judgment coming ! Men have their reckoning days, and God will at last have His. The trumpet shall sound. The dead shall be raised incorruptible. The living shall be changed. All, of every name and nation, and people and tongue, shall stand before the judgment-seat of Christ. The books shall be opened, and the evidence brought forth. Our true character will come out before the world. There will be no concealment, no evasion, no false colouring. Every one shall give account of Himself to God, and all shall be judged according to their works. The wicked shall go away into everlasting fire, and the righteous into life eternal.

These are awful truths! But they are truths, and ought to be told. No wonder that the Roman governor Felix trembled when Paul the prisoner discoursed about "righteousness, temperance, and judgment to come." (Acts xxiv. 25.) Yet the believer in the Lord Jesus Christ has no cause to be afraid. For him, at any rate, there is no condemnation, and the last assize need have no terrors. The bias of his life shall witness for him; while the shortcomings of his life shall not condemn him. It is the man who rejects Christ, and will not hear His call to repentance,—he is the man who in the judgment day will have reason to be cast down and afraid.

Let the thought of judgment to come have a practical effect on our religion. Let us daily judge ourselves with righteous judgment, that we may not be judged and condemned of the Lord. Let us so speak and so act as men who will be judged by the law of liberty. (James ii. 12.) Let us make conscience of all our hourly conduct, and never forget that for every idle word we must give account at the last day. In a word, let us live like those who believe in the truth of judgment, heaven, and hell. So living we shall be Christians indeed and in truth, and have boldness in the day of Christ's appearing.

Let the judgment day be the Christian's answer and apology when men ridicule him as too strict, too precise, and too particular in his religion. Irreligion may do tolerably well for a season, so long as a man is in health and prosperous, and looks at nothing but this world. But he who believes that he must give account to the Judge of quick and dead, at His appearing and kingdom, will never be content with an ungodly life. He will say, "There is a judgment. I can never serve God too much. Christ died for me. I can never do too much for Him."

NOTES. JOHN XII. 44—50.

44.—[*Jesus cried and said.*] The connection between the address which begins here and the preceding verse, is not very plain or easy to understand.

Some think that it is a continuation of the address which ended at the thirty-sixth verse, and that John's comment and explanation in the last seven verses must be regarded entirely as a parenthesis. This is rather an awkward supposition, when we look at the thirty-sixth verse, and see at the end, "These words spake Jesus and departed, and did hide Himself." Unless we suppose that as He was walking away, "He cried and said, He that believeth on Me," etc., the connection seems incapable of proof. Yet it appears most unlikely that our Lord would have said such things as He was departing.

Others, as Theophylact, think that the address before us is an entirely new and distinct one, and delivered on a different day from that ending at the thirty-sixth verse: viz., on the Tuesday, Wednesday, or Thursday, in Passion Week. This certainly appears to me the least difficult view of the subject. It would then mean that the day after the miracle of the voice from heaven, Jesus appeared again publicly in Jerusalem, and "cried and said."

However, it is useless to deny that the abrupt manner in which the verse before us and the following verses come in is a difficulty, and one which we know not exactly how to explain. One thing only is very clear : this was probably one of the last public discourses which our Lord delivered in Jerusalem, and forms a kind of conclusion to His ministry in that city. It is a short but solemn winding up of all His public testimony to the Jews.

It deserves notice, that some, as Tittman, Stier, Olshausen, Tholuck, Bloomfield, and Alford, consider the whole of the passage, from verse forty-four to the end of the chapter, to be not the words of Jesus Christ, but a statement of John the Evangelist himself, concerning the doctrine Jesus taught throughout His ministry, and specially at Jerusalem. From this view, however, I strongly dissent. The beginning, "Jesus cried," etc., seems utterly inconsistent with the theory. There seems no special necessity for adopting it. A plain reader of the chapter would never dream of it.

It is worth remarking, that the Greek expression, "He cried," is very seldom applied to our Lord in the New Testament. It is found in Matt. xxvii. 50; Mark xv. 39; John vii. 28—37, and here. In every instance it means a loud cry, such as any one uses to call attention to what he has to say.

Flacius thinks that the address beginning here is a kind of peroration and summing up of all our Lord's public teaching to the Jews. In it He repeats the proclamation of His own Divine office and dignity,—the purpose for which He came, to be a "light,"—the danger of neglecting His testimony,—the certainty of a final judgment,—and the direct procession of His doctrine from the Father.

[*He that believeth...Me...him that sent Me.*] This remarkable expression seems meant to proclaim for the last time, the great truth so often insisted on by our Lord,—the entire unity between Himself and the Father. Once more Jesus declares that there is such a complete and mysterious oneness between Himself and the Father, that he who believes on Him, believes not only on Him, but on Him that sent Him.—Of course the sentence cannot literally mean that the man who believes on Christ, does *not* believe on Christ. But according to a mode of speech not uncommon in the New Testament, our Lord taught that all who in obedience to His call put their trust in Him, would find that they were not trusting in the Son only, but in the Father *also*.—In short, to trust in the Son, the sent Saviour of sinners, is to trust also in the Father, who sent Him to save. The Son and the Father cannot be divided, though they are distinct Persons in the Trinity : and faith in the

Son gives an interest in the Father. (Compare John v. 24: "He that heareth my word, and believeth on Him that sent Me." And 1 Peter i. 21: "Who by Him do believe in God.")

To draw a wide line of separation between the Father and the Son, as some do, and to represent the Father as an angry Being whom the Son appeases, is very poor theology, and the high road to Tritheism. The true doctrine is that the Godhead of Father, Son, and Holy Ghost is one, and that in the unity of the Godhead there are three Persons, and yet that there is such entire unity between the Persons that he who believes in the Son believes also in the Father.

Zwingle thinks the latent idea is, "Do not think it is a small and insignificant thing to believe on Me. To believe on Me is the same thing as believing on God the Father, and to know Me is to know the Father."

Bucer seems to think that the address in this verse was meant to encourage those who believed Christ to be the Messiah, but were afraid of confessing Him, to come forward boldly, and acknowledge their belief.

Poole says, that in like manner God says to Samuel, "They have not rejected thee, but have rejected Me," meaning not thee *alone.* (1 Sam. viii. 7.)

45.—[*And he...seeth Me seeth him that sent Me.*] This deep and mysterious verse proclaims even more distinctly than the last verse, the unity of the Father and the Son. It cannot mean that any one who saw Christ with his bodily eyes, did, in so seeing, behold the First Person in the Trinity. Such beholding we are distinctly told is impossible. He is one "whom no man hath seen or can see." (1 Tim. vi. 16.) What our Lord seems to mean is this: "He that seeth Me seeth not Me only, as an ordinary man or a Prophet, like John the Baptist. In seeing Me he beholds one who is one with the Father, the brightness of His glory, and the express image of His Person." (Heb. i. 3.) Of course our Lord did not literally mean, "He that sees Me does not see Me." But He meant, "He that sees Me sees not only Me, but through Me and by Me He sees Him that sent Me, for we cannot be divided."

The divinity of Jesus Christ seems incontrovertibly proved by this verse and the preceding one. If to believe in Christ is to believe in the Father, and to see Christ is to see the Father, then Jesus Christ must be equal with the Father,—very and eternal God.

The supposition of some, that the first "seeth" in this verse means nothing more than "seeth by faith," appears rather incredible. At this rate the verse would be only a repetition of the one preceding it. I prefer the idea that "seeth" means literally, "Seeth with his bodily eyes." Yet Bengel says that "seeth" refers to that vision which faith accompanies, and compares it to John vi. 40.

The object our Lord had in view in this and the preceding verse, appears to have been twofold. It was partly to proclaim once more the unity of Himself and the Father. It was partly to encourage all believers in Himself, for the last time, before He was crucified. Let them know that in resting their souls on Him, they were resting not on Him alone who was about to die on Calvary, but on One who was one with the Father, and therefore were resting on the Father.

Chrysostom observes on the expression "seeth Him that sent me,"—"What then ? Is God a body ? By no means. The seeing of which Jesus here speaks is that of the mind, thence showing the consubstantiality."

Barnes observes, that this language could not have been used about any mere man. To say it of Paul or Isaiah would have been blasphemy.

46.—[*I am come a light into the world, etc.*] In this sentence our Lord proclaims once more the great end and object of His coming into the world. He does it by using His favourite figure of light, and comparing Himself to the sun.—"I have come into a world full of darkness and sin, to be the source and centre of life, peace, holiness, happiness to mankind ; so that every one who receives and believes in Me, may be delivered from darkness and walk in full light."

Let us note that the form of language used here seems to teach that our Lord existed before He entered the world. The saints "are the light of the world," but they do not "come a light into the world." This could only be said of Christ, who was light before His incarnation, just as the sun exists and shines before it rises above the eastern horizon.

Let us note that our Lord's language seems to teach that He came to be a common Saviour and Messiah for all mankind, just as the sun shines for the good of all. It is as though He said, "I have arisen on the world like the sun in the firmament of heaven, in order that every one who is willing to believe in Me should be delivered from spiritual darkness, and be enabled to walk in the light of spiritual life."

Once more we may remember that none could give such a majestic description of His mission, but one who knew and felt that He was very God. We never find Moses, or John the Baptist, or Paul, or Peter using such language as this.

The quantity of precious truth taught and implied in this verse is very note-worthy.—The world is in darkness.—Christ is the only light.—Faith is the only way to have interest in Christ.—He that believeth no longer abides in darkness, but has spiritual light.—He that does not believe remains and continues in a state of darkness, the prelude to hell.

The expression, "not abide in darkness," seems to have a latent reference to those Jews who were convinced of Christ's Messiahship, but were afraid to confess Him openly. Such persons are here exhorted not to remain, stick fast, and continue in darkness.

Burgon remarks on this verse, "This verse shows that (1) Christ existed before His incarnation, even as the sun exists before it appears above the eastern hills ; (2) that Christ is the one Saviour of the world, even as there is only one sun ; (3) that He came not for one nation, but for all, as the sun shines for all the world."

47.—[*And if any...hear...believe not.*] Having shown the privilege of those who believe in Him, our Lord now shows the danger and ruin of those who hear His teaching and yet believe not.

[*I judge him not.*] These words can only mean, "I judge him not now." To put more on them would contradict the teaching of other places, where Christ is spoken of as the Judge of all at the last day. Our Lord's meaning evidently is to teach that His First Advent was not for judgment, but for salvation, not to punish and smite as a conqueror, but to heal and save as a physician.

[*For I am not...judge...save the world.*] These words are an expansion and explanation of the preceding sentence, "I judge him not." They are evidently meant to correct the Jewish impression that Messiah was to come only to judge, to execute vengeance, to smite down His enemies, and to punish His adversaries. This impression arose from misapplied views of the Second Advent and the judgment yet to come. Our Lord, for the last time, declares that He came for no such purpose. Wicked as unbelief was, He did not come to punish it now. He came not as a judge at His First Advent, but as a Saviour.

We must take care, however, that we do not misinterpret this sentence. It affords no countenance to the dangerous doctrine of universal salvation. It does not mean that Christ came in order to actually save from hell all the inhabitants of the whole world. Such a meaning would flatly contradict many other plain passages of Scripture. What then does it mean ?

It means that our Lord came at His First Advent not to be a judge, but a Saviour, not to inflict punishment, but to provide mercy. He came to provide salvation for all the world, so that any one in the world may be saved. But no one gets any benefit from this salvation excepting those that believe.—The true key to the meaning of the sentence is the contrast between Christ's first coming and His second one. The first was to set up a throne of grace : the second will be to set up a throne of judgment. The expression in John iii. 17 is precisely parallel : "God sent not His Son into the world to condemn the world, but that the world through Him might be saved." If it were lawful to coin a word, the true exposition of the sentence would be, "I came that the world might be *salvable*."

But while I say all this, I am unable to see how such expressions as this, and John iii. 16, 17, can possibly be reconciled with an extreme view of particular redemption. To say, on the one hand, that Christ's death is efficacious to none but the elect and believers, is strictly true. Not all men are finally saved by Christ. There is a hell, and unbelievers and impenitent people will be found there. —But to say, on the other hand, that in no sense did Christ do anything at all for the whole world, but that He did everything for the elect alone, seems to me utterly irreconcilable with this text. Surely Christ came to provide a salvation *sufficient* for the whole "world."

I am aware that the advocates of an extreme view of particular redemption say that "the world" here does not mean "the world," but the elect of all nations, as compared to the Jews. But this view is not satisfactory, and looks very like an evasion of the plain meaning of words.

Why the same Greek word is rendered by our English translators, "judge" in this verse, and "condemn" in the parallel place in John iii. 17, it is not easy to see.

48.—*He that rejecteth Me...receiveth not my words...judgeth him.*] In this verse our Lord declares positively the future judgment and condemnation of those who reject Him, and refuse to believe His teaching.

The word we render "rejecteth," is only used here in St. John's Gospel. The idea is that of "despising: setting at naught." (See Luke x. 16.) The person described is one who despises and sets at naught Christ Himself, after seeing Him, and deliberately refuses to acknowledge Him as the Messiah, in spite of all the evidence of His miracles. He is also one who will not receive and take into his heart the doctrines preached by Christ. In short, he despises His person, and refuses to believe His teaching.—"Such a man will find at last, though I punish him not now, that there is a judgment and condemnation of him. He will not find that his rejection of Me, and his unbelief, will go unpunished. He has a Judge prepared already. There is one already, though he knows it not, who will witness against him and condemn him."

[*The word...I have spoken...judge him...last day.*] Our Lord here declares that the things He publicly preached to the Jews while He was upon earth, would witness finally against those who did not believe, at the last day, and be their condemnation. They will not then be able to deny that they were words of wisdom, words of mercy, words subversive of their false views, words fully explaining Christ's kingdom, words entirely in accordance with the Scriptures. And the result will be that they will be speechless. The witness of Christ's words will be unanswerable, and in consequence of that witness they will be condemned.

We see here that the words of those who speak for God are not thrown away, because they seem not believed at the time. Christ's words, though despised and rejected by the Jews, did not fall to the ground. Those whom they did not save they will condemn. There will be a resurrection of all faithful sermons at the last day.—Great is the responsibility of preachers! Their words are always doing good, or adding to the condemnation of the lost. They are a savour of life to some, and of death to others. Great is the responsibility of hearers! They may ridicule and despise sermons. But they will find to their cost at last, that they must give account of all they hear. The very sermons they now despise may be witnesses against them to their eternal ruin.

Let us note that our Lord speaks of judgment and the last day as great realities. Let us take care that we always account them such, and live accordingly. The Christian's best answer to those who ridicule his religion is to say, "I believe in a judgment and a last day."

Let us note that condemnation is taken for granted, if not directly expressed. as the portion of some at the last day. Then

let us not listen to those who say that there is no future punishment, and that all persons of all characters, both good and bad,
are at last going to heaven.

Zwingle remarks that the expression, "My word shall judge,"
is parallel to such expressions as, "The law puts a man to death,"
though it is not actually the law, but the executioner that does
it.   The law only shows him to be worthy of death.   So the
works and words of Christ will show the unbelieving to be worthy
of judgment and condemnation.

49.—[*For I have not spoken of myself.*]   In these words our Lord
once more, as if for the last time, declares that mighty truth
which we find so often in St. John,—the intimate union between
Himself and His Father.   "I have not spoken of myself, of my
own independent mind, and without concert with my Father in
heaven."

The object of saying this is evident.   Our Lord would have the
Jews know what a serious sin it was to refuse His words, and not
believe them.   In so doing men did not refuse the words of a
mere man, or a prophet, like Moses or John the Baptist.   They
were refusing the words of Him who never spake alone, but
always in closest union with the Father.   To refuse to receive the
words of Christ, was to reject not merely His words, but the
words of God the Father.

Here, as in many other places in St. John's Gospel, the Greek
does not mean, "I have not spoken *concerning* myself, but out of
or from myself."

[*But the Father ..gave...commandment.. speak.*]   Here our Lord
explains and enforces more fully what He said of "not speaking
from Himself."   He declares that when He came into the world,
the Father gave Him a "commandment," or a commission, as to
what He should say and speak to men.   The things that He had
spoken were the result of the eternal counsels of the ever blessed
Trinity.   The works that He had done were works which the
Father gave Him to do.   The words which He spoke were words
which the Father gave Him to speak.   Both in His doing and
speaking nothing was left to chance, unforeseen, unprovided, or
unpremeditated.   All was arranged by perfect wisdom, both His
words and His works.

When we read of the Father "sending" Christ, and giving
Christ a "commandment," we must carefully dismiss from our
minds all idea of any inferiority to God the Father on the part of

God the Son. The expressions are used in condescension to our weak faculties, to convey the idea of perfect oneness. We are not speaking of the relation that exists between two human beings like ourselves, but between the Persons in the Divine Trinity.—The "*sending*" of the Son was the result of the eternal counsel of that blessed Trinity, in which Father, Son, and Holy Ghost are co-equal and co-eternal. The eternal Son was as willing to be "sent" as the eternal Father was to "send" Him.—The "*commandment*" given by the Father to the Son as to what He should teach and do, was not a commandment in which the Son had no part but to obey. It was simply the charge or commission arranged in the covenant of redemption, by all three Persons in the Trinity, which the Son was as willing to execute as the Father was willing to give.

The distinction between "say" and "speak" in the Greek is not very clear. Burgon thinks the phrase is meant to include "every class of discourse; as well the words of familiar intercourse, as the grave and solemn addresses." But I am not satisfied that this can be proved.—"A. Lapide" says that "to say is to teach and publish a thing gravely, and to speak is to utter a thing familiarly." Bengel, however, distinguishes them in precisely the contrary way!

There certainly seems to be an intention in the verse to refer the Jews to the well known words of Deuteronomy, concerning the Prophet like unto Moses. "I will raise up a Prophet from among their brethren, like unto thee, and will put my words into His mouth, and He shall speak unto them all that I shall command Him." Our Lord's hearers, familiar from their infancy with Scripture, would see at once that Jesus claimed to be the promised Prophet. The Father's words were in His mouth. He spoke what was commanded Him. (See Deut. xviii. 18.)

50.—[*And I know...His commandment...life everlasting.*] The meaning of this sentence seems to be, "I know, whether you like to believe it or not, that this message, commandment, or commission, which I have from my Father, is life everlasting to all who receive it, and believe. You, in your blindness, see no beauty or excellence in the message I bring, and the doctrine I preach. But I know that in rejecting it you are rejecting life everlasting."—Thus Peter says to our Lord, "Thou hast the words of eternal life" (John vi. 68) : that is, we know Thou hast a commission to proclaim and publish eternal life.—Thus our Lord says, "The words that I speak are spirit and life." (John vi. 63.)

Poole and others say this sentence means, "I know that the

way to life everlasting is to keep His commandments." But I cannot think this is the meaning.

Hall paraphrases the sentence, "The doctrine which by His commandment I preach unto you, is that which will surely bring you to everlasting life."

[*Whatsoever I speak...as Father...so I speak.*] This sentence seems intended to wind up our Lord's public discourses to the unbelieving Jews at Jerusalem. "Whatsoever things I am teaching now, or have spoken to you all through my ministry, are things which the Father gave to Me to speak to you. I am only speaking to you what the Father said to Me. If therefore you reject or refuse my message, know once more, for the last time, that you are rejecting a message from God the Father Himself. I speak nothing but what the Father said to Me. If you despise it, you are despising the God of your fathers, the God of Abraham, and Isaac, and Jacob."

Let us remember that the holy boldness of this last verse should be a pattern to every minister and preacher of the Gospel. Such a man ought to be able to say confidently, "I know, and am persuaded, that the message I bring is life everlasting to all who believe it; and that in saying what I do, I say nothing but what God has showed me in His Word."

END OF VOL. II.